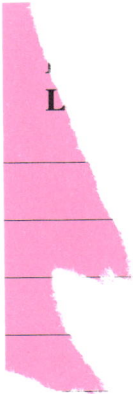

WHAT IS THEORY?

Also available from Continuum:

Deconstruction and Critical Theory, Peter V. Zima
Philosophy of Modern Literary Theory, Peter V. Zima

WHAT IS THEORY?

Cultural Theory as Discourse and Dialogue

PETER V. ZIMA

continuum

Continuum International Publishing Group
The Tower Building, 11 York Road, London SE1 7NX
80 Maiden Lane, Suite 704, New York, NY 10038

British Library Cataloguing-in-Publication Data
A catalogue record for this book is available from the British Library.

ISBN: HB: 0–8264–9050–6
        9780826490506

Library of Congress Cataloging-in-Publication Data
A catalog record for this book is available from the Library of Congress.

Typeset by Aarontype Limited, Easton, Bristol
Printed and bound in Great Britain by Biddles Ltd, King's Lynn, Norfolk

A German version of this book was published by A. Francke Verlag, Tübingen, 2004, under the title *Was ist
Theorie? Theoriebegriff und Dialogische Theorie in den Kultur- und Sozialwissenschaften.*

Contents

Preface

The word "theory" is related to the ancient Greek verb *theorein* which means "to view" or "to observe". So theory in this etymological sense could be somewhat generally defined as "observation". However, nowadays our conception of theory is somewhat more concrete. It means "scientific knowledge" as opposed to religious contemplation or artistic intuition.

The etymological background is of some importance here: for in the modern context it reminds us of the fact that theory is a very specific way of viewing objects and of relating them to one another within a special type of discourse. The word "discourse" implies that we are dealing with linguistic structures and that, in the realm of cultural and social sciences, theory can only be described and understood as a linguistic construct.

So far, the latter has not been adequately analysed. For decades, social scientists have been dealing with concepts such as "culture", "ideology", "language" or "discourse" without ever attempting a viable definition of the general concept of theory.

At the end of the twentieth century, in 1999, a German philosopher had to admit "that so far no generally accepted definition of the concept of theory (...) has been submitted by the theory of science". Like many others, he resorts to basics when pointing out that theories are in many cases conceived of as "systems of sentences".[1] Even Jürgen Mittelstraß, a contemporary German philosopher of science, opts for this kind of minimal definition in one of his more recent works.[2] The Introduction to this book will show that so far theory discussions have not gone beyond formal definitions of this kind.

Hence the principal aim of *Part One* is to define theories as linguistic structures: as discourses or semantic and narrative units which cannot be reduced to the sum total of their sentences, propositions or hypotheses. This purely formal notion of theory can only be superseded if theory is seen as a discourse and defined in terms of the specific (cultural, ideological and linguistic) character of cultural and social sciences.

From this point of view, discourses are to be considered as ideological, philosophical, historical or literary narratives which vary from culture to culture, from ideology to ideology. A case in point is functionalist sociology as it developed after the Second World War in the USA. In retrospect it appears as a consensus ideology adapted to the needs of a particular society and its culture. Similarly, European sociological theories narrate social developments within the frameworks of discourses marked by particular semantics and ideological interests.

To give an example, Alain Touraine retraces the development of modern French society by adopting a culturally specific starting point, i.e. the opposition between social movements on the one hand and state or economic organizations on the other. His ideological engagement comes to the fore whenever he views this development *in the perspective* of the social movements which he considers as forces of emancipation. Even Niklas Luhmann's seemingly impartial description of social differentiation is by no means neutral, for it opposes the narratives of Marxism and Critical Theory – as well as Touraine's sociology of action, movement and emancipation. At the same time, it expresses particular social interests, which will be dealt with in chapter 9.

In *Part One*, theories produced in the realm of cultural and social sciences will be defined as discourses or semantic and narrative structures based on ideological interests and cultural particularities. It will be shown in conjunction with older and more recent publications by the author that, although theoretical discourse thrives on its ideological (liberal, conservative, Marxist or feminist) motivations, it is also threatened by them as a discourse aiming at criticism and knowledge. At any moment cultural or social theory can be blinded and destroyed by its own ideological engagement and degenerate into an ideology which identifies itself monologically with the real world, thus excluding all competing discourses.

In view of the threat posed by ideologies aiming primarily at social action, and not at knowledge, the question arises how to deal with the ideological engagement which seems unavoidable in the human sciences, whose discourses are inseparable from social conflict. In chapters 3 and 4, it will appear that the postulate of *Wertfreiheit* (value-freedom), introduced into the discussion by Max Weber and reinstated by critical rationalists such as Karl R. Popper and Hans Albert, fails to answer the most pressing questions, because in the social sciences discourses can only be understood adequately as reactions to social, economic and cultural problems, such as unemployment, inflation, the environment, etc., and as attempts to solve these problems. Such attempts cannot be divorced from value judgements and hence cannot be *wertfrei* (value-free) in the Weberian sense. The ideologically and politically tinted character of anthropological, sociological and psychological semantics illustrates this fact.

Within this context, the refutability or "falsifiability" of hypotheses and theories as postulated by Popper becomes problematical because the process of refutation does not take place among atomized individuals but among (liberal, conservative, feminist or Marxist) groups of scientists, whose theoretical discourses are at the same time ideological languages. Whatever is considered as "refuted" ("falsified") within one group may still be considered as valid in another. In view of such complications, Popper's idea that scientific theories ought to be refutable seems to be impracticable in the world of social science.

In *Part Two*, an alternative to this critical-rationalist approach is mapped out from the perspective of Adorno's and Horkheimer's Critical Theory and of Mikhail M. Bakhtin's literary hermeneutics. One of the results is a dialectical and dialogical meta-theory which relates conflicting theoretical positions to one another in order to test them in a systematic confrontation. Where incompatible perspectives collide, each of the two theories in question reveals its strengths and its weaknesses, its insights and its blind spots. By opening up new perspectives, by constructing an object differently, the competing theory reveals pitfalls and problems which our favourite approach obscures. Testing theories within heterogeneous scientific groups and their languages (sociolects) is one of the key ideas of *Part Two*.

On this level, the Dialogical Theory presented in this part of the book may also be considered as a critical development of Popper's and Hans Albert's idea of refutability and testability. However, the new model no longer aims at a final refutation or falsification: it is geared, more realistically, towards Otto Neurath's notion of *Erschütterung* (shock). Neurath was among the first to criticize the formalism of Popper's *Logic of Scientific Discovery* (1934), suggesting that the principle of "falsification" or refutation should be replaced by that of *Erschütterung*. In *Part Two* and *Part Three*, this principle is reinterpreted in a dialogical perspective: as a revelation of theoretical flaws by a dialectical encounter of opposites, of incompatible theoretical positions.

Encounters of this type are brought about in *Part Two*, where the approaches of Popper and Lyotard, Davidson and Mannheim, Lukács and Glasersfeld, Luhmann and Bourdieu, Habermas and Foucault are related to one another. They not only contradict but also complement one another as one theory reveals what the other obliterates and vice versa.

In *Part Three*, Dialogical Theory is presented as a meta-theory which develops Adorno's and Horkheimer's Critical Theory by orienting it towards discourse semiotics, theory of science and dialogical hermeneutics (chap. 11). Instead of opting for negativity in the sense of Adorno, critical discourse revives Adorno's concepts of *non-identity* and *alterity* which are redefined in a dialogical context. Alterity in particular is dissociated from Adorno's notion of artistic mimesis and presented in a Bakhtinian, Popperian and constructivist perspective. Rationality is no longer derived from a symbiosis between art and theory but from a dialogical consciousness based on the idea that a theoretical discourse is never identical with reality, that it *constructs* its objects and that these constructions are to be tested in an open dialogue with others, i.e. with heterogeneous theoretical positions.

On this level, Dialogical Theory appears as a meta-theory of scientific communication. One of its central theses, derived from the critique of Weber's *Wertfreiheit* and Popper's notion of refutation, can be summed up as follows: the testing of scientific hypotheses and theories which Popper and other critical rationalists quite rightly demand should not merely have an intersubjective, but also – and above all – an inter-collective or inter-discursive character, i.e. it should take place between heterogeneous groups of scientists. The idea is that the discourse of the Other ought to be taken into account a priori: not so much for ethical but rather for epistemological reasons (chap. 12).

This idea of inter-discursive or inter-collective criticism, which was extensively discussed in *Ethik und Sozialwissenschaften* (Ethics and Social Sciences) (4, 1999), is the main topic of chapters 13 and 14 which also deal with past and present discussions between ideologically heterogeneous groups and their theories: between Marxism and Russian Formalism, Critical Rationalism and Critical Theory, Speech Act Theory and French Deconstruction.

These discussions seem to confirm one of the key hypotheses of this book: namely that the encounter of heterogeneous points of view is a more serious test than discussions *within* a group of scientists and their sociolect. In some cases such discussions may be meaningful and yield new insights; in many cases, however, they tend to confirm established scientific and ideological dogmas. One of the aims underlying this book is to break up such dogmas in order to open up new perspectives.

In times marked by ecological, feminist, ethnic and religious commitments, it seems necessary to stress the importance of the *concept of ideology* in all cultural and social sciences and to redefine this concept on a socio-semiotic level (cf. chaps 2 and 15). The grand ideology in the sense of an international utopia may now look obsolete; however, "local" ideologies orienting groups and movements continue to have a considerable impact on all social and cultural sciences, all of which would wither away if they lacked ideological motivation. However, this impact often turns out to be a negative factor transforming the discourse of theory into a dualistic and monological structure which pretends to be identical with its object, with "reality". It seems important, therefore, to bear in mind that ideologies play an ambivalent role in the development of theories: they can provide important stimuli; they can also ruin theoretical reflection (cf. chaps 2 and 12).

This critique of ideology, which seems indispensable to a viable concept of theory in the social and cultural sciences, also sheds light on the contemporary relevance of Critical Theory in the sense of the Frankfurt School and on Adorno's idea from the 1960s that the failure of European socialism does not imply the inevitability or desirability of late capitalism.

Whoever refuses to accept the commercial manipulation by the media, the systematic exploitation of nature and human beings and the progressive destruction of environment, health and climate, will also reject the merchant's idea that the market – masked as consumption – fosters solidarity among nations and individuals.

As a permanent source of modern ambivalence, the market is also a source of war, especially in a world economy marked by an increasing scarcity of resources and by a permanent struggle for privileged access to markets and raw materials. The truism that consumption is only possible as long as a profitable production process continues unhampered ought to prevent theoreticians from confusing postmodern market society with its pluralistic façade constructed and reconstructed by ideologists.

The pluralistic tolerance practised in this society is in reality a grudging acceptance of cultural otherness and of the "others" until they turn out to be unbearable or unprofitable (cf. chap. 15). This book is an attempt to go beyond this kind of formal tolerance which is also responsible for the indifferent juxtaposition of theories. Such coexistence in indifference is replaced by a critical and auto-critical dialogue which aims at improving interaction and increasing coherence in the humanities.

NB: Dialogic Theory itself became a topic of discussion in Germany in 1999. The reader will find most of the critical comments and the author's replies in the Notes.

Introduction: Problems and Definitions

After the theoretical and methodological discussions of the 1970s and 1980s, theoretical problems are often viewed with scepticism, if not with outright hostility, so the question "What is theory?" might well irritate those sceptics who believe that we can do very well without an answer. Others may believe that the answers provided so far are quite satisfactory.

Traditional practice seems to confirm such reactions: a closer look at various sociological works on theory reveals that the concept of "theory" is hardly ever explained. The fact that a collective volume edited by Giddens and Turner and entitled *Social Theory Today* (1987)[1] leaves this concept undefined is understandable. However, the reader who subsequently resorts to a monograph such as *The Structure of Social Theory* (1984) by Johnson, Dandeker and Ashworth in order to find a viable definition in a linguistic or logical sense, will also be left in the lurch, because the authors divide the theoretical realm according to traditional philosophical criteria: empiricism, subjectivism, substantialism and rationalism.[2] Hardly anybody will object to this classification, for it is well known that the social sciences have inherited the controversies between empiricism, idealism and rationalism from philosophy. However, the *structure* of theory is not really a topic of the book – and at any rate is not defined.

This argument also applies to the more recent study by Max Haller entitled *Soziologische Theorien im systematisch-kritischen Vergleich* (*Sociological Theories Systematically and Critically Compared*) (1999). Although the author does comment on the multitude of sociological theories and distinguishes various types, he does not offer a general definition of "theory" which would apply to all of them, but is content to point out "that the concept of theory formation refers to the symbolic aspects of human experience, as opposed to the mere perception of facts".[3] Unfortunately, this description is equally applicable to ideologies or religions and does not really correspond to other definitions which will be dealt with below. At this stage, one is reminded of Rainer Greshoff's understatement "that the way the word 'theory' is being used is far from uniform".[4] This diagnosis is borne out in the realm of literary criticism, as we shall now see.

In their pioneer study, *Theory of Literature* (1949), Wellek and Warren are quite oblivious of meta-theoretical reflections of this kind: although they define the concept of literature, they seem to treat the complementary concept of theory as a kind of ornament not worth bothering with.[5] A similar situation prevails in Franz K. Stanzel's otherwise thorough and systematic work, *A Theory of Narrative* (1979). Although it contains an implicit theory of narrative perspectives, the latter is neither reflected at a meta-theoretical level nor confronted with alternative concepts such as Greimas's discourse semiotics or Genette's narratology.[5]

Why is this necessary, a sceptical observer of recent theoretical discussions might ask? It is necessary if interested readers are to realize that literary narrative can be constructed differently, so that (in Genette's or Greimas's perspective) novels and their narrators are made to appear in a completely different light.[7] This awareness of alternative constructions is important if the notion of pluralism is taken seriously in the sense that attempts are made to relate theories to one another (cf. chap. 12).

Unlike Stanzel who seems content to use "theory" in its common sense or colloquial meaning, Gerhard Pasternack's *Theoriebildung in der Literaturwissenschaft* (*Theory Formation in Literary Science*) (1975), a book written in the heyday of theoretical and methodological debate in Germany, promises a thorough inquiry into the meaning of "theory". Unfortunately, the author does not even raise the question of a general definition.[8] In the "Epistemological Presentation" he refers to the dependence of theories on paradigms and explains under the heading "Materialist-Dialectical Theory and Science of Literature": "Historical-materialist science sees itself as a revolutionary break with traditional theory."[9] Sentences such as this are often found in philosophical, sociological or psychological works of the 1970s. They raise crucial questions without providing satisfactory answers. Are "theory" and "science" to be used as synonyms? What is meant by "dialectic"?

Vincent Descombes adopts an ironical tone when he reminds us of the fact that, in post-war French philosophy, the word "dialectic" carried euphoric connotations and that any question concerning a definition was dismissed as a kind of sacrilege.[10] This allergy towards definitions has helped to discredit both "dialectics" and "theory".[11]

The results of this decline of theory are summarized by two relatively recent works, one of which deals more specifically with literary theory, while the other has a more general scope: Antoine Compagnon's *Le Démon de la théorie* (1998) and Terry Eagleton's *After Theory* (2003). The common denominator of these two very different books seems to be that theory – sociological or literary – has had its day. But what exactly is (or was) theory? Neither of the two authors raises this question and the reader is left with the uneasy feeling that something is supposed to be buried that has never seen the light of day.[12]

At this stage, the theory-sceptics, who are not that easy to convince (which is probably a theoretical virtue), are most likely to repeat their questions: What do we need theory for? What's the point of insisting on a definition?

This time, the answer can be relatively short. Considering that the Greek word *theoría (theorein)*[13] means perception and that *all our perceptions* are guided by cultures, ideologies or theories, it seems necessary to distinguish ideologies from theories and to consider the immersion of theories in cultures in order to understand one's own arguments. For we are socialized in cultural situations marked by ideological and theoretical languages, which contribute decisively to the development of our perception, our thought and subjectivity. If we wish to think and act with a certain amount of autonomy instead of being determined by whichever cultures, languages, ideologies and theories happen to be influential at a certain period of time, we shall be keen to find out what theory is, how it is structured, how it functions and how it differs from culture, ideology, language or science.

In a scientific context, this reflexive and auto-critical attitude seems to matter more than anywhere else. A concrete concept of theory ought to enable cultural and social scientists to reflect the development of their theories on a historical, social and linguistic level and to recognize in their objects contingent (not arbitrary) constructions. "Text", "culture", "society", "psyche" – and "theory" – can only be adequately understood as theoretical constructions whose historical, genetic aspects should always be borne in mind.

1. Theory: Structure and Function

In a first step, it seems possible to distinguish heuristically two notions of theory which are to be found both in the philosophy and in the sociology of science: the *structural* and the *functional*. In both cases we are dealing with ideal types in the sense of Max Weber, who writes about the *Idealtypus* that it comes about in a process of abstraction and condensation. Some salient features of empirical reality are selected and compounded in order to form a "unified conceptual scheme".[14] Here it becomes clear that a theory geared towards ideal types constructs its objects by abstracting from empirical data on the basis of a specific relevance, selection and construction.

Structural and functional conceptions of theories are ideal types in the Weberian sense insofar as hardly anybody considers the structural or the functional aspects of a theory in isolation. In most cases the structure of a theory is related to its social function. It is nevertheless possible to argue that the philosophy of science tends to focus on the structure of theories, while historical and sociological approaches tend to highlight functional problems.

Structural in the colloquial sense of the word are numerous definitions of "theory" which are to be found in philosophical and sociological dictionaries: "Theory as opposed to mere (...) empirical reality is any unit of knowledge in which facts, models or hypotheses are compounded to form a whole (...)."[15] But what exactly constitutes the coherence of such a unit? How are facts, hypotheses and models related to one another? And how are the latter to be distinguished? Such questions are left open. Philosophical definitions of this kind are hardly improved on in a sociological dictionary, where "theory" is defined as an "empirically founded and coherent whole of propositions concerning aspects of reality accessible to human beings".[16]

More sophisticated is the definition put forward in another sociological dictionary: "A theory is a system of related propositions. It has to be (a) logically consistent and free from contradictions; (b) it has to be informative, i.e. its sentences have to be formulated in such a way that they can be related to the real world and tested by facts; and (c) it has to contain certain rules of correspondence, according to which the operationalization of its postulates, i.e. the translation of the assumptions and concepts used in its hypotheses, is made possible in observations and experiments."[17]

In spite of its length, the definition proposed by Wenturis, Van hove and Dreier in *Methodologie der Sozialwissenschaften (Methodology of the Social Sciences)*, is less precise, less concrete than the one quoted above:

> In a first attempt to answer the question "what is theory" the latter can be described as a (theoretical) scheme related to certain facts. This very general conception can be specified in the sense that a theory is any hypothesis, generalisation or law (be it deterministic or statistical) or a variant of the latter. In addition, it is possible to consider a single sentence as a theory.[18]

Although the authors attempt to justify their last statement by referring to Popper's *Logic of Scientific Discovery* (1934), it is hardly convincing. For individual sentences tend to be ambiguous and to take on a definable meaning only if they are integrated into a discourse considered as a transphrastic, i.e. semantic and narrative, structure. Only in special cases can an isolated, but relatively complex sentence, which renders the gist of a theoretical discourse, be considered as the equivalent of a theory, as its "summary".

One need not be a fervent deconstructionist in order to realize that the definition in *Methodologie der Sozialwissenschaften* is at least partly incompatible with the two preceding definitions of "theory". Unlike the first two definitions which declare "sentences" and "hypotheses" to be *components* of a theory, Wenturis, Van hove and Dreier are prepared to extend the notion of "theory" so as to make it coincide with notions such as "hypothesis", "generalization", "law" and even "sentence".

In what follows (especially in chap. 2), it will be shown that the problem is far from trivial and that it cannot be solved as long as "theory" is not defined in a semiotic context, i.e. as a *transphrastic structure or discourse*. This problem crops up for the first time in Popper's early writings referred to by the authors of *Methodologie der Sozialwissenschaften*, who believe that it is occasionally possible to identify "theory" and "sentence". For Popper points out: "Scientific theories are universal statements." (In the earlier German version, Popper uses the term *Sätze*, sentences: "Wissenschaftliche Theorien sind allgemeine Sätze."[19])

The structural point of view is crucial to his work, which will play an important part in the sixth chapter, because it revolves around the idea that the form or structure and not the content of theories is essential. Theories, Popper argues, ought to be structured in such a way as to make them refutable or "falsifiable". As an alternative to the criterion of empirical verification, endorsed by most members of the Vienna Circle, Popper proposes (in 1934) refutability or "falsification" as the new criterion: "But I shall certainly admit a system as empirical or scientific only if it is capable of being tested by experience. These considerations suggest that not the *verifiability* but the *falsifiability* of a system is to be taken as a criterion of demarcation."[20]

It is not the content of theoretical statements which is decisive, according to Popper, but the way they are formulated, which makes refutation possible. Popper explains: "*It must be possible for an empirical scientific system to be refuted by experience.*"[21] He gives two examples: "Thus the statement 'It will rain or not rain here tomorrow' will not be regarded as empirical, simply because it cannot be refuted; whereas the statement, 'it will rain here tomorrow' will be regarded as empirical."[22] Whoever feels irritated by a nondescript rhetoric announcing "changeable weather" or by horoscopes warning us about the "traffic dangers", will tend to agree with Popper.

However, Popper relates refutation in the scientific sense to an axiomatic system modelled on physics which is hardly applicable to cultural and social sciences:

The attempt is made to collect all the assumptions which are needed, but no more, to form the apex of the system. They are usually called "axioms" (...) The axioms are chosen in such a way that all the other statements belonging to the theoretical system can be derived from the axioms by purely logical or mathematical transformations.[23]

The problem here is that most theories in the social sciences have a *narrative*, not a purely logical or mathematical structure (cf. chap. 2). Hence it seems legitimate to ask whether the principle of refutation or "falsification" is at all applicable to them. In the fourth chapter, this question, which Popper's critics have kept raising ever since Otto Neurath brought it up in 1935,[24] will be dealt with in some detail.

More radical and more precise than Popper in the mathematical sense, Wolfgang Stegmüller proposes to define "theory" on a structural level:

> The mathematical structure of a theory will be divided up into a *structural frame*, a *structural core* and an *enlarged structural core*. *Theory* as such will be defined as a non-linguistic entity, i.e. a binary structure, consisting of a structural core C and a class of intended applications I.[25]

On the one hand, a definition of this kind is encouraging because it raises hopes that "theory" will be defined here with utmost mathematical precision; on the other hand, it is disappointing because precision in this particular sense presupposes the non-linguistic character of theories.

Stegmüller's explicit "renunciation of the 'statement view' of theories"[26], which eliminates their linguistic structures, so that they can no longer be conceived of as "*classes of sentences*"[27], may offer certain advantages to the natural scientist who may be able to treat different theories as being equivalent or to reduce one theory to another: "It ought to be possible to speak of the equivalence of *different* theories based on completely *different* conceptual schemes."[28] Its main disadvantage seems to be the fact that Stegmüller's model is based on the particularities and needs of physics and hence inapplicable to theories in the cultural and social sciences.

His attempt to apply this model to Freud's psychoanalysis begets distortions and misunderstandings, because a key concept such as *repression* (*Verdrängung*), which is closely related to the concept of the *unconscious*, is treated by Stegmüller as a secondary term. Other key concepts such as *Ego*, *Id* and *Super-Ego* are omitted altogether. Along with these concepts (which constitute the actantial model of psychoanalytic discourse), the narrative character of psychoanalysis and its therapies is eclipsed.[29]

Stegmüller's otherwise quite stimulating reconstruction of Marx's Political Economy also obliterates the narrative structure of this theory and isolates one of its aspects: the economic model.[30] (This problem will be dealt with in more detail in chap. 13, 2.) Considering such formal, mathematical attempts at reconstruction which cast new light on some aspects of the reconstructed theories while completely obscuring others, one wonders whether it is actually possible to speak of equivalent theories or parts of theories in the cultural and social sciences.

Even if "equivalence" is not taken to mean formal identity, but merely an "intuitive idea" (Stegmüller), implying "that from equivalent theories 'the same empirical consequences can be deduced' ",[31] the applicability to social sciences is not at all certain. In these sciences, theories articulate − as will be shown later on − individual and collective interests. This is one of the reasons why they cannot possibly be treated as equivalents or reduced to one another. They are in no way interchangeable because they crucially contribute to the constitution of subjectivity, both on a collective and an individual level.[32]

Pierre Bourdieu's predominantly functional approach to scientific theories reveals to what extent this is the case; it will be discussed in more detail in the ninth chapter. At this stage, it may be sufficient to point out that Bourdieu is interested less in the structure, the formal aspects of theories, but more in the way they function in the *scientific field (champ scientifique)*, i.e. within the institutional context. In this context, he explains, they fulfil "a pure − purely scientific − function and a social function",[33] namely with respect to the individuals and groups acting in the scientific field.

In other words: we are dealing on the one hand with cognitive processes, on the other hand with strategic conflicts involving *symbolic capital* (reputation, prestige, etc.) and a redistribution of assets and roles in the field. A scientific discovery the value of which nobody contests may entail the "symbolic murder"[34] of a rival who was pursuing the same discovery by availing himself of another theory.

"Theory" is presented here both as an instrument of knowledge and as a strategy designed to ensure individual or collective predominance in the scientific field. It is not by chance that Bourdieu speaks of "ideology" in this particular case:

> In other words, I do believe that quite a lot of works which are being referred to as "theoretical" or "methodological" are little more than ideologies justifying certain forms of scientific competence. And an analysis of the sociological field would undoubtedly reveal that a strong correlation exists between the kind of capital different scientists dispose of and the kind of sociology which they defend as being the only legitimate one.[35]

The danger underlying this functional perspective consists in reducing theories to their strategic role in the scientific field, thus forgetting their linguistic structure and their cognitive value. The fact that Bourdieu tenaciously denies this forgetfulness inherent in his approach[36] will not induce anybody to overlook the absence of a structural definition of "theory" in his "sociology of sociologies". Unlike Popper or Stegmüller, he has never described "theory" as a structure. How can we distinguish theories from ideologies or "field strategies"? How can we describe their structures without neglecting their functions? Bourdieu provides no satisfactory answers to these questions. For this reason, a clear structural and functional distinction between ideology and theory seems indispensable (cf. chap. 2) in order to obtain a viable definition of theory as discourse, i.e. as a semantic and narrative structure.[37]

The discursive level is bypassed entirely by Niklas Luhmann, who defines theories as communications "articulated in sentences"[38] and also highlights the factor of social domination in the scientific field in order to focus on the functioning of theories within the autonomous, *autopoietic* (self-producing and self-maintaining)[39] subsystem of science. According to Luhmann, the latter is based on the distinction *true/untrue (wahr/unwahr)*.[40] The *communication* and *production of knowledge* within this system is the actual object of Luhmann's preoccupations and analyses, not the structure of particular theories: "The autopoiesis of the system simply demands that the communication about truth or untruth should continue, that is to say the communication within this symbolically generalized medium."[41]

In spite of all the differences and incompatibilities which lie between Luhmann and Bourdieu and which will be discussed in the ninth chapter, Luhmann's approach is also geared towards the functional question of how knowledge and truth are being produced by communication within the subsystem of science. In this context, even Popper's Critical Rationalism and his insistence on refutability appear as strategies and functions in an autonomous subsystem[42] rather than as proposals for a viable – i.e. falsifiable, mathematically definable or critical – theory structure.

On the whole it can be said that the functional and structural conceptions of theory are complementary in many ways – although they have so far not been systematically related to one another. This is why in the following chapters attempts will be made to reveal the links between structural and functional aspects of theories, especially in the light of the fundamental distinction between the theoretical and the ideological function of discourse (chap. 2).

2.   Theory Defined in Relation to its Objects

Starting from Max Weber's notion of the ideal type, a third way of defining "theory" seems possible, namely in relation to its *object* or *objects*. The idea of a theory conceived in view of a particular object might shock the universalist, who is not entirely wrong in assuming that a good theory ought to be capable of explaining just about everything.

In the ideal world he seems to have in mind, this would probably be the case. However, the real world is rather different, and even Luhmann's all-encompassing theory of the social system which has been applied to virtually all social phenomena – from the economy to art – tends to yield trivialities: for example when Luhmann explains artistic autonomy in an institutional context, relying almost entirely on arguments which the Russian Formalists put forward at the beginning of the twentieth century – without having the slightest idea what a systems theory of society and art might look like.[43] Like Hegel's systematic philosophy, Luhmann's sociology tends to subordinate the particular object to its own grand design and to ignore its specific features.

In *Social Theory and Social Structure* (1949, 1968), the North American sociologist Robert K. Merton considers the "grand theory" with similar scepticism and pleads in favour of a *theory of the middle range*. He distinguishes it from working hypotheses of current research (occasionally considered as "theories", as was pointed out earlier on) and from "all-inclusive systematic efforts to develop a unified theory that will explain all the observed uniformities of social behavior, social organization and social change".[44]

In contrast with a grand theory, a theory of the middle range serves to guide empirical research and does not aim at society as a whole, but only at "delimited aspects of social phenomena", i.e. at particular objects.[45] As examples Merton mentions the reference group, social mobility or role conflicts.[46]

He considers Durkheim's sociology of suicide as a model of middle range theory. In his well-known study *Suicide* (1897), Durkheim attempts to show that the suicide rate is not simply an individual, psychological phenomenon, but a social fact which increases with decreasing social solidarity. This is why it is more frequent in urban than in rural areas. A particular role is played by the family (as a more or less integrated community) and the religious factor. While the suicide rate is relatively high in individualistically organized Protestant groupings, it is relatively low in more integrated Catholic and Jewish groups. Merton concludes: "Durkheim's monograph, *Suicide*, is perhaps the classical instance of the use and development of middle-range theory."[47]

This concept of theory which is based on Anglo-American empiricism and David Hume's scepticism could be justified as follows: the object of research ought to be clearly delimited in order to assure applicability and empirical testability of the theory in question. However, Merton's own example shows that an object-oriented definition of "theory" can be dicey.[48] For Durkheim's well-known study can hardly be understood independently from his *theory of society*, i.e. from the process of social differentiation which gradually replaces mechanical solidarity (based on the resemblance of individuals) by organic or functional solidarity. The latter is not solidarity in the colloquial or psychological sense of the word but functional interdependence which tends to weaken the feeling of solidarity in the sense of collective consciousness. This development which is concomitant with industrialization and professional differentiation explains why suicide becomes a major problem in late modern market society.[49]

In other words, Durkheim's analysis of suicide should not be considered in isolation as a "theory of the middle range", for it is part and parcel of an all-encompassing social theory most of which is contained in Durkheim's fundamental work *The Division of Labour in Society* (1893).

In this context, it may well be asked whether theories of the "middle range" actually exist as autonomous structures: whether they are not embedded in general social theories which they tacitly imply. If this were the case, theory should not simply aim at particular objects, but at the nexus between theory formation and the corresponding general social theory. Here the relevant question seems to be: How is a particular notion of theory related to the encompassing theory of society and how does the latter construct itself as a meta-theory, i.e. as a reflection upon its own genesis and structure? (Cf. the last section of this introduction and chap. 11.)

Dealing with the relationship between theories and their objects, Niklas Luhmann aptly points out: "Not the object guarantees the unity of theory, but theory guarantees the unity of the object, according to the dictum that everything that constitutes a unit for an autopoietic system is a unit by virtue of the autopoietic system."[50] (Luhmann considers "science" as an autopoietic, self-generating system and scientific theories as subsystems: cf. chap. 9.)

His anti-empiricist thesis seems to be borne out by Merton's own definition of theory, which is somewhat rudimentary, and suggests that the scientist ought to avoid defining a theory exclusively in relation to its object: "Throughout this book, the term sociological theory refers to logically interconnected sets of propositions from which empirical uniformities can be derived."[51] However, which are the factors relating these "sets of propositions" to one another? Once again, "theory" is not envisaged as a coherent discourse.

This criticism also applies to another object-oriented approach: to Barney Glaser's and Anselm Strauss's Grounded Theory which was developed in conjunction with American Pragmatism, Merton's Functionalism and Mead's Symbolic Interactionism.[52]

Grounded Theory can best be understood as an inductive hermeneutic whose hypotheses are closely related to the analysed facts in an open-ended process of theory building.[53] Anselm Strauss and Juliet Corbin have listed four salient features of Grounded Theory: (1) it corresponds to the described phenomenon; (2) it contributes to a better understanding of it; (3) its statements are so general that variations and transformations of this phenomenon can be accounted for; and (4) finally, it ought to make an effective control of these three phases of research possible.[54]

In a continuous process of adjustment to the analysed phenomenon and its variations, the theory in question is "saturated" by the absorption of all available information so as to become adequate to its object. It is designed as an open structure. "The strategy of comparative analysis for generating theory puts a high emphasis on theory as process (. . .)",[55] conclude Glaser and Strauss.

The idea that theory is an open process and not a closed system, corresponds to one of the main tenets of Dialogical Theory, whose subject, as will be shown in chapter 2, maintains a permanent openness vis-à-vis its objects, bearing in mind that the latter may at any time be constructed differently by other theoreticians. Unfortunately, this dialogical and constructivist approach is entirely absent from Grounded Theory. The latter seems to be firmly anchored in an epistemological realism and based on the idea of *adequacy to its object*, not on the idea of *object construction*. "A good grounded theory," writes Brian D. Haig, "is one that is (1) inductively derived from data, (2) subjected to theoretical elaboration, and (3) judged adequate to its domain (. . .)."[56] But who will decide that adequacy has been reached at any given moment?

Whenever the constructivist moment of thought is suppressed, a dialogical orientation is missing. A theory aiming at *object adequacy* will invariably tend to identify monologically with its objects. It lacks the insight that it is merely a possible discourse and not identical with the real world or parts of it, i.e. its proponents neglect theory as discourse, as a contingent semantic and narrative structure. Very much like Merton whose influence they acknowledge, they fail to reflect on the historical and social conditions of their theorizing.

These critical remarks concerning some object-oriented theories lead to the following provisional conclusion: the subject of theory constructs its objects within the framework of its discourse which it tests and adapts on an empirical level and in a permanent interaction with other theories.

Moreover, it analyses the linguistic and social context of its own origin and development (cf. chap. 15).

Leaving aside all idealist speculations, one might say that without theory there would be no scientific objects: without physics, no *magnetic field*, without biology, no *umbellifers* (just flowers), without psychoanalysis, no *unconscious*, without literary theory, no *omniscient narrator* and without sociology, neither *institutions* nor *reference groups*, nor *artistic* and *scientific fields* (Bourdieu).

It may nevertheless be meaningful to investigate the relationship between a theory and its object in order to find out more about the nature of theories. Since Wilhelm Dilthey's somewhat dogmatic, but by no means meaningless distinction between human sciences whose aim it is to understand socio-cultural contexts, and natural sciences which explain phenomena in conjunction with the principle of causality,[57] some groups of scientists (e.g. the Vienna Circle and later on the Althusser Group)[58] adhere to the idea of a unified science, while others (supporters of hermeneutics, dialectics or ethnomethodology) continue to differentiate.

In recent years, Johann August Schülein has made an attempt to add new aspects to this debate by proposing a fundamental distinction between *denotative* and *connotative theories*. This not entirely unproblematic delimitation is probably based on the assumption that "denotative theories" are not to be identified with the natural sciences, while the expression "connotative theories" is not to be read as a simple synonym of the cultural and social sciences.

Nevertheless, there is substantial evidence in Schülein's work that "denotative theories" are related to objects of nature and are guided by corresponding interests, while connotative theories deal with social, self-producing (or "autopoietic", Schülein) objects and are therefore guided by hermeneutic understanding in the sense of Dilthey. "A closer examination reveals", explains Schülein:

> that nomological and autopoietic realities confront the symbolic system with quite different problems. If one accepts this basic distinction, one soon realizes that nomological reality can best be represented within a *denotative symbolic system*, while autopoietic reality is adequately dealt with by a *connotative symbolic system*. [Author's translation].[59]

In this context, "connotation" implies a hermeneutic understanding of social actors and their logics, for Schülein takes "theories of the family and the firm, of management, therapy and politics, etc."[60] to be "connotative" theories in the sense of social science. He explains the notion of connotative theory as follows: "It has to adapt to the specific logic of the topic in question without eliminating its reflexive distance."[61]

In the 1970s, this reflexive attitude based on understanding was referred to by Anthony Giddens as "double hermeneutic", for "sociology, unlike natural science, deals with a pre-interpreted world".[62] In other words, the objects of social science are also subjects who interpret reality and whose interpretations may depart from those of the scientist.

This is plausible enough. However, readers familiar with semiotics would like to know why this "double hermeneutic" or subject-subject relationship is considered as having a connotative character. For in linguistics "connotation" refers to the "secondary meaning" of words which comes about whenever a word is used that evokes a specific register or context, for example, in an expression like "refined cuisine", the second part of which evokes the context of French gastronomy. On *this* level, "connotation", which is always based on a primary meaning (cuisine = cooking), is distinguished from "denotation" which has an exclusively primary character.[63] It would have certainly been helpful, if Schülein had clearly marked off his concept of connotation from the current linguistic concept most readers are familiar with.[64]

In spite of this somewhat confusing terminology, Schülein's object-oriented distinction between denotative and connotative theories is stimulating, because it shows that theoreticians ought to take into account the specific character of their objects if they wish to avoid forcing them into their conceptual schemes (as Stegmüller does with psychoanalysis). It is also useful, because it reveals the existence of "hybrid" objects located between the "denotative" and the "connotative" realm: for example climate and the biological evolution, both of which are increasingly being influenced by human or social action.[65]

In the third chapter, the relationship between natural and cultural or social sciences will be discussed in more detail. It will appear that similarities and differences are possibly in equilibrium – especially, if the linguistic, cultural and ideological particularities of the social sciences are taken into account. A lot depends on how the relationship between these two types of sciences is constructed. Moreover, the possibility of constructing a unified science in the sense of the Vienna Circle should not be excluded a priori.

3. Theory as Discourse and the Task of Philosophy

It is not meaningful, at this stage, to anticipate the key arguments of the second chapter and to define "theory" as a discourse in a socio-semiotic context. However, a preliminary definition seems indispensable if an alternative to the definitions mentioned so far is to take shape. *Theory is an interest-guided discourse whose semantic and narrative structure is developed and reflected upon by a self-critical subject who is aware of the theory's historical, social and linguistic origins.*

Unlike the definitions of theory commented on so far, this definition goes well beyond the formal conceptions of theory as a "system of sentences or propositions", because the notion of discourse encompasses a lexical reper- toire, a semantic and a narrative syntax which jointly guarantee a certain amount of coherence. The expression "interest-guided" means that the speaking subject, which is frequently a collective subject (of psychoanalysis, Critical Rationalism or Critical Theory), does not choose lexical units or semantic distinctions at random, but in conjunction with a social view- point and corresponding collective interests. The coherence of a theoretical discourse thus appears as based on lexical, semantic and syntactic deci- sions made by the subject of enunciation in accordance with particular social interests.

What seems essential here, is the distinction between a purely *phrastic* (sentence-oriented) discourse theory, first developed by Zellig Harris[66], and a *transphrastic* semiotic of discourse. While Harris attempts to under- stand discourse as a succession of sentences, semioticians such as Greimas, Halliday or Stubbs start from the assumption that a discourse is substan- tially more than the sum of its sentences: namely a narrative structure whose semantic foundations determine the meaning of each sentence involved.[67] Ultimately, this meaning is grounded in the *ideological interests* of the individual and collective speaker – interests semioticians such as Greimas tend to neglect (cf. chap. 2).

These arguments may sound somewhat abstract; they should become more concrete when they are applied. For it becomes clear that the semantic and narrative discourse structure is quite often contained in individual words or expressions which may function as synecdoches. Thus an expres- sion such as "state monopoly capitalism", which was at the centre of Marxist-Leninist discourse after the Second World War, contains the narra- tive structure of this particular discourse: the state has to intervene system- atically in order to avert or mitigate the cyclic crises of capitalism, etc. Habermas's well-known title *Modernity – an Incomplete Project* (*Die Mod- erne – ein unvollendetes Projekt*, 1980) announces a critical discourse, whose subject takes up some of Adorno's and Horkheimer's arguments when plead- ing in favour of a critical and self-reflexive completion of the Enlightenment programme. The social interest or engagement of the discourse subject can hardly be overlooked in this case. It turns against all postmodern thinkers who try to slow down or reverse the modern movement of emancipation.

In exceptional cases, a single sentence may contain the structure of the discourse it belongs to. "Thus postmodernity", argues the German philosopher Wolfgang Welsch, "is a situation where the ideas of modernity need no longer be invoked, because they are being realized."[68] As in the case of Habermas, the relationship of modernity and postmodernity is *narrated*. However, it is evaluated very differently. For in Welsch's discourse, postmodernity as multiplicity and pluralism appears as the realization of modern projects of emancipation, not as an attempt to foil them.

Each of the two discourses in question constructs the semantic units "modernity" and "postmodernity" differently, i.e. within the framework of two different, contradictory narratives. In what follows, an attempt will be made to understand theories on a meta-theoretical level as discourses or interest-guided narratives (cf. chap. 2). It will become clear that this construction is a more adequate description of theories in the social and cultural sciences than the formal definitions commented on above. At the same time, a concept of theory will be developed which takes into account the specific character of these sciences and eventually opens onto a Dialogical Theory.

As was pointed out in the Preface, this theory functions as a meta-theory mediating between two points of view: the point of view of a theory of science whose object is scientific and theoretical development, and the point of view of a sociology of science which reflects critically upon this development in a social and historical context.

As a Dialogical Theory (cf. *Part Three*), this meta-theory is linked to the social position of the reflecting individual in the sense of Adorno's and Horkheimer's Critical Theory which it develops and transforms on a socio-semiotic level.[69] The idea that this theory should no longer be geared towards the negativity of art, but towards alterity, which is also a key concept underlying Adorno's thought, is an important aspect of this development. The idea of alterity yields a dialogical orientation. For it is dialogue with the other theory and the other subject that enables us to test hypotheses seriously and view theories, including our own, critically (cf. chap. 11).

The notion of a critical meta-theory, as it is mapped out here, could already be found – albeit in an allusive form – in Adorno's post-war philosophy which, on the one hand, aims at overcoming the scientific division of labour,[70] while attempting, on the other hand, a critical reflection of its own discursive premises.[71] This kind of philosophy is at the same time a critique of discourse that reflects upon its attitude towards its objects without falling prey to objectivism or empiricism. Unlike Merton's approach it refuses to be determined by its object.

This meta-theoretical reflection upon one's own object as an object construction in the research process could also be called methodology:

"Methodology is a meta-theory of the research process; its objectives are the critical evaluation of its results, the question how they came about and proposals concerning the improvement of research practice." Methodology in this sense also deals with the "construction of theories and their testing".[72]

In this context, philosophical reflection as critical meta-theory has the task to overcome the established division of labour so as to be able to propose a philosophical and socio-semiotic concept of theory, thus giving a new impulse to debates in the human sciences and introducing a new mode of theory testing.

The term "socio-semiotic" marks out the ground covered by this book. As it is impossible – for reasons of competence and coherence – to consider all cultural and social sciences in detail, this book focuses on philosophical reflection, on semiotics and literary criticism in the cultural sciences and on sociology in the social sciences. Disciplines such as history, politics or social anthropology are dealt with briefly, mainly in chapters 2 and 5.

The author does hope, however, that this inevitable selection will not discourage scholars, whose disciplines are not represented here, from relating the questions raised by this book to their own scientific and theoretical experience.

Part One

Theoretical Discourse in the Cultural and Social Sciences: Definition

The definition of theory as an interest-guided discourse may have conveyed the impression that the central argument of the book aims at a particularization of the concept of theory. It should therefore be pointed out that the author is neither a partisan of abstract universalism nor a supporter of postmodern particularism (in the sense of Lyotard or Zygmunt Bauman). His approach is a dialectical mediation between these two extremes.

It seems important to him to recognize the irrational character of a rationalist universalism which Karl R. Popper has inherited from the Vienna Circle in spite of all his critical remarks. For this kind of universalism entails a systematic neglect of cultural, ideological and linguistic particularities in scientific discussions and in theory formation. However, in the human sciences theories are in virtually all cases linguistic constructs, and the irrational element in the various brands of rationalism (of Logical Positivism, Critical Rationalism or certain games theories) consists in simply ignoring cultural and linguistic particularities. For many rationalists, human beings are rational, calculating and rationally acting individuals, whose socio-cultural identities are discarded.

At the other end of the theoretical spectrum, not only the possibility of a "universal language"[1] in the sense of the early Vienna Circle is denied, but also the possibility to relate different "language games" (Wittgenstein, Lyotard) to one another. Lyotard describes this postmodern tendency towards particularization and incommensurability in some detail, when he explains:

As for what you call the French philosophy of recent years, if it has been postmodern in some way, this is because it has also stressed incommensurabilities, through its reflection on the deconstruction of writing (Derrida), on the disorder of discourse (Foucault), on the epistemological paradox (Serres), on alterity (Lévinas), on the effect of meaning by nomadic encounter (Deleuze).[2]

These *incommensurabilités*, as Lyotard puts it, are the incompatible particularities of a fragmented, pluralized society.

In what follows, a socio-semiotic concept of theory will be mapped out, which takes into account the coexisting and colliding particularities, without however sacrificing the principles of validity and rational communication defended by Critical Theory. The idea is to mediate dialectically and dialogically between the particular and the universal (cf. *Part Two* and *Three*), without accepting Adorno's paradox of a paratactic, i.e. non-theoretical theory.[3]

However, this type of mediation cannot succeed as long as the concept of theory remains abstract and vague (theory as a "system of sentences or propositions"). In this form it cannot possibly take into account the particular points of view and interests which are *also* articulated in theories. It may succeed in an approach where theory is conceived as a linguistic structure in the semiotic sense: as *a discourse produced in particular socio-cultural and linguistic contexts and driven by an ideological engagement.*

If one adopts this perspective, it is crucial not to lose sight of the fundamental ambivalence of ideology. In chapter 2, it will become clear that the latter is both the motor of theory and its most dangerous adversary. Although ideological engagement in the Marxist, feminist or liberal sense may vitally motivate theoreticians, it may also blind them if it becomes too powerful.

In this socio-semiotic context it will become clear – in the last two chapters of *Part One* – why the concepts of *Wertfreiheit* and *paradigm*, which were introduced into the debate by the sociology and the history of science, are not applicable in the realm of cultural and social sciences. They abstract from the cultural particularities and the ideological interests articulated in theoretical discourses. The very idea of a "coexistence of different paradigms" in sociology, anthropology or literary criticism illustrates this fact as much as the expression "multi-paradigm-science".[4] The existence of a multitude of paradigms in a particular discipline is a symptom of ideological interference and of the impossibility of a unified paradigm accepted temporarily by all scientists.

Chapter 1

The Cultural Character of Theory

The title gives rise to several questions: What is specifically cultural about theories in the human sciences? Are not all human creations cultural? And: What is meant by culture?

In the last resort, all phenomena produced by humans and not by nature can be called social or cultural. Hence the thesis according to which all scientific theories have a cultural character is a truism because it is far too abstract. However, if we succeed in giving it a more concrete form, it can be "activated" and applied.

Its applicability depends on how the key concepts of "culture" and "theory" are related to one another. A concrete relationship is only conceivable if the definition of "culture" does not turn out to be too abstract as in the case of the anthropologist Clyde Kluckhohn, who takes a very general view of the matter: "The anthropological term designates those aspects of the total human environment, tangible and intangible, which have been created by men."[1] Somewhat more concrete is Talcott Parsons' definition in *The Social System* (1951): "It is a question of beliefs, of particular systems of expressive symbols, or even of patterns of moral value-orientation when only 'acceptance' rather than commitment in action is involved."[2] The smallest common denominator underlying all definitions seems to find its most recent expression in Klaus P. Hansen's concise description: "It [culture] encompasses the totality of the customs and habits of a collective."[3] (Here one can hardly avoid the impression that the most recent definitions are not necessarily the best ones.)

All three definitions may be informative in certain respects; however, they do not seem to form a sound basis when it comes to establishing a link between "culture" and "theory" considered, for the time being, as an "interest-guided discourse".

In order to relate this concept of theory to the notion of culture, the latter will be defined here as a *problem complex: as a social and historical problematic which finds its expression in non-verbal and verbal sign systems.*[4] In the next chapter it will be viewed more concretely as a *socio-linguistic situation,* i.e. reduced to its verbal components in order to make it correspond to the verbal character of theories.

The word "problematic" suggests that culture is a dynamic unit, an historical constellation of problems to which religious, ideological, artistic and scientific groupings react in many different ways. Thus the homogeneity of the problematic consists in the similarity of its problems, whereas its heterogeneity consists in the diversity of reactions to these problems: to the destruction of the environment, globalization, the equality of women or the process of European integration.

The dynamic character of culture conceived as a problematic allows for a link-up between the concepts of culture and theory. *As interest-guided discourses, theories and complexes of theories react in very different ways to the problems of a culture.* Considering that these problems differ from nation to nation, from society to society, it is hardly surprising that theoretical reactions to cultural problems and processes of theory formation are very different in Britain, Germany, France or the USA. The fact that this tendency towards particularization is countered by intercultural scientific communication and cross-cultural theorizing is just as important, however, and will be dealt with in the following sections.

1.   Processes of Rationalization

The fact that national and regional cultures are by no means hermetically sealed systems, but historical constellations linked to one another by supra-national and interregional developments, is amply illustrated by Max Weber's analyses of the process of rationalization in Europe. Although this chapter cannot deal with these analyses in detail, it starts from Weber's central assumption that scientific development as a whole is part and parcel of this process. Insofar as they are its products, both the natural sciences and the human sciences can be considered as culturally determined.

They all evolved within a secularized European culture which, in the course of centuries, moved away from myth, religion or tradition and in the final stages of its development only acknowledged the different brands of rational thought we know today. In a secularized modern society marked by scientific progress, the question (raised by some Romantics) is no longer *whether* reason is to determine social evolution, but *which* reason. In this constellation or problematic, the common denominator of all sciences – from physics to the science of religion[5] – seems to be the criterion of exact conceptual definition, rational argument and empirical proof.

It goes without saying that this criterion is one of the results of rationalization as described by Weber and his heirs. It is a crucial aspect of the kind of scientific progress Weber comments on: "Scientific progress is only a fraction, but the most important fraction of that process of intellectualization to which we have been subject for millennia (...)."[6] Further on, Weber refers to the "intellectualist rationalization through science".[7] The assumption that this rationalization forms the basis of all modern sciences and of every single scientific argument is certainly not an illusion. Therefore one can only agree with Jürgen Mittelstraß who concludes: "In this respect, it seems legitimate to assume that *all* sciences bear witness to one and the same rationality produced by the modern world."[8]

On the basis of this assumption, Weber could try to justify his postulate of a *value-free (wertfrei)* science, a science situated well beyond the never-ending struggles among value judgements and value systems. "This means, however," explains Wolfgang Schluchter, "that a 'free' empirical science is a value to be preserved, that it is 'valuable'."[9]

The fact that this kind of science is governed by "instrumental reason"[10] in the sense of Max Horkheimer has been emphasized time and again. At the same time, the question concerning an alternative science, a science not based on instrumental thinking, has been raised. However, philosophers like Gernot Böhme no longer doubt that in modern societies the instrumental type of reason predominates: "The idea that science can also be different, is repressed and forgotten, and every single scientific approach is anxious to parade as science (in the sense of modern science) in order to be able to compete – psychoanalysis is a case in point."[11] Even Max Weber's ideal of a *value-free (wertfrei)* empirical science bears witness to this compulsive adaptation, which is contested here by an alternative conception of theory.

The question whether Weber's ideal is a rationalist illusion will not be dealt with here, but in the fourth chapter. However, it is good to remind ourselves of the fact that Weber's *understanding sociology (verstehende Soziologie)* can be conceived as a rationalist component of the process of rationalization and that a critic of Weberian sociology like Manfred Hennen has long since realized to what extent *understanding* or *Verstehen* "is a rationalist registration of facts".[12] In other words, Weber's notion of reason is particular to a certain type of culture, for it is inseparable from philosophical traditions such as the Neo-Kantianism of the Heidelberg School founded by Rickert, Windelband and others.

Even the process of rationalization is not a universal or universally uniform phenomenon which permeates all cultures in the same way, but a development originating in Europe – as Weber himself points out.[13] The explanations of the cultural foundations of this process (and of all the theories it helps to generate) are quite heterogeneous and cannot be commented on in detail.

It seems worthwhile, however, to examine two of these explanations and to compare them briefly. While C. A. van Peursen believes that rationalization in China did not evolve in accordance with European patterns of thought, because Chinese geometry and algebra "were always related to events in the real world",[14] Richard Münch suggests that, although "rationalized domains with specific laws" did exist in China and India, they did not *interpenetrate*:

> Thus in China, for example, a highly developed technology did exist and in India a highly rationalized philosophy and mathematics, but neither in China nor in India do we find the rational experiment as a salient feature of modern science, in which theory and practical technology, rational logic of proof and empirical research interpenetrate each other instead of being kept separate.[15]

How does this diagnosis compare with van Peursen's opinion that in China geometry and algebra "were always related to events in the real world"? It seems that processes of rationalization in different cultures can be interpreted in many ways ...

What matters here, however, is not this problem but the idea that rationalization in the sense of Weber can assume *culturally specific forms* and hence cannot be considered as a homogeneous phenomenon with global validity.

As far as the difference between natural and human sciences goes, a difference hinted at in the Introduction, this idea seems to result in a paradox: namely in the discovery that, although all sciences are products of Weber's process of rationalization (sociology as much as physics), natural sciences bring forth universally accepted theories and schemes, whereas cultural and social sciences seem incapable of doing so.

While the period system of chemical elements can claim universal acceptance – in spite of all the cultural particularities of the process of rationalization within which it came about – the literary systems of periodization developed in Europe are inapplicable in Asia or Africa. Even within Europe the Italian way of defining literary styles in accordance with centuries (e.g. *stile seicentesco*) is partly incompatible with the English, the French or the German. Similarly, it is virtually impossible to translate the German name for the *Sturm und Drang* period into English or Italian.[16] How is this to be explained?

2.   Culture as a Problematic: The Cultural Determinants of Human Sciences

On a very general level, it can be explained in conjunction with the fact that natural sciences are dealing with problems the solution of which presupposes *cognitive* involvement, while cultural and social sciences are dealing with problems which imply not only a cognitive but also an *ideological* involvement. It goes without saying that in *both* cases involvement is an emotional and social attitude that may lead to criticism, disagreement and conflict. However, the natural scientist can only criticize colleagues, not nature (the weather can be complained about but not criticized), whereas cultural and social scientists are frequently compelled to criticize, because they confront social problems (not just "value judgements") that cannot be solved without an explicit or implicit political engagement.[17]

"The concept of culture is a value concept,"[18] writes Weber; he ought to have added that it is a value concept because it attracts or provokes criticism. What Walter Benjamin has to say about the historical materialist illustrates the problem: "For what he observes in the vast area of cultural goods appears to be of an origin which makes him shudder." Then follows the well-known sentence: "There is never a document of culture without being at the same time a document of barbarism."[19] Adorno's book *Prisms* carries the subtitle *Critique of Culture and Society*. A comparable "critique of nature" in a physical, chemical or biological sense is only conceivable as a joke.

Somebody might object that, although Benjamin and Adorno are widely recognized as critics of culture, this should not prevent us from considering the possibility of a "value-free" (*wertfrei*) theory of culture and society. For: "Weber insisted (...) quite emphatically on the fundamental difference between 'value relations' and 'value judgements': if we say, for example, that something is important with respect to political freedom, then we neither support nor oppose political freedom."[20] At first sight (cf. chap. 4), this may seem to be a plausible argument; however, the situation changes significantly if we go beyond the controversies about value judgements in order to consider *problems* and *problematics*.

For as soon as we substitute "relations to problems" for "value relations", we discover that a neutral or value-free attitude is not possible in the realm of human sciences, because unlike values, problems have to be solved: for example the related problems of inflation and unemployment, of cultural discrimination with respect to the accumulation or lack of "cultural capital" (Bourdieu) or of an environment threatened by economic growth. Such problems can hardly be described without political and ideological involvement, i.e. within the framework of a neutral theoretical observation. They certainly cannot be solved in a neutral way. For the very hypothesis that certain social groupings are being discriminated against because their access to "cultural capital" is fraught with difficulties, implies criticism and provokes counter-criticism.

At this stage, somebody might argue that politicians should solve social problems, while scientists ought to describe them "objectively" or "neutrally". This objection is naive, for we know that Popper's suggestion to replace a holistic (Hegelian-Marxist) approach to society by pragmatic *piecemeal social engineering*[21] is as much a reaction to concrete problems as most (controversial) definitions of "society", "the state" or "art". Naturally, a proposal to define "theory" in a certain way is also to be understood as an attempt to solve a social problem. Such an attempt can never be neutral or free of value judgements.

This is why criticism and evaluation are to be found at the very roots of cultural and social sciences. Feminist sociology, linguistics or literary theory bear witness to this fact as much as Critical Theory or Popper's Critical Rationalism whose principle of "falsification" is inseparable from his ideals of an "open society" and a liberal world order.[22] This is one of the reasons why Popper's theses are generally welcomed in Britain and the USA, where entrepreneurial spirit and liberal ideology have always been strong, while they are considered with a certain amount of scepticism in France, where state interventionism has a long tradition and political philosophy diverges significantly from its Anglo-American counterpart.[23]

Even Luhmann's theory of social systems is far from being value free (in spite of its technological rhetoric); it can best be understood as a global reaction to Marxism, Critical Theory and the German debates of the 1970s and 1980s. When the author of *Social Systems* (1984) observes with satisfaction "the extinct volcanoes of Marxism",[24] he announces his own sociological alternative which contains a new sociological orientation and new proposals for solving ecological problems[25] (generally neglected by Marxists). It is a well-known fact that all of his proposals are as controversial as those of the past. Johann August Schülein has a point when he remarks: "While Schrödinger's equations are understood by all physicists in the same way, it is by no means clear how Luhmann's theory of 'ecological communication' is to be understood (this becomes obvious in various reviews) and how it is to be assessed (as these reviews also show)."[26]

While Luhmann can hope to challenge Marxism and Critical Theory in a post-war Germany reconstructed along North American consensus principles, a completely different philosophical and sociological scenario develops in post-war France, where several sociological theories (Bourdieu,

Touraine) analyse mechanisms of domination, mobilizing social movements against economic exploitation and state bureaucracy. In contrast to
Pierre Bourdieu who introduces concepts such as *symbolic capital*, *symbolic violence* and *authorized language* (*langage autorisé*) in order to show to what extent
actors can be excluded from the embattled social fields,[27] Alain Touraine
concentrates on a theory of social action geared towards the *social movement*
as *historical subject*.[28] His notion of social movement is culturally specific insofar as it revives certain anarcho-syndicalist ideas and can be linked to the
principle of *autogestion* (workers' self-administration);[29] at the same time it
is critical of culture and society insofar as it defends the social subject against
the economic system and the state apparatus. The fact that he considers the
problem of the subject from the point of view of the subject as movement can
hardly be overlooked: "The subject comes about both in its conflicts with
the state apparatus as well as by virtue of its respect of the other as subject;
the social movement is a collective action aiming at the defence of the subject against the power of commerce, the economic enterprise and the
state."[30] One is hardly surprised to find that Luhmann does not appreciate
this kind of sociology which reacts to a socio-cultural problematic so different from his own.[31]

Another example illustrating the cultural specificity of sociological
theory, and of sociological terminology in particular, is the Dutch concept
of *pillarization* (*verzuiling*). A short definition of this phenomenon could be:
the organization of society along denominational, ideological or ethnic
lines called metaphorically *pillars* (*zuilen*). J. E. Ellemers explains: "*Verzuiling* or Pillarization is usually considered as the particular way in which
Dutch society has been organized along denominational lines. The Pillars
(*Zuilen*), which form the basis of this system, are made up of different
denominational groups."[32] Although this very useful concept can be
applied to different societies and cultures, one becomes aware of its specifically Dutch origin whenever one tries to translate it into English or French
and explain it to an English-speaking or French-speaking sociologist.

Sociology is not the only discipline to oscillate between a critical stance
and a scientism fascinated by exactness;[33] literary criticism seems to be in a
similar situation. Considered in an intercultural context,[34] this cultural
science appears as a brand of criticism in the English-speaking world as
well as in Romance countries, while it is defined as a science in the Germanic
and Slav cultures.

Unlike in the English-speaking world, in France, Italy and Spain, where
the frontiers between literary criticism and literary theory often appear
as blurred (cf. *critique littéraire/théorie de la littérature*, *critica letteraria/teoria
della letteratura* or *crítica literaria/teoría de la literatura*)[35], in Germany, the

Netherlands and the Slav countries, literary criticism in the evaluative, journalistic sense is an *object* of the *science* of literature (*Literaturwissenschaft, literatuurwetenschap, literaturovedennie*).[36] This means that the demarcation line separating practical, journalistic criticism from literary science is far more pronounced in Central and Eastern Europe than in Britain or the Romance countries. It is more rigidly institutionalized in Germany or the Netherlands than in the USA where a deconstructionist such as Geoffrey H. Hartman can present the literary critic (not scientist) as an author *sui generis* who writes literature about literature.[37]

In this context, one may understand French expressions such as *psycho-critique* and *sociocritique*. They refer to psychoanalytic and sociological approaches which are predominantly text-oriented and therefore considered as components of literary criticism in the sense of *critique littéraire*. Insofar as it avoids empirical sociological research, French *sociocritique* is primarily literary criticism and not sociology (of literature).[38]

These examples are meant to illustrate a fundamental dilemma of human sciences: owing their existence to the processes of rationalization described by Max Weber, they aspire towards scientific exactness and universal validity; at the same time, however, they face the necessity to react critically to national and regional problems within a specific social and cultural problematic. In each country they are confronted with *specific discussions* and *patterns of communication*, which may not exist elsewhere. In view of such problems, it is hardly surprising that their hypotheses and theories do not enjoy as global an approval as, for example, the periodic table in the world of chemistry.

3.   Institutionalization of Theories

Theoretical discourses not only function within socio-cultural problematics, but are at the same time linguistic aspects of particular institutions embedded in these problematics. Every now and then a theory or a theory compound may acquire a dominant position in the institutions, thus influencing the problematic as a whole and distinguishing it from other problematics.

A case in point is situated on the borders of philosophy and politics. It is the work of Benedetto Croce (1866–1952), which had a considerable impact on cultural life in Italy during the first half of the twentieth century and still continues to provoke controversies. Adapting Hegel to the needs of the twentieth century and of Italian culture,[39] Croce designed an idealist philosophy geared towards the interests and expectations of the liberal and conservative Italian public. He defined concepts such as "history", "politics" and "art" in accordance with these expectations.

Antonio Gramsci's polemical but otherwise quite realistic assessment of Croce's position in the Italian institutions shows to what extent Croce's work reproduces the entire socio-cultural problematic, thereby securing a hegemony status. According to Gramsci, it articulates the ideas of the whole political class, of all the relevant national groups and movements.[40]

The fact is that Croce's anti-fascist stance in the 1920s and during the Second World War helped to maximize his influence in post-war Italy. In 1943, he founded the new Liberal Party whose chairman he was until 1947; in 1944 he became minister after the collapse of fascism. This is why his idealism not only had a lasting impact on Italian philosophy, but also influenced Italian historiography and literary criticism. One of the reasons why Comparative Literature continues to have a difficult stand in Italian universities is due (among other things) to Croce's well-known thesis that each literary work is a unique aesthetic phenomenon which can neither be subsumed under generic concepts nor meaningfully *compared* with other works.[41]

Processes of institutionalization in other cultures only rarely lead to this kind of cultural hegemony (in the sense of Gramsci). However, it seems certain that Auguste Comte's philosophy and Emile Durkheim's sociology have dominated French discussions for decades after Durkheim's death, while in Germany Weber's "understanding sociology" continues to occupy a dominant position in spite of the impressive presence of Luhmann's systems theory. (In this sense the foundation of a Max Weber Institute in Weber's native town of Erfurt in the 1990s can be seen as a symptom.)

Paul Claval quite rightly treats Comte's positivism as a *founding myth* (*mythe fondateur*) which asserted itself in French universities after the revolutions of 1830 and 1848.[42] This positivist myth, which gave birth to the word *sociology*, was later revived by Durkheim and his collaborators (P. Fauconnet, M. Mauss, M. Halbwachs).[43] The influence of the Durkheim School on neighbouring disciplines can hardly be overestimated. It paved the way for Gustave Lanson's sociological theory of literature, for Lévy-Bruhl's ethnology and Henri Berr's science of history. All of these theoretical approaches were over-determined by the problematic founded by Saint-Simon and Comte. It may be sufficient to mention Lanson's lecture "L'Histoire littéraire et la sociologie"[44] delivered at the Ecole des Hautes Etudes in response to Durkheim's invitation.

It is hardly surprising, in this context, that contacts between French and German sociology were very sparse at the beginning of the twentieth century. The word "sociology" had assumed quite different meanings to the west and to the east of the Rhine. While German Weberians took sociology to be a hermeneutic science (*verstehende Wissenschaft*) in the sense of the New Kantians

Lask, Rickert and Windelband[45], who were primarily interested in individual understanding, Comte's disciples were dealing with social facts on a collective level, treating them as "things".[46] This is a substantial difference.

It probably accounts for the fact that, though contemporaries, Durkheim and Weber never took notice of each other. Edward A. Tiryakian confirms the assumption that this ignorance was not due to a lack of information but to a refusal to communicate:

> If this is true, then one can assume that nationalism was the decisive factor in both cases. Since each of them identified with his country as a whole more than any other Frenchman or German of the period (possibly a reflection of the social character of sociology?), each of them may have developed a nationalist resentment towards the other in spite of acknowledging scientific universality: precisely because each saw in the other not only the most competent representative of social science in his own country, but also the imposing symbol of a hostile culture.[47]

Here it becomes clear to what degree "culture" implies a system of values and value judgements. However, we may assume that, apart from national antagonisms, substantial differences between scientific languages or sociolects were also involved (cf. chap. 2).

The plausibility of this assumption is borne out by more recent publications, such as Pierre Ansart's *Les Sociologies contemporaines* (1990). In this work, the theories of Weber, Simmel and Schütz are commented on, but they are overshadowed by representatives of French sociology such as Tocqueville, Comte, Durkheim, Balandier, Bourdieu, Crozier and Touraine. Luhmann is conspicuous by his absence – not only in Ansart's introduction but also in English equivalents. The fact that only two or three of his (minor) works have so far been translated into French is yet another intercultural phenomenon a comparative scientist might be interested in.

Another such phenomenon is the striking absence of Luhmann and his school from an American publication like *Global Sociology*[48] by Robin Cohen and Paul Kennedy. Would Luhmann's notion of "global society" (*Weltgesellschaft*) not have fitted in with the authors' topics and preoccupations? Why is it missing? Why is it also missing in Anthony Giddens's voluminous introduction to Sociology? Chapter 16 of this work carries a title which makes a discussion about Luhmann's "global society" almost inevitable: "The Globalizing of Social Life".[49] In this respect, German introductions to sociology seem to have a broader intercultural basis.[50] (Needless to add that the intercultural perspective is based on the assumption that

Giddens's "globalization" and Luhmann's "global society" are quite different concepts – and that the differences are due to cultural idiosyncrasies.)

Hence it seems meaningful to adopt the additional hypothesis that in the
realm of social science certain theories acquire intercultural recognition
only in the course of time – if at all.[51] This hypothesis is confirmed by Raymond Boudon's *Etudes sur les sociologues classiques* (1998) which deals quite
thoroughly with authors such as Max Weber, Vilfredo Pareto, Max Scheler
and Adam Smith. In a more recent work, Bruno Péquignot and Pierre
Tripier discuss Georg Simmel and Norbert Elias at some length.[52]

However, counter-examples of a rapid assimilation of contemporary foreign theories also exist. Thus Patrick Peretti-Watels's *Sociologie du risque*
(2000) can be read as a prompt and creative response to Ulrich Beck's *Risi-
kogesellschaft* (1986) that also exists in English.[53] In this context, one could
use Rainer Winter's notion of "transnationalization"[54] which he himself
applies mainly to the field of "cultural studies". Is this "transnationalization", as exemplified by the transcultural idea of a "society and a sociology
of risk" a symptom of "globalization"? Does it announce the emergence of a
global, intercultural problematic and terminology in the human sciences?
It seems difficult to answer in the affirmative, especially since an expression
such as "cultural studies" is so idiosyncratic that so far it could not be adequately translated into French or German. It is not by chance that the English term is being used – and more so in the German-speaking than in the
Romance world.

Whoever ventures a closer look at international semiotics, will also tend
to answer in the negative. For in this discipline – very much like in post-war
Comparative Literature[55] – two heterogeneous traditions with different
terminologies seem to coexist: the North American and the Franco-
European.[56] Although the semiotic theories developed by Charles Sanders
Peirce and Charles William Morris as a continuation of John Locke's *semiotic* do contain Kantian elements (Peirce) and ideas of the Vienna Circle
(Morris), they are deeply rooted in American pragmatism which is very
remote from the kind of French rationalism Saussure and his followers
(Hjelmslev, Greimas) grew up with. The terminologies of these two schools
can hardly be said to have a common denominator. The eclecticism of
Umberto Eco's semiotics is partly due to the fact that it is meant to be a
synthesis of these two currents of thought.[57]

The mutual disregard Tiryakian observes between Durkheim and Weber
can also be detected between the representatives of the two culturally
heterogeneous semiotic schools. In their semiotic encyclopedia (1979),
Greimas and Courtés deal with the terms *semiology* and *semiotics* without
even mentioning Peirce and Morris. Their presentation is oriented towards

the approaches of Saussure and Hjelmslev. An analogous disregard for German (and sometimes Russian) semiotics can be found in British and American publications.[58]

It may have become clear at this stage that the universal character of internationally recognized mathematics, physics or computer studies has no counterpart in the realm of human science. So far, no universally, inter-culturally valid semiotic, sociology or literary theory has been invented.

Very much like literary criticism, semiotics is divided into antagonistic spheres, because its representatives deal with socio-cultural problems – and not simply with inanimate "objects". Time and again they feel obliged to take sides, to evaluate, to criticize. A case in point is Julia Kristeva's dis-tinction (of the 1960s) between a critical and self-reflecting *semiology* (*sémio-logie*) and an American *semiotic* marked by positivism and a "technical discourse".[59]

This engagement, like all the others, highlights the fact that culture as a complex network of problems challenges all of its scientists. They cannot abstain from acquiescing or criticizing – and from doing so in discourses which come about in cultures and are moved by ideologies.

Chapter 2

The Linguistic and Ideological Determinants of Theories: Theory as Sociolect and Discourse

In the human sciences, theories are only conceivable as linguistic constructs, because so far nobody has succeeded in adequately representing historic events, action sequences in dramas and novels or social developments with the help of formulae acceptable to natural scientists. Although the use of such formulae in text linguistics and semiotics (especially by Greimas and his group) may occasionally prove to be enlightening, it also yields trivialities. The appearance of scientific exactness becomes a substitute for exactness in the sense of instrumental rationality, in the sense of mathematics or physics.

Instead of aspiring towards scientism and its formal ideals, cultural and social scientists ought to aim at a precise description of the linguistic structures and mechanisms of their discourses.

Some time ago, the historian Werner Schiffer made an attempt to analyse the narrative structures of theories in conjunction with Arthur C. Danto's philosophy. He seems quite confident that textual analysis is an adequate solution, and his confidence evokes the social and linguistic situation of the 1970s, when semiotics occupied a dominant position in academia: "Nevertheless, in contemporary discussions, everyone seems to heed the call for textual analysis in the realm of social sciences and their self-reflection."[1] At present, not everybody could be persuaded to agree with this somewhat categorical statement. Although theory as a narrative, i.e. semantic and syntactic structure has been analysed by historians and especially semioticians[2] the self-reflection of social sciences on a narrative level, advocated by Schiffer, continues to have a utopian tinge to it. Years of interdisciplinary distrust and disregard may have taught another historian, Philipp Sarasin, to be both more circumspect and more realistic. In 2003, he reminds us of the resistance theories of discourse meet with among historians.[3]

This is why this chapter is based on concrete semiotic models and on the definition of discourse as a social, semantic and narrative structure.

Hopefully, this kind of interdisciplinary approach will avoid the one-sidedness of purely sociological, semiotic *or* historical analyses of discourse, ideology and theory and will counter at least some of the negative effects of the scientific division of labour.

However, it seems difficult to understand theory as a linguistic structure, as long as the discourse of theory has not been located in a linguistic, cultural and social context, where it appears as a reaction to religious, philosophical and ideological languages – without the speaking subject being always conscious of its reactions and long-term intentions. For this reason it seems necessary to take into account the role of subjectivity in theoretical (and ideological) discourse.

1.   Socio-Linguistic Situations, Sociolects and Discourses

Wherever "determinants" are evoked, the suspicion arises that some kind of determinism will be the result and that theoretical perception will be considered as entirely determined by language in the sense of Sapir's and Whorf's well-known thesis. These two linguists seem to rely heavily on the notion of the unconscious: "The fact of the matter is that the 'real world' is to a large extent unconsciously built up on the language habits of the group."[4] A complementary thesis was presented by Louis Althusser who invokes Lacan's analyses of the psyche in order to prove that ideology can turn unwitting individuals into subjects, because it is unconscious.[5]

Although useful, both theses are self-contradictory, insofar as they illustrate to what extent some individuals (e.g. the authors of the theses) are perfectly capable of reflecting critically on their own linguistic and ideological determination. One can consider them as theoreticians in order to distinguish them from spontaneously living people who tend to identify with "their" culture, language and ideology, so that their subjectivity appears (to social scientists) as a triple over-determination. On closer scrutiny, however, it becomes clear that even theoreticians such as Sapir, Whorf or Althusser, who have analysed virtually all aspects of over-determination, do not carry the process of self-reflection far enough.

It goes without saying that this process cannot possibly be continued until it reaches the non plus ultra of self-analysis. The idea is to define the *cultural problematic*, mapped out in the first chapter, as a *linguistic problematic* that can be reflected upon in discourse.

The very possibility of a global reflection of this kind makes us recognize the extreme and one-sided character of the Sapir-Whorf thesis and provokes a corresponding critique:

The strong version of Whorf's hypothesis, therefore, that posits that language determines the way we think, cannot be taken seriously, but a weak version, supported by the findings that there are cultural differences in the semantic associations evoked by seemingly common concepts, is generally accepted nowadays.[6]

The weak version may have been formulated too weakly in this sentence, for it does not take into account the possibility that our thought and speech *can* be globally over-determined by the social and linguistic situation we live in.

If this *socio-linguistic situation* is conceived of – in analogy to culture – as a problematic, i.e. as a dynamic, ever-changing constellation of problems and reactions to these problems by individuals and groups, then it becomes possible to describe socio-cultural conditions in linguistic terms. The idea is not to reduce social factors to linguistic ones, but to allow for a semiotic description of contexts in which theories as discourses develop and interact. A description of this kind is indispensable if structures and functions of theories are to be explained.

In the human sciences one of the fundamental problems is the fact that theoretical discourses form symbioses with religious, literary, ideological and scientific languages in order to articulate the social interests of individual and collective subjects.[7] Such collective languages will be called *sociolects*. Although this term is frequently used by Greimas and his group, it will acquire a slightly different meaning here.[8]

In this perspective, the socio-linguistic situation appears as a variable historical problematic: as an open-ended interaction of similar, incompatible or hostile sociolects, all of which react to historically specific problems in order to interpret and solve them. On this level, no substantial difference or dichotomy between social sciences and ideological languages can be postulated.

While at the beginning of the twentieth century Max Weber reacted to the bureaucratic tendencies in his society by upgrading the role of politicians and charismatic leaders,[9] Talcott Parsons wrote a systematic albeit discreet apology of the North American social system after the Second World War.[10] More recently, the French sociologist Alain Touraine responds to some of the most pressing problems of late modernity by espousing the cause of critical and progressive social movements.[11]

This kind of engagement can also be observed in literary and art theory, both marked by a symbiosis between theory formation and artistic practice. While the early Russian Formalists adhered to the precepts and programmes of the futurist avant-garde which inspired some of their key concepts, the Czech Structuralists derived some of their basic theorems from the experiments of French and Czech Surrealism and Czech Poetism.[12] The aesthetics and poetics of the *Tel Quel* Group around Sollers and Kristeva were in turn inspired by the Nouveau Roman in the sense of Butor, Robbe-Grillet and Claude Simon. They all show to what extent the *objects* of human sciences provide the theories and their subjects with ideas and terminologies (cf. chap. III, 4).[13]

Both the sociological and literary examples reveal that socio-linguistic situations are at the same time historical problematics undergoing perpetual change, because certain sociolects which were at the centre of philosophical and scientific debates are gradually made to yield their dominant position to new sociolects which articulate new collective interests linked to new problems. Such problems are rarely *solved* in the cultural and social sciences; rather, they are *superseded* by emerging problems which are pushed towards the centre of the problematic by new groups, organizations or movements.

Thus in post-war France, Marxism, phenomenology and existentialism ("les trois H", as Descombes puts it: Hegel, Husserl, Heidegger)[14] were superseded by sociolects such as semiotics, psychoanalysis, feminism and deconstruction during the transition from modernism to postmodernism. In most European countries, "culture" and "media" tend to become the central problems towards the end of the twentieth century for a majority of social scientists, and notions such as "literature", "art" or "ideology" are increasingly being considered in a "cultural" or "media" context.

The sociolect as an ideological, scientific, literary, philosophical or religious group language is merely a *theoretical construct* which combines a great variety of discourses (as semantic and narrative structures: cf. chap. 12) held together by lexical, semantic and syntactic affinities. In other words, a sociolect can be considered as the lexical and semantic repertoire used by individual and collective subjects in order to produce discourses and to construct (consciously or unconsciously) their own subjectivities. The sociolect as linguistic repertoire could thus be considered as *the totality of real and potential discourses produced by a social group in the course of time.*

The psychoanalytic, Marxist, deconstructionist or feminist sociolect determines the semantic relevance criteria, the classifications and definitions at the disposal of the speaking subjects. Although the latter are free to decide and choose, their choice is usually limited because it is determined by the semantics of the sociolect they speak.[15] The subject narrates the feminist, psychoanalytic, Marxist or rationalist "reality" which is always a construct based on a sociolect or a number of complementary sociolects. (In this context, the sociolect could also be considered with Yuri Lotman as a *secondary modelling system* – cf. chap. 12, 1 – i.e. as a collective language which transforms the primary or natural language in order to produce secondary meanings invested with particular interests.)[16]

The ideological or theoretical construct comes about as the subject of discourse introduces, in accordance with the *relevance criteria*[17] of its sociolect, certain semantic distinctions which make it possible to narrate and explain particular events and actions: why women are under-represented in scientific institutions, why the Soviet Union fell apart or why social differentiation in the sense of Luhmann yields autonomous, autopoietic systems. In all of these cases, the subject reacts to concrete social and linguistic problems: for example to the question whether the post-modern era is or is not an era of cultural and aesthetic de-differentiation (e.g. of the reading public).[18]

The concrete existentialist, feminist or Marxist discourse not only intro-duces particular relevance criteria and the corresponding semantic distinc-tions, but also decides which are the relevant *deep structures* and the corresponding *semantic isotopies*. The latter are defined by Greimas and Courtés as "regular recurrence[s], on the syntagmatic axis, of classemes which guarantee the homogeneity of discourse as enunciation".[19] By *classeme* they mean a general concept (like "active", "passive", "nature", "culture", etc.) which constitutes a class of semantically related words or a semantic iso-topy. Isotopies as semantic structures are interrelated on a conceptual or metaphorical level (e.g. in the semantic opposition *active/passive* or in the poetic analogy between "life" and "journey") and guarantee the coherence of ideological, theoretical or literary discourses. However, this coher-ence comes about both on a semantic *and* on a *syntactic* and *narrative* level.

The narrative dynamics of discourses are partly due to the interaction of *actants* (acting instances) which appear on positively or negatively *connoted* isotopies, thereby contributing to the development of the latter. Jürgen Link explains: "The recurring actants usually coincide with the recurring classemes of the underlying isotopy. In such actants, the isotopy thus appears at the text surface."[20] In other words, actants very often represent general concepts or classemes such as "politics", "economics", "good" or "evil".

In addition to the actants of enunciation (the speaking subjects), the most important of which are the *sender* and the *recipient*, Greimas distinguishes the following actants *within* a discourse or an utterance: the *addresser*, the *counter-addresser*, the *subject*, the *anti-subject* and the *object*. The subject and the anti-subject are symmetrically accompanied by *helpers* and *opponents*.[21] It goes without saying that the subject's or hero's helpers are the opponents of the anti-subject or anti-hero and vice versa.

The relationship between the addresser and the addressee is described by Greimas as follows: "The addresser (a social authority which assigns

an important mission to the hero) endows the hero with the role of addressee, thereby establishing a contractual relationship; for it is assumed that
the fulfilment of the contract involves a reward (...)."[22] This scheme is to
be found in most legends or fairy tales, where a king (*addresser*) sends out a
knight (*addressee, subject*) in order to wrest a captive princess (*object*) from
a dragon (*anti-subject, anti-addressee*) who guards her on behalf of an enemy
king (*anti-addresser*).

It also structures most detective stories and underlies many of Ian Fleming's James Bond novels. Thus James Bond as subject or addressee can be sent
out by the British Government, a metonymic representative of the "free
world", in order to defeat a secret agent acting on behalf of the "Eastern
Bloc" or the "Axis of Evil" on the isotopy (semantic level) of "totalitarian-
ism" or "fundamentalism". In such cases, the object can be a secret weapon
or formula.

Commenting on Fleming's novels, Umberto Eco pointed out that, within
the well-known black and white scheme, the villain or anti-subject is invariably endowed with defects which enable the almost perfect Bond to defeat
him and ward off a deadly menace.[23]

Greimas calls such defects and the corresponding strengths *modalities*, distinguishing *virtualizing* ("must", "wish"), *actualizing* ("to be able to", "to
know") and *accomplishing* ("to do", "to be") *modalities*.[24] The function of
this terminology is easily explained. In order to achieve something in a
fairy tale or a novel, in daily life or politics, I have to have certain abilities,
aspirations and the will to act. This is why in political discourse, frequently
structured by a polemical dualism, competence plays such an important
part: the *speaking subject* (*sujet d'énonciation*) claims explicitly or implicitly to
dispose of all positive modalities and asserts or insinuates that the opponent
(government or opposition) lacks will, competence or coherence.

Stemming from one or several sociolects, a political, literary or scientific
discourse thus appears as a *semantic and narrative structure based on an actantial
model and a corresponding distribution of modalities*.[25] (Greimas, who starts from
Vladimir Propp's functional analysis of the Russian fairy tale,[26] develops
this analysis by reconstructing it on a semantic basis, by introducing
Lucien Tesnière's concept of *actant* and by applying the new semiotic
theory not only to literary or mythical but also to political, commercial
and legal texts.)[27]

At this stage, somebody might object that this kind of analysis may be
applied to fairy tales or political rhetoric, not however to scientific discourse
which – we might assume or hope – has nothing to do with heroes, anti-
heroes, opponents or villains. Are philosophical and scientific theories not
supposed to stay aloof from value judgements, are they not meant to be

"objective"? An answer to this question can only be obtained if we are prepared to have a closer look at several such theories in order to find out how
their discourses function and what "makes them tick".

2.   Ideology and Theory: The Discourse of Theory

In the human sciences, theories without an ideological engagement hardly
exist, for most of them pursue a political goal: the proletarian revolution,
equality for women or a liberal social order, an "open society". Norbert
Elias addresses this issue when he points out:

> The problem human scientists have to grapple with cannot be solved by
> an attempt to renounce their function as members of a group in favour of
> their scientific function. They cannot possibly cease to be involved in the
> social and political matters of their group and their time, they cannot
> avoid being concerned by them. Moreover, their own participation,
> their engagement is one of the prerequisites for their understanding of
> those problems which they are expected to solve as scientists.[28]

If we now try to translate these ideas into the socio-semiotic language of this
book, we obtain the following paraphrase: all theoretical sociolects and their
discourses are ideological in the sense that they articulate group interests
which can be understood as discursive reactions to particular problems or
aspects of a problematic. Groups react to these problems by adhering to certain relevance criteria underlying the deep structures, isotopies and actantial models of their discourses. The following model analyses may illustrate
some aspects of this socio-semiotic practice.

   Karl Marx's and Friedrich Engels's *Manifesto of the Communist Party* (1848)
is based on a fundamental opposition which functions as a deep structure:
the antagonism between capital and workforce and the corresponding contrast between semantic isotopies and actantial functions. While the subject
actant "proletariat" can be observed to act on the semantic levels or isotopies of "wage labour" and "revolution" (the latter being at the same time
addresser in the sense of "history" or "historical revolution"), the anti-
subject "bourgeoisie" acts on the isotopy of "capital" (at the same time
anti-addresser in the sense of "reaction" or "anti-history"). Within this
model, the communists fulfil the function of "authentic helpers" who –
unlike the other opposition parties – always "represent the interests of the
movement as a whole".[29] The object is the "classless society", a completely
new world. Speaking of the proletarians, Marx and Engels conclude: "They

have a world to win."[30] One of the essential, but often neglected features of
this discourse is the fact that the authors construct their historical narrative
around *collective actors or actants*. The subtitle "Bourgeois and Proletarians" is
followed by the famous sentence: "The history of all hitherto existing society
is the history of class struggles."[31]

A closer look at Georg Lukács's *History and Class Consciousness* (1923) shows
to what extent the Marxist sociolect is developed by a Neo-Marxist discourse on the level of *modalities*. One of the fundamental ideas underlying
this work is the postulate that the proletariat is cognitively superior to the
bourgeoisie, because it is able to adopt the point of view of totality: "That
is to say, if the bourgeoisie is held fast in the mire of immediacy from which
the proletariat is able to extricate itself, this is neither purely accidental nor
a purely theoretical scientific problem."[32] Not the Hegelian background is
important here,[33] but the fact that Lukács, more so than Marx, attributes
certain positive modalities (of knowledge and ability) to the proletariat
and withholds them from the bourgeoisie as anti-subject. In this respect,
his discourse hardly differs from the ideological discourses of politicians or
writers like Ian Fleming who endow their heroes with almost magical modalities. The Marxist intellectual of the 1920s puts so much faith in the historical mission of the working class that he is finally blinded by his own
ideological engagement – as Lukács himself recognizes after the Second
World War.[34]

At this stage, someone might point out that we have left this kind of Marxist mythology far behind and are now ready to exchange it for Max Weber's
sociology or Niklas Luhmann's systems theory. However, a closer look at
these theories reveals that they are no less ideological, political than the
Marxist ones. For ideological reasons they cannot rely on the same degree
of consensus natural sciences meet with. The "strong consensus"[35] George
Couvalis evokes in conjunction with these sciences does not seem to obtain in
the social and cultural sciences, because their semantics are fraught with
ideological interests.

In Max Weber's *Economy and Society* (1921), for example, we come across
the following sentence concerning the charismatic principle: "In this purely
empirical and value-free sense it is, however, the specifically 'creative', revolutionary power of history."[36] In Weber's discourse, which is based on a
liberal-nationalist and individualist ideology shaken by the crisis of liberalism between the wars,[37] charisma is an individual characteristic: "By charisma we mean a personal quality which is considered as extraordinary
(...)."[38] In view of the fact that Weber's "understanding sociology" has frequently – and correctly – been interpreted as a reaction to Marxism
within the socio-cultural problematic of the 1920s, a comparison with

Marx's and Engels's actantial model seems to make sense. The comparison shows that Weber's narrative is not only based on a different semantic opposition, namely on that between the isotopies "bureaucracy" and "charisma", but is also constructed around a completely different actantial model. The *collective actant* "proletariat" is replaced by the *individual actant* "charismatic personality" – possibly as a result of Nietzsche's influence, as Mommsen points out.[39] A substitution of this kind cannot be considered as neutral or "value-free" in the sense of Weber. (The question what *Wertfreiheit* or value-freedom can mean in this context will be discussed in some detail in the fourth chapter.)

Even Luhmann's theory of social systems, often dealt with on purely technical terms, is based on value-laden semantic distinctions and on corresponding actantial models. Even in this case, the subject of discourse reacts to particular social and linguistic problems – and not to others. By virtue of this selection, which is at the same time an answer to the question what is *relevant*, it takes sides. Luhmann's basic distinction between system and environment implies an actantial model that excludes both individual and collective actants (in the sense of Weber's charismatic personality or of Marx's social class). Obeying the logic of progressive abstraction, it also deletes (unlike Weber's model) the concept of nation considered as national society and as a collective actant, because "names such as Italy or Spain ought not to occur in a theory, and were it only for methodological reasons". Luhmann adds: "Parsons was quite circumspect in choosing the title *The System of Modern Societies*."[40] Like Parsons who spoke of the social system in general, but meant North American society, Luhmann tends to ignore all particularities and to replace the individual or collective actants of other theories by an abstract or mythical actant called "system".[41] He writes for example: "When a participating system experiences a situation as being doubly contingent, this has an impact on its behaviour."[42] But are we actually dealing with systems which experience something or behave in certain ways? Is society not more plausibly imagined as a complex interaction of "fields" in the sense of Bourdieu, as an entity which, from country to country and from culture to culture, obeys different political, legal and linguistic rules? Luhmann, who views the notion of culture with scepticism, seems to believe in the system, which he tries to preserve within the framework of a consensus ideology,[43] very much like Marx and Weber believed in the class or the charismatic personality. His attempts to solve contemporary social problems are to be understood within a theoretical context based on the idea of increasing the "irritability" or "sensitivity" of social systems: "The irritability of the systems has to be increased, something that can only be achieved within the context of their self-referential closed circuit functioning. This is precisely what systems theory is about (...)."[44] This proposal is not only an ideological plea for the perpetuation of existing systems by continuous improvement; it also implies a rejection of the class struggle and the charisma-bureaucracy models developed by Marx and Weber.

On the whole, it becomes clear that ideological engagement is the *motor of theory* in the human sciences and that *it can be observed in the semantic and narrative structures of all discourses.* Luhmann's semantic distinction between system and environment produces a discourse very different from that of Habermas which is based on the distinction *system/life world.* In this case, the originally polysemic word "system" acquires two ideologically incompatible meanings.

In conjunction with these short analyses, "ideology" *in the general sense* can now be defined as *an interest-guided discourse produced within one or several sociolects by a speaking subject which constructs its own identity by adopting certain relevance criteria, classifications and isotopies and by narrating social reality or a part of it with the help of an actantial model.*

This definition is not only applicable to political, religious or moral ideologies, but to all theories in the human sciences, none of which can function without ideological engagement. In this case, Karl Mannheim would refer to a "total ideology",[45] because – semiotically speaking – *collective interests are articulated in the lexical and semantic units of discourse as much as in its actantial models and narrative structures.*

This terminological situation seems unsatisfactory because we know that the discourses of Weber, Parsons or Luhmann differ quite substantially from political rhetoric or propaganda. The sociologists themselves are well aware of this fact. Luhmann, for example, points out: "Nowadays one should start worrying when one hears the following remarks in the electoral campaign committee: 'People simply want to know who are the heroes and the villains, and *that*'s something *we* can tell them.'"[46] It becomes obvious here that ideology in a negative or critical sense is dominated by a dualism or manicheism, which serious theoreticians try to avoid.

In accordance with these findings, it now seems possible to present a negative or critical definition of ideology. It is *a discourse whose subject eliminates all ambivalences by constructing dualistic actantial models (hero/villain), identifies its representations with reality and renounces all kinds of self-critical reflection, thereby producing an authoritarian monologue which excludes dialogue with other discourses (sociolects).*[47]

"Ideology" in this sense is both an apology of the real world and false consciousness.[48] As a discourse or linguistic *structure* it does not correspond to a "correct" or "false" *point of view* but can be associated – very

much like the authoritarian character – with a large number of heterogeneous social perspectives.

Although it would be somewhat unfair to suggest that Luhmann, Weber
and Marx lack a sense of ambivalence and critical reflection, it seems that
the negative definition of ideology – which completes the general definition – is in some respects also applicable to their discourses. In fact, it can
be applied to most theories in the cultural and social sciences, since the subjects of their discourses tend to identify monologically with reality and to
forget that they merely propose *contingent constructions of the world* which are
inseparable from their *contingent and particular viewpoints*.

Commenting on his "empirical science of literature", the German media
scientist and literary critic Siegfried J. Schmidt explains that it "was conceived as an alternative to [all] other brands of literary criticism (Literaturwissenschaft)".[49] Monological or ideological projects of this kind have been
popular with philosophers since Plato and Hegel, and it is probably not
unrealistic to assume than in the cultural sciences they are the rule rather
than the regrettable exception.

Luhmann's discourse also appears to be a monologue in this sense:
"Another possibility, the most idle compromise is: 'pluralism'."[50] The ideological intention underlying this unambiguous condemnation of theoretical
pluralism is clear: Luhmann's own systems theory is meant to be institutionalized as the only scientific theory of society. A strategy of this kind can best
be understood within the framework of Bourdieu's theory of the *scientific
field*[51] – and this meta-theoretical explanation of a theoretician's attempt
to secure a monopoly position in the "field" is sufficient to discredit all such
monopolistic delusions of grandeur.

At this stage, it seems meaningful to define the critical and theoretical discourse by contrasting it with the ideological monologue. *Theory is an interest-
guided discourse, whose subject of enunciation reflects upon its relevance criteria, its
semantic and narrative techniques and its actantial models in a particular socio-linguistic
context, presenting them as contingent constructions of an ambivalent reality the complexity of which can only be recognized in a permanent dialogue with other theories.*

The decisive element here is the auto-critical attitude of the speaking subject (of the "narrator"), which is not commented on by Popper, Stegmüller
and Luhmann, and the open structure of theoretical discourse.

All things considered, "theory" thus appears as a paradoxical project
whose subject incessantly tries to reflect upon its ideology (in the general
sense) and to criticize it – without abandoning it, however. For renouncing
all ideological engagement would mean sacrificing theory to relativism and
to indifference defined as "interchangeability of all social values".[52] One of
the flaws of Adorno's and Horkheimer's Critical Theory is the one-sided

definition of ideology as "false consciousness". This definition overlooks the productive, creative role of ideology. It explains why Adorno and Horkheimer never reflected upon their own ideological engagement.

Their case helps to answer the question why some theorists retreat into monologue. They try to hide their contingent ideology (in the general sense) by pretending that it is universally valid (thus turning their discourse into an ideology in the negative sense). They tend to identify "truth" or "true knowledge" with a particular point of view and the corresponding relevance criteria. It goes without saying that their critics categorically refuse to adopt their point of view. This stalemate can only be overcome if the futile question concerning the "correct" (proletarian, conservative, liberal or feminist) point of view is abandoned and rationality located in *the discourse structures of theories*: especially in the attitude adopted by the speaking subject towards its own semantic and narrative techniques.

At this point, a *functional distinction* between theoretical and ideological discourses seems possible with respect to the concept of subject. The structural and the functional definitions complement and elucidate one another. While dualistic ideologies help individuals and groups to become subjects and engage in coherent action by distinguishing "good" and "evil", "justice" and "injustice", theories structured by ambivalence reveal the dialectical unity of opposites without a synthesis. By uniting what ideologies keep rigidly apart, they invite the speaking subjects to reflect critically on their theoretical premises and to practise dialogue.

They are self-ironical in the sense of Musil, "humoristic" in the sense of Pirandello and Unamuno: "For reflection, a fruit of bitter experience, imbued the author with the feeling of contrariness (il sentimento del contrario), which induced him to recognize his wrong (. . .)."[53] This means concretely that what matters in theoretical discourse is the recognition of one's own wrong and the ability to overcome it by reflection, self-irony and dialogue.

More often than not, this ability may turn out to be an obstacle on the subject's path towards unity, identity and coherent action. This is why critical self-reflection is hardly in demand in the world of politics. For this world is (understandably) held together by the ideological desire for coherence, efficient action and palpable institutional success. All of these criteria can turn individuals and groups into ideological subjects in the sense of Althusser[54] and integrate them into dualistic semantic schemes and the corresponding narrative structures (*hero/villain*, etc.).

The fact that in 1968 Critical Theory was thoroughly misunderstood by the protesting students and movements, who invoked the Marxist "unity of theory and practice", explains its transformation into ideology and monologue. One should bear in mind that this tendency towards monologue is inherent in every theory in the human sciences, because theory as a paradoxical structure cannot survive without an ideological engagement.[55]

The theory of theory mapped out here and developed as a Dialogical Theory in *Part Three*, does not pretend to supersede all existing theories. On the contrary, it recognizes their *raison d'être* and merely attempts to mediate critically between them, presenting itself as a contingent construct which, by its openness and its hypothetical character, invites dialogue in a fragmented, pluralized and antagonistic society.

In such a society, it seems hardly meaningful to preach "true knowledge" or "real science" which in the end turns out to be just another hermetic language recognized by a handful of converts. It seems more fruitful to develop an approach permitting us to mediate between the various sociolects and the corresponding scientific groups and to reach a certain level of critical consensus. "Pluralism" in this sense is not an idle compromise we should never agree to, as Luhmann would have us think, but a social fact quite independent of our agreement or disagreement. In *Part Three*, it will become clear that, far from being unpractical, the meta-theory proposed here is geared towards the practice of dialogue.

3. Subjectivity and Reflection

Reflection is a an old philosophical, hermeneutic concept which Althusser and his followers derided because they imagined a general social and linguistic over-determination of all subjects. For them, subjectivity *was* over-determination, subjection and the subject a *sub-iectum*.[56]

Fortunately, the situation is not as one-dimensional as these Spinozists[57] and admirers of Lacan would make us believe. Rüdiger Bubner succinctly summarizes the programme of a critical theory of the subject when he points out: "Reflection can at any moment break the determinism of fate."[58] One could add: even if fate takes on the form of "ideology", "language" or "the unconscious".

So far, philosophers have failed to explain what exactly ought to be the object of reflection. This is why the following concluding remarks will indicate the *three levels* a theoretical subject reflects upon: the level of discourse, the sociolect and the socio-linguistic situation or problematic.

The "discourse as the context of the subject's self-construction and sole source of our knowledge concerning the subject"[59] turns into an object of reflection, when the subject of a theoretical discourse begins to take into account its own lexical, semantic and syntactic-narrative activities. On this level, it may become conscious of the fact that its relevance criteria and semantic distinctions (e.g. *system/environment* [Luhmann], *systems/life world* [Habermas] or *social movement/state administration* [Touraine]) open up narrative perspectives which are quite different from those of other discourses.

Actantial models derived from particular semantics are not always comparable with actantial models originating in other discourse semantics. Hence the subject of theory is well advised to reflect upon its own actantial models and their social origins. In philosophical and scientific debates of the past, for example, in the controversies between Critical Rationalism and Critical Theory, this reflection hardly ever took place. This is undoubtedly one of the reasons why a fundamental affinity between these two approaches was overlooked: their *common* refusal to accept the collective actants of Marxism (i.e. the dichotomy *bourgeoisie/proletariat*). In both cases, in Critical Rationalism and Critical Theory, these antagonistic collectives were replaced by the reflecting individual, who, in the Critical Theory of the Frankfurt School, is inseparable from the human subject as a whole.

However, it would have been important to understand the structure of one's own discourse as "essay" (Horkheimer, Adorno), "thinking in models" (Adorno) or "parataxis" in relation to a sociolect which, after the Second World War, increasingly emphasized the autonomy of the individual subject and similar social values. At least in this respect it was *related* to the critical individualism of Popper and Hans Albert. This argument will be developed in some detail in chapter 11, 2, where the discourse of Critical Theory will be at the centre of the scene.

The reflection upon one's own actantial model and discourse structure is incomplete as long as it does not include what Greimas calls *theoretical modalities* (*vouloir, devoir, pouvoir, savoir,* etc.). What do modalities such as "intend", "must", "can" and "know" mean in my theory? Is it the intention of the subject of theory to criticize the social order? Does theory have to reflect upon itself as an object? Do statements of a theory have to be verifiable, falsifiable or quantifiable? Does a theory pretend to be able to predict social developments? Is "future" its object – and in what sense? What does a theory have to know or detect: its own cultural, linguistic and ideological character – or its translatability into a formal language?

It is obvious that some of these modalities are incompatible and cannot be activated simultaneously. However, it is crucial to think about the modalities of one's own discourse (and about those of other discourses), before one criticizes or "refutes" a competing theory – only to realize some time later that it has survived the radical critique because the latter has missed its intentions, its modalities. Some psychoanalytic or feminist theories may not pretend to be "falsifiable" or "translatable" into formal language; some sociologies may be neither interested in quantification nor in predicting developments, etc. Therefore it does not make sense to criticize them for lacking modalities they never intended to acquire.

Critical reflection ought to go beyond one's own discourse or sociolect in order to take into account the entire socio-linguistic problematic in an inter-cultural perspective. Adopting this perspective, one soon recognizes that some statements concerning the institutionalization of theories are not convincing because they are not reflected upon in context.

In the fourth edition of *Wörterbuch für Soziologie (Dictionary of Sociology)* we read for example: "In the social sciences, the empirical-nomological concept of theory, which bears the imprint of (...) Critical Rationalism, has become dominant."[60] Although this opinion may sound plausible in some ears, it certainly is not the opinion of all sociologists: for neither Luhmann and his disciples nor Anthony Giddens and his followers have adopted this particular approach (Giddens is much closer to hermeneutics than to Popper's rationalism). With respect to the French context, in which Raymond Boudon's Weberian and critical-rationalist (Popperian) sociology is quite marginal compared with Bourdieu's and Touraine's dominant models, this opinion turns out to be outright false.

Finally, the subject's self-reflection ought to take into account the power relations between natural languages. A meta-theoretician or second-grade observer in the sense of Luhmann will hardly be indifferent to the fact that those who allow themselves to be turned into subjects by a dominant language and the concomitant culture (e.g. American English), miss important texts and crucial arguments put forward in other cultures. Cases in point are Habermas who tends to read Derrida in English translation[61] and to rely on American literature on Derrida – or German articles on Greimas and Jakobson, which ignore all the French and Russian comments and discussions on the works of these authors.[62]

The easily observable fact that German social scientists tend to focus on British and American literature[63] while the occurrence of German, French, Spanish and Russian titles in British and American social science is constantly diminishing and rapidly approaching zero, is not insignificant. For theory formation and the construction of our own theoretical subjectivity comes about in our interaction with certain types of natural and scientific language. Whoever disregards this fact and fails to reflect upon the development of his subjectivity, turns into a *sub-iectum*, i.e. an unconscious subject of a consolidated cultural and ideological hegemony.

Naturally, it is impossible to take into account all discussions in all languages, and it may be considered normal – *not rational, however* – that most scientists follow the debates in their own culture and language more intensively than in others. However, theoretical openness, as it is understood here, is accompanied by the rankling question whether the concept of theory has not by any chance been dealt with in a revolutionary manner by a Japanese or Korean author whose book we cannot read. Theory is kept alive by a growing interest in the Other and in otherness; it is paralysed by monologue.

Chapter 3

Theory, Science, Institution and the "Strong Programme"

In view of the fact that "theory" and "science" are frequently used as synonyms, it seems necessary to distinguish the two concepts by relating them to the notion of "institution" which refers to the social context of theory formation.

This context is the main object of the *strong programme* developed in Britain by the two sociologists Barry Barnes and David Bloor. They radicalize Karl Marx's and Karl Mannheim's thesis about the social determination of knowledge, arguing that not only the cultural and social sciences are driven by social interests (as Marx and Mannheim would have it), but also the natural sciences and even mathematics.

The aim of this chapter is to show that this "strong" view of social over-determination is too strong, because it ignores certain differences between cultural and natural sciences which were already mentioned in the Introduction, but will be analysed in more detail here. One of the factors, which the defenders of the *strong programme* seem to overlook, is the difference between the global *process of rationalization* that subordinates all sciences (although not to the same degree) to instrumental, technical reason and the *immediate cultural and ideological determinisms* that can only be observed in the cultural and social sciences. This difference is also neglected by the German author Karin Knorr-Cetina who in some respects relies on the arguments of the *strong programme*.

An alternative to this programme seems to be Georges Canguilhem's structural distinction between ideology and scientific theory in the natural sciences. It will be dealt with in the third section of this chapter.

In the last section, the particularity of the cultural and social sciences will be described both on the structural-discursive and on the functional level. It will be defined with respect to ideological interference and the relationship between the subject of theory and its objects.

1. Theory, Science and Institution

The fact that cultural and social sciences undergo different forms of institutionalization in different countries has already been commented on. It ought to be dealt with in conjunction with the complementary fact that these sciences are ideologically heterogeneous – although they are very often institutionalized under labels such as "sociology" or "anthropology" which suggest homogeneity.

Whereas natural sciences such as physics, astronomy and chemistry differ exclusively on a technical or scientific level, i.e. in relation to their object constructions and methods, the cultural sciences are riddled with ideological antagonisms and conflicts between theories. Disciplines such as sociology, semiotics, literary criticism or history are heterogeneous in the sense that each of them consists of competing theoretical sociolects which are at the same time ideological languages.

Feminist linguistics, feminist literary criticism or Marxist sociology are not "inadmissible intrusions" of the political into the scientific institution, but are to be regarded as types of ideological engagement comparable to conservative, liberal or ecological approaches to these disciplines.

Whenever a particular theoretical group language or sociolect dominates the teaching of sociology, anthropology or literary criticism in a university, the corresponding ideology also dominates. This phenomenon is amply illustrated by the development of scientific schools such as the Geneva School founded by Saussure, the Frankfurt Institute of Social Research which gave birth to Critical Theory or the Constance School which focused on reader response criticism. Rationalism, Marxism and liberal individualism were demonstrably involved in these three instances.

It need hardly be emphasized that the absence of ideological interference in the natural sciences does not imply absence of social interest and conflict. However, their conflicts are of a different nature, for they primarily involve the distribution or redistribution of material, financial resources. Recently, Peter Weingart has shown to what extent the financing of one research programme at the expense of another has become the bone of contention among natural scientists.[1] The crucial difference with respect to the cultural sciences, however, is the fact that such economic and social conflicts *do not result in an ideological interference with the theoretical discourse as a seman-tic and narrative structure.* Although natural sciences come about within the general cultural process of rationalization, their discourses (languages) are *free from ideology.*

A brief example will illustrate this argument. As a metaphor, the physical concept of *magnetic field* is certainly comparable to Pierre Bourdieu's notion of *scientific field*. At the same time, however, these two seemingly so similar metaphors are poles apart. While the expression *magnetic field* enjoys trans-cultural, trans-ideological validity and is being used by physicists all over the world, Bourdieu's expression *scientific* or *literary field* (*champ scientifique, littéraire*) remains an ideological apple of discord appreciated by a sizeable number of feminists, considered with scepticism by certain Marxists and rejected by Weberians and supporters of Luhmann's systems theory.[2]

On balance, one might say that "theory" and "science" are not synonyms, because in the natural as well as in the cultural sciences "science" is the generic term. In both cases, theoretical discourses vie with one another within the framework of an institutionalized science such as physics, sociology or linguistics. Unlike in physics, however, where the coexistence of Newton's and Einstein's models[3] does not entail ideological controversies (between feminists, conservatives or liberals), because it can be discussed in purely theoretical and technical terms, competition in the cultural and social sciences is fraught with ideological conflicts involving the lexical, semantic and narrative levels of discourse (cf. chap. 2). It seems worthwhile to have a closer look at Bloor's and Barnes's *strong programme* in this light.

2. Bloor's and Barnes's "Strong Programme": A Critique

The dilemma underlying the *strong programme*, which applies Marx's and Mannheim's thesis about the social determination of social sciences to the natural sciences, can be summed up in a few words: the programme is enlightening in some respects, because it is based on the assumption that both, the natural and the cultural sciences, develop within specific social and historical contexts so that an archaic tribe on the banks of the river Amazon is incapable of producing astrophysics or psychoanalysis. At the same time, however, it is far too abstract and thus obscures the crucial difference between long-term social processes of rationalization and immediate ideological impact. Lacking a concrete concept of *ideology as discourse*, Barnes and Bloor tend to subsume natural and cultural sciences under the general principle of social determination and to overlook essential differences.

In a slightly different context, H. M. Collins follows the general post-modern trend towards particularization and relativism,[4] when he argues that nowadays science is no longer regarded as the realm of true knowledge, but as a "cultural activity".[5] Barnes, Bloor and Mulkay go a few steps further, when they postulate a causal link between scientific arguments or research programmes on the one hand and social interests on the other.

David Bloor, for instance, refers to studies "which have traced the connections between economic, technical and industrial developments and the content of scientific theories".[6] He cites as examples the causal links between water and steam technologies and "the content of theories in thermodynamics".[7] The question of course is, what is meant by "content" here: the objects as scientific object *constructions*, the subjective *interests* guiding research or the *semantics* of discourse?

This crucial question can hardly be answered in conjunction with the principal four points of the *strong programme*. These points are: (1) the sociology of science is based on a causal argument and thus is "concerned with the conditions which bring about belief or states of knowledge"; (2) it is "impartial with respect to truth and falsity, rationality or irrationality, success or failure" (meaning that it aims at a rational explanation of all phenomena, including the irrational ones); (3) it is "symmetrical in its style of explanation – the same types of cause would explain, say, true and false beliefs"; and (4) it is reflexive: "In principle its patterns of explanation would have to be applicable to sociology itself."[8] Bloor is quite right in arguing against some of his critics who maintain that, within the *strong programme*, causal explanations of certain views invalidate these views. His thesis according to which causation does *not* imply error is correct. (I cannot refute a theory, e.g. psychoanalysis, by pointing out that it originates in ancient myths[9].)

In most cases it is possible to achieve a better understanding of a particular theory by confronting it with the theory it opposes and combats for ideological reasons. In the present case it is the version of Critical Rationalism propounded by Karl R. Popper and especially Imre Lakatos.[10] Lakatos distinguishes between internal and external determinants of scientific evolution. He believes that the internal laws of this process are essential, whereas the external, i.e. social or political, factors are secondary or relatively unimportant.[11] He looks upon the development of science in a perspective similar to that adopted by the Russian Formalists in the case of literature: to them, literary evolution is an autonomous process.[12] In Lakatos's opinion, external, political impacts on science are to be located in the realm of the contingent and the irrational, which make themselves felt in extreme situations: for example in the "German physics" of National Socialism or in the Lyssenko Affair[13] under Stalinism. He is convinced that, on the whole, scientific evolution is to be regarded as a rational, linear and cumulative process.

At this point, Barnes, Bloor and J. Henry object that in reality this process is kept in motion by social conflicts – not merely in crisis situations marked by revolutionary discoveries or inventions, but also in everyday research. They refer to the work of Harry M. Collins in order to show "how conflicting beliefs may be sustained about 'the same experience', and how reasonable human beings may actually take 'the same experience' as inductive confirmation for conflicting beliefs".[14] However, such controversies may crop up at any time in all social contexts, not just in science.

Bloor attempts to illustrate his argument by references to historical examples: among other things to the pseudo-discovery of "N-rays" by the French physicist Blondlot. Bloor shows that British, German and North American physicists were quick to notice the flaws in Blondlot's experiments. Their scepticism was by no means mitigated by Blondlot's membership of the French Academy and his prestige among his compatriots. "The lapse was a personal and psychological failure of competence by Blondlot and his compatriots. They fell short of common and standardised procedures."[15]

It is not quite clear what Bloor means by the last sentence. Should he mean that even in an exact science such as physics negligence and ignorance can occur, then his argument is simply trivial; were he to suggest, however, that in French physics the "standardised procedures" as social facts differed from those in other countries for cultural or ideological reasons, then his own discourse would become questionable. The expression "psychological failure" even casts doubts on his own brand of the *strong programme*, because it suggests that in physics, contingent *psychic factors* may have a certain impact, not however intrusions of cultural and ideological value judgements which would produce culturally or ideologically specific discourses.

In order to prove the existence of such intrusions, Bloor would have to show that after Blondlot's "discovery" a different kind of physics developed in France: by analogy to the specifically French *critique littéraire*, French law,[16] French semiotics or sociology. In reality, he shows that the opposite was the case: namely that Blondlot's mistake was corrected by international, intercultural criticism and that, after this regrettable episode, "French" physics was reintegrated into international physics.[17]

This line of argument also applies to Michael Mulkay's description of the situation of French physics at the beginning of the nineteenth century: "This was so because almost all the influential figures in French physics were rigidly opposed to non-corpuscular optics and because these men controlled the dissemination of legitimate information in this field."[18] It is conceivable, of course, that in some spheres of the natural sciences particular patterns of thought – temporarily – prevail. In this case, however, very much like in Blondlot's case, ulterior developments led to the elimination of the anomaly and to a confirmation of the universal character of international physics whose representatives now rely on electronic data transfer and on international English as a relatively neutral means of communication. In French cultural and social sciences, on the other hand, Auguste Comte's positivism still hasn't entirely disappeared.

This is why Michael Mulkay's arguments are too abstract, too vague, when he attempts to "regard the products of science as social constructions like all other social products".[19] If he means by this that all scientists are socialized subjects whose subjectivity as perception and cognition comes about in cultural contexts, then hardly any objections can be made. At the same time, however, the argument is trivial, for it does not relate the social character of science to the fact that the discourses of all natural sciences are internationally institutionalized and based on an *internationally recognized terminology*.

The problem seems to consist in the fact that the lexical and semantic foundations and actantial models of the natural sciences are beyond political, moral or religious ideologies – not however beyond society and culture, as was shown in the first chapter. Semantic opposites such as *positive pole/negative pole, acid/lye* cannot be used for ideological purposes (without losing their original meaning). This also applies to the object-actants of natural sciences: new alloys, vaccines or proteins.

It is hard to imagine a group of scientists arguing that the protein produced by a competing team is "conservative", "sexist", "subversive" or "favourable to the existing social order". An argument of this kind would be considered as meaningless or a joke. However, it becomes meaningful as soon as it is applied to the concepts, goals or object actants of social sciences such as "classless society" (Marx), "open society" (Popper), "equality", "freedom", "economic growth" or Luhmann's "irritability of systems". The last term quoted here can certainly be defined as "conservative" or "favourable to the existing social order".

The production of proteins – and several other issues – are at stake in Karin Knorr-Cetina's sociological study of the production of scientific knowledge which analyses communication processes in chemical laboratories. One of the key theses of the book, parts of which rely on Barnes's and Bloor's *strong programme*, is that the research of natural scientists is marked by understanding, conflicting interpretations and communication problems accompanied by a search for consensus[20] and that in this respect natural sciences are no different from cultural and social sciences. If differences exist, they are secondary: "To begin with, there is the question whether the methodological practice of the natural and technological sciences is fundamentally different from the symbolic and interpretive, 'hermeneutic' practice of the social sciences. I believe that the answer is no."[21]

Knorr-Cetina's argument, "that interpretation and communication are as much to be found in the actions of the technical and natural sciences as in the actions of our everyday life",[22] hardly goes beyond the basic tenets of the *strong programme* and is therefore beside the point. It stands to reason that natural scientists communicate, are prone to misunderstandings, interpret the results of experiments differently and quarrel about new concepts, trying to get the better of their competitors, especially when financial or material advantages are at stake in scientific institutions. However, they communicate in non-ideological, technical languages – which are nevertheless products of culture and of progressive rationalization (cf. chap. 1).

It may have become clear, at this stage, how important the concept of ideology is, especially if used in contrast to "theory". For not everything that can be defined as "social" is at the same time "ideological". The instructions next to the public telephone or under a computer screen are in all respects products of a highly technical society and culture – but they are not ideological (liberal, conservative, feminist, socialist or revisionist). This also applies to the discourses of the natural sciences, for example, to descriptions and evaluations of experiments.

This distinction between the "social" and the "ideological" is missing in the *strong programme*. Bloor uses the concept of ideology somewhat lightheartedly when he concludes: "(...) Theories of knowledge are, in effect, reflections of social ideologies."[23] The problem in this sentence seems to be the word "reflections". It is quite likely that liberal-individualist patterns of thought underpin Popper's theories which Bloor is referring to.[24] But how? And how likely are they to influence the terminologies of physics or crystallography?

Authors such as Bloor, Mulkay and Knorr-Cetina neglect these questions as much as they neglect the semantics of discourse and thus manage to obliterate some qualitative differences (not incompatibilities) between the sciences of nature and the sciences of culture. Such differences come to the fore whenever the semantics of discourses that structure their actantial models are analysed.

3.   Ideology and Natural Sciences: Canguilhem's Alternative

The French philosopher of science Georges Canguilhem is somewhat more cautious than Barnes and Bloor. He does not simply postulate a causal relationship between social interests and events in the sciences, but distinguishes pre-scientific from scientific phases in the evolution of natural sciences. In his model, the ideology of a "natural science" coincides with the pre-scientific phase of the latter.

In contrast to the *strong programme*, which fails to draw a clear line between scientific and non-scientific phases of development in physics, chemistry or biology, Canguilhem relies on Gaston Bachelard's philosophy of science[25] in order to separate the scientific wheat from the ideological chaff: "A scientific ideology comes to an end, when the place which it occupies in the encyclopaedia of knowledge is filled by a discipline which by its very operation proves the validity of its scientific norms."[26] This development from a pre-science or pseudo-science to a science is of course a social and cultural process taking place within an institutional framework: however, it is a process leading to a *break with ideology*. And this is the crucial point the theoreticians of the *strong programme* overlook – unlike Marx, Engels and Mannheim who were almost instinctively aware of it when they refused to relegate the natural sciences to the realm of ideology.

Naturally, scientific ideologies or pseudo-sciences[27] can exist only in a social and linguistic situation where real sciences have successfully been institutionalized. For the pseudo-sciences imitate their language and their *habitus* (Bourdieu) in order to secure a comparable status in the institutions. "The existence of scientific ideologies", explains Canguilhem, "presupposes the parallel existence of scientific discourses and consequently also an accomplished separation of science and religion."[28]

What is at stake here is not merely Luhmann's question of social differentiation[29] but also, and above all, the qualitative leap from one pattern of thought to another: "What science finds is not what ideology was looking for."[30] This maxim is crucial to Canguilhem's and Bachelard's argument, for a science such as chemistry no longer deals with the problems of alchemy; it poses completely new problems. This also applies to genetics: "What Mendel neglects is everything that interested those who in reality were not his predecessors."[31]

As far as the *strong programme* goes, another distinction made by Canguilhem seems important: the distinction between *scientific ideology* (*idéologie scientifique*) and *ideology of scientists* (*idéologie des scientifiques*). The latter is an ideology authentic scientists (physicists, astronomers, biologists) rely on in order to explain the *function* of their science in society. Canguilhem speaks of *philosophical ideologies* (*idéologies philosophiques*).[32] If Barnes and Bloor had recognized this specific difference instead of speaking generally of the social determination of natural sciences, they may have found that, as far as the natural sciences are concerned, ideology and scientific theory can very well be disentangled – in spite of the complexity of their relationships.

One should bear in mind, however, that in this particular context the relationship between ideology and scientific theory is very different from the analogous relationship in the cultural and social sciences. Unlike the natural sciences, which are marked by a clear break between ideology and scientific theory on the structural (semantic-syntactic) level, sciences of culture and society are at the same time ideologies in the general sense, without necessarily degenerating into ideologies in the negative or critical sense (cf. chap. 2). *Their terminologies and semantics are ideological.*

In other words, every natural science can be used or rather misused for ideological purposes on a *functional level*: for example when its (scientific) results are interpreted and exploited by political discourses in election campaigns – or when a well-known physicist comments in public on the "security" of a nuclear power station quoting "reliable data". However, in this case he does not speak as a physicist, because "security" is an ideological concept and not comparable to scientific concepts such as "voltage", "amperage" or "electron".

In the following sentence taken from the interdisciplinary science of crystallography, not a single word can be considered as "ideological" or "culturally specific". For we are dealing here with a trans-cultural, non-ideological terminology: "For all tetragonal lattice complexes the limiting complexes with cubic characteristic space-group type have been derived."[33] This leads to the conclusion that although the discourses of natural sciences can be used for ideological purposes on a *functional level*, they are free from ideological interference on a *structural*, i.e. *semantic-syntactic level*.

4. The Specific Character of Cultural and Social Sciences

When, in the course of the 1960s, Louis Althusser thought he had discovered a break between science and ideology in the work of Karl Marx, a break analogous to the one observed by Bachelard und Canguilhem, he merely produced a new scientific ideology. His argument is well known and can therefore be summed up in a few words: in his later work, especially in *Capital*, Marx abandons the humanist ideology of his early writings, an ideology inspired by Fichte and Hegel, and lays the foundations of an exact science of history which Althusser compares to the mathematics of Ancient Greece and to Galileo's physics. According to this interpretation, the author of *Capital* discovers a new scientific continent: "the continent of History".[34]

Unfortunately, it is impossible to discuss details of Althusser's structural reading of *Capital* or to criticize it.[35] It may be sufficient to point out that it was soon to be attacked as a new brand of scientism and as a "structuralist ideology"[36] – unlike the discoveries of Thales and Pythagoras. Why exactly? Because some of the salient features of "scientific ideologies" as described by Canguilhem can be found in Althusser's Marxism. This discourse imitates the language and the conventions (the *habitus*, Bourdieu would say) of natural sciences without ever attaining a scientific status in the sense of physics and without ever being universally recognized as a science. To make things worse, it contaminates the terminologies of natural sciences with ideology.

Hence the theoretical experiment of the Althusser Group yielded results none of its members had ever intended. It revealed that Marxism is as prone to ideological interference and scientism as all other cultural and social sciences. The word "science" as such was turned into an element of ideology.

In this situation, the specific task of the social sciences cannot possibly be an optimal approximation to the "hard sciences".[37] Pseudo-scientific experiments of this kind are bound to fail and ought to be replaced by a critical and self-critical *reflection* of one's own general ideology in order to escape ideology in the negative or restrictive sense. This presupposes, however, that the subject of theoretical discourse is *aware of the general-ideological character of its own terminology and semantics* – instead of concealing it by scientism (Althusser) or monologue (Luhmann).

Only this kind of reflecting subject is able to recognize the subordination of all sciences to the needs of capital in a postmodern market society which is increasingly adapting to the exigencies of its own economy. We are dealing here with a century-old process accurately described by Marx in the middle of the nineteenth century: "'Alien' science is incorporated by capital just as 'alien' labour is."[38] A century and a half later, and without even referring to Marx's work, Peter Weingart confirms this trend: "Like the nexus between science and politics, science and the media, the relationship between science and economics is becoming *ever closer*."[39] More than ever, science is transformed into an instrument of capital and a means of domination over nature.

Another specific trait of the cultural and social sciences is their *critical attitude* towards this state of affairs expressed in a type of discourse which refuses to submit to market laws. Ever since market society came into being, this has been a handicap and an advantage of philosophy. In most of its forms it can hardly be used as a means for exploiting nature. Some philosophies even turn against the principle of domination by envisaging – like post-war Critical Theory – a domination-free discourse and a subjectivity reconciled with nature.

Moreover, it is a well-known fact that in the realm of cultural and social sciences subjectivity and criticism are not only to be found in theories, but also in their (social) objects which are at the same time subjects trying to solve problems. The subjective character of cultural objects is probably one of the most widely discussed particularities of human sciences as perceived by hermeneutics since Schleiermacher and Dilthey. In this context, objects appear as co-subjects.[40] Anthony Giddens sums up the problem in a few words: "Sociology, unlike natural science, stands in a subject-subject relation to its 'field of study', not a subject-object relation (...)."[41] Proponents of a unitary and universal science are not easily convinced by such arguments. They argue that even "co-subjects" can be described objectively and scientifically, i.e. without the interference of value judgements.[42]

This idea sounds plausible to many people. For it has to be possible, they argue, to describe the discourses of Fascists without evaluating or criticising these discourses, without taking sides. But what happens in a situation where a social scientist familiar with Fascist and Falangist movements deals with individuals whose ideas are clearly of Fascist and Falangist origin, but who define themselves – with apparent naivety – as "true patriots" in order to avoid being ostracized? Will the social scientist renounce all sociological and historical terminology and exclusively refer to "true patriots" in order to preclude a subjective bias? His colleagues would hardly pardon this kind of naivety. For a critical *and* scientific attitude is only possible if the euphemisms of political propaganda, advertising and rhetoric in general are not taken at face value.

A well-known example taken from sociology are Young's and Willmot's – by now classical – field studies of social stratification in the London suburbs Woodford and Bethnal Green. While working-class families in Bethnal Green define themselves as "working class", working-class families in Woodford, a part of town with a predominantly middle-class character, define themselves as "middle class". It goes without saying that the sociologists explain and critically analyse this kind of self-classification, instead of acknowledging it spontaneously.[43] In short, self-definition and scientific definition by others may very well collide for ideological reasons.

Arguments in favour of a unitary science can be countered even more convincingly if we abandon the lexical level the two examples are situated on in order to examine the semantic and syntactic activities of the subjects-objects. The only sociologist who deals with the semantic processes underlying the subject-subject-relationship in the social sciences seems to be Bourdieu:

> When scientific discourse is dragged into the very struggles over classification that it is attempting to objectify (...), it begins once again to function in the reality of struggles over classification. It is thus bound to appear as either *critical* or *complicitous*, depending on the critical or complicitous relation that the reader himself has with the reality being described.[44]

In other words, each analysis in the cultural or social sciences subsumes the analysed discourses on a meta-level under its own patterns of classification, actantial models and narrative constructions. (This is why the theoretical question concerning the meta-level is so important: Who represents whom and how?) If I reject the self-definition of the respondents as "true patriots" or "middle class", because I detect an ideological camouflage, then I also alter their classification systems, their actantial models and their social narratives in which they act as heroes. (If there is such as thing as a "neutral" attitude in the social sciences, it consists in the refusal to discredit the individuals or groups in question in order to achieve an immediate political effect. Instead of pursuing political goals, the scientist seeks to understand and explain events, behaviour and social actions such as self-definitions, camouflage names, etc. However, this has nothing to do with "objectivity", for the very idea of "concealment" or "camouflage" implies a critical attitude and value judgements.)

Such an attitude comes to the fore in Xavière Gauthier's feminist study *Surréalisme et sexualité* which critically reassesses the discourses of French Surrealism by revealing to what extent the revolutionary rhetoric of the avantgarde conceals a conservative actantial model. Within this model, woman appears invariably as the natural, virgin, patient and submissive objectactant: "Woman as represented by Labisse is thus characterized by the softness of plants, the dense endurance of trees, their patience and their entrenchment, their longevity and their blind vitality."[45] Needless to say that the surrealists and their followers would disagree, mustering a vast array of counter-examples. Marxists and advocates of Adorno's or Benjamin's Critical Theory would reconstruct the object-subject of "Surrealism" in yet another context.

"Tell me how you classify, and I shall tell you who you are."[46] This maxim, put forward by Roland Barthes, lays bare the foundations of subjectivity and applies to both the theoretical subjects and to the objects or cosubjects of all cultural and social sciences.

From these object-subjects all objects of nature differ substantially because they are indifferent to the definitions and classifications of scientists. Barnes, Bloor and Henry are quite right in pointing out "that nature is indifferent to how it is classified".[47]

This fact explains why *prognostics* are so different in the two types of science. Unlike prognostics in natural sciences which cannot be distorted by conscious reactions of the objects (stones, plants, animals) involved, prognostics of social scientists are frequently *taken into account* by the actors concerned and *acted upon*. Thus economic or political prognostics are frequently thwarted by big business, trade unions or politicians who integrate them into their planning thereby falsifying them partly or entirely.

Although the natural sciences differ qualitatively from human sciences because they do not depend on ideological languages and deal with inanimate or indifferent objects, this difference does not justify a dichotomy. For all sciences seem to converge in one crucial point: in their struggle for precision which excludes all hasty generalizations such as the "social character of science".

Chapter 4

Value-Free, "Falsifiable" Theory?
The Relationship between Value-Freedom,
Intersubjectivity and Refutability

"Value-freedom" in the sense of Max Weber, "intersubjectivity" and "falsifiability" in the sense of Popper are linked in many ways which have hitherto hardly been explored.[1] The reason for this somewhat astonishing abstinence might be due to a vague apprehension among critical rationalists that a thorough investigation may cause them a lot of embarrassment.

Embarrassment can hardly be avoided as soon as it becomes clear to what extent falsifiability or refutability *presupposes* a value-free (*wertfrei*) intersubjective discussion. The fact that the *possibility* of such a discussion is tacitly presupposed, is observable in crucial passages of Karl R. Popper's early work *The Logic of Scientific Discovery* (1934, Engl. tr. 1959). In this work, the falsifiability or refutability of hypotheses is clearly understood as an intersubjective approach. At the same time, it is considered as ideologically neutral, i.e. as taking place in a language situated beyond ideological interference.

This idea of language as a universally valid, value-free means of communication was inherited by Popper and his German disciple Hans Albert from the Vienna Circle in spite of Popper's many critical remarks concerning this group of philosophers. His lucid critique of Vienna positivism and its theories of induction does not prevent him from considering scientific language as a universally valid jargon in the sense of his contemporary Otto Neurath[2] and from focusing, very much like Moritz Schlick,[3] on the *sentence* as the essential unit.

However, if we follow Saussure and other rationalists in considering the sentence (the *syntagm*) as the basic unit, we lose sight of the discourse as a whole,[4] thereby preventing ourselves from noticing the social interests and value judgements underlying the semantics and actantial models of discourses. The following analyses are meant to show how, in the theories of Critical Rationalism, this basic oversight consolidates the belief in value-freedom and how this belief becomes the basis of an intersubjectively organized process of refutation ("falsification").

At the same time, it will become clear that the terminological and theoretical complex of Critical Rationalism is bound to disintegrate as soon as discourse as a trans-phrastic unit is introduced – and, along with it, subjective interests.

1. Value-Freedom as a Discursive Problem

In the cultural and social sciences, value-freedom only makes sense if it is interpreted, with Norbert Elias, as critical distance towards one's own ideology in the general sense and towards one's own discourse. This kind of distance not only involves self-criticism but also makes us aware of objections and arguments put forward by competing theories.

At present, it is generally recognized that the different brands of Critical Rationalism are all rooted in a liberal and individualist ideology which is responsible both for the strengths and the flaws of this theory complex.[5]

This ideology does not only manifest itself in Popper's later work and in his autobiographical writings; it can be detected in the early phases of his development, for example in *The Logic of Scientific Discovery*, where the author pleads in favour of the new, the negative method:

> According to my proposal, what characterizes the empirical method is its manner of exposing to falsification, in every conceivable way, the system to be tested. Its aim is not to save the lives of untenable systems but, on the contrary, to select the one which is by comparison the fittest, by exposing them all to the fiercest struggle for survival.[6]

(It is interesting to observe that the original German expression "in möglichst strengem Wettbewerb" [*op. cit.*, p. 16] is rendered in the English socio-linguistic context by Darwin's "struggle for survival", thus accentuating a particular ideology.)

If, in the second half of the second sentence, one replaces the word "systems" by the word "economies" or "firms", one can hardly avoid the impression of listening to a liberal economist such as von Mises whom Hans Albert quotes as saying: "Capitalism is the only conceivable or possible form of social economy marked by the division of labour."[7] Hans Albert attempts to confirm this thesis by turning Popper's principle of falsification or refutation against existing forms of socialism (in the 1980s). After the collapse of communism in Europe, this kind of refutation no longer seems necessary. For capitalism, which might eventually turn out to be its own fatal foe, has no serious competitors any more. But what has happened to *value-freedom*, to Weber's *Wertfreiheit?*

Hans Albert, who deals more thoroughly with it than any other critical rationalist (Popper or Topitsch), does consider it as a linguistic problem, but completely neglects the semantic and narrative levels of discourse. Following Weber,[8] he starts from the assumption that value-based criteria of relevance concern exclusively the scientist's *choice of an object* (e.g. "family and environment" rather than "social class" or "stratification"), not, however, the actual *object analysis*. This leads him to believe "that the whole value problem is thus transformed into a meta-scientific problem of relevance, as it is moved onto the level of basic decisions". He adds: "Such value-orientations may thus have an impact on the way a question is objectively formulated, but the question itself can be dealt with without the interference of value judgements."[9]

"Objective", "sachlich" tends to become a magic formula in this discourse, especially when Albert adds:

> The discussion can thus be related to objective criteria which may be interesting in relation to some particular values. On the linguistic level, this can best be achieved by transforming all statements involved into a descriptive language in order to avoid being misled by normative expressions.[10]

But what exactly is meant by "objective criteria", and what does a (purely) "descriptive language" look like in the human sciences? The problem is not solved by Albert's additional advice in a footnote to "replace value-laden concepts by objective criteria".[11] This advice is presumably meant to avoid a relapse into ideological language.

However, ideological interests are inherent both in the lexical repertoire and in the semantics of a discourse and the corresponding sociolect. Scientific "competition" in the sense of Popper is a liberal-Darwinist concept,[12] and Max Weber's methodological individualism is based on the (by no means value-free) semantic opposition between bureaucracy and charisma, an opposition that can best be understood as a reaction to the crisis of the liberal-individualist social order at the end of the nineteenth century. Hans Albert continues to defend this order by introducing the principle of value-freedom and by banning all collective factors from the discourse of social science.

Mommsen intuitively addresses the crucial point when he remarks: "Weber's great sociology was by no means entirely value-free; its radically individualist premises (...) can only be grasped in relation to the European humanist tradition and its esteem of the individual (...)."[13] Albert misses this point when he objects: "This means that methodological individualism is to be taken as an example of the violation of the principle of value-freedom. In this respect even natural science is not free from value judgements!"[14]

This argument is simply wrong, because it ignores the fact that, unlike those of the social sciences, the semantics and the actantial models of natural sciences do not articulate ideological interests. No physicist will reject scientific concepts such as "amperage" or "nuclear fission" without ceasing to be a physicist; at the same time, however, concepts of the social sciences such as "strong programme", "social role", "posthistoire" (Gehlen) or "charisma" provoke protracted and even passionate controversies.

Weber's individualist actantial model evoked indirectly by Mommsen is not only rejected by Marxists, but also appears as highly controversial to advocates of Luhmann's systems theory, partly because it stands for a terminology considered as obsolete, partly because it proposes solutions which seem unacceptable: for example the upgrading of politics and the politician vis-à-vis bureaucracy and the bureaucrat.[15] The solutions envisaged by systems theory are situated beyond the liberal-individualist model. It pleads in favour of improving the "irritability" (sensitivity) of systems and thus seeks to contribute to the solution of social problems in its own specific way. This is quite legitimate, of course. Less legitimate seem to be attempts to declare certain ways of solving problems as "neutral", "purely technical" or "value-free".

Social problem-solving is also situated at the centre of economics whenever the efficiency of the economic system as a whole, of individual branches or firms is at stake. This also applies to business management. If management consultants and economists were merely to describe an ailing business in a value-free fashion, instead of examining it critically and proposing solutions to its problems, they would not hold their jobs for long.[16] Far from being a purely technical matter, their analyses and reform proposals contain value judgements, ideological elements – and they are very often queried, especially if they involve "rationalizations" at the expense of the employees. (How *rational* are such "rationalizations" from a sociological point of view?)

For these reasons, a "strict neutrality of scientific propositions"[17] does not exist in the cultural and social sciences. Hans Albert's recourse to magic formulae such as "technical approach" or "descriptive language" is merely conducive to confusion. The solution consists in recognizing the role of (general) ideology in all theories and in reflecting upon the effects of ideological engagement in one's own discourse in order to avoid ideology in the negative or critical sense.

This engagement need not be denied or suppressed, as was shown in the Introduction to this book; it ought to be recognized as inevitable and potentially creative: as long as it does not produce ideology in the negative sense, thus blocking theoretical reflection and dialogue.

Ideology in the negative sense becomes manifest in Critical Rationalism whenever its proponents attempt to shield their individualism against all kinds of critique.[18] They tend to overlook the existence of group languages expressing interests and value judgements and of discourses articulating such value judgements on a semantic and narrative level. In any case, Thomas S. Kuhn is not entirely wrong when he remarks about Popper's logic of scientific discovery: "Rather than a logic, Sir Karl has provided an ideology; rather than methodological rules, he has supplied procedural maxims."[19]

The following sections are meant to show that intersubjective testing and intersubjective refutation ("falsification") of theories or theoretical propositions is only conceivable, if the social and linguistic problems discussed here are (conveniently) overlooked.

2.   Refutability, Intersubjectivity and Discourse

One can wholeheartedly agree with Hans Albert when he points out: "The principle of value-freedom can (...) be considered as part and parcel of a methodological conception based on the idea of a free, critical discussion. It is the core of a general philosophical orientation one could refer to as Critical Rationalism."[20] Whoever tends to relate Karl R. Popper's Critical Rationalism to the slogan of "falsifiability" and to associate the principle of value-freedom with Max Weber's *understanding sociology* (*verstehende Soziologie*), may be surprised by this attempt to put the notion of value-freedom at the centre of Critical Rationalism.

This surprise fades away, as soon as one realizes that even in Popper's early work, *The Logic of Scientific Discovery*, the principle of refutation or falsification presupposes value-freedom. Reviving Kant's individualist and idealist approach, Popper sees arguments, objections and refutations as situated in a neutral and universally accepted language, when he writes: "A justification is 'objective' if in principle it can be tested and understood by anybody."[21] Whatever applies to explanations in the Kantian sense, also applies to refutations: "Now I hold that scientific theories are never fully justifiable or verifiable, but that they are nevertheless testable. I shall therefore say that the objectivity of scientific statements lies in the fact that they can *be inter-subjectively tested*."[22] In a remark added later on, the expression "inter-subjective test" is replaced by the expression "inter-subjective critique" and related to the "idea of mutual rational control by critical discussion".[23]

In *Conjectures and Refutations*, published almost thirty years after his first major work (in 1963), Popper emphasizes – in contrast with Neurath and other members of the Vienna Circle – that he does not envisage a purely scientific language beyond metaphysics. He even considers the possibility of discovering the mythical origins of scientific theories ("originate in myths")[24] and repeats the central thesis of *The Logic of Scientific Discovery*, namely that the criterion of refutability provides the only means of tracing a demarcation line between science and non-science. "Thus testability is the same as refutability, and can therefore likewise be taken as a criterion of demarcation."[25] Immediately the question arises: Who tests and in what language? It will be dealt with later.

For observation is not only *"observation in the light of theories"*[26] (as sentences or statements), as Popper would have it, but also in the light of theoretical discourses which are at the same time *ideological languages*. Three factors seem to be responsible for Popper's silence on this subject: his liberal individualism which ignores the role of collective phenomena; his (complementary) Kantianism which tends to gloss over idealistically the historical and social nature of language; finally, his fixation on the sentence (the syntagm in the sense of Saussure) which makes him overlook discourse as a trans-phrastic unit and the corresponding sociolect[27]: what Halliday calls "the sociosemantic nature of discourse".[28] By thus abstracting from social and linguistic reality, Popper can genuinely believe in a neutral or "value-free" language.

It is quite surprising to see how often the word "sentence" is repeated in *The Logic of Scientific Discovery* and in some preliminary works. The refutation of a theory comes about in conjunction with "basic sentences", Popper claims in his main early work and in a commentary published in 1978: "By empirical refutability or falsifiability of a theory I mean the existence of observation sentences ('basic sentences', 'test sentences') the truth of which would refute the theory or prove it wrong."[29] By considering the sentence as the crucial linguistic unit and criterion of refutation, Popper loses sight of the discourse as a collective construct expressing particular interests.

This problem also crops up in Popper's fluctuating definitions of the concept of theory: "Scientific theories are universal statements. Like all linguistic representations they are systems of signs or symbols."[30] So what exactly are they: sentences (*Sätze*, German version, *op. cit.*, p. 31), statements, representations, systems of signs – or symbols? Further on, Popper envisages a trans-phrastic (but not discursive) definition, when he mentions a theoretical system made up of a "set of statements, the axioms".[31] Here, theory clearly goes *beyond* the sentence.

However, all examples Popper uses in order to illustrate the process of refutation or falsification are based on the sentence: "There are no white ravens." "There is no perpetual motion machine." "There is no electrical charge other than a multiple cf the electrical elementary charge."[32] It becomes clear, at this stage, that the linguistic level of testing is neutralized by the orientation towards the sentence (by the elimination of discourse) and by the complementary orientation towards the natural sciences or everyday common sense. For all of the sentences quoted here can in fact be tested at any time without ideological interference. Anyone who knows what a raven or a perpetuum mobile is can refute the corresponding sentence, as soon as he encounters one of these two phenomena.

The chance of bringing about a swift refutation or "falsification" diminishes dramatically as soon as we deal with sentences belonging to definable discourses and sociolects in the social sciences: "There is no unconscious without repression." "There is no modern society without a conflict between bureaucracy and politics." "There is no capitalist economy without cyclic crises." "There is no society without literature."

The first three sentences, which can unambiguously be attributed to psychoanalysis, Weberian sociology and Marxism, may be falsifiable in the formal, Popperian sense; however, in practice they turn out to be irrefutable. It is not difficult to find the reason: they stand for discourses or semantic and narrative structures produced within specific sociolects which cannot at any time be tested intersubjectively by all rational individuals. For most of these individuals belong to particular groups and speak group languages some of which are incompatible with the discourses quoted here.

While psychoanalysts, many feminists and advocates of Critical Theory will accept the sentence "There is no unconscious without repression", it will be rejected by most critical rationalists, supporters of empirical psychology and Luhmann's systems theory alike. The critical rationalist is unlikely to be impressed by its refutable form, because he continues to regard with suspicion the semantics and the narrative structures of psychoanalysis as a whole. It goes without saying that this also applies to seemingly "refutable" sentences from Marxism.

To the problem of the sociolect and its interest-guided discourses one can add the problem of interpretation *within a discourse*. When exactly is it possible to speak of "cyclic crises" in a capitalist economy? What Marxists define as "cyclic crises", because they cannot help looking forward to the "last battle", disciples of Keynes or Hayek tend to define as "recessions" which can be overcome with or without state interventions. Thus each discourse constructs its objects differently – in accordance with the relevance criteria and semantic foundations (isotopies) of its sociolect. The question is to what extent such object constructions are comparable.

Considered in this context, a seemingly refutable statement such as "There is no society without literature" can lead to endless and fruitless discussions. For "literature" as a value-free or neutral concept encompassing all written and oral traditions is hardly conceivable. On this level, different aesthetics, canons and stylistics, political, feminist and postmodern poetics of de-differentiation[33] compete with one another and propose partly incompatible definitions.

Popper who, in the course of his controversies with Kuhn (cf. chap. V), rejected the idea of linguistic or ideological frameworks (i.e. the notion of incompatible noetic systems), would undoubtedly also reject the related concepts of "sociolect" and "discourse" as "irrational myths". He would most probably relegate them to the realm of what Hans Albert calls "collective subjectivism".[34]

In *The Logic of Scientific Discovery*, he nevertheless envisages the possibility that intersubjective criticism in a neutral language, as advocated by himself and his followers, might fail: "If some day it should no longer be possible for scientific observers to reach agreement about basic statements this would amount to a failure of language as a means of universal communication. It would amount to a new 'Babel of Tongues'."[35] In this passage, Popper describes fairly accurately the present, postmodern situation in the cultural and social sciences, where the applicability of the intersubjective principle is highly restricted by the overriding principles of intercollectivity or interdiscursivity (used as synonyms here).

In these sciences, virtually all social and linguistic relations between individual subjects are *at the same time* relations between groups and ideological or theoretical group languages all of which give shape to individual subjectivity. In other words, individual subjects cannot observe and argue neutrally, because they owe their subjectivity and their language to specific sociolects which they keep changing by critical reflection. (About the position of the individual subject in language, Paul Valéry remarks in a dialectic spirit: "Sometimes I adapt it to my point of view, sometimes it changes my point of view."[36])

Advocates of Critical Rationalism who continue to defend the principle of refutability or falsifiability can now adopt two lines of argument. They can argue that this principle is only applicable in the natural sciences – and that different "degrees of testability"[37] (Popper) have to be taken into account. They can abandon this relatively secure position and claim that it is also to be applied to the cultural and social sciences. Here only the second option is of any interest, because we are dealing primarily with these sciences and because the critical rationalists have actually adopted it.

In *The Open Society and its Enemies* (1945), for example, Popper criticizes Karl Mannheim's sociology of knowledge, suggesting that, by introducing the concept of "total ideology", it blocks the intersubjective testability of propositions or hypotheses. He concludes:

> The only course open to the social sciences is to forget all about the verbal fireworks and to tackle the practical problems of our time with the help of the theoretical methods which are fundamentally the same in *all* sciences. I mean the methods of trial and error, of inventing hypotheses which can be practically tested, and of submitting them to practical tests.[38]

However, "the verbal fireworks" Popper is prepared to gloss over in a rationalist manner, constitute individual and collective subjectivities which cannot develop outside of collective languages and their discourses. We can only put forward views or arguments because we have been socialized in certain socio-linguistic contexts, because we grow out of these contexts which we subsequently reflect on critically, having occupied positions in new contexts. We thus develop our subjectivity. A speech independent of a speaking subject and of particular socio-linguistic contexts does not exist. In this respect, every discussion is a dialogue between subjects whose dynamic identities tend to coincide with their discourses in progress and their changing sociolects.[39]

Rationalists can only afford to ignore this social and linguistic situation of the subject because they concentrate on isolated sentences borrowed from the natural sciences, on sentences which may occur in any discourse – independently of all ideologies. Quite right: there is no such thing as a perpetuum mobile. This statement will be endorsed without much ado by feminists, Marxists and the disciples of Bourdieu or Luhmann, because they can consider it as perfectly neutral.

However, in *The Logic of Scientific Discovery*, Popper goes one step further when he extends the principle of falsification to include "occurrences": "Instead of speaking of basic statements [in the German version: *Basissätze*, *op. cit.*, p. 55] which are ruled out or prohibited by a theory, we can then say that the theory rules out certain possible occurrences, and that it will be falsified if these possible occurrences do in fact occur."[40] One need not be a fervent follower of Deleuze[41] in order to recognize the problematical character of the word "occurrence". When is an earthquake an earthquake, a coup d'état a coup d'état, a crime a crime? Popper goes on to extend the scope of falsification even further, when – in spite of the self-critical remark that the word "occurrence" is vague[42] – he suggests that a falsifiable theory "rules out, or prohibits, not merely an occurrence, but always *at least one event*" [German version: *Vorgang*, i.e. series of events, *op. cit.*, p. 57].[43]

In the cultural and social sciences, this amounts to saying that whole narrative sequences based on actantial models are to be refuted. On this level of discourse, a Leninist, for example, might attempt to refute the thesis that "the collapse of the Eastern Block proves the impossibility of socialism" by pointing to China's successful economy. A liberal economist or political scientist might very well interpret this argument as a self-goal of the Leninist and remind him of the fact that capitalism and market economy are very much in evidence in contemporary China – in spite of the government's communist rhetoric. The Leninist in turn could answer (especially if he is a Chinese Leninist) that China has developed a successful model by integrating market laws into a planned economy controlled by the party. What matters here are not the strongly simplified historical contexts, but the fact that "occurrences" or "series of occurrences" are narrative constructions which each discourse will model differently (but not arbitrarily), because reality is always ambiguous and hence can be interpreted in many different ways. This is why all attempts to relate "occurrences" to theories in order to test or refute them are doomed to failure.

In this respect, Imre Lakatos also embarks on a risky venture when, in his constructive critique of Popper's falsification principle, he suggests that, instead of testing theorems or theories, we ought to test series of theories, i.e. whole research programmes which invariably turn out to be complex narrative structures: "First, I claim that the typical descriptive unit of great scientific achievements is not an isolated hypothesis but rather a research programme."[44] He adds: "Sophisticated falsificationism thus shifts the problem of how to appraise *theories* to the problem of how to appraise *series of theories.*"[45]

Here one can only repeat what was said of Popper's ambitious critique of "series of occurrences": the larger the criticized units the more intricate and arbitrary becomes the process of refutation. Eventually, Lakatos's arguments tend to coincide with the well-known ideological positions of Critical Rationalism: Freudian psychoanalysis and Marxism appear to be "degenerating" scientific programmes, whereas Critical Rationalism and some natural sciences are defined as "progressive" research programmes – *quod erat demonstrandum*.

All things considered, Andrew Sayer is quite right when he remarks about the falsification principle "that it is virtually impossible to put into practice".[46] This kind of critique is reminiscent of Otto Neurath's sceptical remarks about *The Logic of Scientific Discovery* in 1935: "Wherever Popper replaces the 'verification' of a theory by 'testability', we replace 'falsifiability' by *'disturbance'* (*'Erschütterung'*) of a theory (. . .)."[47] However, this kind of "disturbance" is not a "modest refutation" but something quite different: a matter of discretion.

This argument also applies to the compromise expression proposed by Russell Keat and John Urry: "reasonable abandonment".[48] This new formula simply shifts the problem to a higher, more abstract level. When is something "reasonable"? What seems reasonable to one person may seem wildly exaggerated to another, for example, for ideological reasons. For the question whether my faith in a theory is "shaken" or not also depends on political and economic factors: for example on the collapse of socialism in Eastern Europe, which may entail a general scepticism towards Marxist theories or a major ecological crisis, that casts doubts on an ever-expanding economy and on theories advocating economic growth.

The difficulty in applying Popper's falsificationism to the social sciences was analysed in detail by the French sociologist Jean-Claude Passeron whose work *Le Raisonnement sociologique: L'espace non-poppérien du raisonnnement naturel* (1991) has so far been ignored both in the English- and in the German-speaking world. (The reason for this ignorance seems to be mainly linguistic and cultural.)

Passeron focuses on the form of Popper's principle of falsification and argues that this form cannot possibly function in the social sciences: "The empirical test of a theoretical statement can never, in sociology, take on the logical form of 'refutation' ('falsification') in the sense of Popper."[49] The reason for this is the linguistic heterogeneity of social sciences which, unlike the natural sciences, reproduce the heterogeneity of everyday language: "Among groups which talk about the world in different languages, empirical proof does not decide anything (. . .)."[50]

In other words, the social sciences cannot be shielded by artificial languages against particular interests and value judgements which polarize natural language. This also means that the collective languages of the social sciences are always related to particular historical situations ("séries de configurations historiques singulières")[51] and hence cannot be tested within the framework of a purely logical, universally valid language. In the context of this chapter, one could say that the rules of verification or refutation vary from socio-linguistic situation to socio-linguistic situation and from sociolect to sociolect.

The alternative mapped out for the social sciences by Passeron is an interpretative and exemplifying approach that is by no means incompatible with empirical research. On the contrary, it encourages theoreticians to "multiply their empirical investigations and to relate them to one another by interpretative coherence".[52]

Passeron thus rejects Popper's rationalist universalism which is also criticized, in a somewhat different context, by the sociologists Bruno Péquignot and Pierre Tripier.[53] The fundamental problem of this universalism seems to be the refusal to acknowledge the specific character of cultural and social sciences none of which deals with "laws" in the sense of natural science.[54] For in society nothing ever repeats itself in a strict sense and, unlike in a laboratory, it is impossible to conduct experiments "under identical conditions", yielding universally recognized results.

3. Learning from Critical Rationalism: An Outlook

The idea of questioning Critical Rationalism in a dialectical or hermeneutic perspective is certainly not new. More innovative would be the attempt to learn from Popper's challenging experience in order to develop Critical Theory and give it a dialogical turn. It is obvious that any attempt to combine or synthesize the two approaches would merely lead to contradictions and eclecticism. The renewal of Critical Theory as envisaged here consists in an orientation towards alterity and dialogue announced towards the end of the "Introduction" and worked out in *Part Three*. This re-orientation seems to be possible with the help of Popper's philosophy.

The latter's notion of "scientific objectivity" is seen by Günter Witschel as anchored in dialogue: "According to Popper, objectivity is not achieved by the scientist's viewpoint but by social means, by 'mutual criticism', 'a both friendly and hostile division of labour', by 'cooperation' as well as 'competition'."[55] This concise presentation of the dialogical components of Critical Rationalism is at the same time a fairly accurate, albeit partial, description of theoretical dialogue as mapped out in the third part of this book.

What matters in the theoretical context constructed here is no longer the idea of a final and indubitable foundation of knowledge which both Apel and Habermas associate with the "ideal speech situation", but the more realistic idea that the permanent interaction with the Other, with the other theory, will yield new insights. In this sense, Popper's notion of *critical testing* becomes part and parcel of Dialogical Theory.

The orientation towards the Other is also based on the dialectical principle that it is the unity of opposites, of divergent views (without a synthesis), which is singularly well suited for revealing all aspects of a social phenomenon. In short, what is at stake here is an open dialectical totality and an open-ended dialogue in the sense of Bakhtin.

Chapter 5

Paradigms in the Cultural and Social Sciences?

As a polymorphous and innovative concept in the recent history of science, *paradigm* was almost predestined to become a magic word in the cultural and social sciences because it offered individuals and groups a welcome opportunity to develop ever new paradigms. The fact that we are actually dealing with an ambiguous or polymorphous concept was established beyond doubt by Margaret Masterman who found at least twenty-one different meanings of "paradigm" in Thomas S. Kuhn's well-known work *The Structure of Scientific Revolutions* (1962).[1] In the human sciences, such a word opens fascinating perspectives – very much like Bachelard's "epistemological break", Foucault's "episteme" or Popper's "falsification".

Although Kuhn uses the concept of paradigm almost exclusively to describe the evolution of the natural sciences, he sporadically[2] indicates that he does not exclude the possibility of applying it to the cultural and social sciences. Such hints are acknowledged with gratitude by philosophers, literary critics, ethnologists and sociologists who subsequently try to establish new paradigms in their respective disciplines in order to secure institutional success in what Bourdieu calls the "scientific field". In a few cases, their strategy turned out to be successful because some people decided that they could not afford to ignore a "new paradigm" enthusiastically acclaimed by well-known scientists and their followers. However, in the course of time the proliferation of new paradigms met with rising scepticism and suspicion.

What went wrong? It was, one might say, the mechanical transposition of a concept yielded by systematic observation of the natural sciences into the realm of cultural and social theory where it was soon assimilated to well-established notions such as "ideology", "theory", "world view" or "model". If virtually all competent scientists agree that Newton's physics are a paradigm in the sense of Kuhn, then Shakespeare's dramas[3] cannot claim to be a paradigm of this kind – let alone Astrid Lindgren's children's book *Pippi Langstrump*.[4] In this case, a person's "autonomy" in the legal or sociological sense[5] cannot constitute a paradigm, because "individual autonomy" is part and parcel of liberal individualism and other ideologies which are neither paradigms in the sense of Newtonian physics nor aspects of such paradigms. If "paradigm" is transformed into a synonym of "model", "example" or "essence" – as is the case in Edgar Morin's book *Le Paradigme perdu: la nature humaine*[6] – then it loses the meaning given it by Kuhn in spite of the ambiguities he could not avoid.

In what follows, the applicability of the concept of paradigm to the cultural and social sciences will be globally questioned, and alternatives will be proposed towards the end of the chapter. It is to be expected that this kind of criticism will not be appreciated by those among the human scientists who prefer terminological fantasies and fashions. The critic's aim is, however, to develop theoretical terminology by clarification.

1. Towards a Definition of "Paradigm"

An enumeration of all the meanings of *paradigm* (Greek: *paradigma* = example, model) as listed by Margaret Masterman in conjunction with Kuhn's well-known work would probably be somewhat tedious. In order to illustrate the ambiguities of this proliferating concept, it may suffice to name a few: "a universally recognized scientific achievement", "a myth", "a 'philosophy' or constellation of questions", "a textbook", "a whole tradition", "a successful metaphysical speculation", etc.[7] Considering these partly conflicting definitions, one might be inclined to doubt the practicability of the concept in question – or even Kuhn's theoretical competence.

In this situation, it seems preferable to proceed in a constructivist rather than in a deconstructionist way[8] and to look out for a definition which takes into account *all* of Kuhn's key arguments. This approach seems to be not only fairer to Kuhn but also more serious from a theoretical point of view.

The following definition taken from *The Structure of Scientific Revolutions* seems to be both reasonably general and concrete: "A paradigm is what the members of a scientific community share, *and*, conversely, a scientific community consists of men who share a paradigm."[9] This tautological definition was often contested and later revised by Kuhn.[10] However, not the tautology is the main problem here but "that which is common". What exactly is it?

Later definitions by Kuhn make it clear that it is a *specific language*. In a preface written in 1976 for a German collection of articles published under the title *Die Entstehung des Neuen (The Emergence of the New)* we read: "One thing that binds the members of any scientific community together and simultaneously differentiates them from the members of other apparently similar groups is their possession of a common language or special dialect."[11]

Within the context mapped out here, one could also say that a paradigm in the sense of Kuhn is a *sociolect*. This translation into the language of semiotics would be almost superfluous if it were not followed by the addendum that it is a technical and scientific, not an ideological sociolect. For according to Canguilhem (cf. chap. 3, 3), ideological or metaphysical languages occur only in the pre-scientific phases of an emerging science. Commenting on the development of the theory of light, Kuhn himself writes: "Instead there were a number of competing schools and subschools, most of them espousing one variant or another of Epicurean, Aristotelian, or Platonic theory."[12] He adds: "Each of the corresponding schools derived strength from its relation to some particular metaphysic, and each emphasized, as paradigmatic observations, the particular cluster of optical phenomena that its own theory could do most to explain."[13] During this phase of its development, explains Kuhn, optics were "something less than science".[14] Here, the object of discussion is obviously the pre-scientific or pre-paradigmatic state of physical optics whose scientific development was subsequently initiated by Newton. However, Kuhn reminds us of the fact that this is not the state-of-the-art modern, Newtonian optics can be related to. It can be better understood as a break with metaphysical "optics".[15]

His arguments bear a striking resemblance to those of Georges Canguilhem. It will be remembered that Canguilhem refers to the pre-scientific state of a natural science as a "scientific ideology" whose problems have virtually nothing to do with those of the science which is about to supersede it. With George Couvalis one could also speak of a "*pre-paradigm* stage" marked by "deep disagreement about fundamental theory and a great deal of fairly random fact-gathering which does not follow any kind of accepted procedure".[16] In short, the new scientific constellation as described by Canguilhem roughly corresponds to Kuhn's paradigm.

These considerations converge towards a general definition of the concept of paradigm in accordance with the fundamental intentions of Kuhn's work. *A paradigm is an interculturally recognized technical and non-ideological sociolect which allows for intersubjectively and experimentally testable and applicable solutions within a universal community of scientists.*

In other words, it is a sociolect understood and spoken in a particular phase of development of a natural science by all scientists concerned and not rejected by some groups of scientists as being pseudoscientific or ideological. (It should be immediately added, however, that the universal validity of such a sociolect excludes neither controversies nor conflicts.)

It is interesting to note that this universal character of a technical and scientific sociolect is confirmed by Albert Einstein in conjunction with

Newton's physics. Einstein explains: "Until the end of the 19th century it was the programme of all theoretical-physical research. All physical events were to be related to masses obeying Newton's laws of motion."[17] This universal character of paradigms in the natural sciences is also recognized by Barry Barnes who speaks of the "universal acceptance throughout a scientific field".[18]

Based on a paradigm, "normal science" in the sense of Kuhn presupposes the *universalism* described here. For "normal science" is relatively homogeneous and, as Kuhn points out, "holds creative philosophy at arm's length"[19], thus avoiding ideological interference.

It is important to remember that, according to Kuhn, even the anomalies which trigger off scientific revolutions (i.e. changes of paradigms) are recognized as such *within* a universally accepted paradigm: "Anomaly appears only against the background provided by the paradigm."[20] This means that without a *paradigmatically valid universal language* there can be no ascertainable anomalies precipitating revolutions.

From what has been said so far, it follows that every paradigm is a sociolect (a "special language" in the sense of Kuhn), but not every sociolect is a paradigm. Hence "sociolect" is the more general term. A nationalist, liberal or conservative ideology can be defined as a sociolect, not as a paradigm, however. For it is exclusively spoken and understood by those who adhere to it and is rejected or ignored by others. It is particular and, in extreme cases, restricted to a small group of true believers or fanatics. Although such extreme cases hardly ever occur in the cultural and social sciences, the theoretical sociolects, which form the substance of these sciences, are culturally and ideologically determined and therefore never universally recognized. In this respect, they are radically different from paradigms in physics, astronomy or chemistry.

Thus the language of Luhmann's systems theory is used in the German-speaking world by many social scientists; it is (partly) understood in wider circles and often rejected there. In English-speaking and French-speaking countries, it is rarely used – and even more rarely understood. A comparison with quantum mechanics or crystallography which enjoy world-wide acceptance casts light on the particular, culturally and ideologically restricted character of this sociological group language.

Continuing efforts to apply Kuhn's concept of paradigm to the cultural and social sciences are best understood by analysing some of the definitions and application attempts in this part of the scientific world. It ought to become clear that especially the definitions omit essential elements of the definition proposed here in conjunction with Kuhn's work.

2.   The Applicability of the Concept of Paradigm in the Cultural and Social Sciences

Numerous applications of this concept to the cultural and social sciences were made possible, as pointed out initially, by several hints in *The Structure of Scientific Revolutions* and in some of Kuhn's articles. In one of these, Kuhn discusses the paradigmatic consensus which came about in optics towards the end of the seventeenth century, in chemistry in the course of the eighteenth century. He explains that in "parts of biology no very real consensus developed until after the first third of the nineteenth century".[21] He adds: "This century appears to be characterized by the emergence of a first consensus in parts of a few of the social sciences."[22]

Apart from these direct references to the social sciences, there is another reason why cultural and social scientists feel encouraged to claim the notion of paradigm for their disciplines. Kuhn quite rightly points out that the natural sciences are not as monolithic as some of his own descriptions of "normal science" suggest. For it seems possible to interpret one and the same paradigm in different ways: "In short, though quantum mechanics (...) is a paradigm for many scientific groups, it is not the same paradigm for them all."[23] This means, however, that the paradigm which is supposed to constitute meaning is itself constructed on a meta-level. This meta-level is left undefined by Kuhn.

In the natural sciences, a revolutionary situation may emerge marked by a coexistence of competing paradigms: of the Newtonian and the Einsteinian paradigms in physics, for instance.[24] This tendency towards paradigmatic pluralism is illustrated by other remarks in Kuhn's works: "The very existence of science depends upon vesting the power to choose between paradigms in the members of a special kind of community."[25]

Kuhn seems to contradict himself when he claims elsewhere: "In that pattern, development occurs from one consensus to another, and alternate approaches are not ordinarily in competition."[26] If this were the case, the "normal scientist" could certainly not choose among competing paradigms. A choice of this kind is only conceivable in a revolutionary phase, when the consensus within a normal science disintegrates in the face of proliferating anomalies and the contours of a new paradigm begin to emerge. However, Kuhn explicitly states that this revolutionary situation is "relatively rare"[27] in the scientific tradition.

Maybe cultural and social scientists overlooked or ignored the passages quoted here when they decided to apply Kuhn's concept in their disciplines. Whatever their actual attitude may have been, the fact is that they adopted the principle of "co-existing rival paradigms", thereby highlighting those among Kuhn's statements which seem to justify the application of his key concept to their domain.

Kurt Bayertz seems to have found an explanation for this situation:

> Although Kuhn's description is mainly geared towards the natural sciences, it seems to suit the social and cultural sciences even more, because it is not so strongly linked to formal logic and the distinction between science and philosophy, a distinction which is hardly viable in these disciplines.[28]

However, the comparison of Kuhn's and Canguilhem's histories of science has revealed that both, Kuhn and the French philosopher, *do* distinguish between pre-scientific and scientific stages of development.

The real problem underlying a contemporary application of the concept of paradigm to the cultural and social sciences is due to the problematic definitions of this concept. One can only agree with Gerhard Schurz, when he objects to the simple identification of "paradigm" and "world vision" or *Weltanschauung.*[29] The definition he himself proposes – "paradigm as a *cognitive system*" – is a lot more concrete, especially since he distinguishes four components: the theoretical component (the core of a theory, hypotheses about laws, models); the empirical component (cases in point); the methodological component (rules and principles, epistemology, i.e. epistemological assumptions, normative assumptions) and finally, the programmatic components (the research programme).[30]

If one compares this rather complex definition with the one proposed here, one is struck by an omission: Schurz does not mention the non-ideological, technical language shared by a community of scientists. It thus becomes possible to apply the concept of paradigm not only to Newton's physics, the behaviourist theory of learning and Darwin's theory of evolution, but also to Freud's psychoanalysis.[31]

The language of psychoanalysis, of course, is neither interculturally valid nor free from ideological elements.[32] Even before Freud's death, two psychoanalytic sociolects developed which significantly departed from Freudian language: the psychoanalytic theories of Carl Gustav Jung and Wilhelm Reich. One of the crucial differences between these three types of discourse come to the fore when their actantial models are examined. While Jung and Reich introduce collective actants and actors – albeit in very different social and linguistic contexts : the collective unconscious (Jung); the class in the Marxist sense (Reich) – the Freudians continue to focus on the individual and the individual unconscious and reject both Jung's and Reich's terminologies.

In other words: Freud's psychoanalysis is an ideological and theoretical sociolect originating, very much like some novels by Svevo, Musil and Broch,[33] in the crisis of Central European culture at the turn of the century – and not a paradigm in the sense of Newtonian physics. Could one present Freudian psychoanalysis, paraphrasing Einstein, as a "programme for every kind of psychological research"? The answer must clearly be "no", if one takes into consideration Jean Piaget's or Wilhelm Wundt's psychology and empirical psychology in general. Moreover, it seems impossible to integrate Jung's and Reich's sociolects into the Freudian programme, especially if one bears in mind Reich's attempts to bring about a synthesis between psychoanalysis and Marxism.[34]

Gratzl and Leitgeb virtually sacrifice their originally precise definition when they try to illustrate "paradigm in the most general sense"[35] by referring to Shakespeare's dramas: "Shakespeare's dramas are a paradigm in this sense for the drama production within a particular group of playwrights in the 19th century (...)."[36] This assessment may be valid for England and Germany; it certainly does not apply to France where, in spite of all innovations (e.g. Voltaire's), seventeenth-century Classicism continued to survive.[37] The situation hardly becomes clearer when the authors add: "The group of playwrights is a human community in the 18th century."[38] From a sociological and an intercultural point of view, it is difficult to view it as a homogeneous community because the Spanish and the French playwrights of that period differ substantially from their English or German counterparts. This kind of "paradigm" can hardly be compared with Newton's universally (albeit temporarily) recognized physics. For it lacks the intercultural and trans-ideological validity of paradigms in natural sciences. In Shakespeare's case, the Czech Structuralists would speak, somewhat more realistically, of an *aesthetic norm.*[39]

In this perspective, Kurt Bayertz quite rightly criticizes the excessively generous use of the word "paradigm" by some literary critics who turn prestigious interpretations (e.g. Dilthey's interpretation of Goethe, Engels's interpretation of Balzac) into paradigms: "This kind of usage tends to eliminate the decisive function attributed by Kuhn to paradigms in the fully developed sciences of nature: namely the function of uniting all the scientists active in a particular field of research."[40] In order to pre-empt misunderstandings, one ought to add immediately that this process of unification is a *linguistic* process: the creation of an international technical language transcending all ideological and cultural boundaries.

The hypothesis put forward here that cultural bias and ideological engagement prevent universally recognized paradigms in the sense of physics or crystallography from emerging in the cultural and social sciences is confirmed by Gerhart Arnreiter's and Peter Weichhart's article on "Rival Paradigms in Geography". Schurz introduces this article by pointing out that "around 1969 a change took place in German-speaking geography (...)".[41] This change resulted in a shift from landscape geography to a geography of space analysis. The very notion of a "German-speaking geography" is somewhat puzzling. Is there such a thing as a German-speaking physics or computer science? Is it not the case that these two disciplines have been communicating for decades in a universally accepted English lingua franca?

The article published by Arnreiter and Weichhart highlights the role of ideology in geography and especially in human geography. Here a development can be traced from a qualitative and behaviouristic turn to a humanist turn and subsequently to a Marxist and a feminist turn.[42] We are not dealing with a succession or an exchange of paradigms in the sense of Kuhn, i.e. with revolutions triggered off by interculturally and intersubjectively observable anomalies within cognitive systems. What is at stake here are ideological antagonisms and conflicts between institutionalized groups.

Such conflicts are argued out within a socio-lingustic problematic where certain groups of scientists try to further their interests and have their sociolect recognized in the institutions. If their strategies are successful and their group language comes to dominate the relevant institutional sector, the impression that a new paradigm has emerged may prevail for a certain period of time. But in reality, a particular group of scientists has succeeded in positioning its ideological and theoretical language at the centre of the scientific problematic and in relegating competing sociolects to the periphery.

It soon becomes clear that, more often than not, this kind of strategy is only successful within a particular national culture and a specific socio-linguistic problematic – and not in others. In their analyses of German geography, Arnreiter and Weichhart emphasize "that almost simultaneously with the paradigmatic shift in German geography from the landscape concept and from idiographic geography to a positivistically-oriented theory of space, at least three fully fledged groups of paradigms coexisted and competed in the English-speaking world".[43]

Moreover, it seems crucial that the authors of this article are unable to discern the emergence of a normal science within recent German geography. For they point out: "Thus an authentic 'normal science phase' in the sense of Kuhn, a phase during which the options of the paradigm could have been put into practice in empirical research, could not really materialize in the German-speaking world."[44] In this particular world, proponents of "landscape geography" ended up competing with followers of "behaviouristic", "emancipating", "feminist" and other "paradigms".[45]

The authors conveniently omit the conclusion which seems to impose itself, namely that it is virtually impossible, in this case, to speak of a paradigm in the sense of normal science, in the sense of a universally, interculturally accepted "special language" as defined by Kuhn and Einstein. However, they do tell us, albeit between the lines, that instead of speaking of paradigms in (human) geography, we ought to speak of competing ideological-theoretical sociolects whose constellation depends to a large degree on the cultural and linguistic problematic as a whole.

It nonetheless happens occasionally, as suggested above, that a particular theoretical sociolect comes to dominate a social science for a certain period of time and that its hegemony can easily be mistaken for a paradigm in Kuhn's sense. Thus the anthropologist Justin Stagl can refer to "Malinowski's paradigm" in ethnology or social anthropology:

> During the period between the First World War and "de-colonization" (roughly 1920 to 1960), a period which can be considered as the "classical phase" (...) of ethnology, this combination of holistic field work and model-building theory dominated ethnology. In what follows, I shall call it Malinowski's paradigm.[46]

However, at the end of Stagl's article, this "paradigm" turns out to be an ideology:

> Whatever the aspirations of individual ethnographers may have been at that time, the heroic scientism of Malinowski's paradigm fulfilled the function of an ideology for ethnology as a profession by offering it an opportunity to consolidate its position in the academic world.[47]

The key word here is: "scientism". In physics, crystallography or chemistry, "scientism" is inconceivable, because the only relevant distinction here is the distinction between science and non-science. Scientism, which is so persistent in the cultural and social sciences, is comparable to what Canguilhem calls "scientific ideology": to a pre-scientific discourse pretending to be scientific in order to improve its status in academic institutions. In his work *Sociology and Scientism* Robert C. Bannister in the USA analyses the influence of positivism, Protestantism and Darwinism and shows what function these ideologies fulfilled in the attempts of the "founding fathers" of American sociology to relate all research to "hard facts".[48]

When S. N. Eisenstadt and M. Curelaru set out to describe complementary or antagonistic "paradigms" in sociology, they actually deal with ideological and theoretical complexes. The "individualistic", "sociologistic", "cultural or culturalistic" and "environmental paradigms", which they distinguish in conjunction with Pitirim Sorokin's sociology of culture, are far from being universally, interculturally accepted languages. They are "local" ideologies defended by some groups and rejected by others – within one and the same period of time. For sociologists have never succeeded in agreeing on an internationally recognized, homogeneous language.[49]

Moreover, the ideological impulse makes itself felt within Eisenstadt's and Curelaru's own discourse, when they decide to define Marx's model of society as a "closed system" and to narrate the history of sociology as a gradual opening process initiated by Max Weber's approach: "The greatest 'opener' of the closed system approach, of course, was Weber."[50] The inconspicuous "of course" is the symptom of an ideological monologue which prevents readers from asking questions and from taking into account divergent opinions, for example, Ernst Bloch's interpretation of Marxian dialectics as a revolutionary *opening* of Hegel's system.[51]

The result of these considerations can be summed up in a few words. In the cultural and social sciences, we are not dealing with paradigms in the sense of Kuhn (i.e. internationally valid, albeit changing technical languages), but with theoretical languages which are at the same time culturally specific ideological sociolects.

This does not mean that cultural sciences are pre-paradigmatic or pre-scientific, as is often being suggested. It means that they are *non-paradigmatic*, because, as was shown in the second chapter, they *depend* on ideologies (in the general sense) for *motivation*. Unlike the sociolects of cultural and social sciences, the paradigms of natural sciences are value-free, universally valid technical languages whose terminologies (*atom, molecule, protein, gene*) cannot be linked to particular ideological or political viewpoints – in spite of the fact that they could only evolve within certain socio-cultural processes of rationalization (cf. chap. 1). The idea of "German physics" propagated by the National Socialists turned out to be a chimera, and one may safely assume that there will never be such a thing as Marxist or feminist physics.[52]

3. Paradigms, Socio-Linguistic Situations and Sociolects

When Wolfgang Stegmüller suggests that it ought to be possible to overcome the incommensurability of paradigms postulated in Kuhn's work[53] by reducing the "weaker" theory to the "stronger" one, he also indicates that the whole discussion about paradigms revolves around the natural sciences. One of his fundamental aims is to reconcile Kuhn's

theory of paradigms with a cumulative and rationalist approach to the evolution of science:

> For if a superseding theory "reproduces all the achievements of the super-
> seded theory" and offers additional ones, then, in spite of the "incommen-
> surable" character of the two theories (i.e. the heterogeneity of their
> structural cores), it seems possible to speak *of an accumulation of knowledge
> across the revolutionary phases.*[54]

This idea "that the superseded theory can be reduced to the alternative
theory"[55] is quite plausible, as long as one can rely – like in the natural
sciences or in computer science – on a neutral sphere of non-ideological
intersubjectivity, where a general consensus concerning achievement
or lack of achievement is possible, albeit in the long run. The second
chapter has shown that in the cultural and social sciences no such sphere
exists, because in these sciences ideological and theoretical subjectivity comes about in discourses and the corresponding sociolects. What
Kuhn says about inter-paradigmatic communication seems to be valid
here: "Each group uses its own paradigm to argue in that paradigm's
defense."[56] In order to characterize communication in the human sciences,
one could replace the word "paradigm" by the word "sociolect" *in this
particular sentence.*
    Usually, this kind of lexical substitution is impossible, because – as was
shown – "sociolect" is the more general concept which also encompasses
ideological and theoretical languages. Unlike paradigms in natural sciences
which can, at least in principle, be reduced to more complex, more sophisticated paradigms, sociolects in the social sciences cannot be reduced, because
an ideological engagement is irreducible to another. Thus a feminist theory
of society cannot be reduced to a critical-rationalist or a Marxist approach
without ceasing to be a feminist theory. (The fact that even relatively heterogeneous theories can be *combined* in many different ways is well known:
cf. *Part Three.*)
    Considering that intersubjectivity is problematical in the human sciences,
because speakers of a particular sociolect tend to apply the criteria of this
sociolect to discourses of their own group and to those of competing groups,
it seems well-nigh impossible to assess the performance of a theory or a
"paradigm" by relying on universally accepted criteria, i.e. on criteria
recognized by the whole scientific community.
    While Luhmann and his followers are convinced that their theory of the
social system is far superior to Max Weber's action-oriented approach,
Rainer Greshoff declares at the end of a lucid and detailed analysis "that

whatever can be explained with the help of Luhmann's concepts, can also be dealt with using Weber's concepts – and even more".[57] It goes without saying that Luhmann's followers would disagree. However, this is not what matters here.

The crucial point is that a cultural or social science is very rarely dominated by just one sociolect (cf. Stagl's comments on Malinowski above). And this is the reason why a *science* such as sociology, anthropology or semiotics can neither be understood as a paradigm nor as a sociolect. It can best be described as a coexistence of competing or related sociolects, i.e. as a section or model of a particular socio-linguistic situation. This fact is amply illustrated by Arnreiter's and Weichhart's brief presentation of German geography which reveals a constellation of competing sociolects kept in motion by ideological inputs. In other words, they describe aspects of a changing socio-linguistic situation.

The fact that such a situation is at the same time a problematic in the sense of the first chapter, becomes apparent when a German literary critic like Hans Robert Jauß suggests that a paradigmatic change becomes inevitable in literary criticism (or "literary science" in the German sense?), "whenever a paradigm and its methodological axiomatic are no longer able to satisfy the demands a science of literature has to meet".[58] But whose demands does Jauß refer to and what exactly does he expect this discipline to do? He expects it to break with the text-oriented interpretation in general and with production-oriented Marxism in particular and to devote itself to reader-response criticism and the historical reception of literature.

It is difficult to doubt the importance of the readership for literary history. However, one should not underestimate the ideological stakes of this radical re-orientation of German criticism in the 1960s and 1970s. It was meant to counterbalance Marxism and Critical Theory in the "literary field" (Bourdieu) by recurring to the indigenous hermeneutic tradition and (in Iser's case) to phenomenology. Like many of their contemporaries, some German philologists recognized in Kuhn's key concept a welcome ideological camouflage and a promising institutional strategy.[59]

Part Two

The Unity of Opposites:
Prolegomena to a Dialogical Theory

The idea that extremes meet is an old wisdom revived by dialectical philosophy and promoted by Hegel to the rank of supreme law. Although the critical project of uniting the opposites is inspired by Hegel's basic insight "that what is self-contradictory does not resolve itself into a nullity, into abstract nothingness",[1] the solutions proposed in the following chapters avoid the synthesizing movement of Hegelian dialectics. This movement is clearly perceptible in Hegel's *Science of Logic*, where we read about definite negation: "It is a fresh Notion but higher and richer than its predecessor; for it is richer by the negation or opposite of the latter, therefore contains it, but also something more, and is the unity of itself and its opposite."[2]

This kind of unity, which underlies Hegel's entire "system of concepts",[3] was already questioned in the nineteenth century by young Hegelians[4] and finally abandoned by Horkheimer's and Adorno's Critical Theory in favour of an open, negative dialectic. The latter is succinctly explained by Adorno: "Even *in extremis* a negated negative is not a positive."[5] The contradiction can neither be overcome (*aufgehoben*) in a Hegelian manner, nor systematically contained, nor synthesized by a monological discourse whose subject pretends to be identical with reality.

In what follows, contradictory positions will not be synthesized; rather, their coincidence will be interpreted dialogically: as a possibility to connect contradictory perspectives in the hope that each of them will cast light on the blind spots of the other. The idea is to become aware of the whole by relating its extremes to one another without ever aiming at a closed Hegelian totality which excludes dialogue.[6]

In this process, the negativity of Critical Theory as non-identity of subject and object will be oriented towards the Other, towards alterity in Bakhtin's sense (cf. *Part Three*). Only if the subject of discourse realizes that its objects are constructions, i.e. not identical with the real, is it likely to open up to the counter-arguments and alternative constructions of the Other. It will abandon ideological monologue as soon as it realizes that this monologue prevents it from gaining new insights and staying open to experience: "Thought need not be content with its own legality; without abandoning it, we can think against our thought, and if it were possible to define dialectics, this would be a definition worth suggesting."[7]

"Thinking against oneself without abandoning oneself", without toying with the idea of relativism. Such is the stance of a dialectical and dialogical theory which relates contradictory positions to one another in order to accentuate the limits of each position, to become aware of its own limits – and in order to put an end to the sterile coexistence of theories in pluralism.[8] In *Part Three*, this method of "thinking or arguing against oneself" yields a Critical Theory aiming at dialogue and ready to absorb a crucial moment of Critical Rationalism: the critical test which replaces any kind of ultimate justification (e.g. Habermas's notion of an ideal communication situation presumed to be inherent in all types of communication).

The dialectical idea of uniting the opposites occupies a prominent position in the early work of Walter Benjamin, which plays a crucial part in the development of Critical Theory. In his book on German tragedy (*Trauerspiel*), Benjamin explains: "On no account can the representation of an idea succeed, as long as the circle of its possible extremes has not been traced out."[9] What is at stake here is undoubtedly a dialectical totality, not however a closed Hegelian one, but an open structure inviting dialogue.[10]

Where extremes meet, it is hardly surprising to find Benjamin's idea, albeit in a different form, in the work of a contemporary author whom nobody would think of relating to Benjamin the essayist: Niklas Luhmann. This sociologist aims at "discovering similarities of items which initially appear as disparate".[11] He explains: "A specifically scientific performance of theories only comes about when the abstraction of the perspectives underlying comparisons reaches a point where items which are clearly disparate turn out to be comparable (...)."[12] Luhmann obviously hopes that the common denominator of dissimilar phenomena will be revealed by the kind of theoretical system he has in mind.

This, however, is not the idea underlying the following chapters all of which aim at a confrontation of different theoretical models. Such a confrontation serves the purpose of mutual elucidation and criticism. It goes without saying that this train of thought moves neither towards relativism nor towards eclecticism, as superficial observers might suspect, but towards a contrastive and multi-dimensional understanding of the theories involved.

The main goal of *Part Two* is to relate the contrasting notions of theory to one another and to present the latter both in a universalistic and a particularistic, a realist and a constructivist, an individualist and a collectivist perspective. The aim of this approach is not only to discover some hidden flaws within theories but also to gain insight into the complementary character of contrasting perspectives. In all cases, theories are highlighted whose main object is scientific, theoretical communication and the testing of theories in conjunction with the concept of truth.

Chapter 6

Between Universalism and Particularism: Popper and Lyotard (Kuhn, Winch)

The aim of this chapter is not a synthesis of universalism and particularism, of Popper's and Lyotard's theories, but a contrastive comparison which reveals the strengths and flaws of both approaches. The idea is to show that these two incompatible theories are also complementary, because each helps us to detect the shortcomings of the other.

Popper is certainly right when, continuing the rationalist-analytic tradition, he maintains that "it is logically impossible for two incompatible theories both to be true".[1] In the present case, he might argue that universalism and particularism simply cannot be reconciled. Either we dispose of a universally spoken language or we are trapped in mutually exclusive frameworks and cannot communicate. *Tertium non datur*.

Nevertheless, a third possibility seems to exist: the possibility of establishing a dialectical link between extreme positions in order to reveal the interdependence of universalism and particularism. This interdependence is due to the fact that all aspirations towards universal validity are vitiated as long as the subject of discourse refuses to take into account the social and linguistic particularities it encounters in the course of argument.

A concrete universalism, which avoids glossing over the particular in an abstract and rationalist way, can only be a type of thought which takes seriously the main arguments put forward against the modern rationalist and Hegelian tendency towards unification by Lyotard, Adorno, Bauman and Winch – without, however, yielding to a one-sided postmodern particularism. The universal character of thought, conceptualization and criticism ought not to be abandoned.

A systematic overcoming of contrasting positions in Hegel's sense is not envisaged here, especially since the dialogical approach proposed in *Part Three* is not a synthesizing truth situated beyond the extremes, but an open process in the sense of Bakhtin. By relating the opposites to one another, one can hope to obtain insights or moments of truth, not however the one static truth in the metaphysical sense. Popper and Schlick already pointed out that the process of knowledge is interminable.[2]

In these preliminary remarks, followers of Critical Theory may have recognized one of their basic concerns: the reconciliation of the particular with the universal. However, this reconciliation is not to be brought about (as in Adorno's case) with the help of mimesis, essayism and paratactic writing, but rather by an orientation of theory towards alterity and dialogue. This orientation is by no means incompatible with Adorno's and Horkheimer's approach, for it is implicit in the mimesis of essayistic writing.

The question why the author chose to relate Popper's and Lyotard's discourses to one another can be answered in one sentence: these discourses correct each other in crucial points which are at the same time their fundamental weaknesses.

1. Popper's Universalism as a Critique of Kuhn's "Framework"

In the previous chapter, Kuhn was presented as a universalist who sees "paradigm" as a universally, albeit temporarily, valid collective language. The fact that the concept of "paradigm" presupposes heterogeneous and competing sorts of reason, which appear and disappear in the course of scientific evolution, was not commented on. However, it is quite prominent in Popper's criticism of Kuhn's key concept.

Some of the arguments he puts forward in his debates with Kuhn could also be directed against Lyotard. His fundamental aim is to refute Kuhn's particularism contained in one of the basic ideas of *The Structure of Scientific Revolutions*, namely that each paradigm represents a particular rationality that is incompatible with the rationalities of other paradigms. In extreme cases, paradigms are incommensurate.

Popper must have found such extreme cases particularly irritating because he tried to prove that paradigms as noetic or linguistic "frameworks" are "myths" which dissolve whenever they are subjected to rational analysis. As a Kantian he puts forward both rationalist and individualist arguments when he explains with unmitigated optimism how noetic "frameworks can be overcome":

> I do admit that at any moment we are prisoners caught in the framework of our own theories; our expectations; our past experiences; our language. But we are prisoners in a Pickwickian sense: if we try, we can break out of our framework at any time. Admittedly, we shall find ourselves again in a framework, but it will be a better and roomier one; and we can at any moment break out of it again.[3]

Although Popper rejects the idea of the Vienna Circle that a universally valid artificial language (in the sense of Carnap and Neurath) is possible in philosophy,[4] he nevertheless holds on to the Kantian idea that colloquial language is a generally valid means of communication enabling us to overcome all linguistic barriers. It is not by chance that he develops the arguments quoted above by referring to relations between *natural* languages in order to demonstrate that all types of language are always comparable and translatable. He concludes, by way of example, that a large number of Hopi Indians and Chinese have learned very good English. In "The Myth of the Framework", he explains in conjunction with Benjamin Lee Whorf's theory of language (cf. chap. 2) that "in actual fact most human languages seem to be intertranslatable".[5] By pursuing this line of argument, he glosses over all the linguistic residues[6] which cannot be translated (idioms, puns, syntactic constructions), but which may decisively mould the subjectivity of speakers, thus impeding communication by semantic shifts and misunderstandings — even in philosophical and scientific discourses.

It is hardly surprising therefore that Popper's rationalist argument culminates in the thesis that even paradigms in the sense of Kuhn are comparable and translatable. In Popper's perspective, Newton's and Einstein's physical theories do not appear as incommensurate paradigms, but as comparable and compatible systems: "(. . .) It follows from Einstein's theory that Newton's theory is an excellent approximation."[7]

The question is, of course, how a theoretician (in this case Popper) *constructs* objects such as "language", "discourse" or "theory". If these objects are constructed in a universalistic perspective which highlights the signifieds or the content plane (in the sense of Hjelmslev),[8] then the argument is likely to lead to the idea of mutual understanding; if, however, they are constructed in a particularistic manner, whereby the expression plane and the "differing" signifiers in Derrida's sense are stressed, then the argument is more likely to lead to non-translatability and a communication failure.[9]

Popper obviously follows the path to universalism and thus overlooks two crucial points: the impossibility of translating a theoretical-ideological sociolect into another and the fact that communicating scientists are made into subjects by "their" theories-ideologies (most of which are well established before individuals arrive on the scientific stage). Even if this insight is not interpreted deterministically, because it is always possible to reflect one's own ideological discourse or even to abandon it, it stands to reason that a feminist sociologist will refuse to have her discourse translated into a critical-rationalist or a Marxist one. A translation of this kind would negate her interests and her subjectivity.

Although the sociolects of feminism, Critical Rationalism or Marxism are not incommensurate because they can be compared or even combined, they cannot be translated into one another. For translation is based on the notion of *equivalence* – problematical though it may seem.[10]

An approximate equivalence may exist between natural languages;[11] it does not exist between ideological or ideological-theoretical languages. In this respect, Popper's comparison of "frameworks" with natural languages is misleading. The subjectivity of a Chinese woman is not put in question when she speaks English as a second language or as a bilingual speaker. But one cannot expect a feminist to "use" the language of Marxism or Critical Rationalism (except in quotations). For by doing so she would give up her (feminist) subjectivity.

While all ideologies can be expressed in natural languages (though they may undergo changes for cultural and linguistic reasons, as the Maoist brand of Marxism shows), ideological sociolects are separated by qualitative differences, because they express particular interests which are by definition untranslatable. There is a certain naivety in Popper's criticism of the Freudians and Marxists during the interwar period. He blames them for confining themselves to their respective "frameworks": "I mean people like the Marxists, the Freudians, and the Adlerians. None of them could ever be shaken in his adopted view of the world. Every argument against their framework was by them so interpreted as to fit into it (...)."[12] These critical remarks can easily be turned against Popper himself who was never seen to vacillate in his belief in a liberal individualism.[13] This "framework" prevented him from becoming aware of collective factors, group languages or paradigms in the sense of Kuhn.

It is therefore hardly surprising to find that it is precisely Thomas S. Kuhn who considers matters in a sociological perspective and from a collective point of view and who reminds Popper of his ideology: "Rather than a logic, Sir Karl has provided an ideology; rather than methodological rules, he has supplied procedural maxims."[14]

The concept of ideology, which is being used here in the sense of "general ideology" (cf. chap. 2), does not, however, exclude a universally valid "logic of scientific research", as will be shown in chapter 12.

Within a theoretical-ideological sociolect, theory represents the universalistic impulse which aims beyond the particularistic limitations of ideology (in a general sense). In this situation, it is important to be aware of the dialectical tension between ideological particularism and theoretical universalism. Popper does not recognize this task; he rather ignores or denies the existence of the particular by dismissing it as a "myth".

He justifies his universalistic approach both by adopting an individualist and Kantian stance and by considering the natural sciences, whose languages are ideologically neutral, as the only relevant models of scientific discourse. It is therefore hardly surprising that he cannot find "frameworks" in the psychoanalytic or Marxist sense in physics: "(. . .) I could find nothing of the kind in the debates of the physicists about Einstein's General Theory, although it too was hotly debated at the time."[15] A natural science like physics is situated beyond ideological particularities and interests. Popper detects them in the social sciences only to deny their existence in an abstract and rationalist way − instead of pondering on the liberal and individualist *particularity* of his own discourse.

2. Lyotard's Postmodern Particularism as a Polemical Complement cf Critical Rationalism

Bakhtin was among the first to recognize the polemical character of a dialogue marked by a competition of voices. In the novel, the narrator's or hero's voice is constantly being challenged and qualified by competing voices.[16] Lyotard's late writings not only qualify his own Marxist discourse of the 1970s, but put the entire universalistic tradition, both in its rationalist and in its Hegelian-Marxist forms, into perspective.

His radical critique of modernity is summed up by the postmodern sociologist Zygmunt Bauman: "The war against the local, the irregular and the spontaneous was merciless (. . .)."[17] Popper seems to continue this struggle for universal reason, when, in "The Myth of the Framework", he turns against an "irrationalism" whose advocates decompose truth into a multitude of "local" truths.[18]

Lyotard turns the tables on the universalists, when, continuing Adorno's train of thought, he reminds Habermas and his followers that "rationality is reasonable only if it admits that reason is multiple".[19] However, this is the very idea Popper contests and combats in his criticism of Kuhn's "framework". For him there is only one reason whose concrete manifestation is the refutable theory.

At this stage, readers of Lyotard's work could object that the arguments of the postmodern thinker and those of the critical rationalist cannot be compared, because Lyotard does not deal with scientific or theoretical discourse but with *all* forms of language, i.e. with political, juridical, moral discourses. "My interlocutors", remarks Lyotard, "often take *language* in the sense of an idiom, a theory, even a culture. I'm willing to accept these meanings with the exception, nonetheless, of the sense of theory."[20] He subsequently explains why he does not consider "theory" (which he leaves undefined) as a language in the sense of *langue*: "because theory belongs entirely only to the cognitive genre".[21] Paradoxically, this restrictive and somewhat arbitrary attitude towards "theory" induces him to reject Kuhn's thesis about the "incommensurability of scientific paradigms".[22]

This rejection of Kuhn's particularistic approach will only surprise those who are unaware of the specific character of Lyotard's "genres of discourse" and his way of classifying them. Unlike Kuhn, he is not interested in the heterogeneity of science or scientific practice, but in the incompatibility of legal, ethic, aesthetic and cognitive forms of speech. He holds these *types of language* (*langages*) to be heterogeneous; scientific language, however, appears to him as a homogeneous whole. This is why, in *La Condition postmoderne*, he argues "that the language game of science desires its statements to be true".[23]

By adopting this point of view, however, he ignores the heterogeneity of science which appears to him as a homogeneous "cognitive genre" or "language game". This means that his particularism is of a different kind than Kuhn's. It is based on a different notion of language and on a different classification of linguistic forms.

Nevertheless, Lyotard agrees with Kuhn insofar as he also rejects Popper's idea of universal reason. This rejection becomes manifest in his fundamental thesis according to which the invasion of one genre by the other, "in particular of ethics and law by the cognitive, in the Aristotelian sense of dialectics",[24] represents a *tort*, as Lyotard calls this kind of injustice.

For discourse genres considered as "frameworks" (Popper) are heterogeneous and governed by very different, possibly incommensurate patterns or criteria of reasoning. Their contact can easily lead to a *Widerstreit* in the sense of Kant or a *différend* in the sense of Lyotard who takes over and adapts the Kantian term (translated into English as *conflict*).[25] Every attempt to settle such a *conflict* by appealing to a universally valid metalanguage, in the hope of transforming it into a *law suit* (*litige*, Lyotard), overlooks the heterogeneity of the colliding discourses and causes a *tort*, an injustice.[26] A conflict in this particular sense breaks out as soon as it becomes clear that the concern of the plaintiff (e.g. the "labour power", "force de travail", Lyotard) cannot be expressed in the language of the defendant (e.g. "capital", Lyotard).[27]

What Lyotard has to say about language games and later on about genres of discourse is reminiscent of Kuhn's explanations of paradigms:

The examination of language games, just like the critique of the faculties, identifies and reinforces the separation of language from itself. There is no unity to language; there are islands of language, each of them ruled by a different regime, untranslatable into the others.[28]

If for a moment one disregards the fact that these arguments are not aimed at scientific languages, but exclusively at political, ethical, aesthetic or religious language games or genres of discourse, then one is again confronted with Kuhn's problem of particular and incompatible systems of thought. For once again we are dealing with hermetic languages none of which can be translated into another.

The paradox of philosophy seems to consist in the fact that a critical rationalist and universalist such as Popper invokes Kant when defining his own thought "as an attempt to carry further Kant's critical philosophy",[29] whereas Lyotard starts from Kant's *Critique of Judgement* in order to demonstrate the heterogeneity of language and thought.

Here it not only becomes clear that even philosophical works are ambiguous and can be interpreted and used in many ways, but that they contain constant elements most of which can be re-interpreted in different periods of social development. In this particular case, the central issue seems to be Kant's separation of subject and object, reason and imagination, concept and beauty. This separation which Hegel, following Fichte, was determined to overcome by conceptual thought, was rediscovered and accentuated by Lyotard's postmodern critique. Symmetrically, Hegel's dialectics of mediation and unification are rejected by a postmodern thought whose proponents frequently invoke Adorno's work in order to justify their enhancement of the particular.[30]

Lyotard's defence of the latter – of the particular language or culture – is directed against the global unification of societies and cultures by world capital: "The differends between phrase regimens or between genres of discourse are judged to be negligible by the tribunal of capitalism."[31] Towards the end of *The Differend*, no ambiguity remains: "The only insurmountable obstacle that the hegemony of the economic genre comes up against is the heterogeneity of phrase regimens and of genres of discourse (. . .)."[32]

In spite of his linguistic "separatism", Lyotard himself tends to cross the borders between language games and genres of discourse, whenever he combines economic and political, psychological, ethical and aesthetic approaches: for example, in his attempts of the 1970s and 1980s to develop theories inspired by Marx and Freud or Kant and Wittgenstein. He thus contributes to the construction of a postmodern thought marked by eclecticism.

At times it is difficult to avoid the impression that he is determined to separate at all costs what is generally considered as closely related: for example when he speaks of the "invasion of one genre by another, namely of ethics and law by the cognitive mode" (cf. above). Could modern ethics and law survive without cognitive foundations, i.e. without being closely linked to philosophy and jurisprudence?

As was pointed out earlier on, Lyotard neglects the fact that group languages (technical or ideological languages), far from being homogeneous units or hermetic monads, are in reality products of a social and linguistic situation marked by dialogue and intertextuality, that is to say by interpenetration of linguistic genres. A "pure" and isolated genre of discourse which remains unrelated to other types of language hardly exists. A closer scrutiny reveals that each sociolect is a – sometimes unstable – synthesis of more or less heterogeneous discourses. Lyotard's own work illustrates this fact optimally, for it tends to combine dialogically and critically all the dominant languages of the 1960s, 1970s and 1980s – without causing too many *torts*.

Situated at the centre of this chapter, the tension between the particular and the general also makes itself felt in Peter Winch's well-known study *The Idea of a Social Science and its Relation to Philosophy* (1958, 1990). Like Lyotard, Winch invokes Wittgenstein's language games and could be read as a precursor of postmodern particularism, insofar as he blames rationalism, and especially the rationalist sociologist Vilfredo Pareto, for subjecting magic thought to the criteria of scientific discourse: "On the other hand, to try to understand magic by reference to the aims and nature of scientific activity, as Pareto does, will necessarily be to *mis*understand it."[33] In this case, one could also speak of a *tort* in the sense of Lyotard. Magic thought would appear to be a completely different "sentence rule system" the rules of which are incompatible with Pareto's rationalist science. The two systems could be considered as incommensurate.

In this context, it is hardly surprising that, long before the Popper-Kuhn controversy broke out, Winch blamed the critical rationalist for considering social institutions merely as theoretical constructs, thereby neglecting the different types of collective consciousness they articulate. "The ways of thinking embodied in institutions", he explains, "govern the way the members of the societies studied by the social scientist behave."[34] They are autonomous ways of life and "genres of discourse", Lyotard would add, which cannot be assimilated to the rationality of science. Winch's expression "standards of rationality"[35] is reminiscent of Lyotard's "multiplicity of reasons".

Considering the relationship between the universal and the particular in modern and postmodern contexts, especially Winch's preface to the second edition of his book (1990) seems to be relevant. For in this preface he tries to mitigate the particularistic tendency underlying his arguments of the 1950s. Although different social spheres such as morals, religions and science are autonomous, they are intertwined: "Different aspects of social life do not merely 'overlap': they are frequently internally related in such a way that one cannot even be intelligibly conceived as existing in isolation from others."[36]

It is not by chance that this self-criticism is almost identical with the arguments advanced here against Lyotard. It confirms the hypothesis that sociolects evolve in a particular socio-linguistic situation and are intertextual (dialogical) in character. Thus the terminology of formalist and structuralist theories of literature is closely linked to the poetic practice of futurist and surrealist avant-gardes. In a completely different context, Robert C. Bannister discovers the importance of North American Protestantism for the development of sociological positivism. The goal is a "strategy for legitimating science within the confines of American Protestant culture".[37] Language games or sociolects are no monads; on the contrary, they survive and develop by virtue of interpenetration. This is one reason why their discourses cannot be incommensurate.

3.   From the Unity of Opposites to Dialogue

Popper's dictum, according to which "it is logically impossible that of two incompatible theories both be true" (cf. supra), is certainly correct, as long as it is considered from a purely formal point of view. Contradictory statements such as "the earth is flat" and "the earth is a spherical object" are mutually exclusive and cannot both be true. However, complex theories of language, culture and society cannot be as easily divided into "true" and "false" ones.

One of the key problems seems to be that, due to certain taxonomies and actantial models, a theoretical discourse may reveal those aspects of reality and those moments of truth which a competing discourse hides by virtue of introducing completely different semantic and narrative techniques. Peter Winch's mature self-criticism is a case in point. As soon as the subject of a discourse turns a difference into an opposition or indeed an incommensurability, the discourse moves in a different direction on the classification plane. "Overlapping" thus turns into "separation", "separation" into "incompatibility" or "incommensurability", etc. Winch's case is interesting because it illustrates the *reversibility* of this semantic process. The subject of discourse may very well return from "separation" to "overlapping", etc. In other words, we are dealing here with problems of relevance, classification and construction (cf. chap. 2).

Even Lyotard tends occasionally to put his own particularistic approach into perspective: for example, by admitting in conjunction with Donald Davidson's philosophy that different patterns of thought are intertranslatable:

> But the hypothesis of a scheme would prohibit this entity being described in any way other than by means of a scheme. Wherein this hypothesis turns out to be intrinsically aporetic. And how would I know my interlocutor was using a scheme other than mine, unless I could translate it into my language?[38]

Such considerations also cast serious doubts upon Lyotard's own statements concerning the *différend (conflict)* and the incommensurability of "discourse genres", because all of these genres presuppose a common language: namely the natural language within which they evolve (cf. *Part Three*).

In this context, it seems meaningful to relate the opposites or extreme positions to one another. For on a meta-discursive level they appear as partial views which will only further theoretical (dialogical) knowledge if considered simultaneously, if juxtaposed. In conjunction with Popper's and Lyotard's theories this can be taken to mean that universalism without particularism turns abstract and irrational, while a particularism divested of its universalistic counterpart leads to irrationalism and relativism.

Popper's belief that reason is by definition universal will not be contested by anyone who continues to adhere to a critical theory of society − be it in the sense of Critical Rationalism or of the Frankfurt School. However, Lyotard's and Adorno's counter-belief that a reason which ignores the particular becomes unreasonable seems to be equally valid. Popper's own discourse turns irrational whenever its rationalist subject is unaware of the impact of its own liberal-individualist ideology on Critical Rationalism. It is not by chance that Kuhn, the sceptical observer of this kind of rationalism, points out that Sir Karl has founded his method on an ideology (cf. supra).

One of the basic tasks of dialogue is to make ideologies appear, to make interlocutors aware of them. Clearly, this mechanism will only yield results as long as "ideology" is not a priori regarded as "the ideology of the other", but as one's own ideology. (In the present case, the ambivalent, self-critical individualism of Critical Theory is at stake: cf. chap. 11.) Dialogue itself is set in motion by the idea that opposites complete and correct each other, by Pirandello's *sentimento del contrario*: "the feeling for the opposite".[39]

In this case, dialectics fulfils the function of stimulating the self-consciousness and the self-irony of all individual and collective instances involved. It reveals to each of them to what extent its truth is merely a partial truth which needs supplementing by its opposite. As a rhetorical technique, this approach was well known to ancient sophistry; however, it need not lead to sophistry or relativism.

Commenting on this problem, Adorno remarks in *Minima Moralia*:

> *Warning: not to be misused.* The dialectic stems from the sophists; it was a mode of discussion whereby dogmatic assertions were shaken and, as the public prosecutors and comic writers put it, the lesser word made the stronger. (...) But as a means of proving oneself right it was also from the first an instrument of domination, a formal technique of apologetics unconcerned with content, serviceable to those who could pay: the principle of constantly and successfully turning the tables. Its truth or untruth, therefore, is not inherent in the method itself, but in its intention in the historical process.[40]

What exactly is the "intention in the historical process" of a dialogue driven on by the dialectical linking of opposites? It is meant to keep the theoretical discourse open by protecting it from becoming petrified in ideological monologue, in collective dogmatism. In this respect, dialogical thought can be regarded as the opposite of Hegelian dialectics which, according to Ernst Bloch,[41] is marked by a movement towards systematic conclusion. Thus Critical Rationalism is only useful and true when its counterpart is also taken into account. This also applies to Lyotard's philosophy of the *différend* (the conflict of languages): it only appears as meaningful as long as the idea of a universally valid reason is not abandoned.

Chapter 7

Intersubjectivity and Perspective:
Davidson and Mannheim

The importance of intersubjectivity in the sense of an intersubjectively controlled perception of reality increases steadily as the numerous mimetic theories of cognition are put in question. Wherever such theories are criticized and abandoned as remnants of a naïve realism, for example, in Rorty's approach,[1] intersubjective testing of perception and argument is often recognized as a valid alternative and a new criterion of truth.

Since Edmund Husserl's transcendental phenomenology,[2] the object is increasingly being viewed "as the object of a common, intersubjectively accessible world"[3] and not as a realistic representation in the mimetic sense. This idea not only prevails in Critical Rationalism (cf. chap. 4), but also in Jürgen Habermas's conception of an intersubjectively shared *life world*, partly derived from Husserl's phenomenology, partly from Mead's sociology of action and Anglo-American Speech Act Theory. Even some proponents of Radical Constructivism use the notion of *intersubjectivity*[4] without bothering to clarify the fundamental concept of *subjectivity* and to explain how individual and collective subjects interact in discourse.

The widespread use of this concept in very different sociolects, both in the English- and the German-speaking world (in the French-speaking world its use is quite limited), may at least partly account for the fact that it hardly ever undergoes incisive criticism: neither in epistemology nor in the theory of science.

This seems to be a good reason for subjecting it to sceptical scrutiny by analysing its usage in some of Donald Davidson's works and by relating it dialectically to Karl Mannheim's concept of *perspective*. This comparison ought to reveal what Davidson's approach conceals by systematic omission and what Mannheim obliterates by his notion of "free-floating intellectuals": the indelible character of ideological languages. Although the unhampered communication advocated by both thinkers seems to be possible in the last resort, it remains wishful thinking under the – idealized – conditions each of them has in mind.

Intersubjectivity and *perspective* are theoretically related insofar as Mannheim's idea that each individual subject is situated in a collective context
or perspective seems plausible. By ignoring the existence of collective subjects and perspectives as *conceptual schemes*, Davidson is able to present intersubjective communication as a relatively uncomplicated matter. In this
respect, his point of view is akin to Popper's, although he differs from Critical Rationalism – among other things – by presupposing a common value
system underlying all communication. Mannheim in turn differs from a
postmodern philosopher like Lyotard by his efforts to overcome the collective particularities he discovers – long before postmodernism.[5]

1.   Davidson: Subjectivity, Intersubjectivity and Language

Unlike Popper who compares cognitive frameworks (in the sense of Kuhn's
paradigms) with translatable natural languages, thus enabling himself to
dismiss them as myths, Davidson investigates the translatability of heterogeneous noetic systems which he calls *conceptual schemes*. However, following
a rationalist train of thought, he tends to dissolve them in an individualist
and universalistic discourse. Thus Allen Hance can conclude that for Davidson "the idea of a conceptual scheme is but one more dogma of empiricism".[6] But what exactly are Davidson's arguments?

   Dealing with Whorf's theory, he objects that on the one hand this linguist
considers the language of the Hopi Indians and English as incommensurate
systems, but on the other hand continues to comment on Hopi sentences in
English. He objects to Kuhn's approach with analogous arguments: "Kuhn
is brilliant at saying what things were like before the revolution using –
what else? – our post-revolutionary idiom."[7]

   He consolidates this universalistic approach by anchoring it in a consensus theory of society. The only possibility of solving communication problems, he declares, consists in assuming a "general agreement on beliefs".[8]
In this perspective, even disagreements are considered as embedded in
global consensus or "agreement".

   One of his central notions, the notion of *charity*, can be deduced from
his consensus point of view. It is well known that the direction a discourse
takes and even the goal it is moving towards, depend on its relevance criteria: on the normative answer to the question what matters in a society,
what "makes it tick". In Davidson's eyes, *consensus* appears to be the decisive factor, and one of the key modalities permitting us to stabilize or
bring about this consensus, in matters of knowledge as well as in practical
matters, is *charity*. At this stage a "framework" and translation problem

crops up – because, from a French or German point of view, this word seems to be in need of explanation (whatever the translations in other languages may be).[9]

It calls for clarification because Davidson defines "charity" on at least three different levels: (1) as a social and psychic attitude; (2) as a principle of coherence ("a degree of logical consistency in the thought of the speaker");[10] and (3) as a principle of correspondence which "prompts the interpreter to take the speaker to be responding to the same features of the world that he (the interpreter) would be responding to under similar circumstances".[11] The correspondence principle seems to be inseparable from the social and psychic factors mentioned in the first instance. In order to solve the seemingly formal problems of coherence and correspondence, Davidson invokes a kind of empathy the existence of which can only be presupposed if one accepts his consensus view of society and inter-individual communication.

Those who refuse to adopt this view may wonder why an interpreter should be assumed to respond "to the same features of the world" as the speaker – even if "similar circumstances" are granted. For the antithesis seems at least as plausible as Davidson's thesis: namely that speaker and interpreter (i.e. two different discourses) are likely to respond to very different features of the world – even under "similar circumstances". In this case, charity in the sense of "correspondence between speaker and interpreter" would collapse. But what exactly does this word mean on an etymological level?

Let us return to Davidson's text and use it as a starting point: "Since charity is not an option, but a condition of having a workable theory, it is meaningless to suggest that we might fall into massive error by endorsing it."[12] In this sentence, the subject of discourse goes to extremes and even seems willing to grant a problematical concept such as *charity* a kind of immunity from critique and doubt. It seems "meaningless" even to subject the concept in question to further scrutiny.

Eventually, charity appears as a kind of fate ordinary mortals cannot help submitting to:

> Charity is forced upon us; whether we like it or not, if we want to understand others, we must count them right in most matters. If we can produce a theory that reconciles charity and the formal conditions of a theory, we have done all that could be done to ensure communication. Nothing more is possible, and nothing more is needed.[13]

If we wish to understand others, argues Davidson, we must "count them right in most matters". The cautiously interjected word "most" seems to

guarantee the option of tactical retreat, just in case a naïve or radical interlocutor takes this statement to be applicable to discourses of National
Socialism, Fascism or Marxism-Leninism. Charity for everybody – for the
sake of mutual understanding? But what is the original meaning of charity?

The Latin word *caritas* means, among other things, esteem, love, charity.
In French and Italian, *charité* and *carità* mean charity in the religious sense:
"la charité chrétienne", "l'amour du prochain en vue de Dieu",[14] though in
Italian a more secular meaning seems to prevail. Although it is easy enough
to render the general meaning of the word charity in other languages, the
word as used by the American philosopher causes substantial problems.

As was pointed out before, Davidson's charity is primarily an evaluative
attitude towards others. If we wish to understand them, "we must count
them right in most matters". Moreover, we are expected to presuppose
that our interlocutors are coherent and that, under similar circumstances,
they refer to the same features of the world as we do (cf. supra). Although
all of these criteria are different in character, their common denominator
could be defined as "good will towards the other" in a hermeneutic sense.
Elsewhere, however, Davidson follows Quine's theory and defines charity
as a projection of one's own truth criteria into the sentences of the other:
"In either case, the principle directs the interpreter to translate or interpret
so as to read some of his own standards of truth into the pattern of sentences
held true by the speaker."[15]

At this stage, two fundamental problems of the notion of charity come to
the fore. In Davidson's discourse, it lacks a coherent definition, because
counting others "right in most matters" is a far stronger criterion than the
assumption concerning the other's coherence; and projecting some of our
own "standards of truth" into the "sentences" of the other is yet another
matter. While the first criterion is a risky concession to a potentially dangerous or irresponsible interlocutor, the third criterion could be interpreted as
an attempt to encroach upon the autonomy of the other by subjecting her or
his speech to our own standards of truth. In this case, Davidson seems to
gloss over a potential *différend* in the sense of Lyotard. The second problem
regards the intercultural status of *charity* and the translatability of this
notion into other languages (cf. supra). The difficulties encountered by a
translator in this particular case seem to indicate that the "idea of a conceptual scheme" ought not to be dismissed light-heartedly, because the word
charity as used by Davidson has become the keystone of a *conceptual scheme*
which stubbornly resists intercultural and inter-ideological use.

For it is difficult to imagine a philosopher like Lyotard invoking the idea of
charity (translated by him as *charité*)[16] in order to overcome *différends* between
different types of languages. Similarly, philosophers in the German-speaking

world will feel barred from using a word like *Nächstenliebe* (= *charity*) or even *Nachsichtigkeit* (= *leniency*), the word used by the German translator, in discussions about theory formation and scientific communication.

In some respects, Davidson's *charity* appears to fulfil a function similar to Habermas's notion of *ideal speech situation* (*ideale Sprechsituation*). Like the latter it "is forced upon us" and therefore has to be presupposed. However, theoretical or everyday communication by no means presupposes *charity*. Although *charity* – very much like Kant's *good will* – can be considered as a condition for everyday communication, it is certainly not the only condition, nor the dominant attitude. (Thus someone may strongly dislike certain religious or political views, because he understands them only too well, while he may admire and cherish other views for lack of understanding.)

In a conflict-ridden society, other conditions of success or failure in communication will be: psychic and social ambivalence, political interests, distrust and a critical attitude. In the present case, criticism turns against the attempt to present language and society as marked by a general consensus granting atomized individuals the possibility of unhampered communication.

For Davidson's idea of intersubjectivity is deeply rooted in the kind of consensus ideology that formed the basis of sociological functionalism and was at the same time criticized as a systematic apology of North American society.[17] Davidson's conception of "subjectivity" does not take into account the obstacles and hurdles encountered in communication. It presents thought as divided into a private and a public sector: "Thoughts are private" and "thought is necessarily part of a common public world".[18] The latter is based on a consensus concerning reality and truth: "Not only can others often learn what we think by noting the causal dependencies that give our thoughts their content, but the very possibility of thought demands shared standards of truth and objectivity."[19] This highly controversial statement is not only at variance with everything Lyotard has to say about the *différend*; it also contradicts the basic tenets of Mannheim's sociology of knowledge, as will be shown in the following section.

However, Davidson seems to think and write in a world unaffected by the social theories of Tocqueville, Marx and Mannheim. Unlike Popper, who regards with scepticism all attempts by the Vienna Circle to produce a "universal jargon" (cf. chap. 6, 1), he invokes Neurath's universalism in order to define *intersubjectivity*: "Language is in its nature, as Neurath insisted, intersubjective; what someone else's words mean on a given occasion is always something that we can in principle learn from public clues."[20] But how are we supposed to react when our interlocutor (e.g. a Leninist) defines "truth" or "freedom" in such a way that these words mean the very opposite of what we take them to mean? In Davidson's work, this question is not raised.

Unlike the anti-realist Rorty who only recognizes the level of inter-subjective communication, excluding what is commonly called the "real world",[21] Davidson imagines the process of knowledge as based on a triangular structure consisting of a speaker, a listener and a world: "two creatures, and each creature with common features of the world".[22] The common views are guaranteed by "the context of a shared world"[23] and "by a shared language".[24]

Expressions such as *common* and *sharing* dominate in Davidson's discourse, which not only postulates the existence of a common reality but also (and in a style strikingly similar to the functionalism of Parsons and Merton) a common system of social values: "Gauging the thoughts of others requires that I live in the same world with them, sharing many reactions to its many features, including its values."[25] Even the attitude towards values and value judgements thus appears as an intersubjective fact situated beyond all linguistic and ideological conflicts.

Such a conception of language, society and subjectivity is only possible if the constitution and self-construction of subjects in sociolects and discourses is overlooked or ignored. This blind spot in Davidson's philosophy of language is due to his orientation towards the isolated sentence (Saussure's *syntagm*). In a context where only "sentences"[26] are being taken into account, discourse as a trans-phrastic, i.e. semantic and narrative structure stays out of sight.[27] Consequently, it becomes impossible to understand subjectivity as a discursive, narrative process of self-creation.

It stands to reason that, in this situation, collective languages which form the basis of individual subjectivity cannot be taken into account. However, they are situated at the centre of Karl Mannheim's sociology of knowledge, which seems to cast light on those aspects of the cognitive process Davidson leaves in the dark.

2.   Mannheim: Ideology and Perspective

In contrast to Davidson who, like Rorty, follows the precepts of North American individualism and pragmatism, Karl (Károly) Mannheim starts from the premises of the Budapest-based "Sonntagskreis" ("Sunday Circle") whose members were strongly influenced by Hegel's hermeneutics and by Marxism. Eva Karádi quite correctly points out that the various positions within the Circle (Lukács, Mannheim, Arnold Hauser) are all marked by an "anti-liberal theory of alienation".[28]

It is hardly surprising that this theory which envisages a social order beyond liberal individualism is particularly alert to the role played by the collective factor in science, art and everyday life. What Mannheim calls "the roots of thought in social Being" ("Seinsverbundenheit des Denkens")[29] or *perspective*, when commenting on Georg Lukács's *History and Class Consciousness* (1923), is comparable to Popper's, Davidson's and Kuhn's concepts of *framework*, *conceptual scheme* and *paradigm*. It goes without saying that one can only compare what is not identical, not synonymous. Nevertheless, all of these concepts refer directly or indirectly to young Mannheim's idea that thought, even original scientific thought, is collective in character. For this particular reason theoretical communication cannot be imagined as an interaction between atomized individuals.

The group is always present and represented in the individual's thought, which means that even purely individual statements can be attributed to a collective consciousness: "If, however, the particular consciousness of the individual is built around schemes of experience which continue to function even when the group responsible for these schemes is not present as such, then it is legitimate to attribute certain ideas to certain groups (. . .)."[30] In some respects, this idea not only corresponds to Lukács's concept of *class consciousness* (cf. chap. 8), but also to Lucien Goldmann's concept of *world view* (*vision du monde*), which also refers to an *attributed consciousness* (*zugerechnetes Bewußtsein*, Lukács), i.e. a construction in the Weberian sense of *ideal type* and not to the empirical consciousness of the individual.[31] For the individual's consciousness cannot be assumed to contain or realize all the components of the corresponding group consciousness.

This consciousness is historical in character, because it adapts to the changing ideological constellation: "The ideologies of the conservative strata (their aims, their political creed, etc.) undergo changes along with the global constellation in which these ideologies have to prove their worth."[32] In the case of "Liberalism" or "Conservatism", we are thus dealing with changing structures whose reconstructions in the works of Collini, Baglioni[33] or Mannheim are but snapshots of historical processes.

We are nevertheless dealing with structures pre-existing and underlying individual consciousness: pre-existing in the sense of Pêcheux' *interdiscours*[34] or of P. Henry's *préconstruit*.[35] The collective subject is part and parcel of our individual subjectivity: "The collective subject within us is present insofar as there are, within our consciousness, community-specific elements of knowledge experienced within a communitarian space."[36] However, individual subjectivity transcends this social condition analysed by Mannheim, insofar as the individual is also "consciousness in general" (Mannheim)[37] and a "personal subject".[38] These specific components point beyond the boundaries of the group and explain how and to what extent *reflection* (not mentioned by Mannheim) is possible. The individual subject may scan horizons lying well beyond the intellectual scope of its group of origin; it may, at the same time, attempt a synthesis of several *world views* or *perspectives*, as Mannheim puts it,[39] thereby discovering the relative character of each.

Far from embracing a collectivist determinism, Mannheim advocates a process of reflection in the course of which the different ideologies or perspectives are objectified and can thus be viewed "from outside", as Foucault would say.[40] On this level, he can certainly be considered, following the sociologist Ilja Srubar, as a precursor of the postmodern critique of meta-narratives: "In this perspective, the most prominent of all meta-narratives is, of course, religion; however, we shall see that, within Mannheim's scheme, also secular meta-narratives occupy positions of reflexively overcome *métarécits.*" Srubar adds "that the exploratory work of postmodernism which can be observed in the theories of Lyotard, Bauman and Beck is quite advanced in Mannheim's thought".[41] In what respects does Mannheim anticipate postmodern problems?

He announces postmodern society by revealing to what extent the fragmentation of life and the concomitant "disintegration of values" (Broch)[42] put into perspective and "pluralize" all forms of consciousness, all ideologies and world views. In such a situation, where the existence of a homogeneous value system can no longer be taken for granted, communication cannot possibly be assumed to take place among atomized individuals, but has to be regarded as an attempt to mediate between ideological groups and their divergent *perspectives.*

The crucial difference between Popper and Davidson on the one hand and Lyotard and Mannheim on the other consists in their contrasting views of this social and linguistic situation. While Popper and Davidson argue that frameworks or conceptual schemes are negligible or can easily be overcome, because eventually all participants can be made to agree on a common language, Mannheim and Lyotard consider such schemes as fatal obstacles which make communications break down in a fragmented postmodern world. Unlike Lyotard who cannot envisage a dialogical solution to what he calls the *différend* (he merely grants the possibility to "bear witness to differends"/"témoigner du différend"),[43] Mannheim does try to relate the diverging collective perspectives to one another.

His theoretical efforts, some of which are complementary to those of the Durkheim School,[44] aim at translating the competing perspectives into one another. In this context, objectivity and intersubjectivity, as defined by Max Weber, Karl R. Popper and Donald Davidson, appear in a new light:

In the case of situationally conditioned thought, objectivity comes to mean something quite new and different: (a) there is first of all the fact that in so far as different observers are immersed in the same system, they will, on the basis of the identity of their conceptual and categorical apparatus and through the common universe of discourse thereby created, arrive at similar results, and be in a position to eradicate as an error everything that deviates from this unanimity; (b) and recently there is a recognition of the fact that when observers have different perspectives, "objectivity" is attainable only in a more roundabout fashion. In such a case, what has been correctly but differently perceived by the two perspectives must be understood in the light of the differences in structure of these varied modes of perception. An effort must be made to find a formula for translating the results of one into those of the other and to discover a common denominator for these varying perspectivistic insights.[45]

Eckart Huke-Didier quite aptly describes this approach as "a basically consensual theory of truth".[46]

Unlike in the model submitted here (cf. *Part Three*), the problem of subjectivity arising within different perspectives (i.e. sociolects and discourses) is not brought up in Mannheim's sociology of knowledge. He continues his explanations using the phrase "once such a common denominator has been found (...)",[47] thus glossing over the subject problem. For in a semiotic context, it is difficult to disregard the question *who* will find the "common denominator". Which perspective, which sociolect does he belong to, and how does he envisage or construct the translation of heterogeneous language structures into one another?

Since Mannheim avoids this question, he can opt for a solution that invariably provokes critical reactions and protests: the idea of a group of *free-floating intellectuals*, who continue to pursue Enlightenment ideals and appear as the ultimate guardians of neutrality or objectivity[48] (a function they already fulfilled in Mannheim's book on Conservatism).[49]

It is impossible, within the scope of this chapter, to deal with all the arguments Marxists and advocates of Critical Theory mounted against this idea.[50] Adopting a Marxist point of view, Kurt Lenk objects: "The insistence on a free-floating intelligentsia as the bearer of the new synthesis remains abstract, because history appears as an endless process and its semantic unity as a 'utopia'."[51]

The abstract character of this conception is due to more concrete factors: to the fact, for example, that intellectuals are, from an ideological and linguistic point of view, a highly heterogeneous group. Far from speaking a homogeneous sociolect, they communicate in many different, partly incompatible languages some of which give rise to conflicting identities. By overlooking or underestimating this problem, Mannheim, whose theory of ideologies and perspectives challenges Davidson's notion of a consensus-oriented communication, tends to confirm the latter on a higher level: on the level of the seemingly detached intellectuals.

However, intellectuals, far from being free-floating or neutral, are in many cases responsible for the production of rival ideological languages. T. S. Eliot aptly points out: "It is not the business of clerics to agree with each other; they are driven to each other's company by their common dis-similarity from everybody else, and by the fact that they find each other the most profitable people to disagree with."[52] Hegel, Croce and Gramsci, Marx, Lenin and Trotsky, Maurras, Déroulède and Alfred Rosenberg were all intellectuals – who would never have agreed on anything substantial. Thus the opposite of what Mannheim believes seems to be true. The apparently free-floating intellectuals can be held at least partly responsible for the ideological and theoretical fragmentation of modern society.

3.   Towards a Reflexive Dialogue

The confrontation between Davidson's consensus-based theory of intersubjective communication and Mannheim's theory of perspectives reveals two complementary aspects of the problem: namely that each theory constructs reality differently and that competing theoretical constructions are both complementary and mutually destructive. This means that consensus and dissent do not exclude one another because it is the dialectic of agreement and disagreement which triggers off a genuine process of knowledge.

According to Bakhtin, the language of the novel is a system of languages which illuminate each other dialogically. If applied to the theoretical dialogue constructed here, this sentence can also be taken to mean that Mannheim's discourse casts light upon the obstacles Davidson avoids instead of overcoming them. Like Hermann Broch's "polyhistorical novel",[53] Mannheim's sociology of knowledge, deeply rooted in the interwar experience of the Budapest-based "Sunday Circle", draws our attention to the fragmentation of the social value system: to the ideological, linguistic and rhetorical fissures that divide our world into segments. It can also be considered as an anticipatory polemic against Davidson's idea of charity: as a radical critique of his attempt to presuppose unity where hermetic groups, divisions and conflicts are the rule, rather than the exception.

Davidson seems to be unaware of the fact that, apart from religious and political sects, even theoretical sects exist: "After all, one often observes that the tighter the relations within a homogeneous cognitive community are, the more sectarian its language becomes; that it produces a terminology of its own, within which the words of the larger linguistic community cease to be meaningful (...)."[54] Whoever considers the consequences of this kind of linguistic sectarianism, will find it difficult to share Davidson's confidence in charity as a means of overcoming social and linguistic bias.

If one adopts Davidson's point of view in order to consider the sociology of knowledge "from the outside" as it were, one can hardly suppress the ironical remark that Mannheim's theoretical efforts end where Davidson's argument begins: at a charity-based attempt by the (hopefully) "free-floating" intellectuals to overcome conceptual schemes or perspectives. Such intellectuals are supposed to accomplish what all of Davidson's charitable individuals are able to do without being "free-floating" or privileged in any other way. The stony detour via colliding perspectives and translations seems to have been all in vain.

It was not in vain. For the Davidson-Mannheim confrontation reveals to what extent *conceptual schemes*, *ideologies* or *perspectives*, far from being figments of our imagination instantly dissolved by good will combined with insight, are real factors to be taken into account in all kinds of communication. If there is anything chimerical in this particular case, it is the idea cherished by *both* Davidson and Mannheim that anyone can think independently of cultures, ideologies, schemes or perspectives. This idea could only take shape, because both thinkers neglect the origins of *subjectivity* in group languages and ideologies.

Although Mannheim is aware of this problem, he does not solve it. Above all, he fails to relate it to the supposedly free-floating intellectuals who (like other people) are unable to rise above their own particular perspectives, which determine their subjectivities to a high degree. Although it is perfectly possible for me to reflect critically upon my own perspective (ideology) and subjectivity in order to modify or develop it, it is impossible to give it up entirely without becoming another person, another subject.

If there is to be a meaningful theoretical dialogue, it will not take place beyond or outside the participating subjects and their sociolects, but only *between* them: in the *real socio-linguistic situation*. Such a dialogue will be based neither on charity nor on objectivity, nor on value-freedom. It will of necessity be polemical.[55] However, this will not diminish its theoretical value.

Chapter 8

Realism and Constructivism:
Lukács and Glasersfeld

In this particular case, as in other cases, the opposites tend to meet: namely in the implicit assumption that the answerability of the question concerning true knowledge is linked to the existence of a generalized social subject or a homogeneous "community of observers". In what follows, the presence or absence of this community and its function in the process of knowledge will be dealt with.

Ernst von Glasersfeld, who is no longer able or willing to presuppose the existence of such a community, starts from the assumption of a fragmented, pluralized society and propounds a Radical Constructivism which replaces the objectivity criterion of traditional epistemology by the notion of construction.[1] In a historical and social situation where no one can venture to adopt a divine or global point of view, we are forced to accept the coexistence of competing constructions. Traditional epistemology which presupposes the intelligibility of the real is replaced by Glasersfeld – who invokes Vico and Kant as his predecessors[2] – by a radically constructivist approach.

By contrast, Georg Lukács, who does not deal with an irretrievably fragmented social world, but relies on the universal aspirations of the proletariat to overcome class antagonism in a classless society, can presuppose the fundamentally intelligible character of reality as such. In this respect, he continues to rely on the epistemologies developed by Hegel and Marx.

At the core of this chapter is not the question whether Glasersfeld's Radical Constructivism of the 1980s and 1990s ought to be preferred to the hermeneutics of totality underlying *History and Class Consciousness* (1923), a work Lukács himself criticized and revoked,[3] but a dialogical confrontation of the two positions. Eventually, such a confrontation might lead to a new and more critical understanding of both.

When adopting an historical perspective, it ought to be pointed out that Radical Constructivism (in a general sense) is deeply rooted in a philosophical and literary modernism which – in the works of Nietzsche, Musil, Valéry and Adorno – has repudiated Hegel's category of totality[4] and gradually turns into Rorty's and Lyotard's postmodernism.

Unlike the world of the modernists and constructivists, Lukács's world continues to be solidly anchored in Hegel's modernity. Lukács's aesthetic plea in favour of a literary realism based on the *typical* and on Hegel's category of *totality* finds its counterpart in his epistemological realism, inspired by Fichte's and Hegel's trust that Kant's *thing in itself* (*Ding an sich*), i.e. reality, can be known.

This excessive idealism, which can hardly conceal its authoritarian traits, considering the vast array of critiques it provoked in the past,[5] may nowadays appear as an anachronism. However, this anachronism does reveal what has been lost and continues to pose problems by its conspicuous absence in Radical Constructivism and elsewhere: the Archimedean point from which theories could be considered, compared and criticized.

1.   Georg Lukács or the Construction of Realism

Even if one advocates moderate and not Radical Constructivism (as is the case here), one will tend to regard any kind of theory as a discursive or semantic and narrative construction rather than as a true or false reflection of reality. Hence it seems plausible to begin by considering the Hegelian discourse of the young Lukács from a constructivist point of view.

In *History and Class Consciousness*, the word "constructed" does occur, but is used perfunctorily and is reminiscent of a Freudian *lapsus linguae* which reveals the forgotten and forsaken, the repressed. The dialectical approach is defended there against bourgeois science: "This dialectical conception of totality seems to have put a great distance between itself and reality, it appears to construct reality very 'unscientifically'. But it is the only method capable of understanding and reproducing reality."[6] One may assume that even the old Lukács would refuse to admit a Freudian *lapsus*, but would insist on the fact that he uses the word "construct" in the sense attributed to it by the detractors of dialectics. At the same time, he would insist on the necessity of representing reality by dialectical means.

Hegel would do the same. In conjunction with Hegel's critique of Kant's "subjectivism" and of his dictum that it is impossible to know the *thing in itself*, John E. Smith remarks: "Hegel was, in this regard, a thorough-going realist: what we know is the things themselves, their properties, unities and relations."[7] Starting from the premise that the real as such is knowable, Hegel blames Kant for his dualism, his refusal to go beyond appearance: "Theoretically the Kantian philosophy is the 'Illumination' or *Aufklärung* reduced to method; it states that nothing true can be known, but only the phenomenal (...)."[8] It will be shown that a radical constructivist like

Glasersfeld links his key arguments to this subjectivist anti-realism defended by Kant and debunked by Hegel.

In Hegel's philosophy itself, for example in the *Science of Logic*, the repressed constructivist moments surface when the author goes on to explain his "definite negation":

> It is a fresh Notion but higher and richer than its predecessor; for it is richer by the negation or opposite of the latter, therefore contains it, but also something more, and is the unity of itself and its opposite. It is in this way that the system of Notions as such has to be formed — and has to complete itself in a purely continuous course in which nothing extraneous is introduced.[9]

Here the system not only appears as an autonomous process but as a *construct* situated outside reality.

The fact that, in spite of the autonomous, indeed hermetic structure of his system, Hegel never doubts its reality, is due to a discursive instance (an *actant* in the sense of Greimas) which guarantees the identity of discourse and world, subject and object: the *world spirit* (*Weltgeist*). Lukács remarks on this subject: "The 'we' that he was able to find is, as is well known, the World Spirit, or rather, its concrete incarnations, the spirits of the individual peoples."[10] Had Lukács at this point said "invented" (in the sense of Glasersfeld and Heinz von Foerster)[11] instead of "found", he could have turned his Marxist critique of Hegel into a constructivist discourse, thereby revealing the mechanisms of Hegel's historical construction along with the narrative and fictional character of the postulated identity between subject and object.

In spite of this missed opportunity, his mention of the *world spirit* reveals the narrative mechanisms of his own construction, which is also based on an identification of subject and object, thought and being. For Lukács also invokes a narrative instance, a collective actant which guarantees truthfulness and a scientific grasp of the real: *the proletariat as subject of history.*

The latter is the "we", the collective agent that not only turns out to be the reference group and *sender* (*destinateur*, Greimas) of the Marxist philosopher, but also the guarantor of true, undistorted knowledge. However, it can only guarantee true knowledge because it is endowed in Lukács's (Marx's) discourse with certain *modalities* or capacities enabling it to overcome class antagonism and to realize human totality. Unlike the bourgeoisie whose social domination is exercised "*in the interest* of that minority",[12] the proletariat represents "*society as a concrete totality*".[13] This is why Lukács can speak of the "authentic class consciousness of the proletariat".[14]

Unlike the proletariat, the bourgeoisie not only represents limited minority thinking, but also stands for a social process of extreme specialization and fragmentation. Like the Austrian novelist Hermann Broch,[15] Lukács believes that the irrationalism of the bourgeoisie is due to the limits and barriers which seal off the "particular rationalistic disciplines"[16] within bourgeois society from one another.

While the bourgeoisie "is held fast in the mire of immediacy",[17] proletarian consciousness guarantees adequate knowledge aiming at reality as a whole, i.e. at Hegel's category of totality:

> Of course, the knowledge yielded by the standpoint of the proletariat stands on a higher scientific plane objectively; it does after all apply a method that makes possible the solution of problems which the greatest thinkers of the bourgeois era have vainly struggled to find and in its substance, it provides the adequate historical analysis of capitalism which must remain beyond the grasp of bourgeois thinkers.[18]

Two aspects of Lukács's historical realism come to the fore in this passage. Different stages of historical thought exist, and the proletarian stage is epistemologically the *higher* one; the proletarian form of thought is more *adequate* to (capitalist) reality than bourgeois forms.

In this context, two arguments seem plausible. Following Lukács's critics of the interwar period, one could argue that *History and Class Consciousness* is an idealist, Hegelian construction made possible by a discourse subject which turns the working class into a mythical "proletariat", i.e. a mythical actant endowed with fantastic cognitive modalities. The complementary argument is that this construction is not simply the pipe dream of a lonely intellectual, but a collective idea of interwar Marxists who justified their revolutionary hopes by linking them to the aspirations of a seemingly revolutionary working-class movement.

This identification with an historical movement gave an intellectual like Lukács the feeling of belonging to a "we" capable of guaranteeing the existence of a knowable reality accessible to all. In a situation where this "we" as an *authoritative community of observers* disappears, the very notion of "reality" turns out to be problematical.

Naturally, one could object that this "we" was a myth and a nostalgic anachronism both in Hegel's and in Lukács's discourse. This is correct, as a functional comparison with archaic societies shows, where doubts concerning "reality", "truth" or "adequate perception" cannot arise, because the *shared belief in a myth* guarantees the authenticity of collective knowledge and experience. In a society where the last remnants of mythical thought disintegrate (e.g. in late modernity), a pluralist and constructivist approach to knowledge and perception appears as the only solution.

Nevertheless, it would be foolhardy to relegate Lukács's (Hegel's) epistemological model to the realm of archaic or anachronistic thought. For it will be shown that the question concerning the relationship between the "we" and the possibility of authentic knowledge continues to haunt contemporary theories such as Radical Constructivism. This question is as important as the complementary question concerning the role of construction in the "identifying" discourses of Hegel and Lukács which was at the centre of this section.[19]

2.   Ernst von Glasersfeld or the Fragmentation of Reality in Postmodernism

As long as one does not leave the realm of philosophy or what the Russian Formalists would have called "philosophical evolution", it is relatively easy to account for the difference between a Marxist such as Lukács and a radical constructivist such as Ernst von Glasersfeld. While Lukács follows Hegel in asserting that reality as such, as a meaningful totality, is knowable and that Kant's inaccessible "thing in itself" is the relic of an Enlightenment rationalism overcome by dialectics, Glasersfeld follows Kant by insisting on the limits of human knowledge.

The fundamental problem of Radical Constructivism tackled by Glasersfeld boils down to the question "*how* it is possible that we seek and even find a structure in the world of our experience that is *not* a reflection of reality".[20] The radical constructivist believes that Giambattista Vico and Immanuel Kant have at least partly answered this question or suggested answers pointing in the right direction:

> As Vico noticed in 1710, the word *factum* is the past participle of the Latin word for "to make". This was one clue that led him to formulate the epistemological principle that human beings can know only what human beings themselves have made by putting together elements that were accessible to them.[21]

Knowledge thus appears as a process of subjective construction.

In order to pre-empt misunderstandings it should be added that Glasersfeld agrees that objects of nature are accessible to knowledge, in spite of the fact that they are not human constructions; but natural scientists can only know such objects as their own constructs and not "in themselves". Thus light is only accessible to them as particle or wave, water as H_2O, etc.

Following Kant, a radical constructivist like Humberto Maturana also holds that our knowledge can only be subjective: "For one does not explain *the* universe or reality *as such*, but only the coherences of one's own experience."[22] But how do we know that the coherence of our particular experience is preferable to the patterns of coherence advocated by our interlocutors or critics?

At this stage, it becomes clear that it is not sufficient to explain the difference between Lukács and Glasersfeld, between Hegelianism and constructivism, by referring to the contrasting positions of Kant and Hegel. It seems necessary to adopt a more comprehensive perspective and take into account the social context.

The latter was already mentioned in conjunction with Lukács's epistemology whose realism was related to the revolutionary confidence of the Hegelian and Marxist: to the (imaginary) solidarity between the radical intellectual and the proletariat. After the failure of the revolution ("even there where it was successful", Adorno), after the transition to a pluralized and fragmented postmodernity, this kind of solidarity is regarded as an illusion of late modernity.

In Glasersfeld's work, both society and language appear as highly fragmented. He blames the *social constructionists* for relying on *shared meanings*: "This is extremely misleading. (...) For there is not just one meaning which exists somewhere outside, independently of speaker and listener, a meaning shared by both of them. There is rather a meaning adopted by one of them and another meaning adopted by the other."[23] Here, Glasersfeld broaches a postmodern problem par excellence, for he comments on the contradictory or incompatible meanings of words and symbols. In his view, there is no common ground for linguistic (semantic) interaction: "In my experience, the notion that word/symbols have fixed meanings that are shared by every user of the language, breaks down in any conversation that attempts an interaction on the level of concepts, that is, a conversation that attempts to go beyond a simple exchange of soothing familiar sounds."[24] Such remarks sound even more radical than what Lyotard has to say about *paralogy* and the *différend*.

They are quite incompatible with the linguistic universalism defended by Popper against Kuhn and other proponents of the framework idea. Along with the notion of a universally valid language, Glasersfeld dismisses the idea of critical rationalists "that the succession of falsification and new hypothesis implies an approximation to the ontic world".[25] These two ideas are related insofar as the postulated existence of a common language justifies the hope of a common conception of reality. Wherever the rationalist discourse starts from a generalized "we" – in whatever shape or form – a critical and sceptical realism seems possible which, although it may question Hegel's and Lukács's identity of subject and object, of discourse and reality, will not doubt the basic principle that reality is accessible to knowledge.

In the case of Glasersfeld, who distinguishes *reality* (*Realität*), defined as "an inaccessible ontological realm",[26] from *reality* (*Wirklichkeit*) as a world accessible to human knowledge and action, this doubt crops up, because the constructivist philosopher advocates a radical individualism and a pluralism which tend to deny the very possibility of conceptual communication – as was shown above. The existence of supra-individual, collective factors (in the sense of Durkheim Marx or Bourdieu) is systematically dismissed by Glasersfeld. In this respect he also appears as Lukács's antipode:

> In other words, no analysis of social phenomena can be successful if it does not fully take into account that the mind that constructs viable concepts and schemes is under all circumstances an individual mind. Consequently, also "others" and "society" are concepts constructed by individuals on the basis of their own subjective experience.[27]

The question is of course how an intellect capable of constructing concepts can come about without socialization, without internalizing social structures or collective (institutionalized) norms and values. Does Saussure not define language as a "set of collective patterns", as an "ensemble des habitudes collectives"?[28]

Glasersfeld contradicts himself, when he considers conceptual systems as incompatible on one occasion and as compatible on the other. On the subject of human communication and other people's choice of words, he remarks: "Although the words they use are the same as ours, the network of concepts they seem to have in mind is incompatible with the one we have built up."[29] However, on another occasion, he would like to reconcile the incompatible languages: "The conceptual structures which are commonly referred to as knowledge, are subjective, not only in the sense that each individual has to create them for himself, but also because the conceptual structures of a single person cannot be compared with those of others." Paradoxically, he goes on to say: "However, this does not mean that they are not, to a large extent, compatible within a society."[30]

There seems to be no final verdict in this case. Are conceptual structures compatible or incompatible? And what happens if we move from one society, from one culture to another? Does compatibility (Glasersfeld's second option) still obtain? The two passages quoted here bear witness to the kind of "undecidability" deconstructionists are so fascinated by and philosophers like Davidson seem to ignore. (What Glasersfeld has to say about "conceptual structures" is diametrically opposed to Davidson's comments on "conceptual schemes".)

The difficulty in deciding is due – among other things – to the fact that Glasersfeld brackets out all collective factors which give rise to individual subjectivity (such as institutions, organizations, groups and their sociolects). The result is that he is unable to propose a concrete, i.e. social definition of individual subjectivity and its concepts. Hence it is hardly surprising that he can only speculate in an abstract way about the compatibility or incompatibility of conceptual structures.

If considered in a social context, this problem appears in a different light. Individual subjectivity is the product of socialization in institutions, groups and sociolects, and intersubjective communication within a sociolect is qualitatively different from communication between sociolects. While proponents of Liberalism easily agree on the idea that "performance has to pay", feminists are likely to discover that "female performance tends to be less rewarded than the male equivalent", both in the business world and the world of science. This is why communication problems can crop up at any time between the two ideological groups, among other things because they may attribute different meanings to the word "justice". The result of these considerations can be summed up in one sentence: within a sociolect, compatibility of concepts and statements can be assumed, while between sociolects incompatibility tends to predominate – without being the rule.

Unlike the universalist Popper, Glasersfeld postulates social and linguistic heterogeneity or even incompatibility on an individual level and thus sacrifices the modern "we" of Critical Rationalism to a postmodern segmentation which is reminiscent of Lyotard's *différend*. However, the constructivist conflict between languages does not erupt between "discourse genres" (Lyotard), but between atomized individuals.

In Glasersfeld's model, the latter are able to communicate in spite of all differences and contradictions. For like Popper, the constructivist invokes intersubjectivity: "In the constructivist model, 'the others' are that which makes it possible for the subject of knowledge to create a higher, an intersubjective reality."[31] But how are the others supposed to intervene in the individual's process of knowledge if the "conceptual networks" of different individuals are incompatible (cf. supra)? How can intersubjective communication come about if the idea of shared meanings "collapses in each discussion" (cf. supra)?

In spite of all the differences which oppose modern Liberalism to Marxism, Popper and Lukács agree on one crucial point: true knowledge presupposes universal consent. While Popper defines this consent negatively by relating it to intersubjective testing of theories or statements, Lukács turns

it into an historical category. A humanity delivered from class antagonism
appears to him as the only reliable source of true knowledge. It is not by
chance that, following Marx, he defines the bourgeoisie as a "minority".[32]
As such it cannot possibly speak for the whole of humanity, for "humanity as
a unit",[33] as Agnes Heller puts it.

Glasersfeld's problem consists in the fact that on the one hand he follows
Popper by opting for the intersubjective principle, but on the other hand
adopts a radical agnosticism which prompts him to doubt the universal
validity of language and to reject the concept of truth.[34] He thus replaces
"truth" by the notion of "intersubjective viability": "Nevertheless, the fact
that the individual needs the corroboration of others to establish the intersubjective viability of ways of thinking and acting, entails a concern for
others as autonomous constructors."[35]

He suggests that we ought to compare our patterns of thought and the
"tricks" we apply with those of our interlocutors: "Thereby our patterns of
thought and our tricks become intersubjective, so to speak, and we thus
attain a higher level of feasibility or viability than when I say: I use it, but I
do not know whether it is valid for anybody else."[36] This is undoubtedly the
case; the question remains, however, how this level can ever be attained, if it
is true that the "conceptual networks" of the interlocutors are incompatible,
as Glasersfeld himself says.

His contradiction consists in the attempt to have his cake and eat it: to
denounce the idea of an intersubjectively valid language as an illusion
and at the same time invoke it for the sake of "viability". This explains why
Glasersfeld can consider different conceptual schemes both as compatible
and as incompatible. For elsewhere in his work we read: "Although a conceptual congruence is not brought about by these means, we do achieve an
adaptation of individual meanings, so as to make them correspond."[37] Such
an "overlapping" of meanings is undoubtedly necessary if the principle of
intersubjectivity is to be saved. But does it actually occur?

In Glasersfeld's case, this is far from certain. Since he individualistically brackets out all collective factors, he is unaware of the presence of
group languages, of "perspectives" (Mannheim) in individual utterances.
Hence he cannot observe how such collective elements guarantee intersubjectivity within a group and how in turn group languages are translated
into one another on the level of a natural language, based on what Saussure
calls *habitude collective*. (For the collective factor not only divides, it also
connects.) However, the question of translation or translatability is not
raised by Glasersfeld.

Caught in such contradictions, Glasersfeld oscillates incessantly between
the poles of compatibility and incompatibility of individual conceptual

systems which all appear to him as contingent and interchangeable. This oscillation appears as a symptom of what Lukács calls the "atomization of the individual"[38] in capitalism. In the postmodern social and linguistic situation, this atomization is exacerbated on all levels.

It should be pointed out, by way of conclusion, that Glasersfeld's constructivist notion of "intersubjective viability" not only presupposes the existence of a real world (which he never denies), but also a knowable *structure* of this world: not only because the word "viability" contains elements of realism (Lat. *via* = way, path), but also because, in this particular case, intersubjective communication can only refer to the "direction of a path" (the actual constitution of reality).

3. Avoiding the Arbitrary

Not all brands of Radical Constructivism are as radically individualistic as Glasersfeld's approach. For the biologists Humberto Maturana and Francisco Varela, who neither advocate collectivist principles nor exhibit a penchant for sociology, not the isolated individual is the measure of all things, but the "community of observers". They advocate the "creation of a system of concepts capable of constructing the phenomenon to be explained in a way that is acceptable to the community of observers (...)".[39]

Nevertheless, they do speak of *the* "community of observers" in general, not of *a* specific community, which might differ socially and linguistically from other communities. However, the previous chapter has shown in conjunction with Mannheim's sociology of knowledge how dicey it is to start from the premise of a culturally, ideologically and linguistically homogeneous community of scientists. Ideas and hypotheses acceptable to one group may be unacceptable to another.

Other supporters of Radical Constructivism also refer to a general observer or a "we" that turns out to be as problematical a postulate as Maturana's and Varela's community. Thus Siegfried J. Schmidt (who introduced Radical Constructivism to Germany) agrees with Maturana and Glasersfeld that Radical Constructivism offers no possibility "to distinguish true from false statements about 'reality' in the sense of a theory of correspondence". For him, the constructivist alternative is quite obvious: "Rather, it [Radical Constructivism] redirects empirical research towards the question how useful the new cognitive frameworks are for us; what we can think and do with their help; how the newly revealed patterns of thought and action affect our goal attainment and the realization of our wishes (...)."[40]

All of this sounds fairly plausible as long as one is prepared to ignore see-mingly insignificant words such as "we" and "us". In reality, they form the basis of Schmidt's own theoretical construction. Who are "we"? Who thinks, decides and acts? Who decides about the usefulness of a theory or a theoretical position? The "cognitive frameworks" advocated as useful by radical constructivists may be rejected as highly questionable or as outright pernicious by critical rationalists, Marxists, feminists or deconstructionists.

We are thus dealing, in Schmidt's case as in the case of Maturana and Varela, with a mythical "we"-actant whose authority may serve to legiti-mize an authoritarian monologue – according to the ideological principle that "we all know what is useful, reasonable or normal". In a highly frag-mented postmodern society, such phrases conjure up an archaic consensus that no longer exists. They suggest that we also belong to this ill-defined mythical "we". This rhetorical manoeuvre is reminiscent of Lukács's discursive trick of identifying the mythical actant "proletariat" with the actually existing – and very real – actant "Communist Party". The conse-quences of this discursive identification were not only detrimental to Marx-ism – as is well known.

Some critics of Radical Constructivism soon realized that this complex of theories is by no means founded on a homogeneous cognitive community: Schmidt's "we" is as empty as Maturana's and Varela's "community of observers" (without however being rhetorically innocuous). Commenting on the testability of theories within constructivism, Josef Mitterer points out: "Who then is to decide on the non-viability of our constructions? – reality or *an* (other) *theory about reality*? Constructivism would increase its stringency if it opted for the second variant."[41] We may assume that this is also Glasersfeld's option.

Unfortunately, it does not solve the problem of intersubjective validity. For whenever two irreconcilable theories collide, it is difficult to find a way out. In such cases, individual or collective value judgements tend to have a decisive impact on argument. André Kukla who comments on quite differ-ent brands of (social) constructivism gives a vivid summary of the dilemma:

> The constructivist thesis is that scientific objects are constituted by the negotiated *victory* of the theory which posits them. But then the objects posited by *defeated* theories should *not* exist. Yet scientists routinely do believe in the theoretical entities posited by defunct theories. Thus the constructivist account fails to explain actual scientific practice.[42]

Kukla refers to "defunct theories"; but this expression itself is problemati-cal, for immediately the question arises who decides whether a theory is actually dead (or still alive). From Imre Lakatos's point of view (cf. chap. 4), Marxism and psychoanalysis may appear as "defunct theories"; in other perspectives, Critical Rationalism or even Radical Constructivism may seem to be finished.[43] Who speaks, who decides?

Considering the disintegration of our society into countless ideological and theoretical groups and languages, it seems futile to continue betting on mythical collectives such as Lukács's "proletariat", Mannheim's "free-floating intellectuals", Maturana's and Varela's "community of observers" or Schmidt's rhetorically appealing "we" – hoping that one of these dei ex machina will do the trick and bring about a consensus.

The abstract intersubjectivity which presupposes a non-existent (homogeneous) community of critical individuals ought to be replaced by an inter-collective dialogue between theories. The *systematic linking of contrasting positions* should replace the vain search for an Archimedean point anchored in an idealized community of observers or intellectuals. The dialectical unity of the extremes ought to make heterogeneous theories reveal their blind spots, their contradictions – and their strengths.

Dialogical Theory as a meta-theory is responsible for this dialectical linkage which is at the same time a decisive test. It operates according to a motto introduced by the radical constructivist Heinz von Foerster: "Dialogue = looking at oneself with the eyes of another."[44]

Chapter 9

System and Field:
Luhmann and Bourdieu

A confrontation between Niklas Luhmann's *system* and Pierre Bourdieu's *field* looks promising from a dialogical point of view,[1] insofar as both concepts refer to processes of *social differentiation*. At first sight, both sociologists seem to agree that modern differentiation yields autonomous spheres whose particular order corresponds to their functional specificity. Religion cannot be replaced by science, the latter cannot be replaced by religion, politics or art. This basic principle is not only adhered to by sociologists from Durkheim and Simmel to Luhmann, but is widely accepted by a secularized common sense ever mindful of the division of labour and of postmodern cultural pluralism.

When Bourdieu himself was asked to comment on the affinities between his sociology of "social fields" and Luhmann's systems theory, he underscored – as was to be expected – the differences and contrasts. Unlike Althusser's *apparatus* and Luhmann's *system*, he explains, his *field* is neither an organic nor a functionalist notion, but an historical concept meant to describe power relations and social struggles: "The field is an area of power relations not just an area of meaning – that is to say of struggles for transformation; hence it is a place of constant change."[2] Unlike Luhmann's system, the field is not an "immanent self-realization of the structure",[3] Bourdieu adds. Unfortunately, it is not quite clear which of Luhmann's works he has in mind. (He mentions the German sociologist only in his most recent publications without referring to specific texts.)

In what follows, the *concept of truth* will occupy the centre of the scene, and both affinities and contrasts between the systems and the "fields" theory will come to the fore. It will be shown that both sociologists foreground structural factors (such as systems or "fields") and either deny the role of individual subjects (Luhmann) or tend to neglect it (Bourdieu). The production of scientific knowledge appears to both of them as a process without subjects (in this respect they come fairly close to Althusser). Truth as "production of truth" (Luhmann) is made possible by the *scientific system* or the *scientific field* (*champ scientifique*). Discourse as a semantic and narrative structure in which the subject of enunciation develops and critically reflects its own social and linguistic actions, is completely ignored by the two sociologists. They both tend to consider language in a purely functional perspective: as a means of communication or as an instrument of power.

However, it will become clear that the contrasts between the two sociological positions are far more pronounced and more informative than Bourdieu's remarks suggest. While Luhmann sees science as a closed "autopoietic" system which generates truth independently of external influence, Bourdieu presents his "field" as an open, but highly disputed area which it is impossible to shield against invasions by non-scientific social actors. Especially the social sciences appear to him as a contested domain open to the influence of neighbouring (economic, political) fields and their heteronomy. It may have already become clear at this stage that, in spite of its resemblance to Luhmann's approach, Bourdieu's functional perspective is actually an inversion of systemic autonomy and "autopoiesis".

In this chapter, the *question concerning the autonomy or heteronomy of the cultural and social sciences* will be considered as the key problem. It is neglected by both sociologists who tend to focus on the *natural sciences*.

1. Luhmann or the Truth of the System

Luhmann's theory of the *scientific system* is part and parcel of his encompassing theory of social differentiation. In modern society, he argues, "since the Enlightenment, since modernity became a topic of discussion",[4] there develops, alongside other differentiated systems such as art, law or the economy, a system of science based on "second degree observation". This means that researchers who observe certain events or processes are themselves being observed and criticized:

> The scientific system is geared towards second degree observation by virtue of eliminating all kinds of prophetic authority in matters of truth and by replacing them with the medium of publication. Whatever the foundations of knowledge, publications are structured in such a way that the advances in knowledge claimed by them can be observed, i.e. that the process of observation itself can be observed.[5]

This self-observation of the system is at the same time the "self-definition of science" and a "reflexive performance".[6] The fact that the scientific system is turned here into a *subject-actant* which adopts certain attitudes, "eliminates", "replaces" or "observes" is not irrelevant, for it raises the question who exactly observes.

One crucial aspect of this approach seems to be the fact that "truth" in this context loses all of its ontological and metaphysical connotations and is integrated into a systemic code based on the opposition *true/untrue*. This functional opposition is viewed by Luhmann in analogy to the codified oppositions of the economic system (*payment/non-payment*) and the political system (*power/non-power*). The "differential code *true/untrue*"[7] is not simply an element or an aspect of the scientific system, but constitutes and structures the latter: "The (autopoietically reproduced) unity of this system consists in the difference between the true and the untrue (not in knowledge as such)."[8] (In other words, the scientific difference between truth and untruth fulfils a function similar to the political difference between power and the lack of power.)

The concept of truth not only ceases to be metaphysical but acquires an impersonal character devoid of subjectivity. Within the scientific system, truth and the search for truth cannot be attributed to groups or individuals. The system as such distinguishes the true from the untrue: "We only speak of truth if the selection of information cannot be attributed to one of the participants."[9] This means that no "privileged positions of truth"[10] can be deemed to exist: neither with respect to individuals nor to objects, assertions (true sentences) or concepts. "Whatever is recognized as truth", explains Luhmann, "is constituted within the system (...)."[11] This is why, according to Luhmann, "the medium of truth does not tolerate different opinions".[12]

This means that the system as such produces truth – very much like the economic system which yields wealth and keeps the circulation of money in motion by inducing payments, or the political system which keeps generating power. In this context, it is hardly surprising that Luhmann speaks of the "circulation of truth within the system"[13] and compares truth as a medium with money.[14]

Luhmann's "truth" is objective and universal insofar as it is generated by the system itself, i.e. independently of particular viewpoints. His way of defining the production of truth does not mean that he is not aware of "criticism" and "conflict". However, like "truth", the latter do not refer to positions of individual scientists or scientific groups, but to systemic functions regulated by the basic opposition between "true" and "untrue": "Conversely, in the case of truth, every communication relies on criticism, that is to say rejection, that is to say conflict, because in this case the code bases validity on universal recognition by everyone (at least symbolically). Every advance in knowledge implies criticism."[15]

These considerations result logically from Luhmann's conception of the scientific system. Without criticism and conflict the grain of truth cannot be separated from the chaff of false knowledge. (At this point, the sociologist cannot help wondering why this mechanism of differentiation, so plausibly described by Luhmann, is so difficult to set in motion in the social sciences. This problem will be dealt with at a later stage.)

Another aspect of this theory's logic is the fact that it answers Mannheim's question concerning the position-bound character of theories and Popper's question concerning the testability of theories in a systemic perspective. Starting from the premise that there is "no context-independent decision between different claims of validity and hence no context-independent evaluation of scientific progress",[16] Luhmann proposes an alternative within his sociology of systems. "What can be offered *instead*", he argues, "is a recursively arranged observation of observation, a contextualization of contexts, a distinction of distinctions, that is to say a cybernetics of second degree observation."[17] Thus validity claims are not decided on by a privileged, superimposed instance, but by the scientific system as such.

A closer look at the discursive level reveals that the crucial point which was identified with the rational individual by Popper, with the proletariat by Lukács and the free-floating intellectuals by Mannheim, is identified by Luhmann with the cybernetically operating system.

It is not by chance that Bourdieu compares his "field" with God. Ever since Nietzsche announced the "death of God", humans have sought to find a privileged viewpoint, a perspective located above or beyond all perspectives. But whenever this kind of super-perspective is presented as the solution to all problems, it turns out to be an idol unable to keep its promise.

Luhmann's systematic sociology promises a global and more accurate explanation of the social functioning of science than traditional theories or philosophies of science.[18] Paradoxically, its weak points surface whenever it is applied to its own domain: to the social sciences.

As long as the systems theory is used to elucidate the evolution and the functioning of the natural sciences, regularly referred to by Luhmann,[19] it has a certain plausibility. Physicists who believed that the atom is the last indivisible element were proved wrong by experimental means; scientists who declared asbestos to be harmless from a medical point of view, had to revise their judgements as being "untrue" in the sense of Luhmann, etc. Almost daily, opinions held in high esteem are thus brought down in the natural sciences.

In the cultural and social sciences, however, we find ourselves in a very different situation, a situation aptly described by Luhmann himself who sporadically doubts the possibility of progress in this area. He points out in

conjunction with Max Weber's theory of European modernity: "As the
latter has never been surpassed, at best repeated on the basis of new data,
even contemporary sociology remains under the spell of this intellectual
experiment."[20] In this context, it is hardly surprising that refutability is
not considered to be a distinctive feature of sociological theories. Commenting on Parsons's systematic sociology, Luhmann writes: "Parsonian theory
has seldom been adequately understood and never adequately refuted."[21]

If this is the case, then it seems legitimate to ask what function "criticism"
has so far fulfilled in Luhmann's system of (social) sciences and what function it may fulfil in future. If, in the realm of social science, it is unable to
decide (krinein) between "true" and "untrue" statements and refute erro-
neous hypotheses, it is useless as a mechanism of control and a means of
scientific communication. Is it conceivable that Parsons's theory remains
"true" in all respects – half a century after the publication of *The Social
System* (1951)? If not everything in this theory is true, then immediately the
question arises what is *generally* recognized as "untrue" and why.

Does not Luhmann himself claim to go beyond Weber and Parsons by
constructing a theory of "autopoietic systems"? But if his claim has any substance at all, it is difficult to understand how a sociologist like Rainer Greshoff can react to it by arguing that Weber's concepts explain all that
Luhmann seeks to explain and even more ... Luhmann's systems sociology
as a whole has provoked interminable discussions between friends and foes
without enabling the system of science (but where exactly is it?) to define as
"true" or "untrue" at least one of the basic tenets of this theory – *in the eyes of
the whole sociological community*. What is considered as "true" by some members of the community, by Luhmann's followers for example, is considered
as questionable or as blatantly wrong by others. Naturally, this also applies
to the theories of Weber, Parsons, Pareto and Durkheim. In this respect, criticism in the social sciences seems to be an open-ended process.

In analogy to the opposition between *true* and *untrue*, underlying the
system of science, Luhmann introduces the opposition between *intact* and
broken for the technical system. Considering what has been said so far, one
could assume that a scientific system which is not able to distinguish correct
from wrong sociological statements (theories) with respect to the basic
opposition between *true* and *untrue* and by relying on institutionalized criticism, is simply "broken" or "defective". This is probably not the case, but
Luhmann's conception of the scientific system is questionable, especially in
view of the problems which keep cropping up in the social sciences.

This argument can be illustrated by a relatively simple example quoted
by Luhmann himself in one of his last interviews. He contends that social
differentiation renders superfluous all distinctions based on sex or race and

declares that, in science, it is unimportant whether somebody is man or woman, African or Chinese, because an invention is exclusively tested within the framework of the opposition *true/untrue*: "The question is whether the invention or the discovery is 'true' or not, and the same thing, of course, in the economy."[22] At this point it becomes clear to what extent Luhmann (very much like Bourdieu, Popper and Kuhn) considers the natural sciences as his primary model.

For in the cultural and social sciences, even in economics, one can hardly speak of "inventions" and it also seems dicey here to define a "discovery" (Glasersfeld would prefer the word "construction") as "true" or "untrue". Thus a woman sociologist might discover that, in scientific discourse, female subjectivity is constituted differently from its male counterpart. Even if there were such a thing as a relatively homogeneous system of science, it could not decide whether this discovery is "true" or "untrue". For feminist sociology is a sociolect or – rather – an ensemble of sociolects which is accepted by some groups and rejected or simply ignored by others. Luhmann not only fails to overcome the dependence of scientific evaluation on ideologies, but simply suppresses the problem.

The scientific system is – if it exists – a social and linguistic space in which ideological and theoretical groups compete with each other. *They* are the critical instances – not the system. Bourdieu, who certainly cannot be deemed a theoretician of the subject, is quite right in referring to the "collective subjects"[23] which oppose each other in the "field" of science. We can only deal with critical discourses of individual or collective subjects addressing other subjects. Every attempt to bypass subjectivity and its quandaries leads to a situation where nothing can be said about the "truth" or the "lack of truth" in social science.[24] The deficiencies of Luhmann's theory do not appear within the system but during a dialectical and dialogical confrontation with the Other.

Among these deficiencies is the "autopoietic" separation of individual systems from one another, a separation inspired by brain research. It has been exposed to growing scepticism in recent years. Thus Thomas Schwinn shows that "social integration (. . .) [is] a structural dimension with its own laws which cannot simply be deduced from the process of differentiation (. . .)."[25] It cannot be reduced to the interaction of systems. Arguing along similar lines, Rainer Greshoff reveals that Luhmann's discourse generates its own blind spots, whenever it attempts to mark off autopoietic psychic systems (systems of consciousness) against social systems defined as systems of communication.[26]

Similar problems of delimitation crop up between the scientific system and the political and economic systems. Those familiar with Bourdieu and Baudrillard[27] ask themselves whether the differentiation process as described by Luhmann is not being countered by a postmodern movement of de-differentiation in the course of which the medieval dominance of religion and the "primacy of politics" in post-war socialism, mentioned by Luhmann himself,[28] are replaced by the preponderance of the economy in late capitalism. If this were the case, one could speak with one of Luhmann's interlocutors of a growing instrumentalization of the scientific system and most other systems by the economy: "(...) Precisely because it needs these systems it determines these systems; it determines their type of operation."[29]

It ought to have become clear at this stage that the analogy between biological organs (e.g. the brain) and social systems, postulated by Luhmann, is highly questionable. For the "autopoiesis" of the brain – analysed by Maturana and Varela – can hardly be compared with the autonomy of institutionalized science. Bourdieu's attempt to shed light on the role of *heteronomous factors* in the field of science is probably one of his major merits.

2.   Bourdieu or the Embattled Field

Any attempt to reconcile Luhmann's systems theory with Bourdieu's theory of fields in a functional perspective would have to be based on the notion of *autonomy*. For each field, each system functions according to specific laws, and it is impossible to be successful in one of the fields – for example in art – if one acts according to heteronomous rules, for example, those of religion or science.

Each field presupposes the subjective[30] appropriation of a specific *habitus*[31] which not only involves the knowledge and the skills of a scientist, an artist or a technical expert, but also a particular social and affective attitude, etc. Moreover, the autonomy of a field is guaranteed by the permanent circulation of a particular sort of capital: "Speaking of a specific kind of capital amounts to saying that this capital is only valid within a certain field and that it can only be converted into another kind of capital in special circumstances."[32] This also means that the autonomy of a field tends to coincide with the specific character of the capital circulating in that field. Comparing the two approaches, one is struck by the fact that Bourdieu replaces Luhmann's notion of *communication* by the notion of *capital* which in turn implies the notion of *social domination*.[33]

Bourdieu, who relies heavily on the work of Marx and on Paul Cassirer's theory of the symbol,[34] distinguishes four kinds of capital: the *economic capital* in its various forms, the *cultural capital* which mainly involves knowledge and skills, the *social capital* consisting of social relations and memberships, and finally the *symbolic capital* as a form to be found in all kinds of capital as soon as the latter are socially recognized as such.[35] The decisive factor is the specific character of each kind of capital which is subject to particular laws of circulation and hence cannot be reduced to other kinds of capital. Thus symbolic capital (e.g. academic titles) cannot be acquired by economic means – except in extreme cases.[36] This also applies to the *habitus* of artists, journalists or scientists.

Nevertheless, Bourdieu's fields are far more open to external influence than Luhmann's autopoietic systems which are conceived as clearly delimited areas whose communication and interaction with other areas is only made possible by translating heterogeneous codes and languages into one another.[37] Unlike Luhmann's systems, the *fields* of science, politics and media do understand the language of economics whose impacts on the rest of society are felt more than ever under late capitalism (cf. below). It should be added that all forms of capital, even social and cultural forms, may be converted into one another by virtue of the time factor.[38] Economic capital may very well facilitate and accelerate the acquisition of cultural capital (e.g. by buying a good education), and cultural or social capital will often contribute – albeit indirectly – to the increase of economic capital.

This idea that different forms of capital are convertible is based on the dialectical category of mediation introduced by Hegel and Marx and adapted by Bourdieu. It is also based on the growing awareness of the fact that contemporary society is rapidly turning into an "economic" society in which the dominant role played by religion in feudalism and by politics in socialism (at least in its Stalinist phase) is played by the economy.[39]

Although Bourdieu does not describe social evolution in this particular way, his most recent publications reveal to what extent the entire intellectual field is marked by the ascendancy of the economic factor. In *Firing Back*, he even ventures to predict that the present trends towards liberalization "grant economic determinisms a fatal stranglehold by *liberating* them from all controls".[40] He considers the "heteronomous intellectuals", who are responsible for the marketing of art and science in the media, as the most dangerous proponents of this economic hegemony: "If it seems to me indispensable to combat these heteronomous intellectuals, it's because they constitute the Trojan horse through which heteronomy – that is, the laws of the market and the economy – is brought into the field."[41] There is no mention here of Luhmann's autopoietic autonomy of systems – or fields for that matter. In Luhmann's world, neither heteronomous intellectuals nor Trojan horses – metonymies of mediation by the exchange value – seem to exist. His constructivist thought is governed (very much like

Glasersfeld's: cf. chap. 8, 2) by Kant's analytic separation, not by Hegel's dialectical mediation.

Elsewhere it becomes clear that Bourdieu's sociology does take into account *different degrees of autonomy*. Not all fields seem to be equally autonomous with respect to economics, politics and the media.

> A highly autonomous field, mathematics for example, is one in which producers' sole consumers are their competitors, that is, individuals who could have made the discovery in question. (I dream of sociology becoming like this, but, unfortunately, everyone wants to get in on the act. Everybody thinks they know what sociology is, and Alain Peyrefitte thinks he has to give me sociology lessons. Well, why not? you may ask, since there are plenty of sociologists or historians only too happy to talk things over with him . . . on television . . .).[42]

It is worth having a closer look at this passage: not only because it implies that different degrees of field autonomy exist, but also because the sociologist of science admits that he can only dream of an autonomy comparable to that of mathematics or the natural sciences. He shares this dream with Luhmann and a large number of social scientists who continue to be haunted by the ghost of exact science. But unlike these scientists, Bourdieu is prepared to analyse the special status of sociology and the social sciences in general.

Unlike the natural sciences, the humanities are permanently involved in social conflicts in which the "truth about the social world"[43] is at stake. Bourdieu believes that the "intellectualist error"[44] consists in seeking to occupy a point of view above these conflicts. An "intellectualist" sociology tries "to say the truth about this world and about the contradictory attitudes towards it".[45] This critique is not only applicable to Mannheim's notion of "free-floating intellectuals", but also to Luhmann's vision of an autonomous system of science capable of distinguishing like an automat between "true" and "untrue" statements or theories (albeit by way of individual critiques). At first sight, such an autonomous vantage point does not seem to exist in Bourdieu's theory.

In his lectures on the sociology of science, held at the Collège de France between 2000 and 2001, he focuses, like Luhmann, on the development of the natural sciences and again regrets the weak autonomy of the humanities: "One may wonder why the social sciences have so much difficulty in winning recognition of their autonomy, why it is so hard to gain acceptance for a discovery outside the field and even within it."[46]

Far from presupposing as unproblematic Luhmann's opposition between "true" and "untrue" theories, Bourdieu doubts its existence. About the scientific field of the social sciences he writes: "Propositions that are incoherent or incompatible with the facts are more likely to perpetuate themselves and even to thrive than in the most autonomous scientific fields (...)."[47] His explanation of this autonomy is quite surprising: the less successful, "those who are scientifically most dominated",[48] are more prone to political or economic heteronomies (e.g. in the media) than their colleagues in the hard sciences and often succumb to the "logic of plebiscites".

In a media society, this kind of heteronomy may occasionally play an important part. However, it cannot be the main explanation for the social particularities and oddities in the cultural and social sciences as discussed by Bourdieu. These can best be explained with respect to the permanent presence of the ideological and political factor *in* the discourses of the human sciences which Bourdieu does not analyse as semantic and narrative structures.[49] In other words, the heteronomy is not external to these sciences but *inherent in their languages* (cf. chap. 2).

By linking heteronomy to the (dys-)functional factors of the field, instead of locating it in the *semantics of social science*, Bourdieu comes close to Luhmann's functional approach, where heteronomies (e.g. corruption) are simply viewed as rectifiable defects. But at the same time he has to admit that, in reality, the social sciences form an area separate from that of the natural sciences – an area whose autonomy remains doubtful.

Involuntarily, he casts doubts on his own construction of society as a compendium of fields, when he speaks of a "university field"[50] and elsewhere even mentions a "linguistic field",[51] a "field of ideological production" and a "field of class struggle".[52] Is it not conceivable that some of these "fields" *overlap* with the "field" of science?

Similar questions crop up when, in *The Rules of Art*, Bourdieu alternately uses concepts such as *literary field* and *field of cultural production*.[53] Does opera function according to the rules of the literary or the musical field? Are rules valid in the worlds of opera and film also applicable to painting? Does film production still obey the "rules of art" – or is it already part of the media world? Where are the borders and the borderline cases? Bourdieu's explanation that "borders are dynamic" and that "fields" can be further divided up (into *sous-champs*) is of little help.[54]

All of these questions are relevant for an unambiguous definition of the concept of "field", for they culminate in the key question: whether there is such a thing as an encompassing scientific "field", that is to say a homogeneous area where physics and psychoanalysis, crystallography and sociology evolve according to the same or similar rules. It goes without saying that such questions can also be addressed to Luhmann whose notion of a science or art system makes heterogeneous elements merge.

Unlike Luhmann, Bourdieu at least takes into account the strategic heterogeneity of the scientific realm. The field of science does not appear to him
as a communication system *sui generis*, but as a "structured field of forces"
and at the same time as "a field of struggles to conserve or transform this
field of forces".[55] This also means that, in each of these struggles, the acquisition of a maximum of scientific and symbolic capital is at stake.

"Criticism" and "truth" are considered by Bourdieu – unlike by Luhmann – as strategic concepts with close ties to power structures. Similarly,
the concept of capital, one of Bourdieu's key concepts, hints at power relations, and the notion of "symbolic or scientific capital" cannot be used
in simple analogy to the early Chomsky's formal concepts of "competence"
and "performance". For society is not only structured by horizontal
differentiation, as emphasized by Luhmann, but also bears the imprint of
vertical differentiation or hierarchy.[56] The expression "symbolic violence"[57] is also applicable to the scientific field which combines processes of
communication with processes of ex-communication. At the same time, it
implies that scientific development is not only marked by understanding, misunderstanding and constructive criticism, but also by destructive
impulses and power struggles.

Nevertheless, it would be an error to reduce "criticism" and "truth"
to pure strategy, pure instrumentality. Bourdieu quite rightly emphasizes the two aspects of field strategies: "They have a pure – purely scientific – function and a social function within the field (...)."[58] He certainly
cannot be blamed for reducing science to pure strategy, to a "function
in the field".

On the contrary, in his last lectures on the sociology of science, he again
seems to agree with Luhmann when he points out that it is not individuals or groups, not the communicating subjects who are responsible for
the emergence of truth, but *the field as such*. The partly incompatible, colliding interests guarantee the impartial and universal character of truth:
"A truth that has undergone the test of discussions in a field where antagonistic interests, and even opposing power strategies, have battled over it
is in no way undermined by the fact that those who discovered it had an
interest in discovering it."[59]

The conflict-ridden heterogeneity of the field is thus considered by Bourdieu as the actual source of scientific progress. Eventually, the field appears
as an all-round, divine observer without a vantage point, as a "geometral of
all perspectives" ("géométral de toutes les perspectives")[60], as a unification
of all possible views. A heading from *Choses dites*, "Objectifying the Objectifying Subject",[61] is reminiscent of Luhmann's "second degree observer".

Like Luhmann's system, Bourdieu's scientific field represents the vantage point, formerly occupied by Lukács's proletariat and Mannheim's free-floating intellectuals.

But unlike Luhmann who explicitly renounces the "Old European" notion of subject,[62] Bourdieu continues to invoke the philosophical and scientific commonplace of intersubjectivity. In the last resort, the truth of the "field" comes about on an intersubjective level: "Objectivity is an intersubjective product of the scientific field (...)."[63] Bourdieu speaks literally of an "intersubjective agreement within the field".[64] As in the case of Luhmann, truth is not conceived of as a "direct reflection of reality",[65] but in a constructivist manner: as a common construct, as a result of competing field strategies.

Bourdieu's *concept of subjectivity* is not very well thought through (if it exists at all). If there is an agreement within the field, it can hardly come about without subjective reflection and responsibility. This means that theoretical testing (of hypotheses) does not occur in an abstract area called "field", but between individual and collective subjects, between those *sujets collectifs* that are also mentioned by Bourdieu.

In *Leçon sur la leçon*, his inaugural lecture at the Collège de France (1982), in which he ponders on the status of the institutionalized lecture, Bourdieu presents the sociologist as a critical and reflecting theoretician who observes and criticizes the function of sociology in the "field". He expects him to defend "that freedom from institutions which is the precondition of all science".[66] However, criticism and freedom are only possible where an autonomous subject examines the events in the "field" from a critical distance, instead of becoming involved to the extent of being blinded. Such a subject will not be content with the idea – reminiscent of Hegel's "cunning of reason" – that the "field" as the sum total of all conflicts and quarrels will eventually yield the truth. (It is not by chance that Bourdieu, the reader of Hegel, speaks of a "ruse of scientific reason".)[67]

The contradiction between the autonomy of the "field" and subjective autonomy, which comes to the fore in some of Bourdieu's lectures, is closely related to the latent contradiction between a critical attitude towards society (missing in Luhmann's work) and a functional approach which (as in Luhmann's case) tends towards systematization and an elimination of the subjective factor. In this respect, Richard Jenkins is quite right when he speaks of an "objectivist point of view"[68] in conjunction with Bourdieu and blames "his inability to cope with subjectivity".[69] It would be important to take Bourdieu's theory seriously without relegating the individual and collective subjects to the periphery of the "field".

3.   Subjectivity, Truth, Dialogue

The comparison of Luhmann's systems theory with Bourdieu's "fields" theory shows: (a) that reconstructing society as a totality of systems or "fields" may yield new insights, but is problematic at the same time, because overlapping or interpenetration of seemingly autonomous spheres is the rule rather than the exception; (b) that the homogeneity of the scientific system cannot be presupposed; and (c) that the dynamics of the cultural and social sciences cannot be adequately understood without a thorough reflection on the role of subjective instances and their languages.

Although a systematic theory of social differentiation may have concrete advantages, because it provides an answer to the question how "art", "science", "law" or "the economy" function, it neglects the numerous transitional phenomena emerging between and across systems — or is unable to explain them. It is undoubtedly one of Bourdieu's merits to have introduced a key concept, namely *field*, allowing a description not only of social differentiation, but also of social de-differentiation. Luhmann tends to consider the latter as an exception or an anomaly. Relying on Bourdieu's theory of "fields", Richard Jenkins speaks of "dominant fields" which "impinge upon weaker fields and structure what occurs within them".[70] Such an idea, for example, that the economic system structures the political or the art system, cannot occur in Luhmann's discourse because it would undermine the notion of autopoiesis, of self-engenderment.

However, by opening the "field" to heteronomous influences, Bourdieu, unlike Luhmann, seems to undermine the construction of his key concept. For if the production of films turns out to be a predominantly commercial matter and not a creation regulated by the laws of the art system, one faces two possibilities: either one excludes the film industry (along with commercial literature, painting and music) from the artistic "field" or one concedes that art as a "weak field" is being increasingly dominated by the stronger "economic field", i.e. the laws of the market. In this case, one might speak with Baudrillard of "trans-aesthetics"[71] — or follow Hegel and announce the "end of art". In both cases, the borders of Luhmann's art system become blurred.

As was shown above, the system of science is dissolved in Bourdieu's theory of "fields" (and here the second point [b] is addressed). Whenever he dreams of a sociological system that would be as autonomous as mathematics (cf. above), he himself casts doubts on the idea of a homogeneous "field" of science. Whenever he speaks of a "contamination of the scientific order by principles of the political order and of democracy",[72] he reinforces such doubts.

They are certainly not dissipated by Luhmann's systems theory. On the contrary, his distinction between the "true" and the "untrue", upon which scientific criticism and scientific selection are supposed to rest, tends to exclude the cultural and social sciences from the system – because their most important theorems and theses are neither "true" nor "untrue", but simply controversial. Luhmann's own theses illustrate this argument: they are considered as absolutely true by some social scientists and rejected by others.

In this respect, they share the fate of virtually all sociological theories, including Bourdieu's theory of "fields". No system, no "field" can unambiguously answer the question concerning the "truth" or "untruth" of Luhmann's or Bourdieu's approach.[73] The dialogical confrontation produced in this chapter seems to be better suited for revealing the strengths and the weak points of the two theories than monologic and systematic discourses aiming *either* at refutation *or* at justification.

At this stage, the third point (c) can be dealt with. Any attempt to integrate the cultural and social sciences into a unitary scientific "system" or "field" in the hope that they will come to resemble the "hard sciences" in the course of time, is doomed to failure. Moreover, it is ideological in the negative or restrictive sense (cf. chap. 2), because it blocks all reflection on the ideological character of the human sciences and tends to confirm the hegemony of the natural sciences in the institutions.

However, ideology in a general sense (as a system of values and political engagement) is not a regrettable defect in the human sciences, but an indispensable starting point for creative research and theory formation. In this respect, Bourdieu's word "contamination" bears witness to a fatal misunderstanding of the social and linguistic context. For Popper's and Glasersfeld's liberal commitment, Lukács's revolutionary engagement and the feminist critique of Freudian psychoanalysis by Juliet Mitchell have yielded new insights, which would have been literally unthinkable without these different kinds of ideological *parti pris*.

The latter is a subjective attitude and an aspect of individual and collective subjectivity. For this reason, no truths situated beyond the competing subjects can exist in the human sciences: truths produced by the "system" or the "field". The discovery or, rather, construction of truth occurs among conscious and critical subjects who, far from being atomized individuals, articulate their interests and insights within particular sociolects and discourses. Theoretical dialogue takes place between *them* and is conceived here in such a way as to replace both "system" and "field".

Chapter 10

Intersubjectivity and Power Structures: Habermas and Foucault (Althusser, Pêcheux)

The hypothesis that Habermas's and Foucault's theories are antagonistic is not only borne out by Habermas's well-known article on the French philosopher[1] and by relatively recent literature on the two thinkers,[2] but also, and even more clearly, by the contrasting questions underlying their respective works. Unlike Habermas, whose early writings explore the possibilities of undistorted communication,[3] Foucault takes the view, since *Madness and Civilization* (1961), that human communication is mediated by power structures. His often quoted dictum that "reason is torture" ("la torture, c'est la raison")[4] not only expresses criticism and protest, but also the idea that human reason is irretrievably involved in the power structures which it helps to consolidate whenever it is turned into an instrument of domination.

In this respect, Foucault appears as a kindred spirit of Adorno and Horkheimer who, in *Dialectic of Enlightenment* (1947), not only map out a history of the subject, but also a complementary history of reason. In spite of the divergent epistemological premises which separate them from Foucault, the authors agree with his diagnosis that enlightened rationalist reason is deeply rooted in the modern domination of nature. In view of this intellectual affinity, it is hardly surprising that, towards the end of his life, Foucault regretted that his encounter with Critical Theory had occurred so late.[5]

No such affinity seems to exist between Habermas and Foucault, because Habermas envisages an *ideal communication situation* based on the hermeneutics of Kant, Husserl and Mead and situated beyond all power structures. As a postulate, this notion of an ideal communication situation is inherent in every real communication because it is tacitly presupposed by all interlocutors.

However, the very possibility of such a presupposition becomes problematical, if something quite different is presupposed: namely the submission of the communicating subjects to the power structures responsible for their subjectivity. In Foucault's, Althusser's and Pêcheux' theories, the whole context of communication is mediated by power structures. In this kind of situation, a free and undistorted subjectivity, as imagined by Habermas, cannot exist: because in this case the basis and goal of communication is not mutual understanding between "equals in a cooperative search for the truth",[6] but domination and its perpetuation.

If Louis Althusser's Lacanian thesis, according to which ideology calls upon individuals as subjects by turning them into subjected beings,[7] is correct, then no undistorted inter*subjectivity* in the sense of Habermas is conceivable. If one adds Pêcheux' idea that the dominant *interdiscourse* pervades all communication, then intersubjective understanding appears as one of the last humanist illusions – along with the dialogue between theoretical discourses as mapped out here.

In what follows, it will be shown that the dilemma brought about by the confrontation between *ideal intersubjectivity* and *power-mediated subjection of individuals* can be overcome. Foucault's (and Althusser's) own work reveals to what extent the reflecting subject is in a position to analyse critically the social, psychic and linguistic structures which make up its subjectivity. This kind of criticism as self-criticism is the basis of individual autonomy and of communication under *real conditions* as described in this book.

1.   Habermas's Intersubjectivity as Ideal and Abstraction

Notwithstanding his critique of a subject philosophy geared, like Adorno's and Horkheimer's Critical Theory, towards the relationship between subject and object, Habermas does not reject the notion of subject. Instead of renouncing subjectivity, he attempts to integrate it into a communicative theory of *inter*subjectivity.

In this sense, Louis Quéré is quite right in defending him against critics who accuse him of having eliminated the concept of subject: "On the contrary, Habermas attempts a reformulation of notions such as autonomy, responsibility and consciousness, notions underlying the modern conception of subjectivity, by replacing the reflexive model with a systematically worked out model of communication (. . . .)."[8]

This is undoubtedly correct; it should be added, however, that Habermas even retains the idea of a self-reflecting subject.[9] The fact that he continues to adhere to the concept of subjectivity is important here, because it will become clear that his theory of intersubjective communication runs counter to this concept.

To begin with, it should be emphasized that, according to Habermas himself, his "theory of communicative action" is also meant to be applied to scientific communication. Several of his texts indicate that this theory is designed to mediate between the segments of a fragmented postmodern society. For Habermas aims at a new "theory of rationality"[10] and attributes to the philosopher "the role of interpreter who mediates between the expert cultures of science and technology, of law and morals on the one hand and the communicative practice of every day life on the other (...)".[11] Hence the assumption that his theory of communicative action is also applicable to the theory of science is legitimate. For it is precisely in scientific or theoretical communication that, in the end, "the authority of the better argument",[12] as Habermas puts it, can be expected to prevail.

What exactly does his intersubjective communication look like? It is based on two complementary assumptions: *universality* and *abstraction*. These concepts are complementary insofar as the universal applicability of communicative rules and validity rules can only be obtained by abstracting from the particularities of the participating subjects. Commenting on the problem of a "multicultural" society, Habermas points out: "And the greater this diversity is, the more abstract are the rules and principles that protect the integrity and egalitarian coexistence of subjects who are becoming increasingly unfamiliar with one another in their difference and otherness."[13]

The central idea of this sentence is clear enough: the greater the differences between the participating individuals and groups, the higher the normative level of abstraction has to be in order to allow for a common denominator of communication.

In some respects, Habermas inverts Lyotard's basic argument. Precisely because the *différend* grows, one ought not to perpetuate it ("témoigner du différend", Lyotard), but try to overcome it by introducing universally valid criteria. On this level, he agrees with Kant, Popper and the Liberals. He himself locates his discourse ethics between a Kantian individualism and a communitarianism influenced by Hegel's idea of "individualization as socialization".[14]

A more detailed scrutiny reveals, however, that Habermas is much closer to Kant than to Hegel, because, in his definitions of notions such as *life world*, *ideal communication situation* and *intersubjectivity*, he persistently abstracts from reality in order to attain the highest possible level of universality. His thought regularly reproduces Kant's epistemological separations (e.g. of different faculties) and neglects Hegel's category of *mediation* (*Vermittlung*). The final result is a Kantian confrontation of ideal and reality and an abstract negation of the subject as a social and linguistic actor. One can only agree with David Owen who argues that, unlike Foucault, "Habermas fails to acknowledge the claims of genealogy",[15] i. e. the production of subjects within social structures.

In order to understand the theory of communicative action, it seems important not to lose sight of two basic distinctions Habermas keeps emphasizing in discussions with superficial critics who tend to ignore them: the distinction between an *ideal* and a *real* (sociological) *life world*[16] and the complementary distinction between an *ideal* and a *real communication situation*. Dealing with the formal or ideal concept of life world, Habermas writes: "It is a concept complementary to that of communicative action."[17] This means that he defines intersubjective communication with respect to an idealized, formal "life world" and with respect to an ideal communication situation.

Whenever he stresses the universal character of the life world and of the ideal communication situation, it becomes clear that we are dealing with abstract generalizations. Since the "ideal communication situation" presupposes the notion of *life world*, the latter deserves closer scrutiny.

This notion was introduced into philosophical and sociological debate by Edmund Husserl and Alfred Schütz.[18] In Habermas's theory of communicative action, it is expected to warrant common linguistic and cultural criteria and the possibility of generalization. As a basis of mutual understanding the ideal or formal (not the real or social) life world is meant to guarantee a common ground of communication. About the "communicating actors" Habermas says:

> The structures of the life world lay down the forms of the intersubjectivity of possible understanding. It is to them that participants in communication owe their extramundane positions vis-à-vis the innerworldly items about which they can come to an understanding. The lifeworld is, so to speak, the transcendental site where speaker and hearer meet, where they can reciprocally raise claims that their utterances fit the world (objective, social, or subjective), and where they can criticize and confirm those validity claims, settle their disagreements, and arrive at agreements.[19]

A few lines further, he refers to a "shared life world" which "is constitutive for mutual understanding *as such*".[20]

At this stage, one cannot help feeling that the "transcendental location" of the formally defined life world is a utopian construction (*ou topos* = no place) which in Habermas's case fulfils a function similar to that of Heidegger's *Being*, Lukács's *proletariat* and Mannheim's *free-floating intellectuals*.[21] In all of these cases, we are dealing with the search for a vantage point permitting us to discuss the social world without becoming involved in its antagonisms and conflicts.

Starting from an "internal connection between structures of lifeworlds and structures of linguistic worldviews",[22] Habermas constructs an

ideal speech situation (*ideale Sprechsituation*) which is to be presupposed as a
guideline in all forms of real communication. He imagines "that those
participating in argumentation *presuppose* something like an ideal speech
situation".[23] He adds:

> The ideal speech situation is characterized by the fact that every consen-
> sus brought about under its conditions can *per se* be considered as a
> rational consensus. My thesis is: *the anticipation of an ideal speech situation* is
> the sole guarantee for the claim that the *de facto* achieved consensus is a
> rational one (. . .).[24]

Like the formal concept of life world, the ideal speech situation excludes
"a systematic distortion of communication".[25] It is only in such idealized
conditions which are kept free from social constraints, argues Habermas,
that "the non-violent constraint of the better argument"[26] may prevail.
Naturally, the question arises who defines the quality of arguments. Arguments considered as "convincing" by one person (or group) may be rejected
as "absurd" by another.

In order to escape from this reality of everyday life, Habermas imagines a
"pure communicative action"[27] with the following characteristics: "effective equality of chances with respect to the roles in a dialogue", "a universal
interchangeability of dialogical roles"[28] or, as he puts it elsewhere: "universal interchangeability of participant perspectives".[29] In order to consolidate
the "intersubjectively shared traditions"[30] of the life world, he prescribes
a homogeneous language for the communicating individuals. Following
R. Alexy, he specifies: "Different speakers may not use the same expression
with different meanings."[31]

One need not be a fanatical follower of Derrida's deconstruction in order
to suspect a hidden philosophical absurdity. Did not Margaret Masterman
show that even one and the same speaker (in this case Thomas S. Kuhn:
cf. chap. 5) uses the word "paradigm" in twenty-one different ways? How
can we possibly succeed in persuading *different* speakers to link a word to
just one meaning, one signifier to one signified?

It is obvious that we can only succeed in doing this if we systematically reduce the real or social subjectivity of communicating individuals
to an abstract or purely conceptual subjectivity in the sense of Kant or
Fichte. In an attempt to exclude social reality from the ideal speech situation, Habermas demands "*institutional measures*" (emphasis in the German
original):

> Because of all these factors, institutional measures are needed to suffi-
> ciently neutralize empirical limitations and avoidable internal and

external interference so that the idealized conditions always already presupposed by participants in argumentation can at least be adequately approximated.[32]

The key word in this quotation is "to neutralize". But are we to consider neutralized and idealized subjects as genuine subjects?

One could object to Habermas by repeating Max Stirner's criticism of Fichte and Hegel: "'Absolute thought' is the kind of thought which forgets that it is *my* thought, that *I* think and that it only exists by virtue of *my existence.*"[33] The materialist objection is decisive in this context, because it reveals to what extent it is not the "ideal speech situation" that is to be *presupposed* in all kinds of communication (Hans Albert shows in his critique of Karl-Otto Apel that this is not the case),[34] but *individual subjectivity which is invariably a social and linguistic phenomenon manifesting itself in discourse defined as a semantic and narrative structure.* In no conceivable situation can individual subjects renounce their discursive and social identity without at the same time renouncing their existence.

Habermas cannot possibly be aware of discourse as a semantic and narrative structure (the latter has nothing to do with his notion of discourse as dialogue or meta-discussion),[35] because he has founded his ideal speech situation on the speech act theory developed by Austin and Searle. This theory is based on the *sentence* as speech act and thus loses sight of the *trans-phrastic discourse structure* underlying individual and collective subjectivity.

Relying on Austin and Searle, Habermas himself defines the speech act as the pragmatic form of the sentence: "A speech act creates the conditions for using a sentence in a statement; but at the same time it has the form of a sentence."[36] However, constative or performative speech acts (e.g. "I promise to come tomorrow") usually have a neutral, impersonal character and are not specific to particular discourses or subjectivities.

This is why Habermas considers the "ideal speech situation" from the point of view of speech act theory. By doing this, by concentrating on the sentence, he is able to neutralize not only the communicated messages, but also the communicating subjects on a cultural, religious and ideological level.[37] He explains: "If, as was suggested here, we classify speech acts as communicative, constative, representative and regulative statements, then we discover that they and only they are the adequate means of communication for the project of an ideal speech situation."[38] Thus individual subjectivity, which comes about in sociolects and in discourses conceived as trans-phrastic, semantic and narrative structures, is a priori excluded from the ideal speech situation.[39]

If, however, we are prepared to learn something from Young Hegelians like Stirner, from Marx and Nietzsche, *we shall presuppose this social and linguistic subjectivity in every conceivable inter-individual communication,* instead of abstracting from it idealistically. But if we adopt this stance, *we can no longer presuppose* the ideal speech situation which negates social subjectivity in a Kantian manner.[40]

If the material, socio-linguistic subjectivity of the interlocutors becomes the starting point, then the interchangeability of communicative roles demanded by Habermas (cf. supra) no longer appears as a reasonable postulate. How can a feminist take the role of a critical rationalist or Marxist without giving up her subjectivity? The "interchangeability of the participants' perspectives" (cf. supra) is as impossible as the interchangeability of subjectivities anchored in discourses. In this context, Habermas's rule according to which "different speakers are not allowed to attribute different meanings to one and the same expression" (cf. supra) becomes untenable. For a critical rationalist is bound to differ from an advocate of Critical Theory when the word "ideology" is at stake. But it is precisely for this reason that he is interesting as an interlocutor. There is no need for me to discuss "ideology" with somebody who agrees with my definition of this concept. Even the "non-violent constraint of the better argument" turns out to be problematical, because each sociolect, each discourse defines a different argument as "better".

These observations and the "cooperative search for the truth"[41] postulated by Habermas lead to the insight that each of us constructs truth differently. (The disputes around positivism and Habermas's discussions with Luhmann seem to confirm this insight.)

Habermas's basic concern seems to be the exclusion of ideologies, power factors and strategies from communication with the help of notions such as "formal life world" and "ideal speech situation". But along with these distorting factors he eliminates individual subjectivity. His principle of intersubjectivity is thus turned into a repressive measure. William Rasch certainly has a point when he writes about Habermas's communicating subjects: "Their communicative reasoning merely reduces the multiplicity of convictions, such that the goal of their discourse – universal consensus – is to have no one thinking differently from anyone else."[42]

There is a striking resemblance between this repressive utopia and the structures of domination described by Foucault. Aiming at universal consensus, Habermas's theory of communication and communicative action ends up by endowing particular points of view (e.g. the pragmatism of Anglo-American speech act theory) with a universal status. Like most idealist approaches, his ideal amounts to a *universalization of the particular.*

Habermas, who seems anxious to include the Other and otherness,[43] has achieved the very opposite by banning social and ideological subjectivity from an apparently repression-free ideal communication. The point is that human communication – be it practical or theoretical – resembles a game. It combines playful and affective moments with the search for knowledge, power and strategic advantage.[44]

One of the best examples is undoubtedly the world of love where egoism and altruism, strategy and solidarity are inextricably interwoven. When she says "I love you", she almost certainly means something else than he does. Who would want to prevent the lovers from attributing different meanings to the word "love"? More often than not, they will agree without unduly worrying about the univocal use prescribed by the philosopher. It is quite likely that this idea remains valid in scientific communication – where the word "science" is being used in all sorts of ways leading to different, but often complementary insights.

2.   From Foucault to Althusser and Pêcheux: Knowledge as Power

Michel Foucault and Max Stirner seem to agree on one crucial point: on preferring the particular, the material and the corporeal to the ideal. It is not by chance that the French philosopher stresses the "technical and strategic"[45] aspects of power. While Habermas insists on delivering the communicating subjects from the constraints of everyday life in order to prepare them for a seemingly repression-free communication, Foucault *presupposes* a subjectivity and a communication structured by power – and not a communication or interaction free from interests and power structures.

For him the individual subject is primarily a subjugated instance: *subiectum*. In this respect Foucault may also be considered as an heir to Horkheimer and Adorno who describe the self-enslavement of the subject within its own system of domination. In *Negative Dialectics*, the idealist glorification of subjective autonomy appears as ideological arrogance: "The ego principle imitates its negation. It is not true that the object is a subject, as idealism has been drilling into us for thousands of years, but it is true that the subject is an object."[46] Foucault analyses the reduction of subjects to objects more vividly than any other philosopher before him and explains – *en passant*, as it were – why it is so difficult to realize free intersubjectivity as imagined by Popper, Davidson and Habermas.

Habermas was quick to realize that, for Foucault, social communication is rooted in power structures: "From the outset, he is interested in the human sciences as media that in modernity strengthen and promote the mysterious process of this socialization, that is, the investment with power of concrete, bodily mediated interactions."[47] Should anyone naively ask how Foucault's subjects communicate, the ironical answer could be: as objects of administration.

In this situation, it is hard to imagine a genuine intersubjective dialogue, and Habermas aptly points out "that killing off dialogical relationships transforms subjects, who are monologically turned in upon themselves, into objects for one another, and only objects".[48] In this context, one may also read his remark that Foucault "raises 'power' to a basic transcendental-historicist concept of historiography as critique of reason".[49]

In this perspective, Foucault's philosophy appears as a radical alternative to Habermas's transcendental model of an ideal speech situation supposedly inherent in every real communication. Foucault does not *presuppose* the ideal, but rather the (apparently) real power structures.

In human reason he claims to recognize a result of the power process which also generates insights and is by no means identical with blindfolded violence. In *Discipline and Punish*, he seems to answer Habermas when he turns against an entire philosophical tradition which rests on the assumption that power and knowledge are incompatible. Foucault's critique of this tradition resuscitates some of the crucial arguments put forward by the Young Hegelians and Nietzsche: "Perhaps, too, we should abandon a whole tradition that allows us to imagine that knowledge can exist only where the power relations are suspended and that knowledge can develop only outside its injunctions, its demands and its interests."[50] Far from being permanently linked to blindness and madness, power also yields new insights. The manifold relations between military strategy and science amply illustrate this thesis.

However, knowledge thus produced is not universal knowledge in the sense of Kant, Popper or Habermas but particular, technical knowledge in the sense of a pluralized and fragmented postmodernity. Very much like Kuhn's paradigmatic rationality, Foucault's reason is limited in space and time. One is reminded of Kuhn's "paradigms" when reading in *The Birth of the Clinic*: "Significant perception is therefore structurally different in the world of the clinical as it existed in its first form, and as modified by the anatomical method."[51] Each one of the two perceptions represents a different scientific episteme which reproduces some salient features of Kuhn's "paradigm". It is a closed system of rules that excludes the use of other rule systems.

In Foucault's world, as in Kuhn's, reason appears as fragmented by epistemological breaks which oppose incompatible modes of thought to one another. All of these cognitive systems appear to Foucault as being instrumentalized and permeated with power relations. This is undoubtedly why he speaks of "reason's domination" ("domination de la raison").[52] (But he refrains from pointing out social groups or classes capable of using knowledge for their specific purposes.)

Truth itself is considered by him as a contingent factor linked to a particular historical episteme (to a paradigm, Kuhn would say). Commenting on Foucault's model, Gilles Deleuze aptly remarks: "There is no model of truth that does not refer back to a kind of power, and no knowledge or even science that does not express or imply, in an act, power that is being exerted."[53] At this stage, a contrast between Foucault and Kuhn comes to the fore. While the historian of science is led to explain paradigmatic changes with reference to anomalies within the old paradigm or by invoking the emergence of competing paradigms, Foucault is obliged to explain the collapse of an episteme in conjunction with declining power.[54]

Two passages from his article about Nietzsche express this idea very clearly. They could be read as postmodern, Young Hegelian and Nietzschean reactions to Habermas's universalist theory. In a first step, Foucault, following Nietzsche, denies the very possibility of power-free, universal communication: "Humanity does not progress slowly from struggle to struggle for a universal reciprocity the rules of which will finally replace war; with each of its violent acts it crosses a rule system and thus moves from domination to domination."[55] Although Habermas does not envisage his domination-free communication as the goal of history, but as a transcendental prerequisite of every real communication, Foucault's arguments may also be applied to his case.

In a second step, Foucault describes the struggle for new and old rule systems as the actual motor of history: "The great game of history boils down to the question who seizes the rules, who dislodges those who are using them, who knows how to use adequate camouflage to pervert them, to use them counter to their actual meaning and against those who enforced them (...)."[56] On the one hand, reason and knowledge thus appear as power-dependent functions, on the other hand, as historically unique and particular constellations that are valid for a while, only to fall into oblivion some time later.

If the development of human knowledge is considered in this perspective, then all pleading for universally acceptable arguments and universal understanding turns into an illusion which is bound to founder as soon as it collides with reality. Wherever knowledge is tied up with particular power structures, individual subjects appear as subjugated beings who are by definition incapable of reflecting and overcoming their social and linguistic

over-determination. In *Discipline and Punish*, the individual is even defined as
a "fictitious atom of an 'ideological' representation of society".[57]

Hence it is not surprising that, following Foucault, Freud and Lacan,[58]
Althusser defines subjectivity as an effect of ideology: of what he calls "ideological state apparatuses". For him, the individual subject's freedom or
autonomy is but an illusion. In reality, the subject is – as in Foucault's
early theory – a product of specific power constellations. It appears primarily as a subjugated being in the sense of the legal subject (or: the monarch's
subject). This is why Althusser deduces the ideological form of subjectivity
from the legal form: "tirée de la catégorie juridique de 'sujet de droit'."[59]

The result of his analyses is his thesis according to which "*ideology interpel-
lates individuals as subjects*".[60] It means that individuals are formed within
power structures such as the state, the church or the school until they
become what they are: subjects, subjugated beings. Althusser describes the
subjectivity of the individual as follows:

> If he believes in God, he goes to church in order to take part in mass, he
> kneels down, prays, confesses, does penance (...). If he believes in Duty,
> he acts correspondingly and in such a way that his actions fit into certain
> ritual practices that "correspond to good manners". If he believes in
> Justice, he will accept the rules of law without contradiction (...).[61]

Althusser keeps emphasizing the unconscious character of the individual's
submission to such forms and the fact that all subjects are convinced they
enjoy full freedom of action. He compares ideology with the unconscious of
Freudian psychoanalysis and asserts that both are "eternal": "*Ideology is eternal, and so is the unconscious.*"[62] The fact that ideology (for instance political ideology) is a modern phenomenon that could hardly be found in
feudalism and that religion cannot be understood as a form of ideology,
does not seem to bother Althusser.[63]

The "eternal" character of ideology implies, however, that ideology is to
be *presupposed* in all cases – like Freud's unconscious – and that an intersubjective communication without or beyond ideology cannot exist. The idea of
a domination-free communication in the sense of Habermas thus collides
with Althusser's central thesis that subjectivity is always ideological and a
product of power structures. If this is the case, then ideological subjectivity
is to be *presupposed* in every scientific or non-scientific discussion – and not
the "ideal speech situation".

Considering these arguments, it is not surprising that Althusser removes
the concept of subject from the process of scientific discovery in which "the
'subject' plays, not the part it believes it is playing, but the part which is
assigned to it by the mechanism of the process".[64] He explains: "Every

scientific discourse is by definition a discourse without a subject, and a 'subject of science' only exists in an ideology of science.''[65]

At this point, Althusser joins Luhmann's systems theory within the context of a postmodern problematic which tends to relegate the notion of subject to the periphery of social evolution. Like Luhmann, he considers "subjectivity" as a humanist myth. In this respect, he is more radical than Bourdieu who not only continues to use the concept of subject, but also the derived concept of intersubjectivity.

The latter is literally inconceivable in Althusserian circles and is tacitly replaced in Michel Pêcheux' work by the concept of *interdiscourse* which has been derived from Foucault's theory of knowledge as power.[66] This concept implies a reversal of Habermas's idea of domination-free communication, for it rests on the assumption that individuals communicate unwittingly within the framework of a dominant discourse: "We shall call this 'complex totality of discourse formations with a dominant' interdiscourse (...)."[67] The interdiscourse as a linguistic manifestation of the dominant ideology and as a mediator between all discourse formations thus appears as a power-ridden constellation within which "intersubjective communication" takes place. The latter is far from being spontaneous or free. Individuals understand each other because they are being *dominated* by one and the same structure.

This is obviously the very opposite of what Habermas means by domination-free communication. One may wonder, however, whether his prescriptive model is not based on an interdiscourse that tactically conceals its claim to power and to the concomitant shaping of subjectivity. If this were the case, we would once again be confronting an uncanny dialectic of reason aiming at a universalization of the particular.

3. Subjectivity and Communication between Determinism and Freedom

The commentary to this confrontation between an idealist model of freedom and a materialist model of over-determination can be relatively concise. While the idealist and universalist approach tends to overlook that subjectivity and intersubjectivity are inseparable from their material (social, ideological, linguistic) context of origin, materialist determinism, as practised by the early Foucault and by Althusser, tends to ignore the active moments of subjectivity: the ability of the individual subject to reflect and criticize, the ability of human beings to change the social conditions they are born into.

With respect to Foucault's and Althusser's theories of subjectivity and communication, one might repeat Marx's critique of materialism in the third thesis on Feuerbach: "The materialist doctrine that men are products of circumstances and upbringing, and that, therefore, changed men are products of other circumstances and changed upbringing, forgets that it is men that change circumstances, and that the educator himself needs educating."[68] What Marx has in mind is the change of the circumstances by the revolutionary class; but his attempt to combine the active moment of idealism with the passive moments of mechanical materialism may very well be repeated in the case of individuals and groups.

Althusser and Foucault themselves show in most of their writings to what extent critical reflection delivers us from the constraints imposed on us by social and cultural structures. While Althusser's theory of "ideological interpellation" makes us reflect on our own over-determination in a new context, Foucault's "archaeology" reveals the link between power and knowledge and in particular the fact that power does not simply blind and stultify those who wield it, but often yields critical knowledge which can be turned against it. Adopting this point of view, Foucault advocates a struggle against power ("lutte contre le pouvoir").[69] Deleuze comments on this critical project: "Theory is by definition against power."[70]

This is also what Habermas has in mind when he deals with the *other* Foucault, the critical, enlightened philosopher: "But while Foucault has hitherto only explored the will to knowledge in modern power formations in order to denounce it, he *now* presents it in a completely different light: as the critical impulse to be preserved and renewed, an impulse which links his own thought to the beginnings of modernity."[71] If this is the case, then we may assume that a thought situated beyond instrumental and ideological manipulation does exist.

This kind of thought will presuppose both factors: the social and linguistic over-determination of the communicating subjects as well as the willingness to understand each other critically and self-critically, a willingness underlying most scientific discussions. However, this willingness is not inherent in such discussions because an ideal speech situation is tacitly presupposed in all cases, but for institutional reasons. Although indifference, cynicism and rhetoric frequently occur, curiosity and thirst for knowledge can be assumed to prevail in an institutional context marked by competition and criticism.

The works of Althusser and Foucault are essential for theoretical dialogue because they show which aspects of one's own subjectivity have to be taken into account in order to prevent a discussion from degenerating into a dialogue of the deaf, similar to the polemics between "positivism" and Critical

Theory in the late 1960s. Intersubjectivity is only meaningful if it is defined as *interdiscursivity*: i.e. as a process in the course of which all participants become aware of the social and linguistic over-determination of their subjectivity and thus avoid the illusion of spontaneous mutual understanding.

Louis Althusser's objection that this kind of reflection does not go beyond the ideological realm can be countered by a critical reference to his own notion of a Marxist science without subjects. This science has not produced any generally recognized (i.e. intercultural, transideological) truths: neither in philosophy nor in the social sciences. In this respect it is reminiscent of Luhmann's system of science without a subject. So far, the opposition between the *true* and the *untrue* underlying this system has not yielded a single generally accepted decision concerning the value or validity of theories or theorems in the social sciences.

Part Three

Dialogical Theory:
A Meta-Theory of Scientific Communication

What results have the prolegomena of *Part Two* yielded? They have shown that the extremes not only meet but also qualify and correct each other. In this light, it appears worthwhile to make heterogeneous theoretical positions collide and compete. For it becomes clear that each truth has its counterpart and that it is therefore advisable never to forget the other side of the coin.

Luhmann's undoubtedly correct insight according to which the process of social differentiation generates autonomous spheres marked by specific laws and dynamics ought to be supplemented by Bourdieu's analysis of a hetero-nomous process of de-differentiation leading to the domination of one sphere (e.g. the economic) over another. A confrontation of Luhmann's and Bourdieu's theories of science has an effect similar to Derrida's juxtaposition of Hegel's philosophy and some of Jean Genet's experimental texts in *Glas*.[1] While Hegel's system is made to reveal some of its blind spots, Genet's avant-garde experiment appears in a new light.

This also applies to the confrontation of Habermas's and Foucault's (Althusser's, Pêcheux') models in the last chapter of *Part Two*. Foucault's and Althusser's idea that language-based power constellations and ideologies turn individuals into subjects or subjugated actors casts doubts upon Habermas's free-floating, idealized intersubjectivity. For it shows that instead of presupposing an "ideal speech situation", we might have to presuppose something rather different: namely the ideological constitution of seemingly free subjects in the process of intersubjectivity. However, this deterministic truth ought to be immediately completed by Habermas's observation that even Foucault eventually turns his concept of reason against power, thus revealing reason's critical dimension. Like Althusser, he shows – *malgré lui*, as it were – that, apart from being socially determined, human thought is also autonomous and capable of reflection and enlightened criticism.

Following these arguments which take seriously the orientation towards the Other in order to break up the monologue of the One, the remaining chapters are meant to develop Adorno's and Horkheimer's Critical Theory by aiming at alterity and dialogue instead of foregrounding essayism and parataxis. This reorientation activates theoretical potentials of the *Dialectic of Enlightenment* and of *Negative Dialectics* which the founders of Critical Theory tended to neglect. By highlighting problems of composition, of essayism, parataxis and mimesis, Adorno burned all the bridges which had linked early Critical Theory to the social sciences.[2] In this respect, Habermas's objections to post-war Critical Theory are fully justified. He quite rightly stresses the critical and liberating tendencies within the social sciences that are frequently glossed over by Adorno and Horkheimer.[3]

In spite of this affinity with Habermas's critique, the Dialogical Theory presented in the third part of the book is a reversal of the Habermasian model. For instead of starting from the ideal speech situation, it starts from the *real* socio-linguistic situation. This means that it includes all those elements Habermas is so anxious to exclude by his transcendental definitions of the life world and the ideal speech situation. However, communicating with others (other scientists) only makes sense when they are recognized in their cultural, linguistic and ideological alterity. This sense is lost when the *alterity* of our interlocutors is sacrificed to abstract rules.

Considered from an epistemological point of view, the orientation towards alterity and the Other may appear as an arbitrary a priori decision or as an unjustifiable hermeneutic postulate: "Dialogical Theory? – A Methodological Conception!" This is meant to be an alternative suggested by Philipp Balsinger in his response to Dialogical Theory which provoked assent, disagreement and polemics in 1999.[4] However, Balsinger's succinct answer does not really provide a serious option (in spite of the exclamation mark), because the critic simply identifies methodology with Paul Lorenzen's constructivism which, far from being universally accepted, is merely a possible approach. Nevertheless, his criticism shows why it is meaningful to envisage a meta-theory of dialogue in the human sciences. Such a theory ought to prevent scientists from identifying monologically a particular approach with "true science" and from imposing it on others.

Although this openness towards the Other cannot in all cases be presumed to form the basis of communication, it is not meant to be a final foundation in the sense of Apel's or Habermas's "ideal speech situation" (criticized early on by Hans Albert).[5] It is rather a heuristic and empirical postulate based on the assumption that individual and collective subjectivity comes about in a permanent social dialogue. Without the others our own subjectivity could not have developed.[6] This is a commonplace of modern hermeneutics, of Mead's sociology and social psychology. "Identity comes about in a dialogical process (...)",[7] remarks the social psychologist Heiner Keupp.

This should be taken to mean that our scientific subjectivity cannot develop without the assistance of others. Even the subject of theory needs "the energy of the liberating, questioning, innovative and unpredictable dialogue,"[8] as Hans-Herbert Kögler puts it. On the one hand, it seeks the Other's confirmation and encouragement in order to make sure that it is not caught up in chimeras and delusions; but on the other hand, it also seeks, as long as it is capable of theoretical reflection and innovation, the "shake-up of familiar opinions by the experience of strangeness".[9]

This exposure to the unfamiliar is what is most missing in contemporary scientific debates – for example in the controversies triggered off in the 1960s by Popper's and Hans Albert's "positivism". The word "positivism" as such suggests that those who were speaking in the name of Critical Theory (Adorno, Horkheimer, Habermas) refused to take into account the critique of traditional positivism which Critical Rationalism contains.

Critical Rationalism is important for the dialogical approach insofar as the latter also attempts to replace the hermeneutic search for a final foundation (be it God, the synthetic judgement a priori or the ideal speech situation) by criticism and critical testing. However, the idea of a critical test is revised here in two crucial respects. Testing does not take place between isolated individuals, but (directly or indirectly) between groups and their sociolects which are latent in most individual utterances. Hence Bourdieu quite rightly considers scientists as "collective subjects"[10] and not as individual geniuses. The second difference between Critical Rationalism and Dialogical Theory is due to the fact that Popper's "falsification" is abandoned by the latter in favour of Neurath's *Erschütterung* or "shake-up". The dialectical clash of heterogeneous models and the testing of a theory in a heterogeneous context (e.g. of the systems theory within Critical Rationalism) may cast doubts on that theory by revealing its fissures and gaps – but it will hardly ever refute it.

One objection to the (meta-)theoretical approach proposed here can easily be imagined. Finally, one could argue, a socio-semiotic brand of Critical Theory is presented as a meta-theory of scientific dialogue. The answer to this objection is as plausible as the objection itself: without a *particular* meta-theory scientific dialogue is left to chance or ceases to be viable.

The choice of Critical Theory can be justified by the fact that it refuses to identify itself (ideologically) with its objects and by its rejection of monologue: a rejection not simply proclaimed, but inherent in a discourse structure aiming at non-identity and constructivism.

It follows from this that the dialogue between heterogeneous theories proposed here does not require participants to abandon or limit their theoretical identities. On the contrary, it requires all interlocutors to defend their theoretical positions in order to make the voice of the Other heard. However, it also presupposes the will and the ability to reflect upon the socio-linguistic context and upon the discourse structures involved, especially one's own discourse structure.

These criteria do not only apply to *contemporary discussions* during congresses, conferences and symposia. They also underlie the *assessment of past discussions* and controversies – for example, of the debates about "positivism" and of the dispute between Russian Marxists and Formalists – which will appear in a new light (chap. 14): not merely as historical events, but also and above all as associations of contrasting positions in the sense of *Part Two*. They are also valid whenever *different theories are compared*, as is the case here, for such comparisons are geared towards the dialectical unity of opposites and exclude ideological dualism.

Naturally, it would be both pretentious and naïve to believe that the arguments put forward here are acceptable to all social and cultural scientists. These scientists might be more easily convinced by the negative argument that the contemporary proliferation of unrelated, monological theories is unsatisfactory in the long run. Those who agree with this negative diagnosis might, after all, be interested in the model proposed here, because it reveals problems they cannot afford to ignore as long as they take their own diagnosis seriously.

Chapter 11

Critical Theory as Dialogue: Ambivalence and Dialectics, Non-Identity and Alterity

Adorno's and Horkheimer's Critical Theory, which is at stake here, provoked protracted discussions and polemics in the 1970s and 1980s.[1] It is rarely being discussed nowadays, and some critics wonder whether its intellectual potential is not exhausted.[2] Others try to demonstrate its relevance to the postmodern constellation by reminding us of the fact that Walter Benjamin, Theodor W. Adorno and Max Horkheimer were among the first to defend the particular against the repressive universalism of the rationalists and Hegelians.[3]

In what follows, no attempt will be made to give Critical Theory this kind of postmodern turn. Rather, it will be shown that Habermas sets out from a somewhat one-sided assessment of the situation when he declares that going beyond Adorno (with Adorno) amounts to adopting a post-structuralist stance: "If one takes seriously Adorno's *Negative Dialectics* and his *Aesthetic Theory* and subsequently tries to go just one step further in order to leave this scene dominated by Beckett, then one has to become a kind of post-structuralist."[4] However, Adorno's negative dialectics cannot possibly be reduced to Beckett's aesthetic negativity, and the theory of communicative action is certainly not the only way out of a scene constructed by Habermas.

The main concern of this chapter is to show (a) that, in their critique of rationalism and Hegelianism, Adorno and Horkheimer mapped out an open dialectic of non-identity which breaks out of the identifying, "realistic" monologue, because it contains constructivist elements; (b) that the critique of identifying, systematic thought implies a self-reflecting turn towards particularity and alterity which (c) makes dialogue possible.

Moreover, an attempt will be made to deduce the concept of theory, provisionally defined in the second chapter, from a dialogically and semiotically reinterpreted Critical Theory and to use it as the base of Dialogical Theory. This deduction will show to what extent notions such as *negativity* and *non-identity* imply a semiotic critique of discourse which has hitherto been neglected.[5]

On a semiotic level, one becomes aware of possibilities which open up before a critical theory of society that need neither turn into "post-structuralism" nor into an idealized intersubjectivity in the sense of Apel and Habermas.

Once it is transformed into a Dialogical Theory aiming at *real* social communication, i.e. at discourses, sociolects and the corresponding collective interests, Critical Theory rediscovers its materialist base which it lost in the idealist hermeneutics developed after the Second World War.

1. Ambivalence, Paradox and Open Dialectics

Adorno's and Horkheimer's Critical Theory is a post-Hegelian and post-Marxist thought which postulates the unity of opposites without trying to overcome them in a synthesis. In this respect, it differs fundamentally from Hegel's systematic dialectics of *Aufhebung* aptly characterized by Pierre Macherey: "Thinking the contradiction implies the will to overcome it, for 'one cannot persist in a contradiction'."[6] Adorno's negative dialectic which owes a lot to Walter Benjamin's "Historico-Philosophical Theses"[7] and to their central idea that progress is a progression towards catastrophe, is in some respects a return to the Young Hegelian critique of Hegel. This critique frequently leads to a rejection of Hegel's synthesizing *Aufhebung* and to a reassertion of the social and historical contradiction in a revolutionary or anarchistic perspective.

With respect to Adorno's philosophy, one could repeat what Ewald Volhard wrote about the sceptical Young Hegelian Friedrich Theodor Vischer: "Vischer's constant aim was to replace the contradictory Either-Or by the even more contradictory figure of As-well-as."[8] In a similar social context, Proudhon, a contemporary of Baudelaire, the Young Hegelians and Vischer, pleads against the synthesizing overcoming of antinomies: "The antinomy cannot be dissolved; this is the fundamental error of the entire Hegelian philosophy."[9] Adorno's later work is also based on this negative-dialectical principle of the insurmountable antinomy which yields the kind of extreme ambivalence that is to be found in many philosophical and literary works of modernism.

Like Nietzsche, an heir to Young Hegelianism,[10] who knew "the sadness of intense happiness"[11] and took the view "that the portion of the universe which we know – I mean our human reason – is not very reasonable",[12] like Charles Baudelaire who believed that "superstition is the source of all truth",[13] Adorno unites the opposites without aiming at Hegelian syntheses.

The result is a late-modern or modernist ambivalence,[14] which tends to dismantle all ideological dualisms by revealing to what extent subject and object, truth and untruth, the general and the particular, ideology and science are intertwined. This ambivalence relates Adorno to modernist writers such as Proust, Musil, Joyce or Pirandello[15] and is itself a combination of two etymologically and dialectically interdependent phenomena: *crisis* and *criticism*. For on the one hand, ambivalence, as an insurmountable coexistence of opposites, bears witness to the impossibility of the Hegelian system, its truth and its "Absolute Knowledge";[16] on the other hand, it is a critical instrument enabling modernist thinkers to deconstruct the dogmatized truths of idealism. Their criticism is revived by postmodernist and deconstructionist thought, whose advocates refuse to overcome or synthesize the contradiction by giving it a destructive slant. For them, philosophical and literary contradictions lead to the disintegration of meaning and to the negation of truth in the sense of Adorno's *truth content (Wahrheitsgehalt)*.[17]

Unlike the deconstructionists, Adorno insists on the importance of concepts such as *truth* and *theory* and transforms extreme ambivalence, brought about by the unity of opposites, into a modernist paradox. In this respect, he again resembles modernist writers such as Kafka and Musil the first of whom lets his protagonist die at the entrance to the "Law", an entrance kept open especially for him, while the second undertakes to write an impossible novel: "? Paradox: to write the novel that nobody can write."[18] Like Kafka and Musil, Adorno aspires towards true knowledge; like the modernist writers, he accepts the paradoxes inherent in such aspirations.

Considering the complicity between Hegel's system and the principle of domination, his diagnostic turns out to be similar to Musil's: "Philosophers are violent individuals, who do not have an army at their disposal and therefore conquer the world by locking it up in a system."[19] But is there an alternative to the system?

Like Musil who envisages an "impossible" essayistic novel, Adorno answers this question by proposing a paradoxical solution: by mapping out a non-theoretical theory which takes into account the unique, the particular. The fact that we are dealing with a paradoxical project was clearly perceived by the editors of the posthumously published *Aesthetic Theory*: "A theory, however, that is sparked by the *individuum ineffabile*, that wants to make amends to the unrepeatable, the non-conceptual, for what identifying thought inflicts on it, necessarily comes into conflict with the abstractness to which, as theory, it is compelled."[20]

The problem outlined here is summed up by Adorno's well-known sentence: "*Ratio* without mimesis is self-negating."[21] This problem is hard to solve, because the mimetic principle, which in this case is meant to re-instate theory as a guardian of reason, is situated beyond conceptual thought. The paradox inherent in this solution is reminiscent of the last scene in Kafka's parable "Before the Law": artistic mimesis which is supposed to save theory in a crisis involving the entire metaphysical tradition is excluded from the conceptual and theoretical realm.[22]

Comparable paradoxes crop up in Adorno's analyses of subjectivity. Our main task, he argues, is to come to the rescue of the faltering subject, because at present "the trace of humanity seems to persist only in the individual in his decline".[23] Daniel Kipfer sums up this paradox: "In this theoretical approach, the eliminated individual thus becomes the only instance which is able to resist the elimination of individuality."[24]

It would undoubtedly be possible to describe Adorno's entire discourse of the post-war period as a paradox-ridden structure. For even the expression "negative dialectics" turns into a paradox if dialectics are defined with Hegel and Marx both as a conceptual-ontological and as an historical progression to ever higher stages of development. "As in Hegel's case", remarks Predrag Grujić, "negativity is for dialectical materialism not a principle of destruction, but of perfection."[25] Even for Adorno, dialectics is not a purely destructive approach (in this respect, he differs substantially from deconstruction).[26] His negative variant, which might be defined as "dialectics in suspense",[27] is meant to provoke reflection, self-reflection and criticism: "Dialectics is the self-consciousness of the objective context of delusion; it does not mean to have escaped from that context."[28] In this perspective, dialectics appears as an insight into the negative, oppressive character of society, not as its systematic, Hegelian apology.

At this point, the path of negative dialectics splits, because *two continuations* are conceivable: one leads to Adorno's thesis that "the whole is the false",[29] the other leads to the insight that breaking out of Hegel's identifying discourse (*Identitätsdenken*, Adorno) can open up constructivist and dialogical perspectives. Both options are based on the critical assumption that subject and object are not identical.

While the idea that the whole is false makes dialectics embrace the aesthetic utopia of art, the alternative proposed here starts from Adorno's notion of non-identity in order to show that it also implies the *alterity of the object and of the other subject*. Whenever the monological and systematic discourse which identifies itself with reality breaks up, the Other's alterity comes to the fore, inviting us to a dialogue. At the same time, it becomes clear that all representations of reality are *constructions* the value of which can only be tested dialogically.

2.   Non-Identity, Alterity and Critique

Naturally, some of these arguments have been anticipated by Adorno's and Horkheimer's Critical Theory. Horkheimer, for example, remarks in conjunction with Hegel's identifying thought which was contested on different levels by the Young Hegelians:

> If knowledge and its object, thinking and thought reality appear not to be identical in the course of their definition, if thought turns out to be what it seems to be empirically, that is to say the thought of certain particular individuals, then it has to abandon its absolutist pretensions and yield to the scientific knowledge of the particular.[30]

It is not by chance that Horkheimer refers here – in an article published in 1932 – to a "scientific knowledge" inspired by pre-war Marxism.

However, two years after the war, in *Dialectic of Enlightenment* (1947), a book he published together with Adorno, it appears that the main representative of this "particularity" has become *art* considered as a mimetic approximation to nature.[31] This aspect of post-war Critical Theory is commented on in *Negative Dialectics*: "What the philosophical concept will not abandon is the yearning that animates the nonconceptual side of art (. . .)."[32]

In *Aesthetic Theory*, artistic mimesis finally comes to represent the particular and non-identical that cannot be subsumed under philosophical concepts of nature: "Nature, to whose imago art is devoted, does not yet in any way exist; what is true in art is something nonexistent. What does not exist becomes incumbent on art in that other for which identity-positing reason, which reduced it to material, uses the word nature."[33] The Other considered as the particular and non-identical appears in this passage as the absent and longed for Other, which does not yet exist and only occasionally appears in the allusions of art.

The opening of dialectics and the orientation of thought towards the Other are not only meant to break the mechanisms of identification; they are also expected to make subjective experience possible. In *Aesthetic Theory*, it becomes clear to what extent the question of experience, a central question in Adorno's thought, is linked to ambiguity, ambivalence and openness. Commenting on the ambiguity of art, Adorno criticizes aesthetic theories which combat this kind of ambiguity because it tends to elude their definitions: "This psychological posture is that of an *'intolerance of ambiguity'*, an impatience with what is ambivalent and not strictly definable; ultimately, it is the refusal of what is open, of what has not been predetermined by any jurisdiction, ultimately of experience itself."[34] What matters most in this context, is the link established by Adorno between ambiguity, openness and experience. Alterity which tends to escape all definitions imposed on it by identifying monologue, can only be experienced within an open discourse.

However, this alterity need not be represented or articulated by an art that can hardly bridge the gap between Critical Theory and contemporary social sciences. Alterity can also be represented by the Other: not necessarily the Other in the sense of Habermas, i.e. a communicating individual divested of all social, ideological and psychic particularities, but the Other in the sense of Bakhtin's "other voice",[35] in the sense of what is radically different.

If Horkheimer and Adorno had envisaged the possibility of turning their Critical Theory into a dialogical approach, they might have conceived it as an open theory inspired by the voice of the Other. For their critique of identifying (Hegelian) thought implies a critique of the monological discourse which is not only a closed system in the sense of Hegel, but an authoritarian rhetoric pretending to be identical with reality.

Elsewhere in Adorno's work, especially in the posthumously published lectures, it actually becomes clear that the author does regard the non-identity of subject and object, of phenomenon and concept as a kind of "openness"; not however as an openness towards the other voice, but as a receptiveness to experience, to the empirical as such:

> (...) In reality – and I am increasingly inclined to take this view – only that which can be refuted, which can turn out to be false, represents the kind of openness I referred to here, the kind of openness that really matters. For the notion of openness evokes all that cannot be subsumed under the identity of a concept and hence contains the possibility of being disappointed.[36]

Some time later, he mentions an affinity between his position and empiricism: "Affinität zum Empirismus".[37] This affinity can best be understood in conjunction with his theory of experience.

However, in the sentences quoted here, affinities of a different kind appear, albeit between the lines: affinities between Critical Theory and Critical Rationalism whose postulate that theories and theorems ought to be refutable, falsifiable by others, also aims at *experience*. For Adorno's sketch of an open thought, thriving on refutability and "disappointment", comes surprisingly close to the principle of refutability propounded by Popper and Hans Albert. If "openness" in Adorno's sense is that "which can turn out to be false", then it contains the idea of falsifiability in the most general sense, in the sense of refutability. The "disappointment" mentioned by Adorno need not be related exclusively to facts or events. For the others, our inter-locutors, can also disappoint or refute us – with their counter-arguments.

Any attempt to deduce Popper's and Lakatos's theories of falsifiability from a few remarks dropped here and there by Adorno would obviously be foolhardy. For it is clear that Adorno's dialectics does not contain Popper's deductive logic of scientific testing. The affinity mentioned here is to be found on another level: on the epistemological level where Hegel's postulate of identity comes under attack from Critical Theory and Critical Rational-ism alike.

Although Popper's critique of Hegel consists mainly of simplifications and distortions, it aims – very much like Adorno's and Horkheimer's critique – at the postulate of identity and at the closure of the system.[38] Popper's alternatives, commented on in the fourth chapter, are well known; they are: openness and refutability (falsifiability). He agrees with Adorno's fundamental idea that a closed system identifying monologically with the real world is hostile to *experience* – and excludes an open discussion about the validity of hypotheses.

The arguments put forward against Critical Rationalism (or "Neo-Positivism", viewed as an instrument of domination) by Adorno and Horkheimer will not be discussed at this stage. They are not relevant here; what matters is the idea that two ideologically divergent theories overlap in one crucial point: namely in their postulate of an open theoretical dis-course which lends itself to testing, refutation and experience. This *partial agreement* between the two theoretical positions is due to their self-critical individualism that was hardly mentioned during the controversies about "positivism".[39] In the last resort, both theoretical models are based on the notions of individual autonomy and critique – in spite of their incompatible attitudes towards capitalism and liberalism.

In this respect, Adorno's and Horkheimer's post-war philosophy is by no means tied up, for better or worse, with artistic mimesis or Beckett's negative scenario, as Habermas would have us believe. It seems perfectly suitable as the starting point of a dialogical meta-theory, as long as its notion of alterity is re-interpreted dialogically.

In the present context, it seems more adaptable to dialogue than Critical Rationalism and Habermas's idealistic brand of Critical Theory, because it takes into account the alterity of the Other. While both Popper and Haber-mas imagine an intersubjectivity situated beyond all *frameworks*, that is beyond all cultural, ideological and linguistic particularities, a Dialogical Theory in the sense of Adorno and Horkheimer aims at individual auton-omy, alterity, heterogeneity and otherness. As such, it appeals to the Other in order to envisage "the concrete possibility of doing things differently".[40]

3.   Alterity, Ambivalence and Dialogue

What kind of cognitive function can alterity fulfil in a scientific discussion? In the first place, it will destroy some of our most cherished illusions: for example the illusion that our discourse (as a semantic and narrative structure) is identical with the real world. At the same time, it will remind us of the fact that reality is ambivalent and hence can be constructed differently by different speakers (cf. chap. 12). Finally, it confronts us with the question, whether the Other's construction is not better, more complex and more coherent than our own.

It seems hard to dodge this kind of question. It is always possible, of course, to react to it by putting forward an ideological justification in order to prove that our construction is the best and will remain the best. However, this ideological tactic of justifying one's approach will prove unsatisfactory in the long run, because it defeats all theoretical objects and eventually forces us to consider the possibility of revising our opinions at least in part. Thus alterity appears as a catalyst in the process of self-analysis and self-criticism. Without the voice of the Other, this process would never be set in motion.

Bakhtin, the theoretician of ambivalence and alterity, analyses polyphony and the role of the Other's voice in Dostoevsky's work. Commenting on the structure of Dostoevsky's novels, he remarks: "In no novel is the multiplicity of tones and styles reduced to a single common denominator. Nowhere is there a discourse-*dominant*, be it authorial discourse or the discourse of a major hero. Unity of style in the monologic sense does not exist in Dostoevsky's novels."[41] Bakhtin continues: "For it must be emphasized that in Dostoevsky's world even *agreement* retains its *dialogic* character, that is, it never leads to a *merging* of voices and truths in a single *impersonal* truth, as occurs in a monologic world."[42]

The refusal to combine or synthesize "voices", which marks both Dostoevsky's and Bakhtin's works, is motivated by modernist ambivalence, defined as a unity of opposites without synthesis. This ambivalence is the product of a post-Hegelian and Young Hegelian thought that rejects – like Adorno's and Horkheimer's Critical Theory – Hegelian and Marxist monologue and its tendency to identify with reality.[43]

Bakhtin's criticism of monologue in a dialogical perspective thus completes Adorno's and Horkheimer's critique of Hegel's identifying thought. For monologue which a priori excludes the voice of the Other is an aspect of the identifying discourse. Since Fichte and Hegel, this discourse tolerates nothing outside itself.

As a result of their polemics against this kind of language, which negates alterity in all of its forms, Adorno and Horkheimer developed Critical Theory, and Bakhtin mapped out his theory of the polyphonic novel. The complementary critiques of Hegelianism voiced by these authors and the origin of their theories in Young Hegelian thought make a combination of Bakhtin's dialogue with Critical Theory seem plausible.

It may have become clear at the beginning of this chapter to what extent alterity and dialogue are inherent in Adorno's and Horkheimer's theories. In this perspective, a renewal of Critical Theory as a *meta-theory of scientific dialogue* appears as an acceptable alternative to Adorno's orientation towards artistic mimesis – which can also be justified by the postulate of non-identity. Underlying these arguments is the idea that Bakhtin's dialogue aims at the alterity of the Other, instead of pleading – with Habermas's theory of communicative action – in favour of the Other's neutralization by a normative speech act theory, which deletes subjectivity along with discourse.

The experience of alterity is the crucial feature of the three dialogical models mentioned in the introduction to *Part Three*: of theoretical comparison or confrontation, of past scientific debates which can be revived at any time, and of contemporary scientific discussions. What matters in all three cases, is the attempt to make the Other's voice heard in order to break up the cultural, ideological and theoretical *doxa* and to make experience possible along with new insights.

Chapter 12

Subjectivity, Reflection and the Construction of Objects in Discourse

This chapter is not only a continuation of the eleventh; it also resumes some of the key arguments developed in the second chapter where theory was defined as a *discourse guided by the interests of a speaking subject and based on an actantial model*. Although it seems neither possible nor meaningful to separate ideology and theory in a dualistic manner, because ideological interests manifest themselves in the lexical, semantic and narrative units of a discourse, the speaking subject can avoid ideology in the negative sense by systematic reflection.

Reflection is a critical element insofar as it reveals the contingent and ambivalent nature of ideology by defining it as an inexhaustible and indispensable source of political commitment that threatens theory with sterility. On the one hand, theory cannot come about without certain liberal, conservative or feminist value judgements which are direct or indirect reactions to social and cultural *problems* demanding to be solved; on the other hand, the subject of theory is well aware of the danger that the contingent and particular character of such value judgements may be overlooked, thus allowing ideological commitment to produce a monologue pretending to be identical with reality.

This type of identifying monologue à la Hegel was criticized by Adorno and Horkheimer, and to a lesser degree by Bakhtin. While the authors of Critical Theory emphasize the non-identity of subject and object, of discourse and reality, Bakhtin reveals the relativity of authoritarian monologue by confronting it with the polyphony of the critical, carnivalesque novel. In spite of the numerous differences, which separate the Frankfurt philosophers from the Russian critic (and are mainly to be found in their divergent attitudes towards popular culture), the critiques of identifying thought and of monologue converge in one crucial idea that remains implicit or latent in both cases: namely in the idea that the objects of cultural and social sciences are not more or less reliable descriptions of reality but *constructions*.

On this level, Bakhtin and the authors of Critical Theory agree with the radical constructivists who reject the idea of a realist discourse corresponding to the real world (cf. chap. 8). While Bakhtin's, Adorno's and Horkheimer's critiques of ideology contain an *implicit constructivism*, the constructivist theories developed by Glasersfeld and Heinz von Foerster contain an *implicit postulate of non-identity*.

Considered in an epistemological perspective, this coincidence in a crucial point is neither enigma nor chance, but due to the fact that both Critical Theory and Radical Constructivism invoke Kant in order to show that, contrary to Hegel's belief, reality as such, as a Kantian "thing in itself", is not accessible to knowledge (cf. chaps 8 and 11).

The contrast between Critical Theory and Radical Constructivism appears in conjunction with the concept of truth. A radical constructivist such as Glasersfeld replaces truth by the functional and pragmatic notion of *viability*: "Constructivism proposes to replace the concept of truth by the concept of viability – which means something like practicability or acceptability."[1] In this context, it is hardly surprising that Glasersfeld regards science as a kind of instrumental thought: "Science, after all, is purely instrumental."[2] In contrast to this instrumentalist approach, Dialogical Theory continues to adhere, like Critical Theory, to the concept of truth, because it rejects all attempts to dissociate theory from social problem solving and from the question concerning a genuinely human society.

This is why it considers social and cultural problems as dialogical problems. A theory of society and culture deals with "pre-constructed" objects, i.e. with constructions produced by individuals and groups which articulate concrete interests. It cannot react neutrally to such interests but only critically – in view of its own notion of truth.

In what follows, the concept of construction underlying Dialogical Theory will be defined in conjunction with the corresponding concept of Radical Constructivism.

1.   Non-Identity and the Construction of Objects

The semiotician Luis J. Prieto was the first to establish a link between constructivism and the critique of ideology. He turned against a "naturalist" thought that presents itself as "the natural discourse" and identifies itself spontaneously, as it were, with the real world:

The knowledge of material reality is ideological if the subject considers the limits and the identity of the object, which it treats as an equivalent of reality, as existing in the real world as such, that is, if the subject attributes to reality the *idea* which it constructed in view of reality. In this case, the subject of ideological knowledge is not conscious of this construction (. . .).[3]

In *Pertinence et pratique* (1975), Prieto proposes a more concrete, sociological concept of the subject by insisting on the fact that a subject always "belongs to a social group" ("sujet faisant partie d'un groupe social").[4]

Prieto's arguments are important because they anticipate the partial agreement between Critical Theory and Radical Constructivism without actually dealing with these currents of thought. Prieto shows that a semiotic aiming at the critique of ideology implies a constructivist (i.e. "anti-naturalist") orientation. However, this kind of semiotic seems to be more akin to Critical Theory than to Radical Constructivism, because it refuses to bracket out the collective factors inherent in individual subjectivity (cf. Glasersfeld in chap. 8, 2) and because it does not give up its critical attitude towards society.

This kind of semiotic is related to Critical Theory and Radical Constructivism by a key idea which also underlies the arguments in this chapter: by the idea that the reflecting subject of discourse is responsible for the critical and theoretical process. This idea ought to be pondered on by all those who invoke Radical Constructivism (along with sociological systems theory or Foucault's philosophy) in order to add plausibility to their belief that the notion of subject has become obsolete. However, Glasersfeld aptly remarks that the subject plays "the central role of constructor".[5] How is this role to be defined in socio-semiotic terms?

Developing the argument of the first two chapters, one might say that the individual or collective subject constructs its objects on three complementary levels: (a) on the level of a natural language (of English, German or Spanish) underlying all specialized languages in the cultural and social sciences; (b) on the level of one or several sociolects all of which are linked (as sociologies, semiotics or literary theories) to certain ideological languages; and (c) on the level of a particular discourse, that is an idiolect,[6] which can be considered as the creative realization of sociolects.

These observations indicate that the subject of theory is at the same time over-determined and free and that both Sartre's existentialism, which only recognizes freedom, and the structuralist theories, which tend to emphasize over-determination, are one-sided.[7]

The subject is over-determined because, as an individual,[8] it is born into a natural language and is socialized, i.e. turned into a subject (in the sense of Althusser) within this language. In the course of secondary socialization, its subjectivity is modelled by ideological and scientific sociolects such as Critical Rationalism or Critical Theory. It can nevertheless escape over-determination by reflecting and creatively readjusting or recomposing its cultures and languages. In this respect, it is akin to the literary subject which changes the language originally imposed on it by others.

The Russian semiotician Yuri Lotman shows to what extent *secondary modelling systems* such as religion, ideology, literature or science are derived from the *primary modelling system* of the natural language: "Secondary modelling systems: semiotic systems constructed on the basis of a natural language but having a more complex structure."[9] Two aspects of this description are important here: the constructivist aspect and the active aspect which is not related by Lotman to a creative subject but to the "secondary modelling system" as such.

Derived, but also detached from the primary system of natural language, this secondary system is in most cases the ideological, literary or scientific sociolect that is permanently being changed by those subjects who speak it, thus using it creatively. This occurs in a social and linguistic situation or problematic in which different sociolects are combined or opposed to each other by individual or collective subjects.

In this context, specific object constructions come about within the frame-work of sociolects and discourses defined as secondary modelling systems. While sociolects as group languages articulating interests decide which con-cepts and semantic oppositions are relevant, thus fixing particular relevance criteria (cf. chap. 2, 1), individual discourses are concrete applications of such collective semantics which they transform into narrative structures, bringing about modifications and innovations. Hence scientific and other constructions of objects can be said to consist of three elements: a lexical repertoire, a semantic code and a syntactic-narrative programme.

Usually, the lexical repertoire has to be decided on at the outset. In sociol-ogy, for example, repertoires of different, partly incompatible sociolects are on offer if we wish to describe and explain social evolution. If I opt for a variant of games theory, I can describe and explain certain events and developments using individual, collective or abstract actants and actors, because the subjects in question can be individuals, organizations or sys-tems. If, however, I opt, on the lexical level, for Luhmann's concept of system, I also choose the concomitant semantic opposition *system/environment* and thus describe social processes using abstract or mythical actants,[10] i.e. systems capable of doing or preventing something, etc. I opt in favour of collective or abstract actants if I decide that Alain Touraine's concept of social movement is relevant because it is defined in contrast with "state apparatus", "economic enterprise", etc.[11]

In all of these cases, ideological value judgements are at the origin of the theoretical subject's constructions. Examples from political science and modern history abound. Both the Falkland or Malvinas war between Argentina and Britain (1982) as well as the second Iraq war (2003) can be narrated and explained in relation to the semantic opposition between *democracy* and *dictatorship*. Although this opposition is not irrelevant, it is likely to yield a binary construction based on a dualistic actantial model (*hero/anti-hero*) marked by ideological naivety. Only when the complementary semantic opposition between *colonization* and *de-colonization* is superimposed, does the construction reveal the ambivalences and contradictions that invite an open discussion. This argument could also be applied to the Napoleonic Wars in which the drive towards revolutionary emancipation and imperial politics (especially after 1804) can hardly be disentangled.[12]

In all of these cases, the question arises what can safely be referred to as a *fact* – if *factum*, as Glasersfeld aptly points out, is derived from *facere* and hence refers to something we have made. Does society actually consist of systems, institutions or movements? Commenting on sociological constructivism in the sense of Latour and Woolgar, André Kukla remarks: "It is not only scientific *beliefs* that are socially constructed – it's scientific *facts*."[13]

This opinion is shared by a radical constructivist such as Ernst von Glasersfeld who observes: "Empirical facts, from the constructivist perspective, are constructs based on regularities in a subject's experience. They are viable if they maintain their usefulness and serve their purposes in the pursuit of goals."[14] Here, as in the eighth chapter, the question concerning consensus crops up. Which subject is responsible for the construction, and who defines viability, usefulness and goals? What seems viable and useful to one person may seem nonsensical or even harmful to another.

Within the context constructed here, it might be possible to call a fact whatever is recognized as such by most scientific groups and sociolects in contemporary society. At the same time, it becomes clear that in the world of science varying degrees of "reality" can be attributed to different object constructions, because the level of acceptance may strongly fluctuate. Thus physical constructions such as *atom*, *electron* or *magnetic field* enjoy a far more solid intercultural and trans-ideological acceptance than, for example, Freud's or Lacan's construction of the *unconscious* or Bourdieu's construction of the *scientific field* which has to compete with Luhmann's equally controversial notion of the *scientific system*.

Carrying this argument to extremes, one could even suggest that the constructs of physics enjoy a social status quite different from that of constructs in the cultural and social sciences. In this case, these two types of constructs would hardly be comparable. This situation is undoubtedly due to the interference of culture and ideology in the humanities (cf. chaps 1 and 2).

Nevertheless, it seems that even in the humanities the existence of universally recognizable facts, of facts independent of specific groups and sociolects, can be presupposed. Unlike a literary critic such as Stanley Fish, who denies the existence of textual facts or invariables,[15] we can safely assume that *pre-existing structures in nature* or *structures designed by authors in literature* exist and cannot be ignored.

The thesis underlying this argument is straightforward enough: in both the natural and the cultural sciences, constructions presuppose the existence of *pre-structured* entities. The fundamental difference between these two types of science consists in the fact that objects of nature come about without the interference of subjects, whereas the pre-structured objects of social sciences presuppose subjective activity.

A relatively simple example is Albert Camus's novel *The Outsider* (*L'Etranger*, 1942) which is divided up into two parts, both in the original and in its translations.[16] This pre-existing structure cannot be ignored by any reader who wishes to understand the novel – nor can this reader afford to ignore the structuring semantic opposition between *water* and *sun*, two elements symbolizing life and death in Camus's text.[17]

Similar binary structures are likely to be encountered by the political scientist who deals with parliaments consisting of two chambers: House of Commons and House of Lords, Assembly and Senate or Bundestag and Bundesrat. Even the changing number of MPs or deputies and the rules according to which they are supposed to act, can be ascertained quite independently from construction processes in scientific sociolects. They are pre-constructed, very much like the binary structure of Camus's *The Outsider*.

Hence the radical-constructivist assertion that *everything* is invented or constructed by the observer is either due to terminological negligence or to an abuse of the verb "to construct". "Our environment, as perceived by us, is our invention",[18] argues Heinz von Foerster.

This is only partly true. My salary bracket, for example, far from being my invention, is pre-constructed ... It goes without saying that the binary structures of a particular novel lend themselves to many different and even divergent interpretations, and similarly, the organizational structures of parliaments are often at stake in constitutional or scientific disputes: for both the literary text and institutional, political reality are fraught with ambiguities. However, certain fundamental structures are given and pre-exist all interpretation. Whoever argues that Camus's novel is "in reality" divided into three or four parts, has to make this new construction plausible to all those who continue to perceive a binary structure. This also applies to the political scientists who maintain — not without reason — that the British Parliament is "in reality" a one-chamber system.

In other words, not everything is constructed or "invented", and Radical Constructivism cannot do without the assumption that reality pre-exists all discourse[19] and that it is structured in a particular way: "For whoever concedes that reality exists independently of human consciousness has to answer the question, whether he can do so without at the same time presupposing that whatever exists out there is *structured* in a certain way."[20] What has been said so far, adds to the plausibility of this thesis put forward by Winfried Franzen. Our object constructions not only presuppose the existence of an independent world, they also presuppose that this world is structured in certain ways.

The radical constructivists themselves assume that structures exist in the real world whenever they refer to obstacles that can prevent the application or realization of theoretical models. The notion of *viability* introduced by Glasersfeld in order to replace the notion of *truth* seems to confirm this idea. This is the reason why Dialogical Theory combines constructivist with realist assumptions — as will be shown in the last part of this chapter.

2.   The Construction of Objects as a Self-Construction of the Subject

The subject of a theory not only constructs its objects; for by doing so, it also constructs itself. In contrast to the subjects of natural sciences who deal with organic or anorganic nature, the subjects of cultural and social sciences define themselves in a permanent dialogue with other subjects: within the framework of a "double hermeneutic" in the sense of Anthony Giddens, whose approach was commented on in the third chapter.

Long before Giddens, Mikhail Bakhtin revived some arguments of classical German hermeneutics in order to analyse the dialectical relationship between the subject and its subject-objects in the humanities:

> The entire methodological apparatus of mathematics and the natural sciences is geared towards the domination of a *thing-like object without a voice*, an object that does not reveal itself in words, *that does not say anything about itself*. (...) Unlike mathematics and the natural sciences, the humanities confront us with the task of reconstructing, reproducing and interpreting the words of others (...).[21]

This means concretely that every cultural or social science is by definition a dialogical science, because it invariably deals with the word of the Other. However, the dialogue with the latter takes place on two levels, one of which will be dealt with in this chapter, the other in the next two chapters.

The first level is the level of object constructions which come about during a dialogue with the other subject; on the second level, these object constructions are submitted to criticism and testing, in the course of which more voices of alterity make themselves heard. On this level, the subject of theory itself is exposed to analysis and criticism – along with its constructions. Such criticism is frequently reciprocated in a dialogical and polemical form: for example, in replies to reviews, etc. In what follows, the first level of object construction will be considered in the light of the subject's self-articulation and self-construction.

The fact that the construction of objects tends to coincide with the self-construction of the theoretical subject was already pointed out by Deleuze and Guattari. They evoke "conceptual characters" ("personnages conceptuels")[22] and mean, for example, Nietzsche's concept of "power", Plato's "idea", Hegel's *Aufhebung*, Marx's "class" or Heidegger's "Being". In their eyes, all of philosophy appears as a process involving the philosopher's self-creation, a process in the course of which fascinating "conceptual characters" are born: "Philosophy does not consist in knowledge; it is not truth that guides philosophy, but categories such as the interesting, the remarkable, the important decide about its success or failure."[23]

In this Nietzschean and postmodern account, philosophy is particularized and personalized to such a degree that it becomes hard to distinguish it from a novel whose author creates unique characters. However, philosophy is theoretical knowledge and often pretends to be intersubjectively and interdiscursively testable knowledge: especially if it defines itself as philosophy of science. Nevertheless, Deleuze and Guattari are not entirely wrong.

For even in the philosophy of science, in sociology and literary theory, it often appears that certain key concepts are inseparable from the discourses of particular theoretical subjects. While complementary concepts such as *community* and *society*, *mechanical* and *organic solidarity* continue to be associated with the sociological theories of Tönnies and Durkheim, the polysemic word "system" can hardly be used as long as it is not defined "in the sense of" Easton, Parsons, Luhmann or Habermas. As soon as it is related to one of these names, it takes on the meaning conferred upon it by a specific discourse and indirectly by a sociolect (e.g. by North American functionalism). In other words, it is linked to the subjectivity of an author (an idiolect) and of a group held together by a sociolect.

At the same time, subjectivity in this sense is only perceptible in a discursive form: that is as a semantic and narrative structure based on particular relevance criteria. Unlike Luhmann, who founds his individual subjectivity – and the collective subjectivity of his followers – by declaring the opposition between *system* and *environment* to be *relevant*, Habermas constructs his subjectivity and his idiolect, by taking the opposition between *systems* and *life world* as a starting point. At the same time, he founds a collective language, a sociolect.

The theoretical subject defining itself individually or collectively as anthropologist(s), sociologist(s) or literary critic(s) is therefore situated in a social and linguistic situation in which virtually all scientific concepts are claimed by particular theories-ideologies. Most of them belong to sociolects defined as secondary modelling systems articulating particular collective interests and negating others.

In this situation, the subject of theory has three possibilities: it can identify with one of the many group languages that are available in society; it can try to combine two or more such sociolects (e.g. deconstruction, psychoanalysis, feminism); finally, it can try to create its own secondary modelling system or idiolect by relying on words of the natural language that have not yet been claimed for specific purposes by individuals or groups. In many cases, all three possibilities are combined successively or in different situations.

It stands to reason, however, that the third possibility envisaged here can only be realized after intensive interaction with other, relatively unknown languages. This means that theoreticians or would-be theoreticians can only form their identity in an open dialogue with other subjects that are simultaneously their objects. Only by dealing for some time with Durkheim, Weber, Popper or Kuhn can younger philosophers or sociologists hope to develop their own discourse, to go beyond Popper by using some of Popper's arguments and to propose more or less convincing alternatives for testing theories.

At this point, a hitherto neglected aspect of theoretical subject formation comes to the fore. The subjectivities of others, the initially new and strange terminologies, become part and parcel of one's own subjectivity. This not only applies to a theory one wishes to appropriate (constructing one's "Popper" or one's "Kuhn") in order to go beyond it; it also applies to literary works, social phenomena or historical events one reconstructs in one's own discourse by using certain semantic and narrative techniques. Such objects are not incorporated "as such", as "things in themselves" (Kant) into theoretical discourse, because as subjects-objects they are dialogical constructions which contribute decisively to the formation of this discourse.

Whoever specializes in medieval literature will tend to consider all of literature in a medieval perspective. In discussions about modernity, the classical philologist is likely to point out that certain phenomena others define as modern are to be found in antiquity. Finally, the sociologist will tend to explain archaic societies by applying modern sociological categories, thereby irritating the anthropologist. All of these cases show that the discourse, in which theoretical subjectivity comes about, is also formed by "its" objects, defined here as object constructions. Going one step further, one might even argue that subjectivity comes about in such constructions.

This is probably the reason why individual scientists and groups of scientists *identify* so strongly with their object constructions. More often than not, those who interpret a novel, an ancient myth or a social phenomenon "internalize" their objects which thus become part of their subjectivity and their narcissistic investment in the self. Marx was not the only one to identify with "his" proletariat; a contemporary sociologist such as Alain Touraine makes no secret of his solidarity with the social movements he analyses without bothering to compare or contrast his analyses with those of Anthony Giddens or Ulrich Beck.[24] And it would be naive to assume that Habermas's notion of *life world* (*Lebenswelt*) and Luhmann's notion of *system* are not affectively laden. It is sufficient to read the works of these authors attentively in order to become aware of it.

Thus a partial identity of subject and object comes about, turning the object as co-subject into the subject's ally within the scientific institution or the "scientific field", as Bourdieu would put it. Long ago, Don Quixote let himself be bewitched by the romance of chivalry but he still seems to attract followers, especially among literary critics, who – like him – identify with their favourite authors, novels or movements such as romanticism or surrealism.

For theoretical dialogue this means that bilateral or multilateral discussions about particular object constructions imply an increase of dialogical complexity, since now a third (further) subjective instance joins the hermeneutic process. In this situation, it is conceivable that mutual understanding is hampered by the fact that a particular theoretical subject – be it individual or collective – identifies narcissistically with its object construction: with the "true" meaning of a poem by Browning or Mallarmé,[25] the "real" social movement, "true" feminist theory or a Polynesian tribe "discovered" by the researchers involved in the discussion. In such cases, the co-subject may very well fulfil the function of the *ego ideal* in the sense of Freudian psychoanalysis.

It is not surprising that, in this situation, criticism can provoke the Other's narcissism and block the discussion – temporarily or permanently.

Hence it seems advisable for all participants to adhere to the principles of non-identity and reflexivity. Both principles may stimulate the self-irony of the subjects involved by suggesting that it is always possible to envisage a different approach. This kind of self-irony is implicit in the concept of *construction* which excludes all kinds of spontaneous or naive identifications with the real world.

3.   The Truth Content of Constructions

The question concerning the truth content of object constructions has so far not been answered in a satisfactory manner. It cannot possibly be answered by simply referring to "viability" or "usefulness for us", because such answers immediately beg the complementary question who defines "viability" and who are "we". This is at the same time a question concerning the possibility of having theories, theorems and object constructions universally recognized − a question that can best be dealt with in an interdiscursive dialogue between groups of scientists. It will be situated at the centre of the next two chapters.

This kind of dialogue is based on the unity of opposites and presupposes *a realist and a constructivist* assumption. It will be shown, by way of conclusion, that these two assumptions complete one another, because the first helps us to avoid the Scylla of arbitrariness, while the other saves us from the Charybdis of identifying thought and monologue.

It was pointed out earlier on that the constructivism inherent in Adorno's and Horkheimer's Critical Theory excludes discursive identification with reality and monologue. Only a reflecting subject that realizes to what extent its objects are merely possible, contingent (but by no means arbitrary) constructions and not reflections of the real, is capable of renouncing monological identification and taking part in scientific dialogue.

This and the second chapter were designed to answer the question what exactly is being reflected: namely the emergence of object constructions within a particular sociolect and (more concretely) within a discourse developed by a subject. The fact that not every statement, every word can be pronounced and simultaneously reflected by a speaking subject has to be taken into account at all times. But only a theoretical subject conscious of the genetic aspects of its object constructions and of its own development within these constructions can hope to initiate a meaningful dialogue with other subjects.

It can ponder on its own cultural and ideological over-determination and that of other discourses in order to maintain the "critical distance" advocated by Norbert Elias (cf. chap. 2, 2). Without this distance between subject and object, a fruitful dialogue is hardly possible.

Only in a situation where a reflexive distance between the subject and its own lexical, semantic and narrative activity exists, is it possible to test the validity of its object constructions in critical discussions. Critical testing is severely hampered or even blocked if the subject of a theoretical discourse refuses to analyse the discursive mechanisms underlying its object constructions and the development of its own subjectivity.

Moreover, the truth content inherent in an object construction can only be empirically tested if one can assume that a reality independent of all observers *exists* and that it is *structured* in a certain way. To put it in Winfried Franzen's words: "The independence of reality's being there implies a certain independence of its being somehow structured."[26] The implicitly realistic notion of "viability" suggests that this is the case (cf. supra and chap. 8).

It is not sufficient to test truth claims concerning object constructions on an intersubjective or – as suggested here – on an interdiscursive level among groups; the test must also include facts. A fact is not only, as Franzen correctly points out, "that copper conducts electricity",[27] but also that water extinguishes fire (long before the appearance of human observers on earth), that the Third Reich was defeated in 1945 and the Soviet Union fell apart in 1991.

Naturally, such events, some of which are due to human action, can be constructed, narrated in many different ways within a multitude of conflicting discourses; but their existence cannot be denied (except by advocates of irrationalism or solipsism). As events they are not really comparable to constructions such as "the end of modernism", "the beginning of postmodernism", Arnold Gehlen's "end of history" or his notion of "post-history". Whoever treats the "end of the Soviet Union" and "the end of modernism" or the "beginning of postmodernism" as theoretically equivalent constructions, uses the key concept of constructivism improperly. Unlike "the end of the USSR", which belongs to a class of facts recognized by historians, political scientists, lawyers and laymen alike, "the beginning of postmodernism" is recognized as a fact only by some groups and not by others.

Whenever a fact such as "the end of the USSR" is considered as an event brought about by human action, i.e. as a *factum* in the sense of the past participle of *facere*, then it has to be made clear that we are dealing with a construction claiming reality status, or an "out-there-ness" character recognized by everybody, as André Kukla puts it: "For if constructions are real (and if relativism is abjured), they must have out-there-ness for everybody."[28] "The end of modernism" and "the beginning of postmodernism" cannot possibly claim this "out-there-ness", and in this respect they share the hypothetical status of Gehlen's "post-history".

Hence it seems dicey to reject globally, as Maturana does, concepts such as "falsifiability", "verifiability" or "confirmation" − merely because they refer to a "transcendental reality which is independent of what the observer does".[29] For this argument leads to the sort of relativism Kukla has in mind. This relativism admits as true whatever is considered to be true by a certain group of scientists over a certain period of time.

Such reasoning may yield the kind of circular argument put forward by Maturana who maintains "that scientific explanations and assertions are universally valid only within the community of observers who accept as a validation criterion for scientific statements the validation criterion applying to their statements".[30] The question is whether the word "universally" is not misplaced here. For whatever is only valid within a particular group can hardly claim universal validity.

This problem has been clearly outlined by Ernst von Glasersfeld whose sceptical remarks could be read as an unintended riposte to Maturana: "It is very difficult to explain that a viability which can only claim validity within one group is only a very weak viability. All things considered, it should be universally valid."[31]

This idea becomes the starting point of Dialogical Theory which would like to test truth claims of theories and their object constructions not merely *within* one scientific group but interdiscursively, i.e. *between* scientific groups and their heterogeneous discourses.

Chapter 13

Interdiscursive Dialogue: Theory

The will to bring about a dialogue between advocates of different scientific theories[1] cannot be presupposed in all cases – in analogy to the "ideal speech situation" – because dialogue takes place under real social conditions which may not only be marked by a will to understand one another but also by a refusal of otherness. One should bear in mind that a latent refusal can also prevail in a situation where all participants outwardly adhere to the dialogical principle.

This applies as much to discussions between individuals during a conference or after a lecture as to sporadically interrupted debates such as those between Russian Formalists and Marxists, between semioticians and deconstructionists or system theorists and Weberians. It also applies to the comparative analyses of theories which do belong to the dialogical realm without always being impartial or balanced. Partisanship and one-sidedness can never be entirely avoided. For the ideological factor which guarantees both engagement and motivation, also reinforces the emotional propensity to enhance the status of one's own position and to belittle the arguments of others.

At this stage, critics of the dialogical approach could object that most theoretical discussions are bound to break down as soon as the narcissistic propensities of the participants begin to surface. Fortunately, such critics are only partly right, because in most cases counter-tendencies such as scientific curiosity can also be observed. Theoretical dialogue thus appears as an ambivalent project oscillating between egocentrism and alterity, and it is irreducible to one of these two poles.

The fact that ego always presupposes the existence of alter, because subjectivity cannot come about without the involvement of others, has already been mentioned in the introduction to *Part Three*. If, however, alterity is indispensable to the development of one's own theoretical subjectivity, then it seems plausible to regard theoretical curiosity, which can be observed in most scientific institutions, as one of the prerequisites and starting points of dialogue. For most scientists realize that without this kind of curiosity they are in danger of abdicating as scientists. The fact that curiosity is frequently accompanied by distrust and ideological rejection is well known and is part and parcel of the ambivalent structure of dialogue, the ambivalence of which may frequently be of a psychoanalytic nature.[2]

Whoever takes this structure into account will not be content to envisage, like David Bohm, a dialogue inspired by pure altruism:

> In a dialogue, however, nobody is trying to win. Everybody wins if anybody wins. There is a different sort of spirit to it. In a dialogue, there is no attempt to gain points, or to make your particular view prevail. Rather, whenever any mistake is discovered on the part of anybody, everybody gains.[3]

One can hardly object to the last sentence. For it is conceivable that truth prevails in dialogue as it prevails or is supposed to prevail in Bourdieu's *field* or Luhmann's *scientific system*. But why should participants abstain from trying to win? Only in a situation pervaded by a spirit of playful competition is there a guarantee that dialogue will not degenerate into polite conversation. The spirit of competition underlying all games is not unfavourable to scientific dialogue.

Among heterogeneous groups and their languages, this kind of spirit tends to prevail as a result of social and ideological conflict.[4] This is one of the main reasons why it seems necessary to reflect the socio-semiotic conditions and the institutionalized rules underlying dialogue. Without such rules, which include a careful reconstruction of the adversary's theoretical position, every discussion is bound to lapse into empty rhetoric or polemic.

Some of Ernst von Glasersfeld's remarks concerning "viability" were quoted towards the end of the previous chapter. They show to what extent communication between different groups is necessary if we aim at the formulation of universally acceptable statements. A "viability" recognized by just one group is indeed a "very weak viability", as Glasersfeld points out. If it is to be strengthened, one has to go beyond the limits and horizons of one's own group. And this is precisely the task of an intercollective or interdiscursive dialogue.

1.   Interdiscursive Communication: Some Prerequisites

A dialogue is doomed to failure if, following Alexy and Habermas (cf. chap. 10), we demand that "different speakers may not use the same expression with different meanings".[5] For it is perfectly conceivable that even within the discourse of one and the same speaker the meaning of a particular expression undergoes certain changes. One need not be a deconstructionist in order to discover semantic shifts in the works of Habermas.[6] It is even more likely therefore that a concept or expression takes on more or less divergent meanings in the course of a discussion involving heterogeneous viewpoints.

Commenting on dialogue in a very general sense, David Bohm quite rightly observes: "In such a dialogue, when one person says something, the other person does not in general respond with exactly the same meaning as that seen by the first person. Rather, the meanings are only *similar* and not identical."[7] It might even be suggested that in such cases it is impossible to safeguard the semantic identity of a word, because the communication situation of the participants is in a permanent flux: not only for pragmatic reasons (people get to know each other, groups and coalitions are formed, etc.), but also on the semantic level.

Every kind of talk, even soliloquy, tends to have a cumulative semantic effect insofar as the concepts in use mean something different at the end of the day from what they meant at the outset. By constantly revising the relevant definitions, the author of a text can see to it that this semantic change is limited to an inevitable minimum. However, in discussions comprising several participants, and especially in debates that go on for years, semantic shifts are often inevitable. As was shown in the fifth chapter, the protracted discussions concerning the concept of *paradigm*, which seems to have acquired as many as twenty-one meanings in Kuhn's famous book, have led to a complete "desemantization" of this word.

It should be added that an a priori fixed semantic identity of a concept or an expression may not even be desirable in scientific dialogues which often aim at a redefinition of concepts (considered too vague) or at an interdisciplinary extension of their meaning (cf. sec. 3).

In view of these considerations, one might be tempted to regard theoretical dialogue with increasing scepticism. Did the first chapter not reveal that theories are both culturally and linguistically over-determined and that a theory often owes its specific character to a culture and a natural language? Moreover, are theories not collective languages articulating specific collective interests in a given social and linguistic situation? One might add that in such a situation every scientist starts from one or several such group languages in order to specify and change them within a concrete idiolect. Thus every new individual discourse contributes – as an idiolect – to the transformation of the linguistic situation as a whole.

Although Lakatos speaks the language of Critical Rationalism, he develops a discourse that differs in many respects from Popper's or Hans Albert's. Habermas's discourse is not identical with Adorno's or Horkheimer's.

A meaningful dialogue can only take place if all participants are conscious of these factors and aware of the impact of ideologies on all discourses involved in a discussion. The question is: Which ideologies as systems of values underlie these discourses and how do they manifest themselves?

Apart from the lexical and semantic levels, it seems important to take into account another two levels of discourse: the *level of enunciation* dominated by the speaking subject (*sujet d'énonciation*, Greimas) and the *narrative level* (*énoncé*, Greimas) based on the actants of a discourse. Both levels are dependent on discourse semantics.

On the enunciation level, it soon becomes clear whether the subject of a discourse is able to reflect self-critically upon its ideological value judgements and to present its objects as object constructions or whether it identifies monologically with the real world, thus obliterating the construction process. In this case, the interlocutor's only option seems to be a constructivist critique of ideology (as critique of discourse) which may or may not promote critical self-reflection and dialogue. (Cf. chaps 2 and 12.)

On the narrative level, the actantial models and modalities of the discourses involved are at stake. They have to be considered if we want to decide whether discourses are structurally comparable or not. If, in the course of the "Positivism Controversy" (between Adorno, Horkheimer, Popper, Hans Albert, *et al.*), somebody had raised the question concerning the actantial models of Critical Theory and Critical Rationalism, certain aspects of the controversy would have come to light which remained in the dark till the very end: among other things the fact that the discourses of both groups are attempts to describe and explain social development and theory formation in relation to individual actants. On this level, it might have been possible to agree on the idea that the autonomous individual is responsible for social and theoretical criticism. At the same time, it would have appeared that in Critical Rationalism this individual is regarded as a representative of liberalism, whereas in Critical Theory he is taken to be the representative of a disintegrated collective actant: the revolutionary proletariat. This fact has far-reaching consequences for the divergent social theories of the two groups, which rely on different modalities. While Critical Theory *wants* an overcoming of capitalism, Critical Rationalism *rejects* the very idea of overcoming and asks instead how capitalism can be adapted and improved (in the sense of Popper's "piecemeal engineering").

The question concerning actantial models is also relevant for the communication between fundamentally heterogeneous types of discourse. For it is hardly meaningful to relate Freud's psychoanalysis and Marxism, Weber's sociology and Luhmann's theory of social systems to one another without considering the actantial models and the modalities of these theories, all of which came about in different social and linguistic situations (cf. chaps 1–2).

While Freud's discourse subdivides individual actants such as *mother, father, child* into infra-individual actants called *ego, id, super-ego*, Marxism focuses on supra-individual, collective actants or classes. Any discussion between these two types of theory would have to take into account differences on the actantial level and corresponding differences on the level of modalities. For the modalities of *will, knowledge* and *ability* (*vouloir, savoir* and *pouvoir* in the sense of Greimas) relevant to the psychoanalytic theory complex might be partly or entirely missing in the Marxist complex and vice versa. Thus Freudian psychoanalysis primarily *wants* to explain individual and not collective action – unlike Marxism and C. G. Jung's psychoanalysis. Such differences are frequently glossed over by "post-structuralist" analogies constructed by authors such as Ernesto Laclau who believes that in Marxism and Freudian psychoanalysis all revolves around "the logic of the signifier as a logic of unevenness and dislocation".[8]

Unlike Critical Rationalism and Critical Theory which are similar on the actantial level (cf. supra), Weber's individualistic sociology and Luhmann's systems theory turn out to be extremely heterogeneous from a semiotic or actantial point of view. Moreover, they set out to solve completely different problems on the level of modalities. Although he does not use the semiotic concept of *actant*, Rainer Greshoff is well aware of the discursive and narrative differences between Weber and Luhmann, when he remarks: "Luhmann continues to associate an action-oriented theoretical foundation of sociology with the problematic idea of subject-relatedness or, more precisely, 'subject-burdening'."[9] He realizes that Luhmann's actantial model is not Weber's: "Luhmann, on the other hand, keeps using 'compact expressions' such as 'the communication/the system does something/produces something'."[10]

It may have become clear at this stage how useful Tesnière's and Greimas's concept of *actant* can be. For it enables us to map out a discourse typology which distinguishes different types of actants: individual, infra-individual, collective, abstract, mythical, etc. From this point of view, theoretical discourses appear both as constructions of reality and narrative structures based on similar, complementary or incompatible actantial models. In both psychoanalysis and systems theory, there is a real danger that infra-individual (*ego, id, super-ego*) or abstract actants (*systems*) are turned into mythical instances whose intentions and actions – *narrative programmes* in the sense of Greimas[11] – cannot be traced empirically.

However, in order to become aware of this danger, it is necessary to reconstruct theoretical discourse as an actantial model and a narrative structure based on this model. This kind of reconstruction presupposes the complementary reconstruction of the sociolect(s) in which discourses and actantial models originate. In the case of Freud and Weber, a liberal and individualistic group language can be held responsible for the individualism of the actantial models. It is also to be found at the origin of the actantial structure of Critical Rationalism – as was shown in the sixth chapter. Unlike these three theories, Luhmann's discourse is anchored in a completely different sociolect: in the language of postmodern managers who have replaced the liberal principles of individual autonomy, courage and competition by a "management of innovation"[12] based on the complementary principles of teamwork, communication and cooperation.

Luhmann himself seems to confirm this hypothesis. While the author of *Social Systems* considers "competition" as a concept "of the 18th and 19th century",[13] the author of *Die Wirtschaft der Gesellschaft* (*The Economy of Society*) points out "that competition cannot be a system, because for intrinsic reasons it cannot be translated into directives for communication and cannot be implemented by interaction".[14] In Luhmann's discourse, "competition" as a liberal concept is thus replaced by the post-liberal notion of "communication". Now it is one of the salient features of post-liberal and postmodern management as described by Burns and Stalker that it tends to replace competition and individual responsibility (i.e. a vertical or hierarchical system) by teamwork and communication. Luhmann's approach can be fully grasped only if the actantial model underlying his discourse is related to this relatively new group language which emerged after the Second World War.

The discourses, actantial models and sociolects mentioned here are so heterogeneous[15] that communication between them seems well-nigh impossible. Even if one is prepared to renounce synonymy in the strict sense, it becomes difficult to compare "critique" in the sense of Critical Theory with "critique" in the sense of Critical Rationalism. A similar argument applies to Habermas's concepts of "system" and "communication" and the (apparently) analogous concepts in Luhmann's systems theory. As was shown earlier on, the semantic opposition between *systems* and *life world* and the semantic opposition between *system* and *environment* yield two completely different discourses based on very different actantial models. The lexical repertoires and the semantics of the discourses underlying the actantial models are quite heterogeneous. Hence the question arises at this point whether these discourses and their sociolects can at all be related to one another and if so, how.

This question can now be answered in conjunction with the previous chapter and with Yuri Lotman's semiotics of culture. As *secondary modelling systems*, discourses and sociolects are embedded in the *primary modelling system* of natural language and can always be related to this primary system and explained with its help in the course of a dialogue.

The problem that crops up here could be viewed ironically as a paradox. The secondary systems (sociolects and discourses) which have laboriously been detached from natural language in order to obtain a clear and unambiguous terminology that is no longer hampered by the ambiguities of everyday language, are to be translated back into natural language. The paradox is only apparent, however: first of all, because the secondary systems are *not to be dissolved but explicated* in natural language (most scientific dictionaries illustrate this process by circumscribing technical terms); secondly, because the secondary systems have come about within the primary system and hence can be derived from it.

This symbiotic relationship between theoretical languages as secondary systems and natural languages as primary systems is clarified as soon as one becomes aware of the ideological inferences in Critical Rationalism and in Luhmann's systems theory. While Critical Rationalism shows traces of a liberal and individualistic sociolect, systems theory can also be understood as a reaction to precisely this sociolect which it criticizes in the name of a post-individualistic management of innovation and a postmodern economy. As ideologies, however, both sociolects belong to everyday language which they have considerably changed. Hence they cannot be separated from it.

Although he uses a different vocabulary, Gadamer refers to this dialectic of primary and secondary languages when he points out: "The 'language games' of science remain related to the mother tongue as meta-language."[16] This sentence shows, on the one hand, that the terminology of semiotics is more precise, because the expression "secondary modelling system" reveals *how* scientific theory is related to the natural language as "mother tongue", i.e. genetically; on the other hand, it shows that every now and again striking similarities between heterogeneous discourses (in this case between semiotics and hermeneutics) can be observed, similarities which will be commented on in more detail in the last section of this chapter.

2.   Reconstruction, Translation, Critique

Critique is mentioned here in the last instance, because it is hardly meaningful to criticize a theory without investigating its social and linguistic contexts. Maturana quite rightly remarks: "A discussion is only possible, if one is prepared to accept the hermeneutic background of another person."[17]

For this reason, some factors were analysed in the previous section which are part of this background: the ideology (in a general sense), the sociolect which yields a particular theoretical discourse and the actantial model of the latter. In what follows, the actual aims of dialogue are at stake: the reconstruction of the Other's discourse, its translation and its critique.

With respect to communication between different discourses, "reconstruction" gives rise to additional questions which were not dealt with in the previous section. Who reconstructs and in what language does he translate the discourse of the Other? The question as such suggests that the processes of reconstruction and translation can hardly be kept apart. For as soon as we embark on a reconstruction, we simultaneously translate the Other's discourse into our language or a language with which we are familiar.

In this context, one can distinguish two kinds of reconstruction as translation: the translation into natural language as primary modelling system and the translation into one's own discourse. Both kinds of translation can further the comprehension and assimilation of the Other's discourse.

The first kind of reconstruction predominates in scientific dictionaries and encyclopedias. The concept of "actant" is thus defined by Greimas and Courtés as follows (only the first sentence of the article is quoted here): "The actant can be identified with the instance which commits or suffers the act, apart from all other determinants."[18] Serving as a summary definition, this sentence has a colloquial character, because it does not contain any technical terms belonging to structural semiotics. This also applies to the partial definition of "repression" in Laplanche's and Pontalis's dictionary of psychoanalysis: "Literally: operation in the course of which the subject attempts to push back certain fantasies (ideas, images, memories) towards the unconscious or to keep them there."[19] Apart from the word "subject" which can be treated as a technical term in the psychoanalytic sense, this passage too contains no technical jargon and is purely colloquial in character.

These considerations not only illustrate the possibility of reconstruction as translation into colloquial or natural language, but can also serve to enhance the plausibility of an argument put forward at the end of the last section: namely that colloquial reconstructions of theoretical discourses are possible – at least in principle and in spite of the difficulties that may crop up at any moment. From the point of view of theoretical dialogue, this is not unimportant, because this kind of dialogue depends on the possibility of explaining (not reducing) the secondary systems within the framework of the primary system of a natural language.

The second possibility of reconstruction is the partial or global translation of the Other's discourse into one's own. It is obvious that in this case omissions, simplifications and distortions are always possible and may irritate our interlocutors who feel misunderstood and misrepresented. For each theoretical discourse as secondary modelling system consists of a certain vocabulary, a particular semantic and actantial model which by definition cannot be assimilated to other models. If it could be assimilated or reduced to these models (in the sense of Stegmüller), it would become irrelevant.

Hence it should become a rule of theoretical dialogue to reconstruct the Other's discourse in such a way as to ensure that our interlocutor can agree with the reconstruction and – in the optimal case – can confirm it phase by phase. Habermas remarks on this subject: "It is always irritating for an author to find that relatively subtle ideas are not just dealt with selectively and tendentiously distorted by a political and even scientific public, but often enough turned into the very opposite of what they originally meant."[20] If, for argument's sake, one disregards malice or lack of competence, the structural problem remains that a reconstruction of the Other's theory in one's own discourse may entail not only distortions and simplifications but also a *tort* or injustice in the sense of Lyotard (cf. chap. 6).

In *Part Two* of this book, several theories were reconstructed within a socio-semiotic context, i.e. as semantic and narrative structures based on actantial models. Even such an approach may lead to distortions, especially in a case where a theory like Habermas's hermeneutic of communication ignores the idea of discourse as narrative structure and is reluctant to admit (for whatever reason) semiotic terminologies.

Distortions may occur whenever attempts are made to reconstruct hermeneutic or dialectical theories such as Freud's psychoanalysis or Marx's political economy in a logical and mathematical set-up and to translate them into the language of formal logic. More often than not, their modalities – *willingness* (*vouloir*) and *capability* (*pouvoir*) – are disregarded in such cases. Are such theories really *meant* to be translated into the languages of logic and mathematics? Are they at all *able* to bring about this kind of translation?

When Wolfgang Stegmüller, for example, sets out to reconstruct psychoanalysis within the framework of his mathematical structuralism (cf. *Introduction*), the question arises whether a structural and mathematical model does not actually *replace* a psychoanalysis founded originally on hermeneutic premises. Stegmüller remarks in this context: "If, in addition to this, the terminology in question offered the possibility to reconstruct theories, whose scientific character has hitherto been in doubt, the structuralist approach would have passed another test."[21] At this point, one might ask, however, which of the two theories is about to be tested: psychoanalysis within the framework of mathematic structuralism or vice versa.

It is quite amazing, however, that in Stegmüller's case Freudian theory is by no means discredited in a logical and mathematical context. On the contrary, Stegmüller concludes his argument by defending the scientific status of psychoanalysis: "Even the simplifying sketch presented here is sufficient to cast doubts on the accusation according to which Freud's theory is a pseudo-scientific project."[22] Psychoanalysts who present their approach as an exact and empirical science,[23] will certainly welcome this diagnosis. The fact, however, that Stegmüller does not consider repression as one of the key concepts of psychoanalysis[24] and at the same time disregards Freud's actantial model (*ego-id-superego*) is bound to arouse the suspicion of insiders. Does Stegmüller's confrontation with the Other not end in a reduction?

This question might also be asked by Marxists or readers of Marx when they are confronted with Stegmüller's attempt to "base the reconstruction of Marx's theory of capital and value 'on the assumption that we are dealing with the work of an economist' ".[25] This attempt yields a scientistic interpretation and brings about a rapprochement between the social scientist Marx and the physicist Newton,[26] a rapprochement reminiscent of Althusser's anti-humanist reading of Marx's work: "We could thus disregard the *practical* and *religious* components which must be detached from all these theoretical aspects, namely Marx's *humanism*."[27] This means, however, that the *object-actant* of Marx's discourse is eliminated: his idea of a classless society. At the same time, its *underlying modality* disappears: the radical critique of capitalism aiming beyond the existing social order.

Nevertheless, Stegmüller's reconstructions do illustrate the importance of dialogues between heterogeneous discourses and their sociolects. Moreover, they show that the Other's discourse (e.g. Freud's psychoanalysis) need not always be negated or belittled; it can also be confirmed or reinstated *in a completely new context*. In this perspective, the "interdiscursive theorems" will be considered here in the last section: *theorems emerging between heterogeneous collective languages*.

However, the primary task of an interdiscursive dialogue is not to have one's own hypotheses confirmed by others, but to have them tested in an open discussion. This is why contrasting positions were related to one another in *Part Two*.

The dialogue between them is a permanent dialectic between agreement and disagreement, coincidence and divergence, translatability and intranslatability.[28] This dialectic was reconstructed by Paul Lorenzen in quite a different context. He imagines three possible situations: in the first situation, certain lexical and semantic units of the Other's sociolect (Lorenzen uses the word *ortho-languages* or *Orthosprachen*) can be translated into one's own language, and a reconstruction in one's own discourse is possible. In the second situation, we may find that the Other's language "contains certain concepts (i.e. conceptual distinctions) we have not yet come across in our own systematic reflection".[29] In this particular case, a translation is not possible, but it is possible to expand and qualify our discourse on a semantic and lexical level.

A case in point is the present attempt to expand Critical Theory in order to make it encompass the concept of "construction" introduced by Radical Constructivism, but also deducible from a basic tenet of Critical Theory: from the postulate of non-identity. It becomes clear at this stage how a theory can be expanded by dialogical means and how it can be made to explore new terrain.

The third situation described by Paul Lorenzen is probably the most interesting one:

> (...) The attempt to translate into one's own ortho-language or to expand the latter in order to make it encompass concepts of [the Other's] text [may] yield contradictions. In this case, it is necessary to test systematically one's own thought and the results submitted by the [other] author.[30]

This is a concise presentation of what was practised here, especially in *Part Two*: a systematic correlation of opposites that leads to critical and self-critical testing.

The dialogue with Critical Rationalism and Radical Constructivism did not lead to a "falsification" of Critical Theory (nor were psychoanalysis and Marxism "falsified" in Stegmüller's scheme), but to an *Erschütterung* in the sense of Neurath. At the end of the dialogical process, it seemed reasonable to redefine negativity in the sense of non-identity and to integrate the latter into a constructivist theory of dialogue.

This kind of critical "shake-up" is undergone by all theoretical positions as soon as they are related to their counter-positions, their opposites (in a comparison or in a discussion). Advocates of each theory are thus compelled to adopt the Other's perspective and to reconsider their ideas in this perspective. In this light, the confrontation between Popper and Lyotard shows that the critical rationalist fails to solve certain problems, because he ignores the particular, while the postmodernist turns it into an absolute and thus refutes the implicitly universalist claims of his own theory. Bringing together the contrasting discourses of Lukács and Glasersfeld reveals that Lukács can only substantiate his claims by invoking a mythical actant (the proletariat), while Glasersfeld's postulate of a universal "viability" presupposes the existence of this or a similar actant. Finally, the fictive dialogue between

Bourdieu and Luhmann reveals to what extent "field" and "system" are exposed to heteronomous forces whose presence casts doubts on the autonomy of both. At the same time, this dialogue makes us wonder whether scientific truth is not after all produced anonymously in a "system" or a "field" and whether the concept of subject used here does not actually obliterate this fact.

What matters then, are direct or indirect confrontations between heterogeneous scientific languages which make all participants consider their discourses and constructions "from the outside" as it were, i.e. with the eyes of the Other. This kind of "estrangement" of one's own language can hardly be regarded as a "falsification" in the sense of Popper; but it certainly can reveal weak spots in all the theories involved.

Coming close to what Neurath calls *Erschütterung*, it seems to be a meaningful alternative to "falsification" which usually comes about in a particular group language and loses its validity in other scientific languages which continue to use the "falsified" theory.[31] In such cases, ideological factors and value judgements play an important part – for they cannot be refuted (as Max Weber knew). Although it does not adopt the principle of falsification, because the latter is hardly applicable in the cultural and social sciences, Dialogical Theory continues to uphold the *negative principle* introduced into the philosophy of science by Popper and Bachelard.[32] For confronting the Other's discourse implies a permanent questioning of one's own position.

Dialogical thought thus appears as a thinking against oneself that is motivated by the presence of the Other. In the following section and in the next chapter, it will be shown that, apart from yielding criticism and doubt, this kind of thought also yields moments of truth which are worth keeping in mind.[33]

3.   Interdiscursive Theorems

The idea situated at the centre of this final section can be summed up in a few words. Theorems which come about between heterogeneous group languages acquire a more general status than theorems accepted exclusively within a particular group of scientists. Once again, we are dealing here with Glasersfeld's postulate that "viability" ought to stretch beyond the boundaries of a collective language.

In a first step, the key constructivist theorem will be considered according to which our theories do not depict reality mimetically, but construct it. This theorem is not only prominent in various brands of constructivism, but – as was shown earlier on – also in Adorno's and Horkheimer's Critical Theory and in Luis J. Prieto's semiotics. It could be summed up as follows: "Reality as a scientific object is invariably a construct of the theoretician."

Naturally, this theorem assumes different meanings within Radical Constructivism (the other constructivisms), Critical Theory and Prieto's semiotics. Therefore a strict synonymy cannot be taken for granted. But in all of these cases, it can be interpreted as a rejection of Hegel's tacit identification of discourse and reality. In Critical Theory and Prieto's semiotics, the theorem in question is however related to ideological and collective factors which crucially contribute to the construction of an object. A radical constructivist and individualist such as Glasersfeld might not recognize the relevance of these factors. Following Maturana and Varela, he might prefer to discuss neurobiological processes instead.

But this is precisely the meaning of an interdiscursive dialogue: to introduce the sentence "Reality as a scientific object is always a construct of the theoretician" into many different discourses and sociolects in order to make it *signify* there, thus enlarging its scope of application. A perfect synonymy or semantic congruence would condemn theoretical dialogue to sterility. This kind of dialogue is set in motion by a limited, controlled polysemy: by an "equivalence in difference",[34] as Roman Jakobson puts it in an article on the linguistics of translation. Thus the main purpose of an interdisciplinary conference dealing with this sentence or theorem could be its concretization in different scientific contexts: in philosophy, semiotics, sociology and biology.

The dissensions that invariably crop up on such occasions are not a handicap. On the contrary, they guarantee the heterogeneity of the viewpoints and the open character of the dialogue. Moreover, they guarantee that, once reached, a temporary consensus is not transformed into a doxa – like many a consensus *within* a scientific sociolect. In an interdiscursive or intercollective dialogue, consensus and dissent are in a dynamic equilibrium, and the always looming dissent virtually excludes the danger of complacent dogmatization within a particular ideology.

Another interdiscursive theorem, one that runs counter to the intentions of this book, could be formulated as follows: "Scientific truth is neither subjective nor intersubjective, but the product of anonymous mechanisms which prevail in the system (Luhmann), the field (Bourdieu) or the scientific process (Althusser)."

One can hardly doubt the ideological and theoretical heterogeneity of the three approaches in question. The contrast between Luhmann's and Bourdieu's sociology was commented on in detail in the ninth chapter; moreover, it is well known that Luhmann adopts a critical stance towards Marxism

and that Bourdieu rejects the Althusserian brand of historical materialism.[35] Hence the theorem has an interdiscursive character and ought to be
taken seriously.

Nevertheless, it cannot claim universal validity – very much like the constructivist theorem. One objection is obvious: Luhmann as well as Bourdieu
and Althusser regard the world of natural science as their model, a world
where ideological and subjective factors hardly have an impact (as was
shown in chapter 3). In the natural sciences, no ideological interference
can be observed on a lexical or semantic level. Advocates of this theorem
would have to show that similar conditions obtain in the cultural and
social sciences. This might prove to be a difficult task, because in these
sciences the "collective subjects"[36] referred to by Bourdieu also act as ideological instances.

The preliminary conclusion could be that this particular interdiscursive
theorem can claim validity in the natural sciences, but is inapplicable to the
humanities. However, one should avoid jumping to conclusions, just
because one feels encouraged by two or three arguments. For processes in
the cultural and social sciences might turn out to be more anonymous than
is generally assumed. Therefore it would make sense to continue testing this
theorem even in the human sciences and to continue arguing against oneself
according to Robert Musil's self-ironical precepts: "Let us discuss things
with ourselves, Mr. Musil. So you seem to have days when you dislike
artists?"[37] There may very well be days when one feels a sudden dislike for
theoreticians and tends to consider the entire theoretical undertaking with a
certain distrust.

Chapter 14

Interdiscursive Dialogue: Practice

The question concerning the possibilities and the scope of theoretical dialogue, which the previous chapter focused on, is followed by the question: "what for?" The latter should not be regarded as a concession to contemporary utilitarianism, but as an attempt to define dialogue in more concrete terms: by showing – among other things – that it can yield new questions and concepts which allow for a more precise and a multidimensional construction of objects.

Initially, two debates will be focused on, one of which has an historical character, while the other has not yet come to an end. In the second part of this chapter, the second debate will be supplemented and completed by a comparison of theories. The aim underlying this approach is not a detailed presentation of the debates, but an elucidation of the central problems, a definition of the contrasting viewpoints and an evaluation of the theoretical confrontation in view of scientific practice.

While the Formalism-Marxism debate, which will be commented on in the first part, deals primarily with the theory of art and literature, the controversies between Derrida and Anglo-American speech act theory are relevant to virtually all cultural and social sciences, because they focus on the role of *repetition* in discourse, i.e. on its importance for the monosemy or polysemy of concepts and statements. The somewhat polemical discussions between Derrida and John R. Searle are supplemented (in the last part of the chapter) by a comparison of Derrida's deconstruction and Algirdas J. Greimas's structural semiotics. This comparison focuses on two key concepts which are related both dialectically and dialogically: *iterativity* and *iterability*.

Although the word "practice" means primarily the applicability of such concepts in scientific texts and in future debates, it also refers to the organization of current theoretical discussions. Like the controversies around Critical Rationalism, which will once more be commented on towards the end of the chapter, such discussions are hampered by misunderstandings, distortions and polemics.

This is why the fundamental question of chapter 13 concerning the reconstruction of theories and theorems is important. For without a context-oriented reconstruction our partner can understand and agree with, a rational dialogue is inconceivable.

Naturally, theoretical discussions are also hampered by ideological interference that can hardly be avoided in the cultural and social sciences whose evolution would stagnate without the ideological impulse. Expressions such as "ecological conception of language",[1] "feminist sociology or linguistics" or "Marxist theory of literature" bear witness to this institutionalized state of affairs. The ambivalence of ideology comes to the fore whenever ideological engagement blocks the theoretical process of communication. The debates between Russian formalists and Marxists, which took place mainly in the 1920s, illustrate some aspects of this problem.

1.   Formalism and Marxism: The "How" and the "Why"

The *formal method* (*formalnyj metod*), as the formalists called their approach, before controversies, polemics and misunderstandings broke out, was conceived as a critical response to a social and linguistic situation dominated by the discourses of metaphysical symbolism and a biographical positivism focusing on historical facts and causal links.

In their controversies with the symbolists, the formalists could rely on their avant-garde allies, the futurists: "The common element linking the futurists and the scientists of poetic language was, apart from the general (...) consensus, their enemy: the symbolists."[2] More strongly than their French counterparts (Leconte de Lisle, Verlaine, Moréas), the Russian symbolists emphasized the search for the unknown, the mysterious. To this metaphysical search the formalists and the futurists opposed a "material" aesthetic of innovation and estrangement. Unlike the symbolists and the positivists, they did not search for hidden essences behind the ambiguities of the literary text, but aimed at a liberation of poetic discourse from the stereotypes of everyday language, from religious and ideological clichés. This liberation could only be envisaged within the framework of an aesthetic based on the notion of artistic autonomy and impervious to all positivist attempts to deduce art from the artist's biography or to treat literature as an historical document.

The formal method could thus be reconstructed within the context of a socio-linguistic problematic marked (among other things) by the polemical interaction of the sociolects of futurism, symbolism, positivism and Marxism. Considering the fact that the formalists opposed both the metaphysical interpretations of the symbolists and the biographical reductionism of the positivists, it is not altogether surprising that they opted (at least partly) in favour of Kant's aesthetic of autonomy: i.e. in favour of an aesthetic based on the idea that the beautiful (art) pleases the senses without being translatable into conceptual language. Like Kant, the authors of the formal method believe that the beautiful pleases "without a concept", and they add that the goal of art is not to express ideas but to bring about a "new perception" of the world: "The purpose of the image is not to improve our understanding of its meaning, but to induce a special perception of the object, so that the latter is 'seen' and not 'recognized'."[3] What matters then, is the liberation of the percipient's imagination from the bonds of everyday communication. Ewa Thompson explains: "Kant's concept might not have been familiar to Shklovsky in its original version; the latter argues, however, along Kantian lines."[4]

The orientation of the formal method towards Kant's theorem "without a concept" ("ohne Begriff") puts the question concerning the formal nature of art at the centre of formalist aesthetics. Some of the well-known formalist titles which emphasize the *how* refer indirectly to this question: "How Gogol's Coat is Made" (B. Eikhenbaum), "How the Don Quixote is Made" (V. Shklovsky).

The fact that this kind of question is somewhat one-sided, because it tends to leave out historical and social factors, is revealed by Shklovky's famous statement: "*A new form does not appear in order to express a new content but in order to replace an old form which has lost its characteristic of an artistic form.*"[5]

What is needed for the reconstruction of the formalist model – apart from the literary and aesthetic components – is also an inquiry into the social and ideological context. As theoreticians who intuitively take Kant's work as their starting point by insisting on the *non-conceptual character of art* and by adopting the perspective of an *idealized observer* (the "new perception"), the formalists place their arguments within an individualist actantial model which corresponds in some respects to the models of Critical Rationalism and Radical Constructivism. All of these discursive models eliminate collective factors.

In the post-revolutionary linguistic situation of the 1920s, the formalist model thus provokes Russian Marxists such as Lev Trotsky and Anatolij Lunacharsky, who derive their arguments from a collectivist actantial model and a strongly simplified Hegelian aesthetic. Instead of adopting the Kantian viewpoint of the individual *observer* or *reader*, they focus, like Hegel and Marx, on the *historical producer* who adopts a stance within the ongoing historical process or the class struggle. On the one hand, they follow Hegel by admitting that art does not primarily address our conceptual faculties but our senses, on the other hand, they also negate, like Hegel, Kant's principle according to which the beautiful (art) pleases "without concept". In the last resort, art appears to them as *translatable* into conceptual thought, as a politically definable phenomenon.

The debates of the 1920s are marked by the conspicuous absence of a systematic *reflection on the aesthetic models* and the *discursive particularities* of the theories involved. No "reconstruction" in the above sense took place. In their critiques of formalism, the Marxists tacitly started from Hegelian premises without bothering to analyse the Kantian and avant-garde premises of the formalists – which are partly contradictory.[6] Most of their arguments are based on Hegel's definition of art as "sensual appearance of the Idea".

Thus Bukharin remarks: "For art, the emotional character of the material is crucial."[7] And Lunacharsky specifies this essentially Hegelian idea when he points out in one of his critical commentaries (1924): "What does the idea in art have to look like, if it is to belong to the ideological realm without being abstract thought? It is obvious that it has to take on the form of an emotion."[8] It is also obvious that this type of question is out of touch with formalism, because Lunacharsky tries to mediate between thoughts and emotions without taking into account the "how" of the works, the problem of artistic or literary techniques. Eikhenbaum, however, stresses this "how" and defines the formalists as "specifyiers": "We are not 'formalists', but 'specifyiers', if you like."[9] In other words, the "how" of the formal method seeks to shed light on the specific character of art and of the individual work: on all those salient aesthetic features which the Marxist and Hegelian focus on the "content" and the "why" leaves in the dark.

The fact is that this "why" dominated the aesthetics of Russian Marxism between the world wars and that it not only underlies Bukharin's arguments, but also those of Trotsky who asserts that only Marxism can *explain* why a certain artistic movement developed in a given historical period.[10] It is precisely this – by no means trivial – "genetic" question that Boris Eikhenbaum explicitly excludes: "The question concerning the genesis of literary phenomena (their links to facts of the social environment and the economy, to the individual psychology or physiology of the author, etc. without end) is explicitly rejected (...)."[11]

This rejection did not exactly further theoretical communication between formalists and Marxists whose dialogue was burdened by ideological rhetoric and the repressive policies of the Marxists-Leninists. In these circumstances, a *reconstruction* of the aesthetic, ideological and linguistic premises of the two groups was hardly possible. Considering all these factors, it is legitimate to ask what meaning a failed dialogue of this kind can possibly have for a better understanding of art.

The answer can be reasonably concise. The collision of two ideologically heterogeneous positions raises two apparently incompatible, but in reality complementary questions: the "how" and the "why".

This is why the confrontation between formalists and Marxists eventually turned out to be so fruitful in retrospect, especially since various contemporaries of the formalists had already attempted to relate these two key questions to one another. Thus Pavel Medvedev places the twofold question concerning the "how" and the "why" at the centre of his book about the "formal method". Formalism, he argues, cannot concede that an external social factor which has an impact on literature, can turn into an internal factor, into a factor of literature's immanent development.[12] Medvedev addresses here the problem of dialectical mediation by postulating that the linguistic, religious, social and economic problems are inherent in the literary text. Hence they cannot be understood mechanically as matters of external influence.

Medvedev, Bakhtin and Voloshinov were among the first who tried to understand artistic and literary forms as social facts and to combine the "how" and the "why". Thus for Bakhtin the polyphony of the novel and its narrative structure can be deduced from the carnivalesque elements of popular culture. For him the forms of language, so meticulously analysed by the formalists, are at the same time social and critical forms.[13] In this case, the interdiscursive theorem could be formulated as follows: "The form as technique is as such a social fact."

This fundamental idea which expresses the unity of the opposites, of the "how" and the "why", was later on worked out by West European scientists such as Tony Bennett in Britain,[14] Edmond Cros and Julia Kristeva in France. Without the impulse emanating from the formalist-Marxist dialogue,[15] neither Edmond Cros[16] nor Julia Kristeva could have mapped out their sociological and psychoanalytic approaches considering the literary text as a semantic and narrative structure.[17]

Commenting on the debates between formalists and Marxists, William Garrett Walton aptly points out: "Each school offered a methodology for part of the problem, but each had significant blind spots."[18] In a dialogue defined either literally as a discussion or metaphorically as a confrontation of theories, this discovery of "significant blind spots" is what matters, what causes a "shake-up" (*Erschütterung*, Neurath) in the theories involved – and eventually yields a better theory. For in this context, new theories can develop which avoid the flaws of their predecessors. This might be regarded

as a kind of progress in cultural and social sciences and as a viable alternative to Popper's principle of "falsification".

2.   Speech Act Theory, Semiotics and Deconstruction:
Repetition as Iterativity and Iterability

In what follows, the controversies between John L. Austin's and John R.
Searle's speech act theory and Derrida's deconstruction, which took
place in the 1970s and 1980s, will lead to a comparison of the theories
involved. The comparison will be augmented by Greimas's concept of
iterativity. This additional element is not an unnecessary increase of complexity, but is meant to relate two contradictory and complementary
notions – *iterativity* (Greimas) and *iterability* (Derrida) – to one another.
The philosophical debate in question is relevant to all kinds of theory formation, because it deals with such general problems as semantic repetition and
theoretical reflection.

What is at stake here is the answer to the crucial question concerning the
possibility of unambiguous definition and of maintaining the identity or per-
manence of meaning in repetition. While Austin's and Searle's speech act
theory agrees with the (otherwise heterogeneous) semiotic theory of Greimas that the repetition of a linguistic unit in discourse does not alter its identity, Derrida believes that repetition invariably entails semantic shifts, so
that the identity of a repeated unit cannot be maintained.

In this case, as in the case of formalism and Marxism, it seems necessary to
reconstruct the ideological and philosophical contexts of the theories
involved, thus filling a gap which contributed to the breakdown of the original debates. While speech act theory adopts as its starting point an individualist rationalism in the sense of Carnap, Frege and Russell, a rationalism
based on the conviction that concepts and statements can be univocally
defined, Derrida radicalizes Nietzsche's theory of tropes, thus casting
doubt on the very possibility of conceptual definition. Unlike Austin and
Searle, who continue to adhere to the idea of an autonomous subject responsible for a particular and univocal intentionality in speech, Derrida tries to
deconstruct individual subjectivity along with its speech acts and the underlying intentionality.

The controversy with Searle was triggered off by a lecture Derrida
delivered in 1971 in Montreal under the title "Signature événement con-
texte". The title of the conference was: "La Communication". In his radical critique of Austin's speech act theory, Derrida questions the very possibility of communication (at least implicitly). He does so by declaring, in

accordance with his theory of language,[19] that the *presence of meaning* (*présence du sens*) is an illusion.

At the same time, he contests Austin's distinction between serious and non-serious speech acts, a distinction which presupposes a stable and always identifiable intentionality. Derrida considers the latter as an illusion, because Austin and Searle themselves have to admit that all speech acts come about in open contexts all of which are marked by a process of *repetition* that invariably subverts what Searle calls "meaning". "Understanding a sentence is knowing its meaning",[20] writes Searle in *Speech Acts*. His remarks in defence of Austin's theory are complementary: "Inasmuch as the author says what he wants to say, the text expresses his intentions."[21] However, the meaning of these intentions is dependent on the context.

In conjunction with Austin's speech act theory, Derrida remarks: "For a context to be exhaustively determinable, in the sense demanded by Austin, it at least would be necessary for the conscious intention to be totally present and actually transparent for itself and others, since it is a determining focal point of the context."[22] But considering that this context remains forever open and cannot be exhaustively determined,[23] a "totally present" and "transparent" intention cannot be expressed in any speech act, especially since the open context implies a repetition with semantic shifts.

Derrida calls this kind of repetition *iterability* (*itérabilité*). In *Limited Inc.*, a long commentary on Searle's reply, he declares: "Iterability alters, contaminating parasitically what it identifies and enables to repeat 'itself'; it leaves us no choice but to mean (to say) something that is (already, always, also) other than what we mean (to say), to say something other than what we say *and* would have wanted to say, to understand something other than ... etc."[24] Iterability thus appears as a process leading to the disintegration of textual coherence.

This deconstructionist argument is by no means obscure, for it contains a certain amount of analytic plausibility. In almost every theoretical discussion, unintended semantic shifts occur. They are often accompanied by phrases like "if I understood your remark correctly ..." or "this is not what I said, wanted to say ...", etc. Among the results of such semantic shifts are the twenty-one meanings of the word "paradigm" ("possibly more, not less", M. Masterman), commented on in the fifth chapter where it was shown how Kuhn's concept fell prey to the process of iterability.

One may well wonder, at this stage, whether iterability is not inherent in all communications and whether it is not an inexhaustible source of misunderstandings which condemns all theoretical discussions to failure: from the confrontation between Critical Rationalism and Critical Theory to the Derrida-Searle debate. It is certainly a factor that ought to be taken seriously, especially if it is enhanced by rhetoric and polemic.

The title *Limited Inc.* as such raises doubts concerning Derrida's willingness to deal seriously with the arguments of his interlocutors. The simple fact that J. R. Searle quotes H. Dreyfus and D. Searle with whom he discussed some of Derrida's objections to speech act theory, is interpreted by the deconstructionist as an attempt by his interlocutor to share responsibility and to hide behind the mask of anonymity. He therefore writes Searle's name as Sarl (*Société à responsabilité limitée*, i.e. Limited Inc.). This kind of satire may amuse some readers, but can hardly be expected to create a climate of confidence and bring about a serious dialogue.

Fortunately, iterability is not the philosopher's stone. For Searle's pragmatic idea that, in the normal run of things, a text expresses the intention of its author (cf. supra), is not only borne out in daily life, where locutionary, illocutionary and perlocutionary speech acts satisfy our communicative needs, but also in Greimas's structural semiotics.

In this theory, the concept of *iterativity* is defined etymologically in view of the phenomenon it refers to (*iter* = path, *iterare* = to repeat) and can be considered as an alternative to *iterability*: "Iterativity is the reproduction on a syntagmatic axis of identical or comparable units which are situated on the same level of analysis."[25] The complementary concept of *isotopy* is defined as "iterativity of classemes on a syntagmatic axis which guarantees the homogeneity of a discourse".[26]

In these definitions, the possibility to *repeat the identical* is clearly presupposed. At the same time, the semiotician envisages a repetition that does not lead to semantic shifting and the disintegration of textual coherence, but to a semantic consolidation of the text. This consolidation is due to the fact that different words or *sememes* in context are linked by a common general concept or *classeme*. The repetition or iterativity of the latter forms the basis of an isotopy. Thus the simple sentence "The pupil eats" (Greimas's example) is coherent, because the words "pupil" and "to eat" both contain the classeme "human". Similarly, Searle's sentence "Understanding a sentence is knowing its meaning" is coherent, because its key words contain the classeme "cognitive".

At this stage, Derrida could intervene in order to point out a weak spot in Greimas's definition of "iterativity": namely the expression "of identical or comparable units". Identical or comparable? Whatever is comparable is *by definition* not identical, and Greimas' tacit concession to the deconstructionist principle of semantic shifting reveals to what extent iterability is inherent in structural semantics – in spite of their rationalist orientation. It is hard to dismiss this argument because it shows that "iterativity" and "iterability" form an indissoluble nexus.[27]

It is relatively easy, however, to turn the tables on the deconstructionist (without sophistic intentions): by showing that whenever Derrida protests against misunderstandings or misinterpretations of his writings, for example, by trying to elucidate the "true" meaning of "iterability",[28] he confirms – in spite of himself – the rationalist postulates of identity and coherence. If the identity of concepts or statements did not exist, iterability would reign supreme and misunderstandings would be impossible. For they can only exist where stable and repeatable meanings are presupposed – and avoidable deviations from these meanings. They are also presupposed by Derrida who is particularly sensitive to misunderstandings.[29]

The result of this debate and of the subsequent comparison can be summed up in one sentence representing an interdiscursive theorem: "Iterativity as repetition of the identical, i.e. as production of meaning, and iterability as disintegration of meaning and negation of identity are aspects of human speech and communication."

The importance of this theorem for the practice of dialogue is clear: it shows how essential the reconstruction of a theory and its context is, if a concept such as "repetition" is at stake, a concept which means virtually the opposite in Derridan deconstruction of what it means in Anglo-American speech act theory and in Greimasian semiotics. At the same time, it shows why iterability cannot be avoided in complex discussions where heterogeneous languages collide. As soon as a concept belonging to a particular discourse (and its sociolect) is used by speakers of other discourses, a shift in meaning occurs. The only remedy against this semantic shifting seems to be the reconstruction of the original meaning or a joint redefinition of the concept involved. Both processes take place on the level of semantic repetition, and are not mutually exclusive.

3.   Rejection, Agreement and Misunderstanding

Both the formalism-Marxism debate and the discussions between Derrida and Searle illustrate what was meant in the second chapter by the "shake-up" or *Erschütterung* (Neurath) of a theory. A theory, considered as a discourse constructing scientific objects, is "shaken" or radically called into question when it collides with competing discourses which construct "the same" object differently.

At this point, a constructivist, who views the notion of reality with scepticism, might argue that we are not dealing with the same object in the two instances, because formalist "art" is not the same thing as Marxist "art", and because "iterability" refers to a phenomenon which has nothing or little to do with Greimas's "iterativity". The two debates show that this is not the case; for the interlocutors are by no means prey to illusion when they believe that they are dealing with the same phenomenon. Both the formalists and the Marxists refer to "art", but they construct it differently. Derrida, Searle and Greimas deal with *repetition* as a semantic and pragmatic phenomenon; but they construct it in very different contexts.

The fact that one group of theoreticians rejects the constructions of the other shows to what extent such constructions can be one-sided, because they come about in relatively homogeneous group languages and in the corresponding monological discourses. It is the dialogical collision of heterogeneous languages which leads to a "shake-up" of theories by exposing their blind spots.

This "shake-up" is caused by the rejection of a theoretical discourse in a heterogeneous sociolect. The interlocutors are not always aware of it or try to ignore it. In the case of formalism and Marxism, it was noticed and evaluated much later, when in the 1960s and 1970s some critics pointed out the shortcomings of both formalism and Marxist aesthetics.

A serious dialogue between Greimas's structural semiotics and Derrida's deconstruction may have just started. The comparison of the two approaches does show, however, especially if it is considered against the backdrop of the Searle-Derrida debate, that even in this case "shake-ups" are inevitable. For Greimas's ambiguous expression "of identical or comparable units" may very well be interpreted as a stopgap, while Derrida's plea in favour of an "ethic of discussion" contradicts the key notion of iterability, because it implies the possibility to fix meanings and repeat them in new contexts. When Derrida asserts that a certain "definition of the deconstructionist [in Searle's discourse] is *false*",[30] he presupposes the existence of a fixed and repeatable definition.

At times, attempts to justify a theory by explaining away its weak spots make the latter even more prominent and irritating. But who recognizes such weak spots in his own discourse? The answer might be: only theoreticians who dispose of a sufficient amount of curiosity and self-irony enabling them to delay emotional and ideological reactions and to expose their own theory to a dialogical critique.

Naturally, the success of such a critique is based on the assumption that interlocutors do not start from preconceived stereotypes and misunderstandings which prevent them from grasping the Other's position and argument. Among such misunderstandings is the term "formalism" which ignores all formalist attempts to locate and explain art and literature in a social context.[31] Misunderstandings of this kind also prevent Derrida and Searle from bringing about a rapprochement, from agreeing on the object in question. Searle's recurring remark that Derrida's Austin is unrecognizable is a case in point.

This remark is reminiscent of Hans Albert's "A Short Astonished Afterword" to the "Positivism Controversy". Commenting on Adorno's inability to reconstruct the position of Critical Rationalism (hastily defined as "positivism"), he quite rightly objects that Adorno, Horkheimer and Habermas tend to identify this brand of rationalism with the logical positivism of the 1920s or 1930s and subsequently put forward "arguments against this approach, without sufficiently explaining and taking into account the position of Critical Rationalism".[32]

This reductionist approach to Critical Rationalism is hardly surprising when one considers Adorno's sentence: "The game of discussion deserves to be regarded with scepticism."[33] This statement not only implies a refusal of dialogue (of communicative reason in the sense of Habermas), but also the will to ignore the arguments of the interlocutors – if need be. Unfortunately, this attitude manifests itself on quite a few occasions in Adorno's discourse: among other things in his commentaries on Heidegger which Derrida quite rightly queries.[34] Nevertheless, Adorno's attempt to reduce Critical Rationalism to "positivism" is surprising for readers of his *Negative Dialectics* and *Aesthetic Theory* who expect the author of these works to respect the particular character of the Other's discourse.

Considering these problems, it would seem that alterity and the particular are better off in a Dialogical Theory aiming at the reconstruction of the Other's position than in an essayistic discourse geared towards models and a paratactic structure. This is one of the main reasons why it was suggested earlier on that Critical Theory be restructured and transformed into a Dialogical Theory by a re-interpretation of Adorno's three central concepts: *non-identity, particularity* and *alterity*.

The idea that non-identity as an aspect of negativity relates Critical Theory to Critical Rationalism must have crossed Adorno's mind in an early phase of the "Positivism Controversy", when he wrote about Popper's position: "By identifying scientific objectivity with the critical method, he turns the latter into the crucial criterion of truth. No contemporary dialectician could demand more."[35] Such sentences show to what extent an apparent agreement can hide a disagreement. They also show how important it is to reconstruct the social and linguistic positions of theories involved in a debate.

The postulate of non-identity does relate Critical Rationalism to Critical Theory. For advocates of both theory complexes reject all ideological and Hegelian attempts to identify a particular discourse with objects and events in the real world. Unfortunately, the common theoretical ground seems to end here, for Popper's "negativity" differs considerably from that of the dialectical thinkers: it implies the refutability of a theory, the possibility of its failure in crucial tests. However, the idea that the postulate of refutability or falsifiability presupposes the non-identity between discourse and reality, leads back to the common starting point.

All three debates which were considered here in some detail reveal the importance of a twofold reconstruction of the Other's position: within the natural (everyday) language and within one's own theoretical discourse. In the optimal case, these two reconstructions are compared, related to one another and genetically explained within the relevant social and linguistic context (cf. chap. 13). It goes without saying that they cannot be identical. However, if they turn out to be mutually enlightening, they may well contribute to a successful dialogue.

In none of the three debates did reconstructions of this kind form the basis of dialogue. The unbiased observer cannot help feeling that most participants were primarily interested in justifying their respective modes of thought. However, the justifying and identifying monologue is always ideological in a critical, negative sense. This is one fundamental reason why it is impossible in the cultural and social sciences to grasp the theoretical aims and goals of theories without taking into account their ideological impetus.

Chapter 15

Communication in a Fragmented Society: Pluralism, Indifference and Ideology

When Dialogical Theory became itself a topic of discussion in 1999, the German literary theorist Friedmar Apel interpreted it as a "plea for kindness".[1] Initially, the author may have been taken in with this somewhat surprising reaction, especially since he never intended to promote wickedness or malice which are bound to undermine all attempts at rational communication. It is nevertheless a misunderstanding, because it overlooks the essential.

The essential in this case is the elementary *question* underlying Dialogical Theory: How can social scientists and groups of scientists communicate in a socially and linguistically heterogeneous world? At this stage, the answer can be summed up as follows: by reflecting upon the structure, the function and the interaction of their theoretical and ideological discourses and by relating them to the social and linguistic situation in which they communicate with their interlocutors. This is not a plea for kindness or goodness, but an invitation to reflection, reconstruction and criticism.

It is at the same time a proposal to stimulate scientific curiosity to such a degree that theoreticians decide to test their hypotheses by exposing them to the criticism of the Other, the scientific stranger. If, for whatever reason, someone wanted to reduce the approach developed here to a popular slogan, the expression "plea for scientific curiosity" might do.

Somebody might object that curiosity abounds and that there is no need to cultivate it. This is by no means certain, especially if curiosity is defined as the will to overcome cultural, linguistic and ideological barriers in order to discover otherness, thereby casting doubts upon one's own engrained opinions or concepts.

For in a strongly pluralized postmodern society which is officially presented as tolerant, indifference (as exchangeability of values) is the reverse of the medal, and this indifference can at any time provoke ideological reactions marked by dualism and dogmatism. Goethe realized that tolerance is a predominantly negative attitude implying rejection and refusal: "As a matter of fact, tolerance ought to be no more than a passing attitude: it must lead to recognition. To tolerate means to offend."[2] It seems worth-while therefore to examine more closely the nexus of pluralism, tolerance and ideology in order to relate it to the problems of theoretical dialogue.

1.   Pluralism and Indifference

Time and again postmodernity has been defined as a pluralist world in which "modernity no longer has to be pleaded for, because it is being realized".[3] This way of looking at things seems plausible, especially if one concentrates on the European political scene which is no longer dominated − as was the case between the world wars − by authoritarian movements, parties and politicians who were a threat to the democratic order. After the collapse of fascism, national socialism and European communism, pluralist democracy seems to be firmly established in Europe − or at least within the European Union.

However, "pluralism" and "tolerance" are phenomena of a market society which, since its origins in the late Middle Ages and the Renaissance,[4] has been dominated by the fundamental principle of indifference as *exchangeability of cultural values* (not as emotional indifference). Merchants are neither interested in the social origin of their goods nor in the political attitudes of their customers. What matters to them is the exchange value and the corresponding profit. From their point of view, the religious, political or aesthetic orientation of customers is indifferent, i.e. interchangeable, because it does not or should not interfere with the exchange process. The paradoxical sentence "customers are always right" expresses this indifference as interchangeability of social values. They are right because they pay, and as long as they pay, their contrasting opinions are irrelevant. Very rarely will shop assistants who share directly or indirectly in the shop's profit discourage a customer (a stranger) from buying an expensive dress or a suit they consider as utterly tasteless. In many cases shop assistants and shopkeepers will tend to conceal their aesthetic opinions or emotions and will even extol a garment they find ugly. Underlying the ambivalence of their rhetoric and their gestures, the exchange value obliterates the aesthetic value.

Even if the exchange principle penetrates into all spheres of social life, the exchange value does not turn into that all-pervading and hence indefinable value Baudrillard has in mind,[5] but in such a situation it becomes increasingly difficult to recognize its opposite, the use value.[6] Whoever criticizes a bestseller on aesthetic or political grounds, arouses the suspicion (especially as a writer) that this kind of criticism is mainly motivated by a deep-seated but ineffable envy. In such cases, the critic is often silenced by the stereotype pseudo-argument: "tastes differ".

This argument confirms the *de facto* interchangeability of all value judgements in a developed market society. At the same time, it shows that indifference is the reverse of the pluralist medal. Otherness is acknowledged with a shrug of one's shoulders. It may very well have its *raison d'être* – but nobody can *prove* it.

This pluralism, defined as an aspect of indifference, is amply illustrated by a study from the 1970s whose authors try to answer the question "What is good style?" on an empirical level. The result is summed up by Eberhard Frey: "The readers' reactions provided several complex answers to the question 'What is good style?'. To begin with, one can say that the answer depends on the readership a book is meant to address."[7]

At this point, a critic might object that this kind of pluralism may prevail in aesthetics and art, which are governed by the idea that "there is no accounting for tastes" – but not in science. This is by no means certain. In literary theory which does pretend to be a science at least from time to time, Stanley Fish has tried to ascertain the "correct" or "acceptable" meaning of a text by purely rhetorical means. In his later work, he denies the existence of textual features and asserts that the text as a whole is a creation of the reader.[8] Later on, he goes beyond the individual reader and attempts to found the "correct" meaning in an "interpretive community": "Indeed, it is interpretive communities, rather than either the text or the reader, that produce meanings and are responsible for the emergence of formal features."[9]

We are dealing here with a radical-constructivist point of view based on the idea that nothing can be said about the real world, i.e. about the text. However, unlike Glasersfeld, Fish does not ponder on the validity of arguments put forward by an interpretive community in the eyes of competing interpretive communities. A meaning considered as "viable" within one interpretive community might be rejected as absurd by another (cf. chap. 8, 2).

Fish tries to solve this problem by rhetorics: "I claimed the right, along with everyone else, to argue for a way of reading, which, if it became accepted, would be, for a time at least, the true one. In short, I preserved generality by rhetoricizing it."[10] Nobody should confuse this solution with general validity in the theoretical sense; for what Fish proposes is a well-established political trick: bamboozling people into believing something.

It becomes clear, in this context, that postmodern authors such as Stanley Fish have once and for all forsaken the idea of an interculturally and

transideologically valid scientific knowledge. They seem content to persuade the members of their group that the interpretations they propose are
temporarily valid. This extreme particularization of theoretical thought not
only corresponds to the radical pluralism of postmodernity, but also bears
witness to the global spread of indifference. For if every single meaning is
irretrievably tied up with the interests of an "interpretive community" and
remains linked to the particular stance of this community, especially since it
cannot be critically related to any real object, then all theoretical constructions turn out to be arbitrary and interchangeable. In this situation, the
most likely (pragmatic) solution is the one that satisfies collective and individual narcissism by ensuring that readers or listeners believe in "our" or
"my" interpretation. Truth thus yields to the dubious art of rhetoric.

Fish's proposal to solve theoretical problems by rhetorical means is bound
to have a disastrous impact on politics. The often inextricable arguments of
economists, politicians and journalists become irrelevant as soon as a media
mogul succeeds in manipulating public opinion by an efficient and visually
stunning rhetoric. What sounds slightly frivolous in literary criticism, a
hybrid discipline rarely attracted by theoretical issues, becomes a serious
threat to democracy when transposed into the realm of politics. For in a
society where it is not the theoretically better economic or political argument that gains the upper hand, but the more efficient rhetoric, democratic
decision-making as such is in danger. In the long run, it may become clear
that the principle of indifference, which makes all points of view and all
arguments appear interchangeable, is incompatible with a democratic
order based on information, rationality and legality.

2.   Ideological Reactions and the Hermetic Character of Theories

Only the neutral observer, the floating voter or the indifferent consumer,
whose sole passion is the special offer or the price increase, can be said to
consider as interchangeable the different religious, ideological or theoretical
points of view. For the religious, ideological and theoretical communities,
these points of view are by no means interchangeable. Each of these groups
is convinced that its beliefs and explanations are true and should on no
account be confused with those of other groups which are considered with
distrust or outright aversion.

While Lyotard spares no effort to dissociate himself from the ideas of such
postmodern authors as Jencks and Oliva,[11] groups of semioticians, psychoanalysts or sociologists defend their unmistakeable theoretical (and ideological) projects – only to provoke polemical or ironical reactions within

other groups. Greimas describes this social and linguistic situation with a pessimistic undertone:

> The story of the Tower of Babel repeats itself. The multitude of discourses which interpenetrate each other and overlap, each of them proclaiming its own criteria of truth that are accompanied by terrorizing or despising connotations, can only yield a situation marked by the kind of linguistic alienation which at best leads to an era of incredulity.[12]

This passage clearly brings out the ideological reactions of discourses to indifference as interchangeability of values. At the same time, Goethe's maxim, according to which "tolerance is an insult", takes on a new meaning within the postmodern context. The tolerant coexistence of theoretical discourses in pluralism can turn unexpectedly into bitter conflict between ideologies. In such cases – as for example during the controversies between formalists and Marxists – the opponent may well be disqualified as "reactionary", "conservative", "technocratic" or "sexist". The "terrorizing or despising connotations" referred to by Greimas frequently accompany such discursive practices.

This is not altogether surprising if one takes into account the fact that the "interpretive communities" invoked by Fish are held together both by their theoretical and ideological convictions and by the antagonisms which oppose them to other groups. If one of the many groups ever succeeded in having its scientific theses accepted on a worldwide, intercultural scale, it would soon cease to exist as a group. It owes its existence to a *polarized pluralism* which, by its intrinsic indifference, keeps provoking strong ideological reactions.

Such reactions are not only directed against the rivals but against indifference itself: "You may believe that we are not substantially different from our opponents, but you are mistaken; our theory is scientific." This frequently articulated claim is not only to be found in philosophical and sociological discourses from Marx to Luhmann, but also in the liberal, conservative or socialist languages of political parties. None of them will admit that it merely expresses specific group interests and hence adopts a particular (not universal) point of view. On the contrary, it will pretend – implicitly or explicitly – to represent universal truth, the majority of "reasonable people", the "silent majority", totality. It thereby contradicts its self-definition as a party, a *pars*.

Such pretentious gestures elicit scepticism and irony, both in the scientific and the political world, and tend to increase the kind of "incredulity" hinted at by Greimas. This "incredulity" can be considered as an aspect of postmodern indifference which is reinforced by the monologic pretensions of the quarrelling scientific and political groupings. In other words: the ideological reactions to the indifference of postmodern market society contribute to an intensification of this indifference. However, this process does not lead to an "end of ideology", as Raymond Aron and the early Daniel Bell would have us believe,[13] but to an exacerbation of the antagonism between indifference and ideology that may engender violence – as the violent actions of anti-globalization movements show.

In this situation, the subject of Dialogical Theory will opt neither for indifference nor for ideological dualism, but will try to think through the dialectic between indifference and ideology. It will refuse to conceal the ideological, particular aspect of its own discourse (in the present case: the viewpoint of Critical Theory), and will reflect it auto-critically. For it is well aware of the dangers emanating from both ideology and indifference. Whoever pleads unilaterally, like Lenin, for a "scientific ideology",[14] destroys theoretical reflection by ideological partisanship; whoever pleads, equally unilaterally, like Fish, in favour of (rhetorical) indifference, destroys theory by relativism or the interchangeablity of all positions. The critically reflecting subject bans both dangers by linking the extremes: indifference and ideology, Fish and Lenin. It tries to argue against itself without giving up the position it has adhered to.

3. Why Dialogical Theory?

This presentation of Dialogical Theory, of its position between indifference and ideology might, in spite of all explanations offered so far, provoke the question what this meta-theory is good for. What has been said so far may have shown that, whatever perpetuates the polarized pluralism described above, will merely prolong the life of hermetic monologues, thus accelerating the fall of cultural and social sciences into disrepute. For unlike the natural sciences which test their hypotheses and theories by experiments and are frequently offered the means to apply them on a large scale, thereby securing social prestige, cultural and social sciences find it difficult to make their function plausible to the general public. In many cases, empirical research relevant to the attainment of practical (economic, political, pedagogical) goals is dissociated from theoretical reflection and theory formation.[15] In a similar anti-theoretical vein, philologists naively assume that it is possible to analyse literary texts without any theoretical prolegomena.

In this situation, Dialogical Theory, defined as a meta-theory of scientific communication, fulfils the task of transforming the sterile juxtaposition of theoretical discourses into a dialogical interaction, thereby increasing the cognitive potential of the cultural and social sciences. Instead of ignoring each other monologically, scientific groups ought to discover the interdiscursive, intercollective approach in order to understand *their own theories* more concretely (i.e. in context).

Commenting on the problems of Dialogical Theory, Heinrich Bußhoff remarks: "Zima's aim is not only to make a dialogue 'between heterogeneous groups' possible, but to *force* these groups to take part in a dialogue."[16] Unfortunately, we are dealing here with one of the many misunderstandings which have burdened the – otherwise fruitful – discussions in the special issue of *Ethik und Sozialwissenschaften* in 1999. What has been said so far ought to have made it clear that it is impossible to force an individual or a group to engage in dialogue.

Dialogical Theory contains concrete proposals for improving scientific communication by orienting it towards the word of the Other, as Bakhtin would say. It is not based on constraints, but – on the contrary – on the free will of individuals to emancipate themselves from the sociolects in which they were socialized and to look for inspiration in "foreign parts" in order to satisfy their curiosity. Whoever rejects dialogue for ideological or psychic reasons, cannot possibly be forced by anybody to develop this kind of curiosity. One might just as well try to persuade someone who feels seasick as soon as he catches a glimpse of the sea to book a cruise.

An argument which was not put forward against Dialogical Theory so far, but was expected by the author, concerns the (inevitably) particular character of this approach: "It is, after all, a particular and contingent theoretical project which cannot claim universal validity." On the one hand, this critique is trivial, on the other hand, it is understandable. It is trivial like any truism, because in the cultural and social sciences every discourse, defined as a semantic and narrative structure, comes about in a culture, an ideology and a language – and therefore has a particular character. Are we to surrender in view of this obvious fact and abandon the goal of rational scientific discussion? It is understandable, because the metatheoretical approach mapped out here is unlikely to be accepted by the entire scientific community.

The author nevertheless hopes that, by giving theoretical discourse a dialogical orientation, he has raised questions that are common to many different approaches in the cultural and social sciences, so that dissidents and critics, who keep theory as an open-ended process alive, will recognize some of their own problems in this book. It is to be expected that they will try to solve them differently, by different means. They can only feel encouraged by Dialogical Theory which, by definition, excludes the "final word". However, it is unlikely that they will be able to avoid or ignore some of the key problems which have been dealt with here: the intercollective character of scientific communication, the self-reflection of the subject, the reconstruction of the Other's discourse in context and the ideological factor in theoretical language.

The central issue would seem to be the *awareness* of these problems and the will to solve them in a joint effort: in the general interest of the cultural sciences which are everywhere in danger of losing their scientific status in the institutions and degenerating into "cultural entertainment" or "culture industry". In order to counter this fatal tendency, the author of this book has tried to activate the critical impulse of theory at crucial points.

Notes

Preface

1. P. W. Balsinger, "Dialogische Theorie? Methodische Konzeption!", in: *Ethik und Sozialwissenschaften* 4, 1999, pp. 602–3. In this book, the discussion occasioned by Dialogical Theory and published by the German periodical *Ethik und Sozialwissenschaften* (Ethics and Social Sciences) in 1999, will be referred to sporadically, especially in chaps 13 and 14.
2. J. Mittelstraß, *Die Häuser des Wissens. Wissenschaftstheoretische Studien*, Frankfurt: Suhrkamp, 1998, p. 28. Mittelstraß quite rightly points out: "The option in favour of a theory is always the option in favour of a system of sentences, not in favour of individual sentences." Nevertheless, the question remains how the semantic coherence of such a system comes about.

Introduction: Problems and Definitions

1. Cf. A. Giddens & J. Turner, *Social Theory Today*, Cambridge & Oxford: Polity and Blackwell, 1987, pp. 9–10.
2. Cf. T. Johnson, Ch. Dandeker & C. Ashworth, *The Structure of Social Theory*, London: Macmillan (1984), 1987, pp. 19–21.
3. M. Haller, *Soziologische Theorie im systematisch-kritischen Vergleich*, Opladen: Leske & Budrich, 1999, p. 38.
4. R. Greshoff, "Notwendigkeit einer 'konzeptuellen Revolution in der Soziologie'? Kritische Überlegungen zu Luhmanns Anspruch am Beispiel von 'doppelter Kontingenz' ", in: *Österr. Zeitschrift für Soziologie* 2, 1999, p. 7.
5. R. Wellek & A. Warren, *Theory of Literature*, London: Peregrine Books (1963), 1968, pp. 36–7.
6. Cf. F. K. Stanzel, *A Theory of Narrative*, Cambridge: Cambridge University Press, 1986.
7. Cf. T. H. Kim, *Vom Aktantenmodell zur Semiotik der Leidenschaften. Eine Studie zur narrativen Semiotik von Algirdas J. Greimas*, Tübingen: Narr, 2002, chap. V: "Der erzähltheoretische Kontext: Greimas, Genette, Stanzel". Kim compares these narrative theories and analyses the methods developed by Greimas, Genette and Stanzel with respect to their narrative relevance.

8. Among the rare exceptions in this area, one could quote: H. Göttner, *Logik der Inter-
    pretation. Analyse einer literaturwissenschaftlichen Methode unter kritischer Betrachtung der
    Hermeneutik*, Munich: Fink, 1973, p. 7; "Classification of Theories of Literature",
    in: *Communication and Cognition* (Ghent), 2, 1978, pp. 157–61. (In her analyses,
    Göttner relies heavily on W. Stegmüller's models.) Cf. also J. J. A. Mooy, "Filosofie
    van de literatuurwetenschap", in: *idem, Idee en verbeelding. Filosofische aspecten van
    de literatuurbeschouwing*, Assen: Van Gorcum, 1981, p. 96, where Mooy mentions
    the low prognostic value and the equally low degree of testability of theories in
    literary criticism.

9. G. Pasternack, *Theoriebildung in der Literaturwissenschaft*, Munich: Fink, 1975, p. 15.

10. V. Descombes, *Le Même et l'autre. Quarante-cinq ans de philosophie française (1933–
    1978)*, Paris: Minuit, 1979, p. 22.

11. Cf. R. Bubner, *Zur Sache der Dialektik*, Frankfurt: Suhrkamp, 1980.

12. Cf. A. Compagnon, *Le Démon de la théorie. Littérature et sens commun*, Paris: Seuil, 1998;
    instead of pleading in favour of theoretical dialogue, Compagnon finally proclaims
    relativism, arguing that literary theory is a "school of relativism" (p. 311). Cf. also
    T. Eagleton, *After Theory*, London: Allen Lane, 2003; Penguin, 2004, in particular
    chap. II: "The Rise and Fall of Theory".

13. Cf. H. Kloft, "Die Theoria der Griechen. Ein Modell und drei Fallbeispiele", in:
    K. L. Pfeiffer, R. Kray & K. Städtke (eds), *Theorie als kulturelles Ereignis*, Berlin &
    New York: de Gruyter, 2001, p. 49.

14. M. Weber, *Soziologie, universalgeschichtliche Analysen, Politik*, Stuttgart: Kröner,
    1973, p. 235.

15. G. Schischkoff (ed.), *Philosophisches Wörterbuch*, Stuttgart: Kröner, 1978, p. 693.

16. B. Schäfers (ed.), *Grundbegriffe der Soziologie*, Opladen: Leske & Budrich, 1986, p. 295.

17. *Wörterbuch der Soziologie*, founded by G. Hartfiel, re-edited by K. H. Hillmann,
    Stuttgart: Kröner, 1972 (3rd edn), p. 758. (Compare the commentary to the 4th
    edn in chap. 3.)

18. N. Wenturis, W. Van hove & V. Dreier, *Methodologie der Sozialwissenschaften*, Tübin-
    gen & Basel: Francke, 1992, pp. 330–1.

19. K. R. Popper, *The Logic of Scientific Discovery* (1959), London & New York: Rout-
    ledge, 2002, p. 37. (*Logik der Forschung* [1934], Tübingen: Mohr-Siebeck, 2002
    [10th edn], p. 31.)

20. K. R. Popper, *The Logic of Scientific Discovery, op. cit.*, p. 18.

21. Ibid.

22. Ibid., p. 19.

23. Ibid., p. 50.

24. Cf. O. Neurath, "Pseudorationalismus der Falsifikation (1935)", in: O. Neurath,
    Gesammelte philosophische und methodologische Schriften, vol. II, eds R. Haller &
    H. Rutte, Vienna: Hölder-Pichler-Tempsky, 1981, pp. 637–9. The Controversy
    between Popper and Neurath is dealt with in detail in: F. Fistetti, *Neurath contro
    Popper. Otto Neurath riscoperto*, Bari: Dedalo, 1985, pp. 66–77: "Lo pseudoraziona-
    lismo di Karl Popper".

25. W. Stegmüller, *Probleme und Resultate der Wissenschaftstheorie und Analytischen Philoso-phie*, vol. II, *Theorie und Erfahrung*, Zweiter Teilband, *Theorienstrukturen und Theorien-dynamik*, Berlin, Heidelberg & New York: Springer, 1985, p. 20.
26. Ibid., p. 141.
27. Ibid.
28. Ibid.
29. W. Stegmüller, *Probleme und Resultate der Wissenschaftstheorie und Analytischen Philoso-phie*, vol. II, *Theorie und Erfahrung*, Dritter Teilband, *Die Entwicklung des neuen Struk-turalismus seit 1973*, Berlin, Heidelberg & New York: Springer, 1986, pp. 419–21.
30. Cf. ibid., pp. 432–49.
31. W. Stegmüller, *Probleme und Resultate der Wissenschaftstheorie und Analytischen Philoso-phie*, vol. II, *Theorie und Erfahrung, op. cit.*, p. 141.
32. Cf. P. V. Zima, *Theorie des Subjekts. Subjektivität und Identität zwischen Moderne und Post-moderne*, Tübingen & Basel: Francke, 2000, chap. V.
33. Pierre Bourdieu, *Science of Science and Reflexivity*, Cambridge: Polity, 2004, p. 54.
34. Ibid.
35. P. Bourdieu, *Choses dites*, Paris: Minuit, 1987, p. 48.
36. Cf. P. Bourdieu, *In Other Words. Essays Towards a Reflexive Sociology*, Cambridge & Oxford: Polity and Blackwell, 1990, p. 198.
37. Cf. P. V. Zima, *Ideologie und Theorie. Eine Diskurskritik*, Tübingen: Francke, 1989, chap. IX: "Reflexion und Diskurs".
38. N. Luhmann, *Die Wissenschaft der Gesellschaft*, Frankfurt: Suhrkamp, 1990, p. 406.
39. Cf. N. Luhmann, *Einführung in die Systemtheorie*, ed. D. Boeck, Heidelberg: Carl-Auer-Systeme Verlag, 2002, p. 100 and also G. Kneer & A. Nassehi, *Niklas Luh-manns Theorie sozialer Systeme*, Munich: Fink, 1997 (3rd edn), p. 56: definition of "autopoiesis".
40. Cf. N. Luhmann, *Die Wissenschaft der Gesellschaft, op. cit.*, pp. 577–8.
41. Ibid., p. 285.
42. Ibid., p. 394 and p. 430.
43. In *Die Kunst der Gesellschaft*, Frankfurt: Suhrkamp (1995), 1997, p. 238, Luhmann puts forward a traditionally formalist argument (in the sense of Russian Formal-ism), when he explains: "The work of art thus draws the observer's attention to the observation of form." Someone might object that Luhmann uses the central formalist thesis within his sociological systems theory. This is undoubtedly true, but with respect to the individual work he hardly goes beyond formalist horizons.
44. R. K. Merton, *Social Theory and Social Structure*, New York: The Free Press, 1968 (enlarged edn), p. 39.
45. Ibid., pp. 39–40.
46. Ibid., p. 40.
47. Ibid., p. 59.
48. One of the numerous critics of Merton's notion of theory is M. Mulkay. In his book, *Functionalism, Exchange and Theoretical Strategy* (1971), Aldershot: Gregg Revivals, 1992, p. 220, he argues: "One difficulty with the notion of middle-range theory is

that it is a residual category; and residual categories are typically susceptible to further sub-division."

49. Cf. Ch. Baudelot & R. Establet, *Durkheim et le suicide*, Paris: PUF, 1990 (3rd edn), pp. 120–1.

50. N. Luhmann, *Die Wissenschaft der Gesellschaft, op. cit.*, p. 407.

51. R. K. Merton, *Social Theory and Social Structure, op. cit.*, p. 39.

52. The genetic context of Grounded Theory is discussed in some detail by B. Péquignot and P. Tripier, in *Les Fondements de la sociologie*, Paris: Nathan, 2000, pp. 197–8.

53. The fact that we are not dealing with some kind of banal empiricism, but with a special brand of empirical hermeneutics, is stressed by Uwe Flick in his presentation of Grounded Theory as a qualitative approach: "In such cases, the research process does not set out from a tabula rasa. The starting point is rather a preliminary understanding of the analysed object or field." (U. Flick, *Qualitative Forschung. Theorie, Methoden, Anwendung in Psychologie und Sozialwissenschaften*, Reinbek: Rowohlt, 1999 [4th edn], p. 60.)

54. Cf. A. Strauss & J. Corbin, *Basics of Qualitative Research: Grounded Theory. Procedures and Techniques*, London & Newbury Park: Sage, 1990, chap. I.

55. B. Glaser & A. Strauss, *The Discovery of Grounded Theory*, Chicago: Aldine, 1967, p. 32.

56. B. D. Haig, "Grounded Theory as Scientific Method", in: Philosophy of Education 1995: http://www.ed.uiuc.edu/EPS/PES-Yearbook/95-docs/haig.html, p. 1.

57. Cf. W. Dilthey, "Die Entstehung der Hermeneutik", in: W. Dilthey, *Gesammelte Schriften*, vol. V, Stuttgart: B. G. Teubner; Göttingen: Vandenhoeck & Ruprecht, 1968, pp. 318–19.

58. Cf. R. Carnap, H. Hahn & O. Neurath, "Wissenschaftliche Weltauffassung – der Wiener Kreis", in: O. Neurath, *Wissenschaftliche Weltauffassung. Sozialismus und Logischer Empirismus*, ed. R. Hegselmann, Frankfurt: Suhrkamp, 1979, pp. 86–91; and also L. Althusser, *Lenin and Philosophy and Other Essays*, New York: Monthly Review Press, 1971, p. 15.

59. J. A. Schülein, *Autopoietische Realität und konnotative Theorie. Über Balanceprobleme sozialwissenschaftlichen Erkennens*, Weilerswist: Velbrück, 2002, p. 139. (Unfortunately, it seems to be the other way around: discourses of the natural sciences can very well be described as secondary connotative systems, while discourses of the social sciences are inconceivable without their denotative functions.)

60. J. A. Schülein & S. Reitze, *Wissenschaftstheorie für Einsteiger*, Vienna: WUV Universitätsverlag, 2002, p. 196.

61. Ibid., p. 197.

62. Cf. A. Giddens, *New Rules of Sociological Method. A Positive Critique of Interpretative Sociologies*, London: Hutchinson, 1976, p. 146.

63. A. Nünning, (ed.), *Metzler Lexikon Literatur- und Kulturtheorie*, Stuttgart: Weimar, 2001 (2nd edn), pp. 330–1.

64. Commenting on the concepts of "denotation" and "connotation", Schülein remarks: "Both concepts have been borrowed from linguistic discussions. There

'denotation' is being used in different discourses, while 'connotation' lacks the necessary conceptual clarity and relevance – as far as I can tell" (*Autopoietische Realität und konnotative Theorie, op. cit.*, p. 139). It seems that the sociologist has somewhat underestimated the linguists and the semioticians – especially L. Hjelmslev's *Prolegomena to a Theory of Language*, Madison, Milwaukee & London: Univ. of Wisconsin Press, 1969, pp. 114–27: "Connotative semiotics and metasemiotics". One could have expected Schülein to take into account at least this "classical" distinction between "denotation" and "connotation", especially since his own distinction seems to serve a different, but not very clear purpose . . .

65. Cf. J. A. Schülein & S. Reitze, *Wissenschaftstheorie für Einsteiger, op. cit.*, p. 194.
66. Cf. Z. S. Harris, "Discourse analysis", in: *Language* 28, 1952.
67. Cf. the comments on Greimas's semiotics in chap. 2 and M. A. K. Halliday, *Language as Social Semiotic: The Social Interpretation of Language and Meaning*, London: Edward Arnold, 1978; M. Stubbs, *Discourse Analysis. The Sociolinguistic Analysis of Natural Language*, Oxford: Blackwell (1983), 1994, p. 7: "It follows that the grammatical, structural units of clause or sentence are not necessarily either the most important units for language study, or the biggest (. . .)." Compare this with G. Brown & G. Yule, *Discourse Analysis*, Cambridge: Cambridge Univ. Press (1983), 1991, chap. IV: "'Staging' and the Representation of Discourse Structure".
68. W. Welsch, *Unsere postmoderne Moderne*, Weinheim: VCH, 1991 (3rd edn), p. 36.
69. Cf. P. V. Zima, *Ideologie und Theorie, op. cit.*, chap. X; and P. V. Zima, *Theorie des Subjekts, op. cit.*, chap. V.
70. Th. W. Adorno, "Wozu noch Philosophie", in: Th. W. Adorno, *Eingriffe. Neun kritische Modelle*, Frankfurt: Suhrkamp, 1971 (7th edn), p. 18.
71. Cf. A. Demirović, *Der nonkonformistische Intellektuelle. Die Entwicklung der Kritischen Theorie zur Frankfurter Schule*, Frankfurt: Suhrkamp, 1999, chap. 5. 4: "Die Notwendigkeit der Philosophie".
72. K. Lenkenau, "Methodologie", in: B. Schäfers (ed.), *Grundbegriffe der Soziologie, op. cit.*, p. 195. "Methods" as objects of methodology would then be concrete procedures such as "data processing", "survey", "observation", "experiment", etc.

Part One
Theoretical Discourse in the Cultural and Social Sciences: Definition

1. Cf. O. Neurath, "Universaljargon und Terminologie", in: *idem, Gesammelte philosophische und methodologische Schriften*, vol. II, eds R. Haller & H. Rutte, Vienna: Hölder-Pichler-Tempsky, 1981, pp. 902–3.
2. J.-F. Lyotard, *Political Writings*, London: UCL Press, 1993, p. 28.
3. A critique of Adorno's notion of parataxis is to be found in: P. V. Zima, "Adorno et la crise du langage", in: *idem, Théorie critique du discours. La discursivité entre Adorno et le postmodernisme*, Paris: L'Harmattan, 2003.

4. R. L. Geiger, "Die Institutionalisierung soziologischer Paradigmen: Drei Beispiele aus der Frühzeit der französischen Soziologie", in: W. Lepenies (ed.), *Geschichte der Soziologie*, vol. II, Frankfurt: Suhrkamp, 1981, p. 140.

1.   The Cultural Character of Theory

1. C. Kluckhohn, "The Study of Culture", in: L. A. Coser & B. Rosenberg (eds), *Sociological Theory*, New York: Macmillan, 1966, p. 40.
2. T. Parsons, *The Social System*, London: Routledge & Kegan Paul, 1951, p. 52.
3. K. P. Hansen, *Kultur und Kulturwissenschaft*, Tübingen & Basel: Francke, 2003 (3rd edn), pp. 17–18.
4. "Modernism" and "Postmodernism" have been defined as cultural problematics in: P. V. Zima, *Moderne/Postmoderne. Gesellschaft, Philosophie, Literatur*, Tübingen & Basel: Francke, 2001 (2nd edn).
5. Cf. C. Koch, "Möglichkeiten und Grenzen der vergleichenden Religionswissenschaft", in: P. V. Zima (ed.), *Vergleichende Wissenschaften*, Tübingen: Narr, 2000, S. 131: "(...) For the relationship between the underlying concept of theory and the corresponding choice of a method is decisive in the science of religion."
6. M. Weber, "Vom inneren Beruf zur Wissenschaft", in: M. Weber, *Soziologie, universalgeschichtliche Analysen, Politik*, ed. J. Winckelmann, Stuttgart: Kröner, 1973, p. 316.
7. Ibid., p. 317.
8. J. Mittelstraß, *Die Häuser des Wissens. Wissenschaftstheoretische Studien*, Frankfurt: Suhrkamp, 1998, p. 133.
9. W. Schluchter, *Rationalismus und Weltbeherrschung. Studien zu Max Weber*, Frankfurt: Suhrkamp, 1980, p. 51.
10. Cf. M. Horkheimer, *Zur Kritik der instrumentellen Vernunft*, Frankfurt: Fischer, 1974, pp. 94–7.
11. G. Böhme, *Alternativen der Wissenschaft*, Frankfurt: Suhrkamp, 1980, p. 13.
12. M. Hennen, *Krise der Rationalität – Dilemma der Soziologie. Zur kritischen Rezeption Max Webers*, Stuttgart: Enke, 1976, p. 41.
13. Cf. M. Weber, *Die protestantische Ethik I. Eine Aufsatzsammlung*, ed. J. Winckelmann, Hamburg: Siebenstern, 1973 (3rd edn), pp. 339–41.
14. C. A. van Peursen, "Rationality: European or Universal?", in: *Higher Education and Research in the Netherlands* 3/4, "Eurocentrism and Science", 1982, p. 17.
15. R. Münch, *Theorie des Handelns. Zur Rekonstruktion der Beiträge von Talcott Parsons, Emile Durkheim und Max Weber*, Frankfurt: Suhrkamp (1982), 1988, p. 488. Münch's theory of interpenetration is presented in: R. Münch, *Die Struktur der Moderne. Grundmuster und differentielle Gestaltung des institutionellen Aufbaus der modernen Gesellschaften*, Frankfurt: Suhrkamp (1984), 1992, pp. 14–20.
16. Cf. P. V. Zima, *Komparatistik. Einführung in die Vergleichende Literaturwissenschaft*, Tübingen & Basel: Francke, 1992, chap. VII.

17. The cultural context of Luhmann's theory is dealt with in: K. L. Pfeiffer, "Theorie als kulturelles Ereignis. Modellierungen eines Themas überwiegend am Beispiel der Systemtheorie", in: K. L. Pfeiffer, R. Kray & K. Städtke (eds), *Theorie als kulturelles Ereignis*, Berlin & New York: de Gruyter, 2001, p. 17: "Nowadays, one easily forgets how intensively Luhmann kept 'interlinking' many of his writings (. . .) with social and cultural, even with personal topics."

18. M. Weber, *Gesammelte Aufsätze zur Wissenschaftslehre*, Tübingen: Mohr-Siebeck, 1951, p. 175.

19. W. Benjamin, *Zur Kritik der Gewalt und andere Aufsätze*, Frankfurt: Suhrkamp, 1971 (2nd edn), p. 83.

20. L. Strauss, "Die Unterscheidung zwischen Tatsachen und Werten", in: H. Albert & E. Topitsch (eds), *Werturteilsstreit*, Darmstadt: Wiss. Buchgesellschaft, 1979, p. 74.

21. K. R. Popper, *The Open Society and its Enemies*, vol. II, *The High Tide of Prophecy: Hegel, Marx, and the Aftermath*, London: Routledge & Kegan Paul (1945), 1963, p. 130.

22. Cf. K. R. Popper, "What does the West Believe in? (Stolen from the Author of *The Open Society*)", in: *idem, In Search of a Better World. Lectures and Essays from Thirty Years*, London & New York: Routledge, 1992, pp. 207–8. (The unity of the "West" is ideologically presupposed here. But are Europe and North America not two very distinct entities?)

23. Cf. D. Lecourt, *L'Ordre et les jeux. Le positivisme logique en question*, Paris: Grasset, 1981, pp. 23–4.

24. N. Luhmann, *Soziale Systeme. Grundriß einer allgemeinen Theorie*, Frankfurt: Suhrkamp (1984), 1987, p. 13.

25. Cf. N. Luhmann, *Ökologische Kommunikation. Kann die moderne Gesellschaft sich auf ökologische Gefährdungen einstellen?*, Opladen: Westdeutscher Verlag, 1986, pp. 177–9.

26. J. A. Schülein, *Autopoietische Realität und konnotative Theorie. Über Balanceprobleme sozialwissenschaftlichen Erkennens*, Weilerswist: Velbrück, 2002, p. 23.

27. P. Bourdieu, *Language and Symbolic Power*, ed. J. B. Thompson, Cambridge: Polity (1991), 2005, Part II: "The Social Institution of Symbolic Power".

28. A. Touraine, *Sociologie de l'action*, Paris: Seuil, 1965.

29. Cf. A. Touraine, *Critique de la modernité*, Paris: Fayard, 1992, pp. 100–1.

30. Ibid., p. 331.

31. Cf. N. Luhmann, *Soziale Systeme, op. cit.*, p. 543 and N. Luhmann, *Die Gesellschaft der Gesellschaft*, vol. II, Frankfurt: Suhrkamp, 1997, p. 1031: "Within the discipline, this 'theory of action' lives on its historical memories."

32. J. E. Ellemers, "Pillarization as a Process of Modernization", in: *Acta Politica* 1, 1984, p. 129.

33. Cf. R. C. Bannister, *Sociology and Scientism. The American Quest for Objectivity, 1890–1940*, Chapel Hill & London, Univ. of North Carolina Press, 1987, chap. VIII: "An Objective Standard".

34. This topic is dealt with in detail in: L. Danneberg & F. Vollhardt (eds), *Wie international ist die Literaturwissenschaft? Methoden und Theoriediskussion in den Literaturwissenschaften: kulturelle Besonderheiten und kultureller Austausch am Beispiel des*

Interpretationsproblems (1950–1990). Stuttgart & Weimar: Metzler, 1996. With respect to the cultural specificity of theory formation L. Danneberg, and J. Schönert point out in this volume: "(...) The construction of evolution in literary history is as dependent on theories and methods that are specific to certain cultures as the interpretation of literary works."

35.   Cf. F. Thumerel, *La Critique littéraire*, Paris: Armand Colin, 1998, chap. III: "Les trois critiques". (There the author deals with "la critique journalistique", "la critique universitaire" – i.e. "science of literature" in the Germanic and Slav sense – and "la critique d'écrivain", i.e. the writer's critical essay.)

36.   Cf. P. V. Zima, "Die Stellung der Literaturwissenschaft zwischen den Kulturen: Eine textsoziologische Betrachtung", in: H. Foltinek & Ch. Leitgeb (eds), *Literaturwissenschaft: intermedial – interdisziplinär*, Vienna: Verlag der Österr. Akademie der Wissenschaften, 2002, pp. 31–4.

37.   Cf. G. H. Hartman, *Criticism in the Wilderness. The Study of Literature Today*, New Haven & London: Yale Univ. Press, 1980, p. 4 and p. 211.

38.   Cf. Ch. Mauron, *Des métaphores obsédantes au mythe personnel. Introduction à la psychocritique*, Paris: Corti, 1983; E. Cros, *Theory and Practice of Sociocriticism*, Minneapolis, Univ. of Minnesota Press, 1988; P. Dirkx, *Sociologie de la littérature*, Paris: Armand Colin, 2000, pp. 88–93 and P. V. Zima, *Manuel de sociocritique*, Paris (1985): L'Harmattan, 2000.

39.   Cf. B. Croce, *Dialogo con Hegel*, ed. G. Gembilo, Naples: Edizioni Scientifiche Italiane, 1995.

40.   Cf. A. Gramsci, *Il materialismo storico e la filosofia di Benedetto Croce*, Turin: Einaudi, 1957.

41.   Cf. B. Croce, *Estetica come scienza dell'espressione e linguistica generale*, Bari: Laterza, 1973 (12th edn), p. 41.

42.   P. Claval, *Les Mythes fondateurs des sciences sociales*, Paris: PUF, 1980, p. 108.

43.   H. Peyré, "Durkheim: The Man, his Time, and his Intellectual Background", in: E. Durkheim, *et al.*, *Essays on Sociology and Philosophy*, ed. K. H. Wolf, New York: Harper & Row, 1960, pp. 23–4.

44.   Cf. G. Lanson, "L'histoire littéraire et la sociologie", in: *idem, Essais de méthode, de critique et d'histoire littéraire*, Paris: Hachette, 1965.

45.   Cf. H. Rickert, "Die Heidelberger Tradition und Kants Kritizismus (Systematische Selbstdarstellung)", in: H. Rickert, *Philosophische Aufsätze*, Tübingen: Mohr-Siebeck, 1999, pp. 376–7: the concept of "understanding"/"Verstehen".

46.   E. Durkheim, *Les Règles de la méthode sociologique*, Paris: PUF, 1987 (23rd edn), pp. 73–4.

47.   E. A. Tiryakian, "Ein Problem für die Wissenssoziologie: Die gegenseitige Nichtbeachtung von Emile Durkheim und Max Weber", in: W. Lepenies (ed.), *Geschichte der Soziologie*, vol. IV, *op. cit.*, p. 24.

48.   Cf. R. Cohen & P. Kennedy, *Global Sociology*, New York: University Press (2000), 2003.

49.   Cf. A. Giddens, *Sociology*, Cambridge: Polity; Oxford: Blackwell (1989), 1993 (2nd edn), p. 527.

50. Cf. G. Mikl-Horke, *Soziologie. Historischer Kontext und soziologische Theorie-Entwürfe*, Munich & Vienna: Oldenbourg, 2001 (5th edn). The author not only deals with British, North American and German sociological traditions, but also comments in some detail on French sociology.

51. It is surprising to find that in J. Duvignaud's collective volume *Sociologie de la connaissance*, Paris: Payot, 1979, Karl Mannheim's Sociology of Knowledge, which has many followers in Britain and Germany, is missing.

52. Cf. B. Péquignot & P. Tripier, *Les Fondements de la sociologie*, Paris: Nathan, 2000, pp. 123–5 and pp. 138–43.

53. Cf. U. Beck, *Risk Society. Towards a New Modernity*, London, Thousand Oaks & Delhi: Sage, 1992.

54. Cf. R. Winter, *Die Kunst des Eigensinns. Cultural Studies als Kritik der Macht*, Weilerswist: Velbrück, 2001, chap. IV.

55. Cf. P. V. Zima, *Komparatistik, op. cit.*, chap. I: "Zur Wissenschaftsgeschichte der Komparatistik", I, 3: "Die 'französische' und die 'amerikanische' Schule".

56. Cf. W. Nöth, *Handbuch der Semiotik*, Stuttgart: Metzler, 1985, pp. 4–6.

57. Cf. U. Eco, *Trattato di semiotica generale*, Milan: Bompiani, 1975, pp. 25–8.

58. Cf. B. Martin & F. Ringham, *Dictionary of Semiotics*, London & New York: Cassell, 2000, p. 168: The name Bense is missing here and in: D. Chandler, *Semiotics. The Basics*, London & New York: Routledge, 2002.

59. J. Kristeva, "La sémiologie comme science des idéologies", in: *Semiotica* 1, 1969, pp. 196–204.

2. The Linguistic and Ideological Determinants of Theories: Theory as Sociolect and Discourse

1. W. Schiffer, *Theorien der Geschichtsschreibung und ihre erzähltheoretische Relevanz (Danto, Habermas, Baumgartner, Droysen)*, Stuttgart: Metzler, 1980, p. 3. Cf. also: F. Ankersmit, *The Reality Effect of the Writing of History*, Amsterdam: Noord-Hollandsche, 1989.

2. It is quite surprising therefore that Greimas and Courtés do not define theory in relation to Greimas's concept of discourse: cf. A. J. Greimas & J. Courtés, *Sémiotique. Dictionnaire raisonné de la théorie du langage*, Paris: Hachette, 1979, pp. 394–6. This definition is to be found in: A. J. Greimas, *Sémiotique et sciences sociales*, Paris: Seuil, 1976, pp. 9–42 and in: E. Landowski, *La Société réfléchie. Essais de sociosémiotique*, Paris: Scuil, 1989, pp. 74–109.

3. P. Sarasin, *Geschichtswissenschaft und Diskursanalyse*, Frankfurt: Suhrkamp, 2003, p. 55–6. In one of his theses, Sarasin highlights the crucial moment of discourse analysis in the science of history: "The most important challenge historiography is confronted with in discourse analysis is not so much the often conjured up danger of transforming past reality into discourse or 'fiction'. More interesting and more intricate is the question where, among all the reconstructed symbolic structures that make up the perceptible social world, we meet up with the limits of these structures and hence with the reality that has engendered them."

4. E. Sapir, in: B. L. Whorf, "The Relation of Habitual Thought and Behaviour to Language", in: *idem, Language, Thought and Reality*, Cambridge (Mass.): MIT Press, 1956, p. 134.

5. L. Althusser, "Idéologie et appareils idéologiques d'Etat", in: *idem, Positions*, Paris: Editions Sociales, 1976, p. 122.

6. C. Kramsch, *Language and Culture*, Oxford: Oxford Univ. Press, 1998, p. 13.

7. It goes without saying that, in the present context, the notion of "interest" refers to material interests and not simply to linguistic differences. W. F. Haug constructs a superfluous dichotomy when he remarks in conjunction with Dialogical Theory: "Is it really the case that scientific schools are primarily 'language groups' and not groups based on material interests?" (W. F. Haug, "Möglichkeiten und Grenzen interparadigmatischer Kommunikation", in: *Ethik und Sozialwissenschaften* 4, 1999, pp. 619–20.) The answer is: they are both. But since "theory" is defined here as "discourse", the collective appears primarily as a language group. The socio-semiotic approach does not ignore social, material interests; it translates them into linguistic interests.

8. Greimas defines sociolects as technical, professional languages, not as ideologies or theories. Cf. A. J. Greimas, *Sémiotique et sciences sociales, op. cit.*, pp. 53–5.

9. Cf. M. Weber, "Der Beruf zur Politik", in: *idem, Soziologie, universalgeschichtliche Analysen, Politik*, ed. J. Winckelmann, Stuttgart: Kröner, 1973, p. 185.

10. Cf. A. W. Gouldner, *The Coming Crisis of Western Sociology*, London: Heinemann, 1971.

11. Cf. P. V. Zima, *Theorie des Subjekts. Subjektivität und Identität zwischen Moderne und Postmoderne*, Tübingen & Basel: Francke, 2000, chap. IV, 4: "Alain Touraines Alternative: Subjekt und Bewegung".

12. Cf. P. V. Zima, *The Philosophy of Modern Literary Theory*, London & New Brunswick: Athlone, 1999, chap. II.

13. Cf. R. Brütting, *"Ecriture" und "texte". Die französische Literaturtheorie "nach dem Strukturalismus"*, Bonn: Bouvier, 1976.

14. Cf. V. Descombes, *Le Même et l'autre. Quarante-cinq ans de philosophie française (1933–1978)*, Paris: Minuit, 1979, p. 13.

15. The dialectic between the subject as basis (*hypokeimenon*) and the subject as a subjected instance (*subiectum*) is commented on in: P. V. Zima, *Theorie des Subjekts, op. cit.*, chap. I.

16. Cf. Y. M. Lotman, *Structure of Aesthetic Texts*, Ann Arbor (Mich.): Slavic Contributions, 1977, chap. II.

17. Cf. L. J. Prieto, *Pertinence et pratique. Essai de sémiologie*, Paris: Minuit, 1975, chap. V: "Pertinence et idéologie" and D. Sperber, D. Wilson, *Relevance. Communication and Cognition*, Oxford: Blackwell (1986), 1993, chap. III, 1: "Conditions for Relevance".

18. Cf. S. Lash, *Sociology of Postmodernism*, London & New York: Routledge, 1990, p. 252 and J. Baudrillard, *La transparence du mal. Essai sur les phénomènes extrêmes*, Paris: Galilée, 1990, pp. 22–42.

19. A. J. Greimas & J. Courtés, *Sémiotique, op. cit.*, p. 197.

20. J. Link, *Literaturwissenschaftliche Grundbegriffe. Eine programmierte Einführung auf struk-turalistischer Basis*, Munich: Fink, 1979 (2nd edn), p. 76.

21. Cf. A. J. Greimas, "Les actants, les acteurs et les figures", in: *idem, Du Sens II*, Paris: Seuil, 1983, pp. 49–66 and J. Courtés, *Introduction à la sémiotique narrative et discursive*, Paris: Hachette, 1976, chap. II: "Composante syntaxique".

22. A. J. Greimas, *Du Sens*, Paris: Seuil, 1970, p. 234.

23. Cf. U. Eco, "James Bond: une combinatoire narrative", in: *Communications* 8, 1966, pp. 91–3.

24. Cf. A. J. Greimas, "Pour une théorie des modalités", in: *idem, Du Sens II, op. cit.*, p. 81.

25. It ought to have become clear at this stage, that this definition of "discourse" is based on structural semiotics and has nothing to do with Habermas's discourse as "discussion". It is somewhat surprising therefore that, in his critical remarks on Dialogical Theory, Dietrich Hoffmann, who relies heavily on Habermas's model, seems to think that "discourse" can only mean what Habermas means by it and that "one cannot simply annex the univocally defined concept of discourse". (D. Hoffmann, "Dialogische Theorie – eine Methode zur Überwindung der Widersprüchlichkeit innerhalb der Wissenschaft?", in: *Ethik und Sozialwissenschaften* 4, 1999, p. 622.) This kind of objection reveals a dramatically limited cultural and linguistic horizon that cannot allow for divergent definitions of discourse by internationally known scientists such as Benveniste, Genette, Greimas, Halliday and Stubbs.

26. Cf. V. Propp, *Morphology of the Folktale*, Austin: Univ. of Texas Press (2nd edn), 1968.

27. Cf. L. Tesnière, *Eléments de syntaxe structurale*, Paris: Klincksieck, 1969.

28. N. Elias, *Engagement und Distanzierung. Arbeiten zur Wissenssoziologie*, vol. I, Frankfurt: Suhrkamp, 1983, p. 30.

29. K. Marx, F. Engels, "Manifesto of the Communist Party", in: K. Marx & F. Engels, *Basic Writings on Politics and Philosophy*, ed. L. S. Feuer, New York: Doubleday-Anchor, 1959, p. 20.

30. Ibid., p. 41.

31. Ibid., p. 7.

32. G. Lukács, *History and Class Consciousness. Studies in Marxist Dialectics*, London: Merlin Press, 1971, p. 163.

33. Lukács's Hegelian perspective is dealt with in: P. V. Zima, "Dialektik zwischen Totalität und Fragment", in: H.-J. Schmitt (ed.), *Der Streit mit Georg Lukács*, Frankfurt: Suhrkamp, 1978, pp. 141–2.

34. Cf. Lukács, "Preface to the New Edition (1967)", in: *idem, History and Class Consciousness, op. cit.*, pp. XXI–XXV.

35. G. Couvalis, *The Philosophy of Science. Science and Objectivity*, London: Sage (1997), 1999, p. 150.

36. M. Weber, *Wirtschaft und Gesellschaft. Grundriß der verstehenden Soziologie*, Tübingen: Mohr (5th edn), 1976, vol. II, p. 658.

37. Cf. R. Bendix, *Max Weber. An Intellectual Portrait*, London: Methuen (1959), 1962, pp. 6–7.

38. M. Weber, *Wirtschaft und Gesellschaft*, *op. cit.*, vol. I, p. 140.

39. W. J. Mommsen, in: "Max Weber und die Welt von heute. Eine Diskussion mit Wilhelm Hennis, Wolfgang J. Mommsen und Pietro Rossi", in: Ch. Gneuss & J. Kocka (eds), *Max Weber. Ein Symposion*, Munich: DTV, 1988, pp. 204–5.

40. N. Luhmann, *Die Gesellschaft der Gesellschaft*, vol. I, Frankfurt: Suhrkamp, 1997, p. 158. (It should be pointed out that comparative social sciences – e.g. comparative politics, comparative sociology – are thus made impossible.)

41. The function of mythical actants in Luhmann's discourse is analysed in some detail in: P. V. Zima, *Theorie des Subjekts*, *op. cit.*, chap. IV, 3: "Die Liquidierung des Subjekts durch seine Allgegenwart".

42. N. Luhmann, *Soziale Systeme. Grundriß einer allgemeinen Theorie*, Frankfurt: Suhrkamp (1984), 1987, p. 169.

43. Cf. ibid., p. 314, where the "testing of a possible consensus" appears to be a central principle.

44. N. Luhmann, *Die Gesellschaft der Gesellschaft*, vol. I, *op. cit.*, p. 185.

45. Cf. K. Mannheim, *Ideology and Utopia. An Introduction to the Sociology of Knowledge*, London & Henley: Routledge & Kegan Paul (1936), 1976, pp. 57–62.

46. N. Luhmann, *Soziale Systeme*, *op. cit.* p. 325.

47. Cf. P. V. Zima, *Ideologie und Theorie. Eine Diskurskritik*, Tübingen: Francke, 1989, pp. 55–6.

48. This is why W. F. Haug's critique of the dual definition of ideology proposed here is beside the point. Commenting on this definition, he reminds us of Adorno's view of ideology as false consciousness: "This [definition] eclipses the 'recognition of ideology as socially false consciousness' (...) part of which is the value-discourse." (W. F. Haug, "Möglichkeiten und Grenzen der interparadigmatischen Kommunikation", *op. cit.*, p. 619.) What is missing in Adorno's Critical Theory is precisely the reflection upon its own particular value system, which is based on such value-laden notions as individual autonomy, artistic autonomy, criticism, utopia and emancipation. This is one of the reasons why his discourse engenders apodictic statements from time to time – and why Critical Theory is being restructured here.

49. S. J. Schmidt, "Allgemeine Literaturwissenschaft – ein Entwurf und die Folgen", in: C. Zelle (ed.), *Allgemeine Literaturwissenschaft. Konturen und Profile im Pluralismus*, Opladen-Wiesbaden: Westdeutscher Verlag, 1999, p. 106.

50. N. Luhmann, *Beobachtungen der Moderne*, Opladen: Westdeutscher Verlag, 1992, p. 61.

51. Cf. P. Bourdieu, *Science of Science and Reflexivity*, Cambridge: Polity, 2004, pp. 94–114: "Sketch for a Self-Analysis".

52. The dialectic between ideology and indifference is dealt with in: P. V. Zima, *Moderne/Postmoderne. Gesellschaft, Philosophie, Literatur*, Tübingen & Basel: Francke, 2001 (2nd edn), chap. V, 1 and in the last chapter of this book.

53. L. Pirandello, "L'umorismo", in: *idem, Saggi, poesie, scritti varii*, Milan: Mondadori, 1977 (4th edn), p. 103. Cf. also "Konstruktion und Dekonstruktion des Subjekts: Unamunos *Niebla* und Pirandellos *Uno, nessuno e centomila*", in: P. V. Zima,

Das literarische Subjekt. Zwischen Spätmoderne und Postmoderne, Tübingen & Basel: 2001, pp. 164–9.

54. Cf. P. V. Zima, *Ideologie und Theorie, op. cit.*, chap. X: "Ambivalenz und Dialektik".

55. Unfortunately, some Marxists keep defending the dualistic monologue of ideology, which tends to block the development of theory, against Critical Theory. Cf. I. Mészárosz, *The Power of Ideology*, London & New York, Harvester & Wheatsheaf, 1989, p. 107. Mészáros is certainly not wrong when he refers to the "positive power of ideology that could only arise out of the *materially felt emancipatory need* of the oppressed people". However, this positive power of ideology (as "ideology in the general sense": cf. supra), which temporarily turns individuals and groups into agents or active subjects, at the same time blinds them and makes them submit to the strategies of a political party, a trade union or another bureaucracy.

56. Cf. M. Pêcheux, *Les Vérités de La Palice*, Paris: Maspero, 1975, pp. 146–7.

57. Cf. P. Macherey, *Hegel ou Spinoza*, Paris: Maspero, 1979, pp. 257–8, where Spinoza's philosophy is presented as a thought without a subject.

58. R. Bubner, "Wie wichtig ist Subjektivität? Über einige Selbstverständlichkeiten und mögliche Mißverständnisse der Gegenwart", in: W. Hogrebe (ed.), *Subjektivität*, Munich: Fink, 1998, p. 246.

59. A. J. Greimas, "Du discours scientifique en sciences sociales", in: *idem, Sémiotique et sciences sociales*, Paris: Seuil, 1976, p. 12.

60. Hillmann, K.-H. (ed.), *Wörterbuch der Soziologie*, Stuttgart: Kröner, 1994, p. 869.

61. Cf. J. Habermas, *The Philosophical Discourse of Modernity. Twelve Lectures*, Cambridge: Polity (1987), 2005, pp. 406–7.

62. Compare the articles on "Greimas" and "Jakobson" in: *Metzler-Lexikon Literatur- und Kulturtheorie*, ed. A. Nünning, Stuttgart: Metzler, 2001 (2nd edn) with the French and the Russian debates as presented e.g. in: J.-Cl. Coquet, *Sémiotique. L'Ecole de Paris*, Paris: Hachette, 1982 or in: *Materialy meždunarodnogo kongressa 100 let R. O. Jakobson*, Moscow: Rossijskij Gosudarstvennyj Gumanitarnyj Universitet, 1996.

63. Cf. e.g. D. Berg-Schlosser & F. Müller-Rommel (eds), *Vergleichende Politikwissenschaft. Ein einführendes Studienbuch*, Opladen: Leske & Budrich, 1997 (3rd edn), pp. 301–44.

3. Theory, Science, Institution and the "Strong Programme"

1. Cf. P. Weingart, *Die Stunde der Wahrheit? Zum Verhältnis der Wissenschaft zu Politik, Wirtschaft und Medien in der Wissensgesellschaft*, Weilerswist: Velbrück, 2001, pp. 75–6.

2. This is what A. Ryan means when he writes in *The Philosophy of the Social Sciences*, London: Macmillan (1970), 1980, p. 85: "It is a good deal less plausible to suppose that Durkheim's notion of anomie or Freud's concept of the unconscious would even in principle yield us anything comparable to the elegance of particle

mechanics." The problem is that "anomie" and "the unconscious" are not located beyond ideological controversies.

3. Space technology continues to rely on Newton's models.
4. A definition of postmodernism as a tendency towards particularization and relativism can be found in: P. V. Zima, *Moderne/Postmoderne. Gesellschaft, Philosophie, Literatur*, Tübingen & Basel: Francke, 2001 (2nd edn), chap. II.
5. H. M. Collins, *Changing Order. Replication and Induction in Scientific Practice*, Chicago & London: Univ. of Chicago Press (1985), 1992, p. 1.
6. D. Bloor, *Knowledge and Social Imagery*, Chicago & London: Univ. of Chicago Press (1971), 1991 (2nd edn), p. 6.
7. Ibid.
8. Ibid., p. 7.
9. Ibid., p. 18: He quite rightly rejects the thesis according to which "causation implies error".
10. Ibid., p. 20: "Popper himself sees science as an endless vista of refuted conjectures."
11. Cf. I. Lakatos, *The Methodology of Scientific Research Programmes*, Cambridge: Cambridge Univ. Press (1978), 1983, pp. 118–21: "Internal and External History".
12. It is interesting to observe to what extent Lakatos's arguments resemble those of the Russian Formalists (especially Tynianov's), who seek to explain literary evolution as an autonomous process.
13. The so-called Lyssenko Affair is analysed in detail by D. Lecourt, in: *Lyssenko. Histoire réelle d'une "science prolétarienne"*, Paris: PUF (1976), 1995.
14. B. Barnes, D. Bloor & J. Henry, *Scientific Knowledge. A Sociological Analysis*, London: Athlone, 1996, p. 73.
15. D. Bloor, *Knowledge and Social Imagery*, op. cit., pp. 29–30.
16. The specific character of French law is dealt with by Ch. Autexier in his article "Von der Rechtsvergleichung zum rechtskulturellen Vergleich", in: P. V. Zima (ed.), *Vergleichende Wissenschaften. Interdisziplinarität und Interkulturalität in den Komparatistiken*, Tübingen: Narr, 2000, pp. 121–5.
17. More recently, Blondlot's case has been commented on in: A. Bammé, *Science Wars. Von der akademischen zur postakademischen Wissenschaft*, Frankfurt: Campus, 2004, pp. 38–41.
18. M. Mulkay, *Science and the Sociology of Knowledge* (1979), Aldershot: Gregg Revivals, 1992, p. 88.
19. Ibid., p. 61.
20. Cf. K. Knorr-Cetina, *Wissenskulturen. Ein Vergleich naturwissenschaftlicher Wissensformen*, Frankfurt: Suhrkamp, 2002, p. 350.
21. K. Knorr-Cetina, *Die Fabrikation von Erkenntnis. Zur Anthroplogie der Wissenschaft*, Frankfurt: Suhrkamp, 1984, p. 247.
22. Ibid., p. 260.
23. D. Bloor, *Knowledge and Social Imagery*, op. cit., p. 75.
24. Cf. A. Ryan, "Popper and Liberalism", in: G. Currie & A. Musgrave (eds), *Popper and the Human Sciences*, Dordrecht, Boston & Lancaster: Nijhoff, 1985, p. 89.

25. Cf. G. Bachelard, *La Philosophie du non*, Paris: PUF (1940), 1983 (9th edn), p. 8: "The scientific spirit can only take shape by destroying the non-scientific spirit." Cf. also D. Gil, *Bachelard et la culture scientifique*, Paris: PUF, 1993, pp. 88–93.

26. G. Canguilhem, *Idéologie et rationalité dans l'histoire des sciences de la vie. Nouvelles études d'histoire et de philosophie des sciences*, Paris: Vrin, 1988 (2nd edn), p. 39.

27. What is meant here is not the notion of "scientific ideology" as used by Lenin. Cf. H.-J. Lieber, *Ideologie*, Paderborn: Schöningh, 1985, p. 65.

28. G. Canguilhem, *Idéologie et rationalité, op. cit.*, p. 39.

29. Cf. G. Simmel, *Über sociale Differenzierung*, Leipzig: Duncker & Humblot, 1890; and N. Luhmann, *Soziale Systeme. Grundriß einer allgemeinen Theorie*, Frankfurt: Suhrkamp (1984), 1987, pp. 325–31.

30. G. Canguilhem, *Idéologie et rationalité, op. cit.*, p. 40.

31. Ibid., p. 41.

32. Ibid., p. 44.

33. E. Koch, W. Fischer, "The Cubic Limiting Complexes in the Tetragonal Lattice Complexes", in: *Zeitschrift für Kristallographie. International Journal for Structural, Physical and Chemical Aspects of Crystalline Materials* 9, 2003, p. 597.

34. L. Althusser, *Lenin and Philosophy and other Essays*, New York: Monthly Review Press, 1971, p. 15.

35. A detailed criticism of Althusser's position can be found in: P. V. Zima, *Ideologie und Theorie. Eine Diskurskritik*, Tübingen: Francke, 1989, chap. V.

36. Cf. H. Lefebvre, *L'Idéologie structuraliste*, Paris: Anthropos, 1971, pp. 111–59.

37. The fact that these sciences are not as uncontroversial, not as "hard" as the general public often tends to assume, does not justify an assimilation to the cultural or social sciences. Cf. *Critique* 661–2, June–July 2002: *Sciences dures?*, pp. 430–1.

38. K. Marx, *Capital. A Critique of Political Economy*, vol. I, Harmondsworth: Penguin, 1976, p. 508.

39. P. Weingart, *Die Stunde der Wahrheit?, op. cit.*, p. 15.

40. Cf. N. Mecklenburg & H. Müller, *Erkenntnisinteresse und Literaturwissenschaft*, Stuttgart: Kohlhammer, 1974, p. 56.

41. A. Giddens, *New Rules of Sociological Method*, London: Hutchinson (1976), 1986, p. 146.

42. Cf. H. Albert, *Kritische Vernunft und menschliche Praxis*, Stuttgart: Reclam (1977), 1984, p. 75. Discussing the social sciences, Hans Albert points out: "They can describe the value judgements of the analysed individuals and groups, explain and predict without becoming themselves involved in value judgements." They cannot, because their discourses frequently collide with the self-presentation and self-interpretation of the analysed subjects.

43. Cf. M. Young & P. Willmott, *Family and Kinship in East London*, London: Pelican (1957), 1969, chap. XI.

44. P. Bourdieu, *Language and Symbolic Power*, ed. J. B. Thompson, Cambridge: Polity (1991), 2005, p. 225.

45. X. Gauthier, *Surréalisme et sexualité*, Paris: Gallimard, 1971, p. 121.

46. R. Barthes, *Essais critiques*, Paris: Seuil, 1964, p. 179.
47. B. Barnes, D. Bloor & J. Henry, *Scientific Knowledge, op. cit.*, p. 73.

4. Value-Free, "Falsifiable" Theory? The Relationship between Value-Freedom, Intersubjectivity and Refutability

1. This problem is dealt with in some detail in: P. V. Zima, *Ideologie und Theorie. Eine Diskurskritik*, Tübingen: Francke, 1989, chap. IV, 2.
2. Cf. O. Neurath, "Universaljargon und Terminologie", in: *idem, Gesammelte philosophische und methodologische Schiften*, ed. R. Haller & H. Rutte, Vienna: Hölder-Pichler-Tempsky, 1981, pp. 911–15.
3. Cf. M. Schlick, *Allgemeine Erkenntnislehre* (1918), Frankfurt: Suhrkamp, 1979, pp. 437–9.
4. Cf. J.-M. Adam, *La Linguistique textuelle. Introduction à l'analyse textuelle des discours*, Paris: Armand Colin, 2005, pp. 38–40.
5. Cf. Y. Hagiwara, "Zum Verständnis von Liberalismus bei Popper und Hayek", in: K. Salamun (ed.), *Moral und Politik aus der Sicht des Kritischen Rationalismus*, Amsterdam & Atlanta: Rodopi, 1991, pp. 63–70.
6. K. R. Popper, *The Logic of Scientific Discovery* (1959), London & New York: Routledge, 2002, p. 20. (Cf. K. Popper, *Logik der Forschung* [1934], Tübingen: Mohr-Siebeck, 2002 [10th edn], p. 16.)
7. L. von Mises, in: H. Albert, *Freiheit und Ordnung*, Tübingen: Mohr-Siebeck, 1986, p. 69.
8. Cf. M. Weber, "Die 'Objektivität' sozialwissenschaftlicher und sozialpolitischer Erkenntnis" (1904), in: *idem, Gesammelte Aufsätze zur Wissenschaftslehre*, ed. J. Winckelmann, Tübingen: Mohr-Siebeck, 1973, pp. 152–6.
9. H. Albert, *Aufklärung und Steuerung*, Hamburg: Hoffmann & Campe, 1976, p. 175. Cf. also K. R. Popper, *Conjectures and Refutations. The Growth of Scientific Knowledge*, London & New York: Routledge & Kegan Paul (1963), 1972, p. 72.
10. H. Albert, *Aufklärung und Steuerung, op. cit.*, p. 175.
11. Ibid.
12. The link between liberalism and Darwinism is analysed in great detail by S. Collini in *Liberalism and Sociology. L. T. Hobhouse and Political Argument in England 1880–1914*, Cambridge: Cambridge Univ. Press (1979), 1983, p. 3 (regarding M. Weber).
13. W. J. Mommsen, in: H. Albert, *Konstruktion und Kritik*, Hamburg: Hoffmann & Campe, 1975 (2nd edn), p. 48.
14. H. Albert, *Konstruktion und Kritik, op. cit.*, p. 48.
15. Cf. "Politik als Kampf – Politik als Beruf" (eine Diskussion mit Ch. Graf von Krockow, M. R. Lepsius & H. Maier), in: Ch. Gneuss & J. Kocka (eds), *Max Weber. Ein Symposion*, Munich: DTV, 1988, p. 34.
16. Cf. W. Cezanne, *Allgemeine Volkswirtschaftslehre*, Munich & Vienna: Oldenbourg, 1997, pp. 199–201, the presentations of the "theory of allocation" and of the "role of the state in market economy". The question concerning the role of the state

continues to provoke controversies. It should be added that each political party employs its own economic experts who tend to confirm its ideology.

17. H. Albert, *Traktat über kritische Vernunft*, Tübingen: Mohr-Siebeck, 1980 (4th edn), p. 62.

18. Cf. H. F. Spinner, *Ist der Kritische Rationalismus am Ende? Auf der Suche nach den verlorenen Maßstäben des Kritischen Rationalismus für eine offene Sozialphilosophie und kritische Sozialwissenschaft*, Weinheim & Basel: Beltz, 1982, p. 85.

19. T. S. Kuhn, *The Essential Tension. Selected Studies in Scientific Tradition and Change*, Chicago & London: Univ. of Chicago Press, 1977, p. 283.

20. H. Albert, *Aufklärung und Steuerung*, op. cit., p. 189.

21. K. R. Popper, *The Logic of Scientific Discovery*, op. cit., p. 22.

22. Ibid.

23. Ibid.

24. K. R. Popper, *Conjectures and Refutations*, op. cit., p. 257.

25. Ibid., p. 256.

26. K. R. Popper, *The Logic of Scientific Discovery*, op. cit., p. 37.

27. Cf. P. V. Zima, *Ideologie und Theorie*, op. cit., pp. 147–8.

28. M. A. K. Halliday, *Language as Social Semiotic: The Social Interpretation of Language and Meaning*, London: Edward Arnold, 1978, p. 128.

29. K. R. Popper, *Die beiden Grundprobleme der Erkenntnistheorie*, ed. E. Hansen, Tübingen: Mohr-Siebeck, 1994, p. XXVI.

30. K. R. Popper, *The Logic of Scientific Discovery*, op. cit., p. 37.

31. Ibid., p. 50.

32. Ibid., p. 48.

33. Postmodernism as a poetics of "de-differentiation" has been defined by S. Lash in: *Sociology of Postmodernism*, London & New York: Routledge, 1990, pp. 11–15.

34. H. Albert, *Kritische Vernunft und menschliche Praxis. Mit einer autobiographischen Einleitung*, Stuttgart: Reclam, 1977, p. 117.

35. K. R. Popper, *The Logic of Scientific Discovery*, op. cit., p. 86.

36. P. Valéry, *Cahiers*, vol. I, éd. établie, présentée et annotée par J. Robinson, Paris: Gallimard, Bibl. de la Pléiade, 1973, p. 393.

37. K. R. Popper, *The Logic of Scientific Discovery*, op. cit., p. 95.

38. K. R. Popper, *The Open Society and its Enemies*, vol. II: *The High Tide of Prophecy: Hegel, Marx, and the Aftermath*, London: Routledge & Kegan Paul (1945), 1962, p. 222.

39. Cf. P. V. Zima, *Theorie des Subjekts. Subjektivität und Identität zwischen Moderne und Postmoderne*, Tübingen & Basel: Francke, 2000, chap. I, 1, c.

40. K. R. Popper, *The Logic of Scientific Discovery*, op. cit., p. 68.

41. Gilles Deleuze's notion of "*event/événement*" is discussed in great detail by F. Zourabichvilli in *Deleuze. Une philosophie de l'événement*, Paris: PUF, 1994, p. 92.

42. K. R. Popper, *The Logic of Scientific Discovery*, op. cit., p. 68.

43. Ibid., p. 70.

44. I. Lakatos, *The Methodology of Scientific Research Programmes*, Cambridge: Cambridge Univ. Press (1978), 1983, p. 4.

45. Ibid., p. 34.
46. A. Sayer, *Method in Social Science. A Realist Approach*, London: Hutchinson, 1984, p. 205.
47. O. Neurath, "Pseudorationalismus der Falsifikation (1935)", in: *idem, Gesammelte philosophische und methodologische Schriften*, vol. II, *op. cit.*, p. 638.
48. R. Keat & J. Urry, *Social Theory as Science*, London & Boston: Routledge & Kegan Paul, 1982 (2nd edn), p. 48.
49. J.-Cl. Passeron, *Le Raisonnement sociologique: L'espace non-poppérien du raisonnement naturel*, Paris: Nathan, 1991, p. 359.
50. Ibid., p. 361.
51. Ibid., p. 377.
52. Ibid., p. 390.
53. Cf. B. Péquignot & P. Tripier, *Les Fondements de la sociologie*, Paris: Nathan, 2000, p. 212.
54. The problem mentioned initially consists in the fact that most historians and theoreticians of science tend to consider primarily the natural sciences and to ignore or deny the specific character of the cultural and social sciences. This diagnosis seems to be interculturally valid, for it applies to such different authors as K. R. Popper and T. S. Kuhn, and even to N. R. Hanson's study *Patterns of Scientific Discovery*, Cambridge: Cambridge Univ. Press, 1958, or to his article "Leverrier: The Zenith and Nadir of Newtonian Mechanics", in: *Isis* 53, 1962. It also applies to the Croatian historian of science, I. Supek. Cf. J. Lelas, *Teorije razvoja znanosti*, Zagreb: ArTresor Naklada, 2000, p. 31: "We also want to remind the reader of the fact that it was I. Supek in our country who, relying on his solid knowledge of physics and its history, in the beginning of the 1970s launched the idea of scientific evolution in the sense of a genealogy of sciences." (Cf. I. Supek, *Teorija spoznaje*, Zagreb: Graficki Zavod Hrvatske, 1974, chap. "Rodoslovlje znanosti" ["The Genealogy of Science"], p. 192.)
55. G. Witschel, *Wertvorstellung im Werk Karl R. Poppers*, Bonn: Bouvier, 1977 (2nd edn), p. 61.

5. Paradigms in the Cultural and Social Sciences?

1. Cf. M. Masterman, "The Nature of a Paradigm", in: I. Lakatos & A. Musgrave (eds), *Criticism and the Growth of Knowledge*, Cambridge: Cambridge Univ. Press, 1970, pp. 61–5.
2. Cf. T. S. Kuhn, *The Structure of Scientific Revolutions*, Chicago & London, Univ. of Chicago Press, 1996 (3rd edn), p. 15 and p. 121.
3. Cf. N. Gratzl & H. Leitgeb, "Was ist ein wissenschaftliches Paradigma? Zur Explikation des Paradigmabegriffes", in: *Forschungsmitteilungen des Spezialforschungsbereiches FO 12 der Universität Salzburg "Theorien- und Paradigmenpluralismus in den Wissenschaften. Rivalität, Ausschluß oder Kooperation"*, edition 23, Dec. 2001, p. 21. Most of the scientists taking part in this research project adhere to the thesis that

the concept of paradigm *is* applicable to the cultural and social sciences. This hypothesis can certainly yield results insofar as it also reveals the limits of applicability. The author is indebted to the Salzburg colleagues Justin Stagl and Paul Weingartner for valuable advice and for making important material available.

4. Cf. A. Sturmatz, *Pippi Langstrumpf als Paradigma. Die deutsche Rezeption Astrid Lindgrens und ihr internationaler Kontext*, Tübingen & Basel: Francke, 2004.

5. Cf. J. Leyrer, E. Morscher & A. Siegetsleitner, "Der Datenschutz als Anwendungsbereich des Autonomieparadigmas", in: *Forschungsmitteilungen des SFB, FO 12, op. cit.*, edition 26, May 2002, p. 4. The "recognition of the autonomy of the person" mentioned by the authors belongs to a liberal and individualist ideology which was adopted by European and North American legal systems and is clearly linked to specific cultural patterns.

6. Cf. E. Morin, *Le Paradigme perdu: la nature humaine*, Paris: Seuil (1973), 1979.

7. M. Masterman, "The Nature of a Paradigm", in: I. Lakatos & A. Musgrave (eds), *Criticism and the Growth of Knowledge, op. cit.*, pp. 61–3.

8. Considering the large number of semantic shifts within Kuhn's text, it is hard to avoid the deconstructionist question whether the repetition of a sign or a word does not always imply changes in meaning. Cf. P. V. Zima, *Deconstruction and Critical Theory*, London & New York: Continuum, 2002, p. 51.

9. T. S. Kuhn, *The Structure of Scientific Revolutions, op. cit.*, p. 176.

10. Cf. T. S. Kuhn, "Reflections on my Critics", in: I. Lakatos & A. Musgrave (eds), *Criticism and the Growth of Knowledge, op. cit.*, pp. 276–7.

11. T. S. Kuhn, *The Essential Tension. Selected Studies in Scientific Tradition and Change*, Chicago & London: Univ. of Chicago Press, 1977, p. XXII.

12. T. S. Kuhn, *The Structure of Scientific Revolutions, op. cit.*, p. 12.

13. Ibid., pp. 12–13.

14. Ibid., p. 13.

15. Ibid., p. 12.

16. G. Couvalis, *The Philosophy of Science. Science and Objectivity*, London: Sage (1997), 1999, p. 92.

17. A. Einstein, *Mein Weltbild*, Frankfurt: Ullstein, 1970, p. 154. (Quoted after: N. Gratzl & H. Leitgeb, "Was ist ein wissenschaftliches Paradigma?", in: *Forschungsmitteilungen, SFB, FO 12, op. cit.*, p. 40.)

18. B. Barnes, *T. S. Kuhn and Social Science*, New York: Columbia Univ. Press, 1982, p. 17.

19. T. S. Kuhn, *The Structure of Scientific Revolutions, op. cit.*, p. 88.

20. Ibid., p. 65.

21. T. S. Kuhn, *The Essential Tension, op. cit.*, p. 232.

22. Ibid.

23. T. S. Kuhn, *The Structure of Scientific Revolutions, op. cit.*, p. 50.

24. Ibid., p. 99.

25. Ibid., p. 167.

26. T. S. Kuhn, *The Essential Tension, op. cit.*, p. 232.

27. Ibid., p. 227.

28. K. Bayertz, *Wissenschaftstheorie und Paradigmabegriff*, Stuttgart: Metzler, 1981, pp. 16–17.

29. G. Schurz, "Koexistenzweisen rivalisierender Paradigmen. Eine begriffsklär-ende und problemtypologisierende Studie", in: G. Schurz & P. Weingartner (eds), *Koexistenz rivalisierender Paradigmen. Eine post-kuhnsche Bestandsaufnahme zur Struktur gegenwärtiger Wissenschaft*, Opladen & Wiesbaden: Westdeutscher Verlag, 1998, p. 9.

30. Ibid., pp. 10–11.

31. Ibid., p. 13.

32. Cf. the critical study by J. Mitchell, *Feminism and Psychoanalysis*, New York: Random House, 1975.

33. Cf. P. V. Zima, *Roman und Ideologie. Zur Sozialgeschichte des modernen Romans*, Munich: Fink (1986), 1999, chaps IV and V.

34. Cf. Y. Buin, *L'œuvre européenne de Reich*, Paris: Editions Universitaires, 1972, pp. 95–8 and also: C. Castilla del Pino, *Psicoanálisis y Marxismo*, Madrid: Alianza Editorial (1969), 1981, chap. 11 C: "La axiología comparada de Marx y Freud".

35. N. Gratzl & H. Leitgeb, "Was ist ein wissenschaftliches Paradigma?", in: *Forschungsmitteilungen, SFB, FO 12, op. cit.*, p. 20.

36. Ibid., p. 21.

37. Cf. Ph. Van Tieghem, *Les Grandes doctrines littéraires en France*, Paris: PUF, 1968, p. 124, where the author mentions "Voltaire's fidelity towards Racine".

38. N. Gratzl & H. Leitgeb, "Was ist ein wissenschaftliches Paradigma?", in: *Forschungsmitteilungen, SFB, FO 12, op. cit.*, p. 21.

39. Cf. J. Mukařovský, "Problémy estetické normy", in: *idem, Cestami poetiky a estetiky*, Prague: Československý Spisovatel, 1971, pp. 35–6.

40. K. Bayertz, *Wissenschaftstheorie und Paradigmabegriff, op. cit.*, p. 110.

41. G. Schurz, "Koexistenz rivalisierender Paradigmen", in: G. Schurz & P. Weingartner (eds), *Koexistenz rivalisierender Paradigmen, op. cit.*, p. 42.

42. G. Arnreiter & P. Weichhart, "Rivalisierende Paradigmen im Fach Geographie", in: G. Schurz & P. Weingartner (eds), *Koexistenz rivalisierender Paradigmen, op. cit.*, pp. 57–71.

43. Ibid., p. 64.

44. Ibid.

45. Ibid., p. 65.

46. J. Stagl, "Malinowskis Paradigma", in: W. Schmied-Kowarzik & J. Stagl (eds), *Grundfragen der Ethnologie. Beiträge zur gegenwärtigen Theorie-Diskussion*, Berlin: Dietrich Reimer Verlag, 1993, p. 97. (Cf. also Stagl's stimulating study *A History of Curiosity. The Theory of Travel 1550–1800*, Chur: Harwood Academic Publishers, 1995, pp. 233–42: the intercultural context of the words "anthropology" and "ethnology".)

47. Ibid., p. 103.

48. Cf. R. Bannister, *Sociology and Scientism. The American Quest for Objectivity, 1880–1940*, Chapel Hill & London, Univ. of North Carolina Press, 1987, chap. VII: "The Authority of Fact".

49. Cf. S. N. Eisenstadt & M. Curelaru, *The Form of Sociology – Paradigms and Crises*, New York & London: John Wiley & Sons, 1976, p. 85.

50. Ibid., p. 103.

51. Cf. E. Bloch, "Hegel und die Gewalt des Systems", in: *idem, Über Methode und System bei Hegel*, Frankfurt: Suhrkamp (2nd edn), p. 83.

52. This does not mean, of course, that physicists cannot or should not comment on the social function or the didactics of their discipline from an ecological, feminist or generally "egalitarian" point of view. But this ideological stance has nothing to do with their scientific discourse as such or with their scientific terminology.

53. Cf. T. S. Kuhn, *The Structure of Scientific Revolutions, op. cit.*, p. 94.

54. W. Stegmüller, *Probleme und Resultate der Wissenschaftstheorie und Analytischen Philosophie*, vol. II, *Theorie und Erfahrung*, Zweiter Teilband, *Theoriestrukturen und Theoriedynamik* (2nd edn), Berlin, Heidelberg & New York: Springer, 1985, p. 291.

55. Ibid., p. 284.

56. T. S. Kuhn, *The Structure of Scientific Revolutions, op. cit.*, p. 94.

57. R. Greshoff, *Die theoretischen Konzeptionen des Sozialen von Max Weber und Niklas Luhmann im Vergleich*, Opladen & Wiesbaden: Westdeutscher Verlag, 1999, p. 313.

58. H. R. Jauß, "Paradigmawechsel in der Literaturwissenschaft", in: *Linguistische Berichte* 3, 1969, p. 54.

59. Cf. P. V. Zima, " 'Rezeption' und 'Produktion' als ideologische Begriffe", in: *idem, Kritik der Literatursoziologie*, Frankfurt: Suhrkamp, 1978, pp. 88–9.

Part Two
The Unity of Opposites: Prolegomena to a Dialogical Theory

1. G. W. F. Hegel, *Science of Logic*, London & New York: Allen & Unwin & Humanities Press, 1969, p. 54.

2. Ibid.

3. Ibid.

4. Cf. F. T. Vischer, *Kritische Gänge*, vol. IV, ed. R. Vischer, Munich: Meyer & Jessen, 1922, p. 482.

5. T. W. Adorno, *Negative Dialectics*, London & New York (1973): Routledge, 2000, p. 393.

6. This also answers the following question by Heinrich Bußhoff: "Does Dialogical Theory contain the category of totality which is at the centre of Critical Theory? What does totality consist in? In the process of knowledge?" (H. Bußhoff, "Dialogische Theorie: Bedingung für Erkenntnisfortschritt in den Sozialwissenschaften?", in: *Ethik und Sozialwissenschaften* 4, 1999, p. 607.)

7. T. W. Adorno, *Negative Dialectics, op. cit.*, p. 141.

8. Cf. T. W. Adorno, *Eingriffe. Neun kritische Modelle*, Frankfurt: Suhrkamp, 1971 (7th edn), p. 21: "Dialectics is not a third point of view; it is the attempt to go beyond

philosophical viewpoints and beyond the arbitrariness inherent in a thought divided into viewpoints."

9. W. Benjamin, *Ursprung des deutschen Trauerspiels*, Frankfurt: Suhrkamp (1963), 1972, p. 31.

10. These explanations can also be related to Bußhoff's question quoted in note 5.

11. N. Luhmann, *Die Wissenschaft der Gesellschaft*, Frankfurt: Suhrkamp, 1990, p. 409.

12. Ibid., pp. 409–10.

6.   Between Universalism and Particularism: Popper and Lyotard (Kuhn, Winch)

1. K. R. Popper, "On Knowledge and Ignorance", in: *idem, In Search of a Better World. Lectures and Essays from Thirty Years*, London & New York: Routledge, 1992, p. 38.

2. Cf. M. Schlick, *Allgemeine Erkenntnislehre* (1918), Frankfurt: Suhrkamp, 1979, p. 405.

3. K. R. Popper, "Normal Science and its Dangers", in: I. Lakatos & A. Musgrave (eds), *Criticism and the Growth of Knowledge*, Cambridge: Cambridge Univ. Press (1970), 1982, p. 56.

4. Cf. K. R. Popper, *Conjectures and Refutations. The Growth of Scientific Knowledge*, London: Routledge & Kegan Paul (1963), 1972, p. 269.

5. K. R. Popper, "The Myth of the Framework", in: E. Freeman (ed.), *The Abdication of Philosophy. Philosophy and the Public Good. Essays in Honour of P. A. Schilpp*, La Salle (Ill.): Open Court, The Library of Living Philosophers, 1976, p. 37.

6. Cf. P. V. Zima, "Der Unfaßbare Rest. Übersetzung zwischen Dekonstruktion und Semiotik", in: J. Strutz & P. V. Zima (eds), *Literarische Polyphonie*, Tübingen: Narr, 1996, pp. 26–9.

7. K. R. Popper, "Normal Science and its Dangers", in: I. Lakatos & A. Musgrave (eds), *Criticism and the Growth of Knowledge, op. cit.*, p. 57.

8. Cf. L. Hjelmslev, *Prolegomena to a Theory of Language*, Madison, Milwaukee & London: Univ. of Wisconsin Press, 1969, p. 47: "Expression and Content".

9. Cf. P. V. Zima, *Deconstruction and Critical Theory*, London & New York: Continuum, 2002, pp. 42–53.

10. Cf. B. Hatim & I. Mason, *Discourse and the Translator*, London & New York: Longman, 1990, p. 8.

11. Cf. R. Stolze, *Übersetzungstheorien. Eine Einführung*, Tübingen: Narr, 1994, chap. V: "Übersetzungswissenschaft im Zeitalter der Äquivalenzdiskussion"; and J. Munday, *Introducing Translation Studies. Theories and Applications*, London & New York: Routledge, 2001, chap. III: "Equivalence and Equivalent Effect".

12. K. R. Popper, "The Myth of the Framework", in: E. Freeman (ed.), *The Abdication of Philosophy, op. cit.*, p. 39.

13. Cf. A. Ryan, "Popper and Liberalism", in: G. Currie & A. Musgrave (eds), *Popper and the Human Sciences*, Dordrecht, Boston & Lancaster: Nijhoff, 1985, pp. 89–91.

14. T. S. Kuhn, *The Essential Tension. Selected Studies in Scientific Tradition and Change*, Chicago & London: Univ. of Chicago Press, 1977, p. 283.
15. K. R. Popper, "The Myth of the Framework", in: E. Freeman (ed.), *The Abdication of Philosophy, op. cit.*, p. 39.
16. Cf. M. M. Bakhtin, *Problems of Dostoyevsky's Poetics*, Manchester: Manchester Univ. Press, 1984, pp. 90–2.
17. Z. Bauman, *Postmodern Ethics*, Oxford: Blackwell, 1993, p. 135.
18. K. R. Popper, "The Myth of the Framework", in: E. Freeman (ed.), *The Abdication of Philosophy, op. cit.*, p. 23.
19. J.-F. Lyotard, *Postmodern Fables*, Minneapolis: Univ. of Minnesota Press, 2003 (3rd edn), p. 127.
20. Ibid., p. 132.
21. Ibid., p. 133.
22. Ibid., p. 133.
23. J.-F. Lyotard, *The Postmodern Condition: A Report on Knowledge*, Manchester: Manchester Univ. Press, 2004, p. 28.
24. J.-F. Lyotard, *Postmodern Fables, op. cit.*, p. 135.
25. I. Kant, *Critique of Judgement (1790) (including the First Introduction)*, Indianapolis & Cambridge: Hackett Publishing Co., 1987, p. 116.
26. Cf. G. Warmer & K. Gloy, *Lyotard. Darstellung und Kritik seines Sprachbegriffs*, Aachen: Ein-Fach-Verlag, 1995, pp. 26–7.
27. J.-F. Lyotard, *The Differend. Phrases in Dispute*, Minneapolis: Univ. of Minnesota Press, 1988, p. 10.
28. J.-F. Lyotard, *Political Writings*, London: UCL Press, 1993, p. 20.
29. K. R. Popper, "On the so-called Sources of Knowledge", in: *idem, In Search of a Better World, op. cit.*, p. 48.
30. Cf. J.-F. Lyotard, *The Differend, op. cit.*, pp. 86–92.
31. Ibid., p. 178.
32. Ibid., p. 181.
33. P. Winch, *The Idea of a Social Science and its Relation to Philosophy*, London: Routledge (1958), 1990 (2nd edn), p. 100.
34. Ibid., p. 127.
35. Cf. also Winch's article on "Popper and Scientific Method in the Social Sciences", in: P. A. Schilpp (ed.), *The Philosophy of Karl Popper*, La Salle (Ill.): Open Court, The Library of Living Philosophers (Book II), 1967, p. 902: "As against this, it is important to point out that standards of rationality are involved in traditions of behaviour and that they may be in mutual conflict."
36. P. Winch, *The Idea of a Social Science, op. cit.*, pp. xv–xvi.
37. R. C. Bannister, *Sociology and Scientism. The American Quest for Objectivity 1880–1940*, Chapel Hill & London: Univ. of North Carolina Press, 1987, p. 19.
38. J.-F. Lyotard, *Postmodern Fables, op. cit.*, p. 128.
39. L. Pirandello, "L'umorismo", in: *idem, Saggi, poesie, scritti varii*, Milan: Mondadori, 1977 (4th edn), p. 156.

40. T. W. Adorno, *Minima Moralia. Reflections on a Damaged Life*, London & New York: NLB, 1974; Verso, 2005, p. 244.

41. E. Bloch, *Über Methode und System bei Hegel*, Frankfurt: Suhrkamp, 1975 (2nd edn), pp. 82–3.

7. Intersubjectivity and Perspective: Davidson and Mannheim

1. Cf. R. Rorty, *Objectivity, Relativism, and Truth*, vol. I of *Philosophical Papers* (2 vols), Cambridge: Cambridge Univ. Press, 1991, p. 204.

2. Cf. E. Husserl, *Zur Phänomenologie der Intersubjektivität. Texte aus dem Nachlaß*, Teil I (1905–1920), II (1921–1928) and III (1929–1935), ed. I. Kern, The Hague: Nijhoff, 1973.

3. S. Rinofner-Kreidl, *Edmund Husserl. Zeitlichkeit und Intentionalität*, Freiburg & Munich: Alber, 2000, p. 523.

4. Cf. S. J. Schmidt, "Der Radikale Konstruktivismus: Ein neues Paradigma im interdisziplinären Diskurs", in: S. J. Schmidt (ed.), *Der Diskurs des Radikalen Konstruktivismus*, Frankfurt: Suhrkamp, 1987, p. 43.

5. Cf. I. Srubar, "Mannheim und die Postmodernen", in: M. Endreß (ed.), *Karl Mannheims Analyse der Moderne*, Opladen: Leske & Budrich, 2000, p. 359 and p. 361.

6. A. Hance, "Pragmatism as Naturalized Hegelianism: Overcoming Transcendental Philosophy", in: H. J. Saatkamp (ed.), *Rorty and Pragmatism. The Philosopher Responds to his Critics*, Nashville & London: Vanderbilt Univ. Press, 1995, p. 103.

7. D. Davidson, *Inquiries into Truth and Interpretation*, Oxford: Clarendon Press, 1984, p. 184.

8. Ibid., p. 196.

9. Joachim Schulte translated it into German using the word *Nachsichtigkeit*: cf. D. Davidson, *Subjektiv, intersubjektiv, objektiv*, Frankfurt: Suhrkamp, 2004, pp. 253–5. However, *Nachsichtigkeit* (or rather: *Nachsicht*) means primarily leniency, clemency, forbearance, not charity. The German word certainly does not correspond to the French word *charité* used by Lyotard as a translation of "charity": cf. below. Thus the word "charity" becomes a good example of what Davidson calls a "conceptual scheme".

10. D. Davidson, *Subjective, Intersubjective, Objective*, Oxford: Oxford Univ. Press, 2001, p. 211.

11. Ibid.

12. D. Davidson, *Inquiries into Truth and Interpretation*, Oxford: Clarendon Press, 1984, p. 197.

13. Ibid.

14. *Le Petit Robert. Dictionnaire alphabétique et analogique de la langue française* (par P. Robert), Paris: SNL, 1976, p. 261.

15. D. Davidson, *Subjective, Intersubjective, Objective*, op. cit., p. 148.

16. Cf. J.-F. Lyotard, *Moralités postmodernes*, Paris: Galilée, 1993, p. 116.

17. Cf. A. W. Gouldner, *The Coming Crisis of Western Sociology*, London: Heinemann, 1971.

18. D. Davidson, *Subjective, Intersubjective, Objective, op. cit.*, p. 52.

19. Ibid.

20. Ibid., p. 174.

21. F. B. Farrell, "Rorty and Antirealism", in: H. J. Saatkamp (ed.), *Rorty and Pragmatism, op. cit.*, p. 161: "Rorty and the loss of the World".

22. D. Davidson, *Subjective, Intersubjective, Objective, op. cit.*, p. 212.

23. Ibid., p. 190.

24. Ibid., p. 210.

25. Ibid., p. 220.

26. Cf. D. Davidson, *Inquiries into Truth and Interpretation, op. cit.*, p. 193 and idem, *Subjective, Intersubjective, Objective, op. cit.*, pp. 88–9.

27. In this respect, Hans Friedrich Fulda is quite right when he points out in his long commentary on Davidson's Frankfurt lecture on "Dialectics and Dialogue" (1992) "that we do not only interpret sentences of individual speakers, but whole dialogues and all that which happens in dialogues to interlocutors and their words often unintentionally". (H. F. Fulda, "Unterwegs zu einer einheitlichen Theorie des Sprechens, Handelns und Interpretierens", in: *Dialektik und Dialog. Rede von Donald Davidson anläßlich der Verleihung des Hegel-Preises 1992. Laudatio von Hans Friedrich Fulda "Unterwegs zu einer einheitlichen Theorie des Sprechens, Handelns und Interpretierens"*, Frankfurt: Suhrkamp, 1993, p. 48.)

28. E. Karádi, "Einleitung" in: E. Karádi & E. Vezér (eds), *Georg Lukács, Karl Mannheim und der Sonntagskreis*, Frankfurt: Sendler, 1985, p. 18.

29. K. Mannheim, "Über Geschichte und Klassenbewußtsein", in: E. Karádi & E. Vezér (eds), *Georg Lukács, Karl Mannheim und der Sonntagskreis, op. cit.*, p. 300.

30. K. Mannheim, *Strukturen des Denkens*, ed. D. Kettler, V. Meja & N. Stehr, Frankfurt: Suhrkamp, 1980, p. 81.

31. Compare with L. Goldmann's concept of "conscience possible" in: L. Goldmann, *Sciences humaines et philosophie*, Paris, Gonthier, 1966, pp. 124–5.

32. K. Mannheim, *Konservatismus. Ein Beitrag zur Soziologie des Wissens*, ed. D. Kettler, V. Meja & N. Stehr, Frankfurt: Suhrkamp, 1984, p. 59.

33. Cf. S. Collini, *Liberalism and Sociology. L. T. Hobhouse and Political Argument in England 1880–1914*, Cambridge: Cambridge Univ. Press (1979), 1983 and G. Baglioni, *L'ideologia della borghesia industriale nell'Italia liberale*, Turin: Einaudi, 1974.

34. Cf. M. Pêcheux, *Les Vérités de La Palice*, Paris: Maspero, 1975, p. 152.

35. Cf. P. Henry, "Constructions relatives et articulations discursives", in: *Langages* 37, 1975.

36. K. Mannheim, *Strukturen des Denkens, op. cit.*, pp. 239–40.

37. Ibid., p. 240.

38. Ibid.

39. Cf. K. Mannheim, *Ideology and Utopia. An Introduction to the Sociology of Knowledge*, London & Henley: Routledge & Kegan Paul (1936), 1976, p. 50 and p. 243.

40. Cf. M. Foucault, *La Pensée du dehors*, Paris: Fata Morgana, 1986.

41. I. Srubar, "Mannheim und die Postmodernen", in: M. Endreß (ed.), *Karl Mannheims Analyse der Moderne*, Opladen: Leske & Budrich, 2000, p. 359 and p. 361.

42. Cf. H. Broch, *Die Schlafwandler. Eine Romantrilogie* (1931–2), Frankfurt: Suhrkamp, 1978, pp. 496–8.

43. P.-J. Labarrière (ed.), *Témoigner du différend. Quand phraser ne se peut. Autour de Jean-François Lyotard*, Paris: Osiris, 1989.

44. Cf. the article by M. Halbwachs, "La Psychologie collective du raisonnement" (1938), in: *idem, Classes sociales et morphologie*, Paris: Minuit, 1972, p. 150.

45. K. Mannheim, *Ideology and Utopia, op. cit.*, p. 270.

46. E. Huke-Didier, *Die Wissenssoziologie Karl Mannheims in der Interpretation durch die Kritische Theorie – Kritik einer Kritik*, Frankfurt, Berne & New York: Lang, 1985, p. 334.

47. K. Mannheim, *Ideology and Utopia, op. cit.*, p. 270.

48. Cf. K. Mannheim, *Strukturen des Denkens, op. cit.*, pp. 275–6.

49. Cf. K. Mannheim, *Konservatismus, op. cit.*, pp. 144–5.

50. Cf. V. Meja & N. Stehr (eds), *Der Streit um die Wissenssoziologie*, 2 vols: *Die Entwicklung der deutschen Wissenssoziologie* and *Rezeption und Kritik der Wissenssoziologie*, Frankfurt: Suhrkamp, 1982.

51. K. Lenk, *Marx in der Wissenssoziologie*, Lüneburg: Dietrich zu Klampen Verlag, 1986 (2nd edn), p. 50.

52. T. S. Eliot in: D. Kettler, V. Meja & N. Stehr, *Karl Mannheim*, Chichester: Ellis Horwood Ltd, 1984, p. 156.

53. Cf. H. Broch, *Schriften zur Literatur II. Theorie*, Frankfurt: Suhrkamp, 1975, p. 115. A comparison between Hermann Broch's and Karl Mannheim's theories of society is to be found in: P. V. Zima, "Irrationalität und Totalität bei Broch, Lukács und Mannheim", in: K. Amann & H. Lengauer (eds), *Österreich und der Große Krieg*, Vienna: Verlag Christian Brandstätter, 1989, pp. 223–5.

54. K. Mannheim, *Strukturen des Denkens, op. cit.*, p. 218.

55. In the present context, "polemical" means neither unfair nor rhetorical, nor sophistic.

8.   Realism and Constructivism: Lukács and Glasersfeld

1. Cf. E. von Glasersfeld, *Konstruktivismus statt Erkenntnistheorie*, ed. W. Dörfler & J. Mitterer, Klagenfurt: Drava, 1998.

2. Cf. E. von Glasersfeld, "Einführung in den Radikalen Konstruktivismus", in: P. Watzlawick (ed.), *Die erfundene Wirklichkeit. Wie wissen wir, was wir zu wissen glauben? Beiträge zum Konstruktivismus*, Munich: Piper, 1985 (3rd edn), p. 26.

3. Cf. G. Lukács, "Preface to the New Edition (1967)", in: *idem, History and Class Consciousness*, London: The Merlin Press (1971), 1990, p. XXIII.

4. The constructivist consciousness of modernism is discussed in: P. V. Zima, *Das literarische Subjekt. Zwischen Spätmoderne und Postmoderne*, Tübingen & Basel: Francke, 2001, chap. VII: "Konstruktion und Dekonstruktion des Subjekts: Unamunos *Niebla* und Pirandellos *Uno, nessuno e centomila*".

5. Hegel's "identifying thought" has provoked a number of critiques which begin in Young Hegelianism and take on radical forms in Adorno's Critical Theory and Lyotard's postmodern thought.
6. G. Lukács, *History and Class Consciousness, op. cit.*, p. 10.
7. J. E. Smith, "Hegel's Critique of Kant", in: J. J. O'Malley, K. W. Algozin & F. G. Weiss (eds), *Hegel and the History of Philosophy. Proceedings of the 1972 Hegel Society of America Conference*, The Hague: Nijhoff, 1974, p. 118.
8. G. W. F. Hegel, *Lectures on the History of Philosophy*, London & New York: Routledge & Kegan Paul and Humanities Press (1955), 1963, p. 426.
9. G. W. F. Hegel, *Science of Logic*, London & New York: Allen & Unwin and Humanities Press, 1969, p. 54.
10. G. Lukács, *History and Class Consciousness, op. cit.*, p. 146.
11. Cf. H. von Foerster & E. von Glasersfeld, *Wie wir uns erfinden. Eine Autobiographie des radikalen Konstruktivismus*, Heidelberg: Carl-Auer-Systeme Verlag, 1999, pp. 122–3.
12. G. Lukács, *History and Class Consciousness, op. cit.*, p. 66.
13. Ibid., p. 50.
14. Ibid., p. 80.
15. Cf. H. Broch, *Die Schlafwandler. Eine Romantrilogie*, Frankfurt: Suhrkamp, 1978, p. 498.
16. G. Lukács, *History and Class Consciousness, op. cit.*, p. 178. (In the German original, Lukács does not speak of "disciplines" but of "rationalistische Teilsysteme", because he does not only refer to the organization of science but to social organization at large [like his contemporary Broch]. Cf. G. Lukács, *Geschichte und Klassenbewußtsein* [1923], Darmstadt-Neuwied: Luchterhand [1968], 1975, p. 309.)
17. G. Lukács, *History and Class Consciousness*, p. 163.
18. Ibid., pp. 163–4.
19. "Identifying thought" as ideology is criticized in: T. W. Adorno, *Negative Dialectics*, London & New York: Routledge (1973), 2000, pp. 216–17 and p. 318.
20. E. von Glasersfeld, "Einführung in den radikalen Konstruktivismus", in: P. Watzlawick (ed.), *Die erfundene Wirklichkeit, op. cit.*, p. 26.
21. E. von Glasersfeld, *Radical Constructivism. A Way of Knowing and Learning*, London & Washington, Falmer Press, 1995, p. 114.
22. H. Maturana, *Was ist erkennen? Die Welt entsteht im Auge des Betrachters*, Munich: Piper, 1994; Goldmann, 2001, p. 53.
23. E. von Glasersfeld, in: "Drittes Siegener Gespräch über Radikalen Konstruktivismus. Ernst von Glasersfeld im Gespräch mit LUMIS", in: E. von Glasersfeld, *Radikaler Konstruktivismus. Ideen, Ergebnisse, Probleme*, Frankfurt: Suhrkamp, 1996, p. 353. (This discussion has not been published in the English edition.)
24. E. von Glasersfeld, *Radical Constructivism, op. cit.*, p. 109.
25. E. von Glasersfeld, "Abschied von der Objektivität", in: P. Watzlawick & P. Krieg (eds), *Das Auge des Betrachters. Beiträge zum Konstruktivismus*, Munich: Piper, 1991, p. 29.
26. E. von Glasersfeld, *Wege des Wissens. Konstruktivistische Erkundungen durch unser Denken*, Heidelberg: Carl-Auer-Systeme Verlag, 1997, p. 47.

27. E. von Glasersfeld, *Radical Constructivism, op. cit.*, p. 121.
28. F. de Saussure, *Course in General Linguistics*, London & New York (1959): Fontana-Collins, 1974, p. 143. (*Cours de linguistique générale*, Paris: Payot, 1972, p. 197.)
29. E. von Glasersfeld, *Radical Constructivism, op. cit.*, p. 121.
30. E. von Glasersfeld, *Konstruktivismus statt Erkenntnistheorie, op. cit.*, p. 37.
31. E. von Glasersfeld, *Wege des Wissens, op. cit.*, p. 59.
32. Cf. G. Lukács, *History and Class Consciousness, op. cit.*, p. 66.
33. Cf. A. Heller, *Philosophie des linken Radikalismus. Ein Bekenntnis zur Philosophie*, Hamburg: VSA-Verlag, 1978, p. 132.
34. Cf. E. von Glasersfeld, *Wege des Wissens, op. cit.*, p. 166.
35. E. von Glasersfeld, *Radical Constructivism, op. cit.*, p. 127.
36. E. von Glasersfeld, *Konstruktivismus statt Erkenntnistheorie, op. cit.*, p. 67.
37. Ibid., p. 100.
38. G. Lukács, *History and Class Consciousness, op. cit.*, p. 91.
39. H. Maturana & F. Varela, *Der Baum der Erkenntnis. Die biologischen Wurzeln menschlichen Erkennens*, Berne & Munich: Scherz Verlag & Goldmann, 1987, p. 34.
40. S. J. Schmidt, "Der Radikale Konstruktivismus: Ein neues Paradigma im interdisziplinären Diskurs", in: S. J. Schmidt (ed.), *Der Diskurs des Radikalen Konstruktivismus*, Frankfurt: Suhrkamp, 1987, p 41.
41. J. Mitterer, *Die Flucht aus der Beliebigkeit*, Frankfurt: Fischer, 2001 (2nd edn), pp. 123-4.
42. A. Kukla, *Social Constructivism and the Philosophy of Science*, London & New York: Routledge, 2000, p. 51.
43. Cf. H. J. Wendel, "Wie erfunden ist die Wirklichkeit?", in: *Delfin* 2, 1989, p. 88.
44. H. von Foerster, in: M. Ceruti, "Der Mythos der Allwissenheit und das Auge des Betrachters", in: P. Watzlawick & P. Krieg (eds), *Das Auge des Betrachters, op. cit.*, p. 31.

9.   System and Field: Luhmann and Bourdieu

1. Cf. C. Bohn, *Habitus und Kontext. Ein kritischer Beitrag zur Sozialtheorie Bourdieus*, Opladen: Westdeutscher Verlag, 1991, pp. 136-9: for a comparison of Luhmann's and Bourdieu's positions.
2. P. Bourdieu (with L. J. D. Wacquant), *Réponses. Pour une anthropologie réflexive*, Paris: Seuil, 1992, p. 79.
3. Ibid., p. 80.
4. N. Luhmann, *Die Wissenschaft der Gesellschaft*, Frankfurt: Suhrkamp, 1990, p. 668.
5. N. Luhmann, *Beobachtungen der Moderne*, Opladen: Wetsdeutscher Verlag, 1992, p. 119.
6. N. Luhmann, *Die Wissenschaft der Gesellschaft, op. cit.*, p. 704.
7. Ibid., p. 170.
8. Ibid., p. 172.

9. N. Luhmann, *Die Gesellschaft der Gesellschaft*, vol. I, Frankfurt: Suhrkamp, 1997, p. 339.

10. N. Luhmann, *Die Wissenschaft der Gesellschaft*, *op. cit.*, p. 198.

11. Ibid.

12. Ibid.

13. Ibid., p. 204.

14. Ibid., p. 253.

15. N. Luhmann, *Soziale Systeme. Grundriß einer allgemeinen Theorie*, Frankfurt: Suhrkamp (1984), 1987, p. 513.

16. N. Luhmann, *Die Wissenschaft der Gesellschaft*, *op. cit.*, p. 667.

17. Ibid., p. 668.

18. Cf. ibid., pp. 62–3.

19. Cf. ibid., p. 8.

20. Ibid., p. 702.

21. Ibid., p. 240.

22. N. Luhmann, in: W. Rasch, *Niklas Luhmann's Modernity. The Paradoxes of Differentiation*, Stanford: Stanford Univ. Press, 2000, p. 199.

23. P. Bourdieu, *Science of Science and Reflexivity*, Cambridge: Polity, 2004, p. 70.

24. The speaking subject's position in theoretical discourse is discussed in: P. V. Zima, *Theorie des Subjekts. Subjektivität und Identität zwischen Moderne und Postmoderne*, Tübingen & Basel: Francke, 2000, chap. I, 1 (d).

25. T. Schwinn, "Differenzierung und soziale Integration. Wider eine systemtheoretisch halbierte Soziologie", in: H.-J. Giegel & U. Schimank (eds), *Beobachter der Moderne. Beiträge zu Niklas Luhmanns "Die Gesellschaft der Gesellschaft"*, Frankfurt: Suhrkamp (2001), 2003, p. 231.

26. Cf. R. Greshoff, "Kommunikation als subjekthaftes Handlungsgeschehen – behindern 'traditionelle' Konzepte eine 'genaue begriffliche Bestimmung des Gegenstandes Gesellschaft'?", in: H.-J. Giegel & U. Schimank (eds), *Beobachter der Moderne*, *op. cit.*, pp. 78–9.

27. Cf. what J. Baudrillard has to say about the de-differentiation of society and about the domination of its different spheres by the economy: J. Baudrillard, *La Transparence du Mal. Essai sur les phénomènes extrêmes*, Paris: Galilée, 1990, pp. 11–50.

28. Cf. N. Luhmann, in: W. Rasch, *Niklas Luhmann's Modernity*, *op. cit.*, p. 204.

29. W. Rasch, in: ibid., p. 207.

30. Cf. A. Accardo & P. Corcuff, *La Sociologie de Bourdieu. Textes choisis et commentés*, Bordeaux: Le Mascaret, 1986, p. 14.

31. The concept of *habitus* as used by Bourdieu was originally introduced into the debate by the art historian Erwin Panofsky. Cf. P. Bourdieu, *Choses dites*, Paris: Minuit, 1987, p. 23.

32. P. Bourdieu, *Questions de sociologie*, Paris: Minuit, 1980, p. 114.

33. Cf. C. Bohn, *Habitus und Kontext*, *op. cit.*, p. 96: "So what is the social that has been introduced along with the concept of power? The fundamental paradigm of the social is for Bourdieu a dynamic market imbued with conflict; and the resulting modes of the social: exchange, struggle and competition."

34. Cf. P. Bourdieu (with L. J. D. Wacquant), *Réponses, op. cit.*, p. 72.

35. Cf. C. Calhoun, "Habitus, Field and Capital: The Question of Historical Specificity", in: C. Calhoun, E. LiPuma & M. Postone (eds), *Bourdieu. Critical Perspectives*, Cambridge & Oxford: Polity and Blackwell, 1993, p. 70.

36. Not always, however. W. Kemp for example describes the flourishing trade in academic titles in the USA, showing at the same time to what extent the academic world is dominated by Luhmann's economic principle *payment/non-payment*: cf. W. Kemp, "Wo Rudi Rüssel einen Lehrstuhl hat. Ein Besuch beim Titelhandel", in: J. Wertheimer & P. V. Zima (eds), *Strategien der Verdummung. Infantilisierung in der Fun-Gesellschaft*, Munich: Beck, 2001.

37. Cf. N. Luhmann, *Soziale Systeme, op. cit.*, p. 245.

38. Cf. A. Accardo & P. Corcuff, *La Sociologie de Bourdieu, op. cit.*, p. 93.

39. Cf. O. Šik, *Plan und Markt im Sozialismus*, Vienna: Molden, 1965, pp. 22–4.

40. P. Bourdieu, *Firing Back. Against the Tyranny of the Market 2*, London & New York: Verso, 2003, p. 38.

41. P. Bourdieu, *On Television*, New York: The New Press, 1998, p. 63.

42. Ibid., p. 61.

43. P. Bourdieu, *Choses dites, op. cit.*, p. 114.

44. Ibid.

45. Ibid.

46. P. Bourdieu, *Science of Science and Reflexivity, op. cit.*, p. 86.

47. Ibid., p. 87.

48. Ibid.

49. Cf. P. Bourdieu, *Language and Symbolic Power*, ed. J. B. Thompson, Cambridge: Polity (1991), 2005, Part II: "The Social Institution of Symbolic Power". The main topic here is the institutionalization and the social effect of discourse, not its structure.

50. P. Bourdieu, *Homo academicus*, Paris: Minuit, 1984, p. 211.

51. P. Bourdieu, *Language and Symbolic Power, op. cit.*, p. 57.

52. Ibid., p. 169.

53. Cf. P. Bourdieu, *The Rules of Art. Genesis and Structure of the Literary Field*, Cambridge & Oxford, Polity and Blackwell, 1996, p. 215 and p. 222.

54. Cf. P. Bourdieu (with L. J. D. Wacquant), *Réponses, op. cit.*, p. 80.

55. P. Bourdieu, *Science of Science and Reflexivity, op. cit.*, p. 33.

56. Cf. B. Schwarz, *Vertical Classification. A Study in Structuralism and the Sociology of Knowledge*, Chicago & London: Univ. of Chicago Press, 1981, pp. 7–8.

57. Cf. P. Bourdieu, *Language and Symbolic Power, op. cit.*, p. 167 and B. Krais, "Gender and Symbolic Violence: Female Oppression in the Light of Pierre Bourdieu's Theory of Social Practice", in: C Calhoun *et al.* (eds), *Bourdieu. Critical Perspectives, op. cit.*, pp. 168–73.

58. P. Bourdieu, *Science of Science and Reflexivity, op. cit.*, p. 54.

59. Ibid., p. 84.

60. Ibid., p. 116. (*Science de la science et réflexivité*, Paris: Raisons d'Agir, 2001, p. 222.)

61. P. Bourdieu, *Choses dites, op. cit.*, p. 112.

62. Cf. N. Luhmann, *Soziale Systeme, op. cit.*, p. 111.

63. P. Bourdieu, *Science of Science and Reflexivity, op. cit.*, p. 83.

64. Ibid.

65. Ibid., p. 76.

66. P. Bourdieu, *In Other Words. Essays Towards a Reflexive Sociology*, Cambridge & Oxford: Polity and Blackwell, 1990, p. 198. (*Leçon sur la leçon*, Paris: Minuit, 1982, p. 55.)

67. P. Bourdieu, *Science of Science and Reflexivity, op. cit.*, p. 77.

68. R. Jenkins, *Pierre Bourdieu*, London & New York: Routledge, 1992, p. 91.

69. Ibid., p. 97.

70. Ibid., p. 86.

71. J. Baudrillard, *La Transparence du Mal, op. cit.*, pp. 22–7.

72. P. Bourdieu, *Science of Science and Reflexivity, op. cit.*, p. 73.

73. Cf. H. Gripp-Hagelstange, *Niklas Luhmann. Eine Einführung*, Munich: Fink, 1997 (2nd edn), pp. 142–6.

10. Intersubjectivity and Power Structures: Habermas and Foucault (Althusser, Pêcheux)

1. Cf. J. Habermas, "The Critique of Reason as an Unmasking of the Human Sciences: Michel Foucault", in: *idem, The Philosophical Discourse of Modernity*, Cambridge: Polity (1987), 2005, pp. 253–4.

2. Cf. S. Ashenden & D. Owen (eds), *Foucault Contra Habermas*, London, Thousand Oaks & Delhi: Sage, 1999.

3. Cf. J. Habermas, *Theorie und Parxis. Sozialphilosophische Studien*, Frankfurt: Suhrkamp (1963), 1972, pp. 42–3.

4. M. Foucault, "La Torture, c'est la raison", in: *idem, Dits et écrits*, vol. III, Paris: Gallimard, 1994, p. 390.

5. M. Foucault, "Structuralisme et poststructuralisme", in: *idem, Dits et écrits*, vol. IV, *op. cit.*, p. 439.

6. J. Habermas, *Justification and Application. Remarks on Discourse Ethics*, Cambridge & Oxford: Polity and Blackwell, 1993, p. 50.

7. Cf. L. Althusser, "Idéologie et appareils idéologiques d'Etat", in: *idem, Positions*, Paris: Editions Sociales, 1976, p. 122.

8. L. Quéré, "Vers une anthropologie alternative. Pour les sciences sociales?", in: Ch. Bouchindhomme & R. Rochlitz (eds), *Habermas, la raison, la critique*, Paris: Les Editions du Cerf, 1996, p. 128.

9. Cf. J. Habermas, *Justification and Application, op. cit.*, p. 49. Discourse as a clarifying discussion aiming at the analysis of "problematical claims to legitimacy", is conceived as a reflexive process.

10. J. Habermas, *Nachmetaphysisches Denken. Philosophische Aufsätze*, Frankfurt: Suhrkamp, 1997 (2nd edn), p. 46.

11. Ibid.

12. J. Habermas, *Theory of Communicative Action*, vol. II, *The Critique of Functionalist Reason*, Cambridge & Oxford: Polity and Blackwell (1987), 2004, p. 145.

13. J. Habermas, *Justification and Application*, op. cit., pp. 90–1.

14. J. Habermas, *Erläuterungen zur Diskursethik*, Frankfurt: Suhrkamp, 1991, p. 203.

15. D. Owen, "Orientation and Enlightenment. An Essay on Critique and Genealogy", in: S. Ashenden & D. Owen (eds), *Foucault Contra Habermas*, op. cit., p. 37. A similar idea is put forward by S. Thompson in his contribution to the collective volume quoted above: "The Agony and The Ecstasy. Foucault, Habermas and the Problem of Recognition", in: S. Ashenden & D. Owen (eds), *Foucault Contra Habermas*, op. cit., p. 198: "(...) The subject is defined by systems of power/knowledge which make the other a sublime outsider."

16. J. Habermas, "Entgegnung", in: A. Honneth & H. Joas (eds), *Kommunikatives Handeln. Beiträge zu Jürgen Habermas' "Theorie des kommunikativen Handelns"*, Frankfurt: Suhrkamp, 1986, p. 372.

17. J. Habermas, *The Theory of Communicative Action*, vol. II, op. cit., p. 119.

18. Cf. E. Husserl, *Die Krisis der europäischen Wissenschaften und die transzendentale Phänomenologie*, ed. W. Biemel, The Hague: Nijhoff, 1962, pp. 105–93: Part III: "Der Weg in die phänomenologische Transzendentalphilosophie in der Rückfrage von der vorgegebenen Lebenswelt aus" and A. Schütz, *Das Problem der Relevanz*, Frankfurt: Suhrkamp (1971), 1982, pp. 179–87: "Die Dimension der Lebenswelt".

19. J. Habermas, *The Theory of Communicative Action*, vol. II, op. cit., p. 126.

20. Ibid.

21. A comparison of Habermas's "ideal speech situation" and Karl Mannheim's "free floating intelligentsia" can be found in: P. V. Zima, *Ideologie und Theorie. Eine Diskurskritik*, Tübingen: Francke, 1989, chap. III.

22. J. Habermas, *The Theory of Communicative Action*, vol. II, op. cit., p. 124.

23. J. Habermas, *Vorstudien und Ergänzungen zur Theorie des kommunikativen Handelns*, Frankfurt: Suhrkamp, 1986 (2nd edn), p. 118.

24. Ibid.

25. Ibid., p. 119.

26. Ibid.

27. Ibid., p. 120.

28. Ibid.

29. J. Habermas, *Justification and Application*, op. cit., p. 50.

30. J. Habermas, *Moral Consciousness and Communicative Action*, Cambridge: Polity (1990), 2003, p. 68.

31. Ibid., p. 87.

32. Ibid., p. 92. (*Moralbewußtsein und kommunikatives Handeln*, Frankfurt: Suhrkamp, 1983, p. 102.)

33. M. Stirner, *Der Einzige und sein Eigentum*, Stuttgart: Reclam, 1972, pp. 381–2.

34. Cf. H. Albert, *Transzendentale Träumereien. Karl-Otto Apels Sprachspiele und sein hermeneutischer Gott*, Hamburg: Hoffmann & Campe, 1975, pp. 136–7.

35. Cf. J. Habermas, *Vorstudien und Ergänzungen zur Theorie des kommunikativen Handelns*, *op. cit.*, p. 122. In discourse, Habermas explains, "problematic claims to validity are discussed". In this book, "discourse" is not defined as a discussion but as a semantic and narrative structure based on an actantial model (in the sense of Greimas).

36. J. Habermas, "Vorbereitende Bemerkungen zu einer Theorie der kommunikativen Kompetenz", in: J. Habermas & N. Luhmann, *Theorie der Gesellschaft oder Sozialtechnologie – Was leistet die Systemforschung?*, Frankfurt: Suhrkamp (1971), 1982, p. 103.

37. The reader will find a more detailed criticism of this attempt at neutralization in: P. V. Zima, *Ideologie und Theorie, op. cit.*, pp. 107–23.

38. J. Habermas, "Vorbereitende Bemerkungen zu einer Theorie der kommunikativen Kompetenz", in: J. Habermas & N. Luhmann, *Theorie der Gesellschaft, op. cit.*, p. 122.

39. It can actually be shown that Habermas highlights the conflictual character of society by orienting the process of socialization towards intersubjective consensus: "Subjects capable of speech and action are constituted as individuals by being integrated into an intersubjectively shared life world as members of particular language communities." (*Erläuterungen zur Diskursethik*, Frankfurt: Suhrkamp, 1991, p. 15.) However, in a society many different rival language communities coexist, and their conflicts can penetrate into the individual's process of socialization, thus creating considerable tensions and conflicts within this individual's psyche and between individuals.

40. The implicit negation of real (social) subjectivity in the theories of Descartes, Kant and Fichte is analysed in: P. V. Zima, *Theorie des Subjekts. Subjektivität und Identität zwischen Moderne und Postmoderne*, Tübingen & Basel: Francke, 2000, chap. II, 1.

41. J. Habermas, *Justification and Application, op. cit.*, S. 50.

42. W. Rasch, *Niklas Luhmann's Modernity. The Paradoxes of Differentiation*, Stanford: Stanford Univ. Press, 2000, p. 32.

43. Cf. J. Habermas, *Die Einbeziehung des Anderen*, Frankfurt: Suhrkamp, 1997 (2nd edn), p. 56.

44. One should add that even strategic action does not exclude attempts to understand the Other, as J. Alexander quite rightly points out and that "conflict and strategy do not imply a lack of understanding". (J. Alexander, "Habermas' neue Kritische Theorie: Anspruch und Probleme", in: A. Honneth & H. Joas [eds], *Kommunikatives Handeln. Beiträge zu Jürgen Habermas' "Theorie des kommunikativen Handelns"*, Frankfurt: Suhrkamp, 1986, p. 95.) The treaties of the great powers which strike a balance between all conceivable interests and eventualities bear witness to this.

45. M. Foucault, "Les Rapports de pouvoir passent à l'intérieur des corps", in: *idem*, *Dits et écrits*, vol. III, Paris: Gallimard, 1994, p. 229.

46. T. W. Adorno, *Negative Dialectics*, London & New York: Routledge (1973), 2000, p. 179.

47. J. Habermas, *The Philosophical Discourse of Modernity, op. cit.*, pp. 242–3.

48. Ibid., p. 246.

49. Ibid., p. 254.

50. M. Foucault, *Discipline and Punish. The Birth of the Prison* (1977), London: Penguin, 1991, p. 27.

51. M. Foucault, *The Birth of the Clinic. An Archaeology of Medical Perception* (1973), London & New York: Routledge, 2003, p. 198.

52. M. Foucault, "Structuralisme et poststructuralisme", in: *idem, Dits et écrits*, vol. IV, Paris: Gallimard, 1994, p. 438.

53. G. Deleuze, *Foucault*, London & New York: Continuum (1988), 1999, pp. 33–4.

54. Cf. J. Piaget, *Le Structuralisme*, Paris: PUF, 1974, p. 114. Piaget criticizes Foucault for not having developed a theory of evolution and for being unable to explain the transition from one episteme to the next. This criticism is only partly justified, because one does find traces of an explanation in some of the articles published in *Dits et écrits*.

55. M. Foucault, "Nietzsche, la généalogie, l'histoire", in: *idem, Dits et écrits*, vol. II, Paris: Gallimard, 1994, p. 145.

56. Ibid.

57. M. Foucault, *Discipline and Punish, op. cit.*, p. 194.

58. Cf. L. Althusser, "Freud and Lacan", in: *idem, Lenin and Philosophy and Other Essays*, New York: Monthly Review Press, 1971, p. 189–220.

59. L. Althusser, *Philosophie et philosophie spontanée des savants (1967)*, Paris: Maspero, 1974, p. 94.

60. L. Althusser, "Idéologie et appareils idéologiques d'Etat", in: *idem, Positions, op. cit.*, p. 122.

61. Ibid., pp. 119–20.

62. Ibid., p. 114.

63. A distinction between religion and ideology is proposed in: P. V. Zima, *Ideologie und Theorie, op. cit.*, chap. I, 2.

64. L. Althusser & E. Balibar, *Reading Capital*, London: NLB, 1977 (2nd edn), p. 27.

65. L. Althusser, "Idéologie et appareils idéologiques d'Etat", in: *Positions, op. cit.*, p. 123.

66. This concept should not be confused with the concept of interdiscursive dialogue proposed here. For the latter excludes the domination of a homogeneous "interdiscourse"; moreover, it presupposes the ability of relatively autonomous subjects to reflect self-critically upon their own discourses.

67. M. Pêcheux, *Les Vérités de La Palice*, Paris: Maspero, 1975, p. 146.

68. K. Marx, "Theses on Feuerbach", in: K. Marx & F. Engels, *Basic Writings on Politics and Philosophy*, ed. L. S. Feuer, New York: Doubleday-Anchor, 1959, p. 244.

69. M. Foucault, "Les Intellectuels et le pouvoir" (a discussion with Gilles Deleuze), in: *idem, Dits et écrits*, vol. II, Paris: Gallimard, 1994, p. 308.

70. G. Deleuze, in: M. Foucault, "Les Intellectuels et le pouvoir", *op. cit.*, p. 309.

71. J. Habermas, "Mit dem Pfeil ins Herz der Gegenwart. Zu Foucaults Vorlesung über Kants *Was ist Aufklärung*", in: *idem, Die Neue Unübersichtlichkeit*, Frankfurt: Suhrkamp, 1985, p. 131.

Part Three
Dialogical Theory: A Meta-Theory of Scientific Communication

1. Cf. J. Derrida, *Glas. Que reste-t-il du savoir absolu?* (2 vols), Paris: Denoël-Gonthier, 1981.
2. Cf. H. Dubiel, *Wissenschaftsorganisation und politische Erfahrung. Studien zur frühen Kritischen Theorie*, Frankfurt: Suhrkamp, 1978, pp. 81–4.
3. Cf. J. Habermas, *The Philosophical Discourse of Modernity*, Cambridge: Polity (1987), 2005, chap. V.
4. Cf. P. W. Balsinger, "Dialogische Theorie? – Methodische Konzeption!", in: *Ethik und Sozialwissenschaften* 4, 1999, p. 604.
5. Cf. H. Albert, *Traktat über kritische Vernunft*, Tübingen: Mohr-Siebeck, 1980 (4th edn), p. 11–15.
6. Cf. P. V. Zima, *Theorie des Subjekts. Subjektivität und Identität zwischen Moderne und Postmoderne*, Tübingen & Basel: Francke, 2000, chap. V.
7. H. Keupp, "Diskursarena Identität: Lernprozesse in der Identitätsforschung", in: H. Keupp & R. Höfer (eds), *Identitätsarbeit heute. Klassische und aktuelle Perspektiven in der Identitätsforschung*, Frankfurt: Suhrkamp, 1997, p. 13.
8. H. H. Kögler, *Die Macht des Dialogs. Kritische Hermeneutik nach Gadamer, Foucault und Rorty*, Stuttgart: Metzler, 1992, p. 7.
9. Ibid., p. 12.
10. P. Bourdieu, *Science of Science and Reflexivity*, Cambridge: Polity, 2004, p. 70.

11. Critical Theory as Dialogue:
Ambivalence and Dialectics, Non-Identity and Alterity

1. Cf. M. Jay, *The Dialectical Imagination. A History of the Frankfurt School and the Institute of Social Research 1923–1950*, Boston & Toronto: Little, Brown & Co., 1973; A. Schmidt, *Zur Idee der Kritischen Theorie*, Munich: Hanser, 1974; R. Wiggershaus, *Die Frankfurter Schule. Geschichte. Theoretische Entwicklung. Politische Bedeutung*, Munich: DTV, 1989 (2nd edn).
2. Cf. "Aus der Tagespresse", in: *Information Philosophie* 5, 2000, p. 49.
3. Cf. S. Best & D. Kellner, *Postmodern Theory. Critical Interrogations*, London: Macmillan, 1991, p. 225: "Adorno's Proto-Postmodern Theory".
4. J. Habermas, "Dialektik der Rationalisierung", in: ders., *Die Neue Unübersichtlichkeit*, Frankfurt: Suhrkamp, 1985, p. 172.
5. Cf. P. V. Zima, *Ideologie und Theorie. Eine Diskurskritik*, Tübingen: Francke, 1989, chap. VI and X.
6. P. Macherey, *Hegel ou Spinoza*, Paris: Maspero, 1979, p. 253.
7. Cf. W. Benjamin, "Geschichtsphilosophische Thesen", in: *idem, Kritik der Gewalt und andere Aufsätze*, Frankfurt: Suhrkamp, 1971 (2nd edn), pp. 80–5.

8. E. Volhard, *Zwischen Hegel und Nietzsche. Der Ästhetiker Friedrich Theodor Vischer*, Frankfurt: Klostermann, 1932, p. 197.

9. P. J. Proudhon quoted in G. Gurvitch, *Dialectique et sociologie*, Paris: Flammarion, 1962, p. 130. Commenting on Proudhon's dialectics, Gurvitch writes: "As an alternative to Hegel's dialectic Proudhon proposes another dialectic: his own. He not only envisages an antinomic, negative and antithetic dialectic which rejects all syntheses; he envisages a dialectical method which looks for diversity in all its details" (p. 131). The proximity to the Young Hegelians and Adorno is striking here.

10. Cf. K. Löwith, *Von Hegel zu Nietzsche. Der revolutionäre Bruch im Denken des 19. Jahrhunderts*, Hamburg: Meiner, 1986 (9th edn), chap. II: "Althegelianer, Junghegelianer, Neuhegelianer".

11. F. Nietzsche, *Die fröhliche Wissenschaft*, in: idem, *Werke*, vol. III, ed. K. Schlechta, Munich: Hanser, 1980, p. 145.

12. F. Nietzsche, *Menschliches, Allzumenschliches*, in: idem, *Werke*, vol. II, *op. cit.*, p. 873.

13. Ch. Baudelaire, "Mon cœur mis à nu", in: idem, *Œuvres complètes*, vol. I, texte établi, présenté et annoté par Cl. Pichois, Paris: Gallimard, Bibl. de la Pléiade, 1975, p. 678.

14. Ambivalence and irony as modernist features are discussed in: A. Wilde, *Horizons of Assent: Modernism, Postmodernism and the Ironic Imagination*, Baltimore & London: Johns Hopkins Univ. Press, 1981.

15. Ambivalence as unity of opposites is a salient feature of Pirandello's works. Cf. L. Pirandello, "L'umorismo", in: idem, *Saggi, poesie, scritti varii*, Milan: Mondadori, 1977 (4th edn), p. 156, where a "sentimento del contrario", a "feeling of contradiction" is mentioned.

16. G. W. F. Hegel, *Science of Logic*, London & New York: Allen & Unwin and Humanities Press, 1969, p. 48.

17. Cf. Paul de Man's remarks concerning Nietzschean contradiction in: P. de Man, *Allegories of Reading. Figural Language in Rousseau, Nietzsche, Rilke, and Proust*, New Haven & London: Yale Univ. Press, 1979, pp. 9–15.

18. R. Musil, "Aphorismen", in: idem, *Gesammelte Werke*, vol. VII, ed. A. Frisé, Reinbek: Rowohlt, 1978, p. 826.

19. R. Musil, *Der Mann ohne Eigenschaften*, in: idem, *Gesammelte Werke*, vol. I, *op. cit.*, p. 253.

20. G. Adorno & R. Tiedemann, "Editors' Afterword", in: T. W. Adorno, *Aesthetic Theory*, London: Athlone, 1997, p. 364.

21. T. W. Adorno, *Aesthetic Theory*, *op. cit.*, p. 331.

22. The non-conceptual character of "mimesis" in the sense of Adorno is commented on in detail in: W. M. Lüdke, *Anmerkungen zu einer "Logik des Zerfalls": Adorno-Beckett*, Frankfurt: Suhrkamp, 1981, p. 68.

23. T. W. Adorno, *Minima Moralia. Reflections on a Damaged Life*, London & New York (1974): Verso, 2005, p. 150.

24. D. Kipfer, *Individualität nach Adorno*, Tübingen & Basel: Francke, 1999, p. 82.

25. P. Grujić, *Hegel und die Sowjetphilosophie der Gegenwart*, Berne & Munich: Francke, 1969, p. 64.

26. The function of contradiction in Derridean deconstruction is discussed in: P. V. Zima, *Deconstruction and Critical Theory*, London & New York: Continuum, 2002, pp. 32–4.

27. Cf. P. V. Zima, "Theodor W. Adorno: dialectique en suspens", in: *idem, L'Ecole de Francfort. Dialectique de la particularité*, Paris (1974): L'Harmattan, 2005 (new edn), pp. 69–71.

28. T. W. Adorno, *Negative Dialectics* (1966), London & New York: Routledge, 2000, p. 406.

29. T. W. Adorno, *Minima Moralia, op. cit.*, p. 50.

30. M. Horkheimer, *Anfänge der bürgerlichen Geschichtsphilosophie. Hegel und das Problem der Metaphysik. Montaigne und die Funktion der Skepsis*, Frankfurt: Fischer, 1971, p. 89.

31. Cf. M. Horkheimer & T. W. Adorno, *Dialectic of Enlightenment* (1947), London & New York: Verso, 1997, p. 19.

32. T. W. Adorno, *Negative Dialectics, op. cit.*, p. 15.

33. T. W. Adorno, *Aesthetic Theory, op. cit.*, p. 131.

34. Ibid., pp. 115–16.

35. Cf. M. M. Bakhtin, *Problems of Dostoevsky's Poetics*, Manchester: Manchester Univ. Press, 1984, p. 250.

36. T. W. Adorno, *Metaphysik. Begriff und Probleme*, ed. R. Tiedemann, Frankfurt: Suhrkamp, 1998, p. 220.

37. Ibid.

38. Cf. K. R. Popper, *The Open Society and its Enemies*, vol. II, *The High Tide of Prophecy: Hegel, Marx, and the Aftermath*, London: Routledge & Kegan Paul (1945), 1962, pp. 41–2.

39. Cf. T. W. Adorno, "Zur Logik der Sozialwissenschaften", in: T. W. Adorno *et al.*, *Der Positivismusstreit in der deutschen Soziologie*, Darmstadt & Neuwied: Luchterhand (1969), 1972, pp. 138–9. Some of the articles published in this volume have been translated into English in: A. Giddens (ed.), *Positivism and Sociology*, London: Heinemann, 1974: especially H. Albert, "The Myth of Total Reason" and J. Habermas, "Rationalism Divided in Two".

40. T. W. Adorno, *Zur Lehre von der Geschichte und von der Freiheit*, ed. R. Tiedemann, Frankfurt: Suhrkamp, 2001, p. 100.

41. M. M. Bakhtin, *Problems of Dostoevsky's Poetics, op. cit.*, p. 250.

42. Ibid., p. 95.

43. Cf. P. V. Zima, Bakhtin's "Young Hegelian Aesthetics", in: *Critical Studies* 2 ("The Bakhtin Circle Today"), 1989, pp. 81–2.

12. Subjectivity, Reflection and the Construction of Objects in Discourse

1. E. von Glasersfeld, *Konstruktivismus statt Erkenntnistheorie*, Klagenfurt: Drava, 1998, p. 43.

2. E. von Glasersfeld, in: "Drittes Siegener Gespräch über Radikalen Konstruktivismus. Ernst von Glasersfeld im Gespräch mit LUMIS", in: E. von Glasersfeld, *Radikaler Konstruktivismus. Ideen, Ergebnisse, Probleme*, Frankfurt: Suhrkamp, 1996, p. 330.

3. L. J. Prieto, "Entwurf einer allgemeinen Semiologie", in: *Zeitschrift für Semiotik* 1, 1979, p. 263.

4. L. J. Prieto, *Pertinence et pratique. Essai de sémiologie*, Paris: Minuit, 1975, p. 148.

5. E. von Glasersfeld, *Wege des Wissens. Konstruktivistische Erkundungen durch unser Denken*, Heidelberg: Carl-Auer-Systeme Verlag, 1997, p. 45.

6. The concept of "idiolect" is defined in Umberto Eco's *A Theory of Semiotics*, Bloomington: Indiana Univ. Press. 1976, chap. 3. 7. 6.

7. Cf. P. V. Zima, *Theorie des Subjekts. Subjektivität und Identität zwischen Moderne und Postmoderne*, Tübingen & Basel: Francke, 2000, chap. V, 1.

8. As in *Theorie des Subjekts* (cf. supra) individuality is distinguished here from subjectivity. In this perspective, the individual appears as a physical and psychic entity without a social and linguistic identity (e.g. the infant), while the subject turns out to be the – always provisional – result of this identity process: cf. *Theorie des Subjekts, op. cit.*, chap. I, 1, c.

9. Y. Lotman, *Analysis of the Poetic Text*, Ann Arbor: Ardis, 1976, p. 19.

10. The "mythical actant", as defined by Greimas and his followers, is an actor whose physical and social existence can be queried for all sorts of reasons: e.g. Hegel's "World Spirit".

11. Cf. A. Touraine, *Critique de la modernité*, Paris: Fayard, 1992, pp. 111–26.

12. Cf. H. White, "Vergangenheit konstruieren", in: H. R. Fischer & S. J. Schmidt (eds), *Wirklichkeit und Welterzeugung*, Heidelberg: Carl-Auer-Systeme Verlag, 2000, p. 338.

13. A. Kukla, *Social Constructivism and the Philosophy of Science*, London & New York: Routledge, 2000, p. 9.

14. E. von Glasersfeld, *Radical Constructivism. A Way of Knowing and Learning*, London: Falmer Press, 1995, p. 128.

15. Cf. S. Fish, *Doing What Comes Naturally*, Oxford: Clarendon Press, 1989, p. 77. A critique of this approach is to be found in: P. V. Zima, *The Philosophy of Modern Literary Theory*, London: Athlone, 1999, pp. 75–80.

16. Cf. A. Camus, *L'Etranger*, Paris: Gallimard (1942), 1957, p. 5 and p. 91 and A. Camus, *The Outsider*, Harmondsworth: Penguin, 1964, p. 11 and p. 65.

17. Cf. P. V. Zima, *The Philosophy of Modern Literary Theory, op. cit.*, chap. IX.

18. H. von Foerster, "Das Konstruieren einer Wirklichkeit", in: P. Watzlawick (ed.), *Die erfundene Wirklichkeit. Wie wissen wir, was wir zu wissen glauben? Beiträge zum Konstruktivismus*, Munich: Piper, 1985 (3rd edn), p. 40.

19. Cf. H. J. Wendel, "Wie erfunden ist die Wirklichkeit?", in: *Delfin* 2, 1989, p. 85.

20. W. Franzen, "Totgesagte leben länger: Beyond Realism and Anti-Realism: Realism", in: Forum für Philosophie Bad Homburg (ed.), *Realismus und Antirealismus*, Frankfurt: Suhrkamp, 1992, p. 43.

21. M. M. Bakhtin, *Die Ästhetik des Wortes*, ed. R. Grübel, Frankfurt: Suhrkamp, 1979, p. 237.

22. G. Deleuze & F. Guattari, *Qu'est-ce que la philosophie?*, Paris: Minuit, 1991, p. 60.
23. Ibid., p. 80.
24. Cf. A. Touraine, *Pourrons-nous vivre ensemble? Egaux et différents*, Paris: Fayard, 1997, pp. 134–9.
25. Cf. S. Agosti, *Lecture de "Prose pour des Esseintes" et de quelques autres poèmes de Mallarmé*, Chambéry: Ed. Comp'Act, 1998, p. 136. Commenting on Mallarmé's poems in general, Agosti remarks: "They have only one meaning, and a very precise one that has to be found out (...)."
26. W. Franzen, "Totgesagte leben länger", in: Forum für Philosophie Bad Homburg (ed.), *Realismus und Antirealismus, op. cit.*, p. 43.
27. Ibid., p. 37.
28. A. Kukla, *Social Constructivism and the Philosophy of Science, op. cit.*, p. 95.
29. H. Maturana, "Wissenschaft und Alltag: Die Ontologie wissenschaftlicher Erklärungen", in: P. Watzlawick & P. Krieg (eds), *Das Auge des Betrachters. Beiträge zum Konstruktivismus*, Munich: Piper, 1991, p. 187.
30. Ibid., p. 190.
31. E. von Glasersfeld, *Konstruktivismus statt Erkenntnistheorie, op. cit.*, p. 93.

13.   Interdiscursive Dialogue: Theory

1. Here the fundamental problem is the dialogue between scientific theories and not − as Hans Nicklas seems to believe − "discussions between ethnic, cultural or religious communities". (Cf. H. Nicklas, "Die dialogische Theorie: Eine Baustelle", in: *Ethik und Sozialwissenschaften* 4, 1999, p. 637.) For discussions among religious and ideological groups are not primarily oriented towards the concepts of knowledge and empirically founded truth, but towards political or legal status and social recognition. It goes without saying that theoretical reflection and a dialogical approach can be useful in such cases where the practical function of theory comes to the fore − especially since a discussion between religious or ideological monologues is impossible. Only "peaceful coexistence" seems to be conceivable here − or conflict.
2. The psychoanalytic concept of ambivalence is defined by Freud as the coexistence of contrasting aspirations, attitudes or feelings.
3. D. Bohm, *On Dialogue*, ed. L. Nichol, London & New York: Routledge, 1996, p. 7.
4. Although the collective factor plays an important part in Dialogical Theory, the latter does not primarily deal with communication between groups, as Erich H. Witte seems to assume, when he remarks: "I had to learn that a group is hardly capable of tackling complex problems, in spite of all the good will of its members." (E. H. Witte, "Teamfähigkeit und Moderation in den Sozialwissenschaften beim theoretischen Diskurs", in: *Ethik und Sozialwissenschaften* 4, 1999, p. 655.) The collective factor which matters here also manifests itself in discussions between individuals, one of whom may speak the language (sociolect) of Critical Rationalism while the other adopts a psychoanalytic point of view. This is why communication within a group or "team" is not a key problem here.

5.   J. Habermas, *Moral Consciousness and Communicative Action*, Cambridge: Polity, 1990, p. 87.

6.   Cf. J. Habermas's use of the word "system" in: *The Theory of Communicative Action*, vol. II, *The Critique of Functionalist Reason*, Cambridge & Oxford: Polity and Blackwell (1987), 2004, pp. 283–99.

7.   D. Bohm, *On Dialogue, op. cit.*, p. 2.

8.   E. Laclau, "Psychoanalysis and Marxism", in: *Critical Inquiry* 13, 1987, p. 333.

9.   R. Greshoff, *Die theoretischen Konzeptionen des Sozialen von Max Weber und Niklas Luhmann im Vergleich*, Opladen & Wiesbaden: Westdeutscher Verlag, 1999, p. 34.

10. R. Greshoff, "Lassen sich die Konzepte von Max Weber und Niklas Luhmann unter dem Aspekt 'Struktur und Ereignis' miteinander vermitteln?", in: R. Greshoff & G. Kneer (eds), *Struktur und Ereignis in theorievergleichender Perspektive. Ein diskursives Buchprojekt*, Opladen & Wiesbaden: Westdeutscher Verlag, 1999, p. 43.

11. The concept of *narrative programme* is defined in: A. J. Greimas, *Maupassant. La sémiotique du texte: exercices pratiques*, Paris: Seuil, 1976, pp. 48–61.

12. Cf. T. Burns & G. M. Stalker, *The Management of Innovation*, London: Pergamon Press, 1961.

13. N. Luhmann, *Soziale Systeme. Grundriß einer allgemeinen Theorie*, Frankfurt: Suhrkamp (1984), 1987, p. 524.

14. N. Luhmann, *Die Wirtschaft der Gesellschaft*, Frankfurt: Suhrkamp (1988), 1994, p. 101.

15. Matthias von Saldern raises an important epistemological question when he remarks: "A key question seems to be who decides which group languages are to be considered as heterogeneous or homogeneous." (M. von Saldern, "Auch Sozialwissenschaftler/innen sind nur Menschen", in: *Ethik und Sozialwissenschaften* 4, 1999, p. 643.) The answer is: the vocabulary, the semantics and the narrative syntax (the actantial model) – together with the ideological positions of the theoreticians involved. Thus Weber's "understanding sociology" and Luhmann's systems theory are linguistically heterogeneous because they are based on different actantial models. At the same time, they are ideologically heterogeneous, because they imply different models of society. Hence homogeneity and heterogeneity are semiotic and sociological concepts.

16. H.-G. Gadamer, "Rhetorik, Hermeneutik und Ideologiekritik. Metakritische Erörterungen zu *Wahrheit und Methode*", in: K.-O. Apel *et al.*, *Hermeneutik und Ideologiekritik*, Frankfurt: Suhrkamp (1971), 1980, p. 79.

17. H. Maturana, *Was ist erkennen? Die Welt entsteht im Auge des Betrachters*, Munich: Piper, 1994; Goldmann, 2001, p. 180.

18. A. J. Greimas & J. Courtés, *Sémiotique. Dictionnaire raisonné de la théorie du langage*, Paris: Hachette, 1979, p. 3.

19. J. Laplanche & J.-B. Pontalis, *Le Vocabulaire de la psychanalyse*, Paris: PUF, 1967: *refoulement/repression*.

20. J. Habermas, *Die Neue Unübersichtlichkeit*, Frankfurt: Suhrkamp, 1985, p. 165.

21. W. Stegmüller, *Probleme und Resultate der Wissenschaftstheorie und Analytischen Philoso-phie*, vol. II, *Theorie und Erfahrung*, Dritter Teilband, *Die Entwicklung des neuen Strukturalismus seit 1973*, Berlin, Heidelberg & New York, 1986, p. 414.
22. Ibid.
23. Cf. "Psychoanalysis as an Empirical, Interdisciplinary Science", International Symposium of the Austrian Academy of Sciences, Vienna, 22–24 Nov. 2002.
24. W. Stegmüller, *Probleme und Resultate der Wissenschaftstheorie und Analytischen Philoso-phie*, vol. II, *Theorie und Erfahrung*, Dritter Teilband, *op. cit.*, p. 421.
25. Ibid., p. 433.
26. Cf. ibid., p. 434.
27. Ibid., p. 448.
28. Commenting on Dialogical Theory, Rob T. P. Wiche tries to divide this process into phases and to formalize it: "1. There are two parties who are prepared to dis-cuss a problem of the social sciences, although it is clear that they do not agree on the solution. There is also a moderator. 2. The parties agree with the principles of Dialogical Theory. (. . .) 3. Party 1 summarizes the problem which is at the origin of disagreement. 4. The moderator asks party 2 whether it is satisfied with this sum-mary. If this is not the case, then party 2 is asked to present its version of the prob-lem. This process is repeated until both parties agree with the definition of the problem. If, at the end of this process, there is no agreement, then no discussion can take place. 5. Party 1 presents its solution of the problem. 6. Party 2 enumerates the weak and the strong points of this solution (. . .). (R. T. P. Wiche, "Dialogische Theorie und dialogische Praxis", in: *Ethik und Sozialwissenschaften* 4, 1999, p. 654.) Adorno and Horkheimer may have disliked this kind of formalization. However, they would have avoided embarrassing misunderstandings if, in the course of the "Positivism Controversy", they had opted for this kind of approach – and for the kind of discursive (actantial) reconstruction proposed here.
29. P. Lorenzen, *Konstruktive Wissenschaftstheorie*, Frankfurt: Suhrkamp, 1974, p. 118.
30. Ibid.
31. Michael Schmid misses the point of Dialogical Theory when he objects: "Zima leads scientific discussions astray when he endows the subjectivity of scientists with methodological importance, instead of supporting the normative claim to the pro-duction of true (but of course not: certain) theories." (M. Schmidt, "Sozialwis-senschaftliche Theoriebildung und Dialogische Theorie. Oder: Brauchen die Sozialwissenschaften einen ideologischen Diskurs?", in: *Ethik und Sozialwissenschaf-ten* 4, 1999, p. 646.) The key problem is due to the fact that the claim, made by vir-tually all scientists, to produce "true theories" is evaluated differently in different scientific groups: namely in the light of their particular collective and ideological interests which Schmid is not aware of (or simply ignores). He thus returns to the metaphysical point zero: to the idealist question concerning theoretical truth independent of social interests. One last remark: the social sciences do not "need" an ideological discourse, because they have several of them. (Günter Endruweit also misreads Dialogical Theory when he criticizes it for "putting the verbal

interactions of social scientists" at the centre of the scene, instead of focusing on object-oriented research. In so doing, he presupposes the existence of a homogeneous scientific community whose members analyse an object. He also seems to overlook the ideological heterogeneity of this community which is responsible for the well-known fact that objects such as "religion" or "art" are constructed in many different and contradictory ways. This is one reason why the subjective factor is crucial – and the dialogue between subjects. [G. Endruweit, "Regeln für interdisziplinäre Forschung statt einer Theorie des Holzwegs", in: *Ethik und Sozialwissenschaften* 4, 1999, p. 614.])

32. Cf. G. Bachelard, *La Philosophie du non*, Paris: PUF (1940), 1983, p. 32: "There is only one way to advance in science, namely to refute existing science (...)."

33. Commenting on Dialogical Theory, Erich H. Witte writes: "It seems to me that the real topic of discussion is not theory formation, but the testing of theories." (E. H. Witte, "Teamfähigkeit und Moderation in den Sozialwissenschaften beim theoretischen Diskurs", in: *Ethik und Sozialwissenschaften* 4, 1999, p. 655.) The basic idea underlying the *Second* and the *Third Part* of this book can be summed up in a few words: "theory formation through theory testing". One of the results of this critical process are the "inter-discursive or inter-collective theorems".

34. R. Jakobson, "On Linguistic Aspects of Translation", in: L. Venuti (ed.), *The Translation Studies Reader*, London & New York: Routledge, 2001, p. 114.

35. Cf. P. Bourdieu, *Ce que parler veut dire. L'économie des échanges linguistiques*, Paris: Fayard, 1982, pp. 207–26.

36. Cf. P. Bourdieu, *Science of Science and Reflexivity*, Cambridge: Polity, 2004, p. 70.

37. R. Musil, *Aus den Tagebüchern*, Frankfurt: Suhrkamp, 1971, p. 31.

14.   Interdiscursive Dialogue: Practice

1. Cf. Fill, *Wörter zu Pflugscharen. Versuch einer Ökologie der Sprache*, Vienna: Böhlau, 1987, p. 9.

2. W. Raible, "Roman Jakobson oder 'Auf der Wasserscheide zwischen Linguistik und Poetik'", in: R. Jakobson, *Aufsätze zur Linguistik und Poetik*, Munich: Nymphenburger Verlagshandlung, 1974, pp. 9–10.

3. V. Shklovsky, "Iskusstvo, kak priëm", in: J. Striedter (ed.), *Russischer Formalismus* (bilingual edition), vol. I, Munich: Fink, 1969, p. 24.

4. E. M. Thompson, *Russian Formalism and Anglo-American New Criticism. A Comparative Study*, The Hague: Mouton, 1971, p. 68.

5. V. Shklovsky, "Svjaz priëmov sjužetosloženija s obščimi priëmami stilja", in: J. Striedter (ed.), *Russischer Formalismus*, vol. I, *op. cit.*, p. 50.

6. The contradiction between Kantian and avant-garde theorems in formalism and structuralism is discussed in some detail in: P. V. Zima, "Jan Mukařovský's Aesthetics between Autonomy and the Avant-Garde", in: V. Macura & H. Schmidt (eds), *Jan Mukařovský and the Prague School*, Potsdam: Univ. of Potsdam, 1999, pp. 72–3.

7.   N. I. Bukharin, "Über die formale Methode in der Kunst", in: H. Günther (ed.), *Marxismus und Formalismus. Dokumente einer literaturtheoretischen Kontroverse*, Frankfurt, Berlin & Vienna: Ullstein, 1976, p. 64.

8.   A. V. Lunacharsky, "Der Formalismus in der Kunstwissenschaft", in: H. Günther (ed.), *Marxismus und Formalismus, op. cit.*, p. 89

9.   B. M. Eikhenbaum, "Zur Frage der Formalisten (Überblick und Antwort)", in: H. Günther (ed.), *Marxismus und Formalismus, op. cit.*, p. 72.

10. Cf. L. Trotsky, *Literature and Revolution* (1924), London: Redwords, 1991, chap. V.

11. B. Eikhenbaum, "Zur Frage der Formalisten", in: H. Günther (ed.), *Marxismus und Formalismus, op. cit.*, pp. 77–8.

12. Cf. P. N. Medvedev, *The Formal Method in Literary Scholarship. A Critical Introduction to Sociological Poetics* (1928), Cambridge (Mass.): Harvard Univ. Press, 1985, chap. III.

13. Cf. M. M. Bakhtin, *Rabelais and his World*, Cambridge (Mass.) & London: MIT Press, 1968, chap. II.

14. Cf. T. Bennett, *Formalism and Marxism*, London & New York: Routledge (1979), 1989, chap. VIII: "Work in Progress".

15. This dialogue was of considerable importance for the sociology of texts developed by the author of this book in: *Textsoziologie. Eine kritische Einführung*, Stuttgart: Metzler, 1980 and *Manuel de sociocritique*, Paris (1985): L'Harmattan, 2000.

16. Cf. E. Cros, *Theory and Practice of Sociocriticism*, Minneapolis: Univ. Minnesota Press, 1988.

17. Cf. J. Kristeva, *La Révolution du langage poétique. L'avant-garde à la fin du XIXe siècle: Lautréamont et Mallarmé*, Paris: Seuil, 1974, p. 214.

18. W. G. Walton, "V. N. Voloshinov: A Marriage of Formalism and Marxism", in: P. V. Zima (ed.), *Semiotics and Dialectics. Ideology and the Text*, Amsterdam: Benjamins, 1981, p. 51.

19. Cf. J. Derrida, *Speech and Phenomena, and Other Essays on Husserl's Theory of Signs*. Evanston (Ill.): Northwestern Univ. Press, 1973.

20. J. R. Searle, *Speech Acts. An Essay in the Philosophy of Language*, Cambridge: Cambridge Univ. Press (1969), 1977, p. 48.

21. J. R. Searle, "Reiterating the Differences. A Reply to Derrida", in: *Glyph* 1, 1977, p. 202.

22. J. Derrida, *Margins of Philosophy*, London: Routledge & Kegan Paul, 1982, p. 327.

23. Cf. J. Derrida, *Limited Inc.*, Evanston (Ill.): Northwestern Univ. Press (1988), 1990, p. 137.

24. Ibid., p. 62.

25. A. J. Greimas & J. Courtés, *Sémiotique. Dictionnaire raisonné de la théorie du langage*, Paris: Hachette, 1979, p. 199.

26. Ibid., p. 197.

27. A protracted discussion about particular aspects of "itarativity" and "iterability" took place in the 1990s: *Der unzitierbare Text. Ein Gespräch, initiiert von Peter V. Zima und herausgegeben von Alexander Schwarz, Tausch*, vol. X, Berne, Berlin & Paris: Lang, 1997 – and in particular the article by O. Keller, "Wiederholung als Äquivalenz und das Problem der Totalisierung".

28.   Cf. J. Derrida, *Limited Inc.*, *op. cit.*, p 62.

29.   Cf. J. Derrida, *Du droit à la philosophie*, Paris: Galilée, p. 452, where Derrida points out that he is disappointed with the various interpretations of his "deconstruction".

30.   J. Derrida, *Limited Inc.*, *op. cit.*, p. 145.

31.   Cf. J. Tynianov, "Literaturnyj fakt", in: J. Striedter (ed.), *Russischer Formalismus*, vol. I, *op. cit.*

32.   H. Albert, "Kleines verwundertes Nachwort zu einer großen Einleitung", in: T. W. Adorno *et al.*, *Der Positivismusstreit in der deutschen Soziologie*, Darmstadt & Neuwied: Luchterhand, 1984 (11th edn), p. 336.

33.   T. W. Adorno, "Zur Logik der Sozialwissenschaften", in: T. W. Adorno *et al.*, *Der Positivismustreit*, *op. cit.*, p. 133.

34.   Cf. J. Derrida, *Positions*, London: Athlone, 1981.

35.   T. W. Adorno, "Zur Logik der Sozialwissenschaften", in: T. W. Adorno *et al.*, *Der Positivismusstreit*, *op. cit.*, p. 134.

15.   Communication in a Fragmented Society: Pluralism, Indifference and Ideology

1.   F. Apel, "Dialogische Theorie und Kanalbauwesen", in: *Ethik und Sozialwissenschaften* 4, 1999, p. 597. The misunderstanding according to which Dialogical Theory is primarily an ethical project predominates in some of the critical commentaries: Cf. G. Hauck, "Peter Zimas Traum von der moralischen Wissenschaft und der natürlichen Sprache", in: *Ethik und Sozialwissenschaften* 4, 1999, pp. 616–17. Even the linguistic concept of natural language which refers primarily to Y. Lotman's "primary modelling system" (chap. 12, 1) falls prey to a misunderstanding. Cf. also D. J. Krieger, "Wissenschaft als Kommunikation", in: *Ethik und Sozialwissenschaften* 4, 1999, p. 627: "The basic aim of Dialogical Theory seems to oppose the tendency towards differentiation characteristic of the contemporary scientific system and should therefore be founded otherwise than on a plea for self-criticism inherited from the Enlightenment " Although the first part of this critical remark is (unfortunately) perfectly correct, the second part is a misunderstanding. For the basic aim of Dialogical Theory is a better understanding of the social and linguistic context in which scientific communication takes place. The basic motivation is better, more concrete knowledge – not ethics.

2.   J. W. Goethe, *Maximen und Reflexionen*, Munich, DTV (*Gesamtausgabe* 21), 1968 (2nd edn), p. 103.

3.   W. Welsch, *Unsere postmoderne Moderne*, Weinheim: VCH, 1991 (3rd edn), p. 36.

4.   The history of tolerance is discussed in its various aspects in a special issue of *Etudes littéraires* 1–2, 2000: *La Tolérance*, eds J.-P. Barbe & J. Pigeaud. Cf. especially the contributions by A. Michel, "A propos de l'Edit de Nantes: la tradition latine et la tolérance", pp. 31–3 and E. Pommier, "Diabolisation, tolérance, glorification? La Renaissance et la sculpture antique", pp. 62–7.

5.   Cf. J. Baudrillard, *L'Echange impossible*, Paris: Galilée, 1999, pp. 14–15.

6. Cf. W. F. Haug, *Kritik der Warenästhetik*, Frankfurt: Suhrkamp, 1976 (5th edn), p. 64. Haug completes Marcuse's (and to a certain degree Baudrillard's very different) description of one-dimensionality, when he writes about the late capitalist world of commodities: "An alternative to the world of commodities will soon become inconceivable." (His approach seems preferable to that of the late Baudrillard who renounces social criticism.)

7. E. Frey, "Was ist guter Stil?", in: P. U. Hohendahl (ed.), *Sozialgeschichte und Wirkungsästhetik*, Frankfurt: Athenäum-Fischer, 1974, p. 160.

8. Cf. S. Fish, *Doing What Comes Naturally*, Oxford: Clarendon Press, 1989, p. 77.

9. S. Fish, *Is There a Text in This Class? The Authority of Interpretive Communities*, Cambridge (Mass.) & London: Harvard Univ. Press, 1982 (2nd edn), p. 14.

10. Ibid., p. 16.

11. Cf. J.-F. Lyotard, *The Inhuman. Reflections on Time*, Cambridge & Oxford: Polity and Blackwell, 1991, p. 127.

12. A. J. Greimas, *Du Sens II. Essais sémiotiques*, Paris: Seuil, 1983, p. 109.

13. Cf. R. Aron, "Fin de l'âge idéologique?", in: *Sociologica I. Aufsätze Max Horkheimer zum 60. Geburtstag gewidmet*, Cologne: Europäische Verlagsanstalt, 1974 and D. Bell, *The End of Ideology. On the Exhaustion of Political Ideas in the Fifties*, London: Collier-Macmillan (1960), 1967.

14. V. I. Lenin's notion of "scientific socialism" and his positive definition of "ideology" are discussed and criticized by: H.-J. Lieber, *Ideologie. Eine kritisch-systematische Einführung*, Paderborn: Schöningh, 1985, p. 65.

15. Cf. J. C. Alexander, "The Centrality of the Classics", in: A. Giddens & J. Turner (eds), *Social Theory Today*, Oxford: Polity, 1987, especially: "The Empiricist Challenge to the Centrality of the Classics", pp. 12–16.

16. H. Bußhoff, "Dialogische Theorie: Bedingung für Erkenntnisfortschritt in den Sozialwissenschaften?", in: *Ethik und Sozialwissenschaften* 4, 1999, p. 607.

Bibliography

Accardo, A. & Corcuff, P., *La Sociologie de Bourdieu. Textes choisis et commentés*, Bordeaux: Le Mascaret, 1986.

Adam, J.-M., *La Linguistique textuelle. Introduction à l'analyse textuelle des discours*, Paris: Armand Colin, 2005.

Adorno, T. W., *Eingriffe. Neun kritische Modelle*, Frankfurt: Suhrkamp, 1971 (7th edn).

Adorno, T. W., *Negative Dialectics* (1973), London & New York: Routledge, 2000.

Adorno, T. W., *Minima Moralia. Reflections on a Damaged Life*, London & New York (1974): Verso, 2005.

Adorno, T. W., "Zur Logik der Sozialwissenschaften", in: T. W. Adorno *et al.*, *Der Positivismusstreit in der deutschen Soziologie*, Darmstadt & Neuwied: Luchterhand. 1984 (11th edn).

Adorno, T. W., *Aesthetic Theory*, London: Athlone, 1997.

Adorno, T. W., *Metaphysik. Begriff und Probleme*, ed. R. Tiedemann, Frankfurt: Suhrkamp, 1998.

Adorno, T. W., *Zur Lehre von der Geschichte und von der Freiheit*, ed. R. Tiedemann, Frankfurt: Suhrkamp, 2001.

Agosti, S., *Lecture de "Prose pour des Esseintes" et de quelques autres poèmes de Mallarmé*, Chambéry: Ed. Comp'Act, 1998.

Albert, H., *Konstruktion und Kritik*, Hamburg: Hoffmann & Campe, 1972.

Albert, H., *Transzendentale Träumereien. Karl-Otto Apels Sprachspiele und sein hermeneutischer Gott*, Hamburg: Hoffmann & Campe, 1975.

Albert, H., *Aufklärung und Steuerung*, Hamburg: Hoffmann & Campe, 1976.

Albert, H., *Kritische Vernunft und menschliche Praxis. Mit einer autobiographischen Einleitung*, Stuttgart: Reclam, 1977.

Albert, H., *Traktat über kritische Vernunft*, Tübingen: Mohr-Siebeck, 1980 (4th edn).

Albert, H., "Kleines verwundertes Nachwort zu einer großen Einleitung", in: T. W. Adorno *et al.*, *Der Positivismusstreit in der deutschen Soziologie*, Darmstadt & Neuwied: Luchterhand, 1984 (11th edn).

Alexander, J. C., "The Centrality of the Classics", in: A. Giddens & J. Turner (eds), *Social Theory Today*, Oxford: Polity, 1987.

Alexander, J., "Habermas' neue Kritische Theorie: Anspruch und Probleme", in: A. Honneth & H. Joas (eds), *Kommunikatives Handeln. Beiträge zu Jürgen Habermas' "Theorie des kommunikativen Handelns"*, Frankfurt: Suhrkamp, 1986.

Althusser, L., *Lenin and Philosophy and Other Essays*, New York: Monthly Review Press, 1971.

Althusser, L., *Philosophie et philosophie spontanée des savants (1967)*, Paris: Maspero, 1974.

Althusser, L., "Idéologie et appareils idéologiques d'Etat", in: *idem, Positions*, Paris: Editions Sociales, 1976.

Althusser, L. & Balibar, E., *Reading Capital*, London: NLB, 1977 (2nd edn).

Ankersmit, F., *The Reality Effect of the Writing of History*, Amsterdam: Noord-Hollandsche, 1989.

Apel, F., "Dialogische Theorie und Kanalbauwesen", in: *Ethik und Sozialwissenschaften* 4, 1999.

Ashenden, S. & Owen, D. (eds), *Foucault Contra Habermas*, London, Thousand Oaks & New Delhi: Sage,1999.

Bachelard, G., *La Philosophie du non*, Paris: PUF (1940), 1983 (9th edn).

Baglioni, G., *L'ideologia della borghesia industriale nell'Italia liberale*, Turin: Einaudi, 1974.

Bakhtin, M. M., *Rabelais and his World*, Cambridge (Mass.) & London: MIT Press, 1968.

Bakhtin, M. M., *Die Ästhetik des Wortes*, ed. R. Grübel, Frankfurt: Suhrkamp, 1979.

Bakhtin, M. M., *Problems of Dostoevsky's Poetics*, Manchester: Manchester Univ. Press, 1984.

Balsinger, P. W., "Dialogische Theorie? – Methodische Konzeption!", in: *Ethik und Sozialwissenschaften* 4, 1999.

Bannister, R. C., *Sociology and Scientism. The American Quest for Objectivity, 1880–1940*, Chapel Hill & London: Univ. of North Carolina Press, 1987.

Barbe, J.-P. & Pigeaud, J. (eds), "La Tolérance", *Etudes littéraires* 1–2, 2000.

Barnes, B., *T. S. Kuhn and Social Science*, New York: Columbia Univ. Press, 1982.

Barnes, B., Bloor, D. & Henry, J., *Scientific Knowledge. A Sociological Analysis*, London: Athlone, 1996.

Barthes, R., *Essais critiques*, Paris: Seuil, 1964.

Baudelaire, Ch., *Œuvres complètes*, vol. I, Paris: Gallimard, Bibl. de la Pléiade, 1975.

Baudelot, Ch. & Establet, R., *Durkheim et le suicide*, Paris: PUF, 1990 (3rd edn).

Baudrillard, J., *La Transparence du Mal. Essai sur les phénomènes extrêmes*, Paris: Galilée, 1990.

Baudrillard, J., *L'Echange impossible*, Paris: Galilée, 1999.

Bauman, Z., *Postmodern Ethics*, Oxford: Blackwell, 1993.

Bayertz, K., *Wissenschaftstheorie und Paradigmabegriff*, Stuttgart: Metzler, 1981.

Bendix, R., *Max Weber. An Intellectual Portrait*, London: Methuen (1959), 1962.

Benjamin, W., *Zur Kritik der Gewalt und andere Aufsätze*, Frankfurt: Suhrkamp, 1971 (2nd edn).

Benjamin, W., *Ursprung des deutschen Trauerspiels*, Frankfurt: Suhrkamp (1963), 1972.

Bennett, T., *Formalism and Marxism*, London & New York: Routledge (1979), 1989.

Berg-Schlosser, D. & Müller-Rommel F. (eds), *Vergleichende Politikwissenschaft. Ein einführendes Studienbuch*, Opladen: Leske & Budrich, 1997 (3rd edn).

Best, S. & Kellner, D., *Postmodern Theory. Critical Interrogations*, London: Macmillan, 1991.

Bloch, E., *Über Methode und System bei Hegel*, Frankfurt: Suhrkamp, 1975 (2nd edn).

Bloor, D., *Knowledge and Social Imagery*, Chicago & London: Univ. of Chicago Press (1971), 1991 (2nd edn).

Bohm, D., *On Dialogue*, ed. L. Nichol, London & New York: Routledge, 1996.

Böhme, G., *Alternativen der Wissenschaft*, Frankfurt: Suhrkamp, 1980.

Bohn, C., *Habitus und Kontext. Ein kritischer Beitrag zur Sozialtheorie Bourdieus*, Opladen: Westdeutscher Verlag, 1991.

Bourdieu, P., *Questions de sociologie*, Paris: Minuit, 1980.

Bourdieu, P., *Ce que parler veut dire. L'économie des échanges linguistiques*, Paris: Fayard, 1982.

Bourdieu, P., *Leçon sur la leçon*, Paris: Minuit, 1982.

Bourdieu, P., *Homo academicus*, Paris: Minuit, 1984.

Bourdieu, P., *Choses dites*, Paris: Minuit, 1987.

Bourdieu, P., *In Other Words. Essays Towards a Reflexive Sociology*, Cambridge & Oxford: Polity and Blackwell, 1990.

Bourdieu, P., *Language and Symbolic Power*, ed. J. B. Thompson, Cambridge: Polity (1991), 2005.

Bourdieu, P. (with L. J. D. Wacquant), *Réponses. Pour une anthropologie réflexive*, Paris: Seuil, 1992.

Bourdieu, P., *The Rules of Art. Genesis and Structure of the Literary Field*, Cambridge & Oxford: Polity and Blackwell, 1996.

Bourdieu, P., *On Television*, New York: The New Press, 1998.

Bourdieu, P., *Firing Back. Against the Tyranny of the Market 2*, London & New York: Verso, 2003.

Bourdieu, P., *Science of Science and Reflexivity*, Cambridge: Polity, 2004.

Broch, H., *Schriften zur Literatur II. Theorie*, Frankfurt: Suhrkamp, 1975.

Broch, H., *Die Schlafwandler. Eine Romantrilogie* (1931–2), Frankfurt: Suhrkamp, 1978.

Brown, G. & Yule, G., *Discourse Analysis*, Cambridge: Cambridge Univ. Press (1983), 1991.

Brütting, R., *"Ecriture" und "texte". Die französische Literaturtheorie "nach dem Strukturalismus"*, Bonn: Bouvier, 1976.

Bubner, R., *Zur Sache der Dialektik*, Frankfurt: Suhrkamp, 1980.

Bubner, R., "Wie wichtig ist Subjektivität? Über einige Selbstverständlichkeiten und mögliche Mißverständnisse der Gegenwart", in: W. Hogrebe (ed.), *Subjektivität*, Munich: Fink, 1998.

Bukharin, N. I., "Über die Formale Methode in der Kunst", in: H. Günther (ed.), *Marxismus und Formalismus. Dokumente einer literaturtheoretischen Kontroverse*, Frankfurt, Berlin & Vienna: Ullstein, 1976.

Buin, Y., *L'œuvre européenne de Reich*, Paris: Editions Universitaires, 1972.

Burns, T. & Stalker, G. M., *The Management of Innovation*, London: Pergamon Press, 1961.

Bußhoff, H., "Dialogische Theorie: Bedingung für Erkenntnisfortschritt in den Sozialwissenschaften?", in: *Ethik und Sozialwissenschaften 4*, 1999.

Calhoun, C., LiPuma, E. & Postone, M. (eds), *Bourdieu. Critical Perspectives*, Cambridge & Oxford: Polity and Blackwell, 1993.

Camus, A., *L'Etranger*, Paris: Gallimard (1942), 1957.

Camus, A., *The Outsider*, Harmondsworth: Penguin, 1964.

Canguilhem, G., *Idéologie et rationalité dans l'histoire des sciences de la vie. Nouvelles études d'histoire et de philosophie des sciences*, Paris: Vrin, 1988 (2nd edn).

Carnap, R., Hahn, H. & Neurath, O., "Wissenschaftliche Weltauffassung – der Wiener Kreis", in: O. Neurath, *Wissenschaftliche Weltauffassung. Sozialismus und Logischer Empirismus*, ed. R. Hegselmann, Frankfurt: Suhrkamp, 1979.

Castilla del Pino, C., *Psicoanálisis y Marxismo*, Madrid: Alianza Editorial (1969), 1981.

Cezanne, W., *Allgemeine Volkswirtschaftslehre*, Munich & Vienna: Oldenbourg, 1997.

Chandler, D., *Semiotics. The Basics*, London & New York: Routledge, 2002.

Claval, P., *Les Mythes fondateurs des sciences sociales*, Paris: PUF, 1980.

Cohen, R. & Kennedy, P., *Global Sociology*, New York: New York Univ. Press (2000), 2003.

Collini, S., *Liberalism and Sociology. L. T. Hobhouse and Political Argument in England 1880–1914*, Cambridge: Cambridge Univ. Press (1979), 1983.

Collins, H. M., *Changing Order. Replication and Induction in Scientific Practice*, Chicago & London, Univ. of Chicago Press (1985), 1992.

Compagnon, A., *Le Démon de la théorie. Littérature et sens commun*, Paris: Seuil, 1998.

Coquet, J.-Cl., *Sémiotique. L'Ecole de Paris*, Paris: Hachette, 1982.

Courtés, J., *Introduction à la sémiotique narrative et discursive*, Paris: Hachette, 1976.

Couvalis, G., *The Philosophy of Science. Science and Objectivity*, London: Sage (1997), 1999.

Critique 661–662, June–July 2002: *Sciences dures?*

Croce, B., *Estetica come scienza dell'espressione e linguistica generale*, Bari: Laterza, 1973 (12th edn).

Croce, B., *Dialogo con Hegel*, ed. G. Gembilo, Naples: Edizioni Scientifiche Italiane, 1995.

Cros, E., *Theory and Practice of Sociocriticism*, Minneapolis: Univ. of Minnesota Press, 1988.

Danneberg, L. & Vollhardt, F. (eds), *Wie international ist die Literaturwissenschaft? Methoden und Theoriediskussion in den Literaturwissenschaften: kulturelle Besonderheiten und kultureller Austausch am Beispiel des Interpretationsproblems (1950–1990)*, Stuttgart & Weimar: Metzler, 1996.

Davidson, D., *Inquiries into Truth and Interpretation*, Oxford: Clarendon Press, 1984.

Davidson, D., *Subjective, Intersubjective, Objective*, Oxford: Oxford Univ. Press, 2001.

Deleuze, G., *Foucault*, London & New York: Athlone, 1988; Continuum, 2006.

Deleuze, G. & Guattari, F., *Qu'est-ce que la philosophie?*, Paris: Minuit, 1991.

Demirović, A., *Der nonkonformistische Intellektuelle. Die Entwicklung der Kritischen Theorie zur Frankfurter Schule*, Frankfurt: Suhrkamp, 1999.

Derrida, J., *Speech and Phenomena, and other Essays on Husserl's Theory of Signs*, Everston (Ill.): Northwestern Univ. Press, 1973.

Derrida, J., *Positions*, London: Athlone, 1981.

Derrida, J., *Margins of Philosophy*, London: Routledge & Kegan Paul, 1982.

Derrida, J., *Limited Inc.*, Evanston (Ill.): Northwestern Univ. Press, 1990.

Descombes, V., *Le Même et l'autre. Quarante-cinq ans de philosophie française (1933–1978)*, Paris: Minuit, 1979.

Dilthey, W., "Die Entstehung der Hermeneutik", in: W. Dilthey, *Gesammelte Schriften*, vol. V, Stuttgart: B. G. Teubner; Göttingen: Vandenhoeck-Ruprecht, 1968.

Dirkx, P., *Sociologie de la littérature*, Paris: Armand Colin, 2000.

Dubiel, H., *Wissenschaftsorganisation und politische Erfahrung. Studien zur frühen Kritischen Theorie*, Frankfurt: Suhrkamp, 1978.

Durkheim, E., *Les Règles de la méthode sociologique*, Paris: PUF, 1987 (23rd edn).

Duvignaud, J. (ed.), *Sociologie de la connaissance*, Paris: Payot, 1979.

Eagleton, T., *After Theory*, London: Allen Lane, 2003; Penguin, 2004.

Eco, U., *A Theory of Semiotics*, Bloomington: Indiana Univ. Press, 1976.

Eisenstadt, S. N. & Curelaru, M., *The Form of Sociology: Paradigms and Crises*, New York & London: John Wiley & Sons, 1976.

Elias, N., *Engagement und Distanzierung. Arbeiten zur Wissenssoziologie*, vol. I, Frankfurt: Suhrkamp, 1983.

Endruweit, G., "Regeln für interdisziplinäre Forschung statt einer Theorie des Holzwegs", in: *Ethik und Sozialwissenschaften* 4, 1999.

Fill, A., *Wörter zu Pflugscharen. Versuch einer Ökologie der Sprache*, Vienna: Böhlau, 1987.

Fish, S., *Is There a Text in this Class? The Authority of Interpretive Communities*, Cambridge (Mass.) & London: Harvard Univ. Press, 1982 (2nd edn).

Fish, S., *Doing What Comes Naturally*, Oxford: Clarendon Press, 1989.

Fistetti, F., *Neurath contro Popper. Otto Neurath riscoperto*, Bari: Dedalo, 1985.

Flick, U., *Qualitative Forschung. Theorie, Methoden, Anwendung in Psychologie und Sozialwissenschaften*, Reinbek: Rowohlt, 1999 (4th edn).

Foerster, H. von, "Das Konstruieren einer Wirklichkeit", in: P. Watzlawick (ed.), *Die erfundene Wirklichkeit. Wie wissen wir, was wir zu wissen glauben? Beiträge zum Konstruktivismus*, Munich: Piper, 1985 (3rd edn).

Foerster, H. von & Glasersfeld, E. von, *Wie wir uns erfinden. Eine Autobiographie des radikalen Konstruktivismus*, Heidelberg: Carl-Auer-Systeme Verlag, 1999.

Foucault, M., *The Birth of the Clinic* (1973), London & New York: Routledge, 2003.

Foucault, M., *Discipline and Punish. The Birth of the Prison* (1977), London: Penguin, 1991.

Foucault, M., *La Pensée du dehors*, Paris: Fata Morgana, 1986.

Foucault, M., "La Torture, c'est la raison", in: *idem, Dits et écrits*, vol. III, Paris: Gallimard, 1994.

Foucault, M., "Les Intellectuels et le pouvoir" (a discussion with Gilles Deleuze), in: *idem, Dits et écrits*, vol. II, Paris: Gallimard, 1994.

Foucault, M., "Les Rapports de pouvoir passent à l'intérieur des corps", in: *idem, Dits et écrits*, vol. III, Paris: Gallimard, 1994.

Foucault, M., "Nietzsche, la généalogie, l'histoire", in: *idem, Dits et écrits*, vol. II, Paris: Gallimard, 1994.

Foucault, M., "Structuralisme et poststructuralisme", in: *idem, Dits et écrits*, vol. IV, Paris: Gallimard, 1994.

Franzen, W., "Totgesagte leben länger: Beyond Realism and Anti-Realism: Realism", in: Forum für Philosophie Bad Homburg (ed.), *Realismus und Antirealismus*, Frankfurt: Suhrkamp, 1992.

Frey, E., "Was ist guter Stil?", in: P. U. Hohendahl (ed.), *Sozialgeschichte und Wirkungsästhetik*, Frankfurt: Athenäum-Fischer, 1974.

Fulda, H. F., "Unterwegs zu einer einheitlichen Theorie des Sprechens, Handelns und Interpretierens", in: *Dialektik und Dialog. Rede von Donald Davidson anläßlich der Verleihung des Hegel-Preises 1992. Laudatio von Hans Friedrich Fulda "Unterwegs zu einer einheitlichen Theorie des Sprechens, Handelns und Interpretierens"*, Frankfurt: Suhrkamp, 1993.

Gadamer, H.-G., "Rhetorik, Hermeneutik und Ideologiekritik. Metakritische Erörterungen zu *Wahrheit und Methode*", in: K.-O. Apel *et al.*, *Hermeneutik und Ideologiekritik*, Frankfurt: Suhrkamp (1971), 1980.

Gauthier, X., *Surréalisme et sexualité*, Paris: Gallimard, 1971.

Geiger, R. L., "Die Institutionalisierung soziologischer Paradigmen: Drei Beispiele aus der Frühzeit der französischen Soziologie", in: W. Lepenies (ed.), *Geschichte der Soziologie*, vol. II, Frankfurt: Suhrkamp, 1981.

Giddens, A. (ed.), *Positivism and Sociology*, London: Heinemann, 1974.

Giddens, A., *New Rules of Sociological Method. A Positive Critique of Interpretative Sociologies*, London: Hutchinson, 1976.

Giddens, A. & Turner, J., *Social Theory Today*, Cambridge & Oxford: Polity and Blackwell, 1987.

Giddens, A., *Sociology*, Cambridge & Oxford: Polity and Blackwell, 1993 (2nd edn).

Gil, D., *Bachelard et la culture scientifique*, Paris: PUF, 1993.

Glaser, B. & Strauss, A., *The Discovery of Grounded Theory*, Chicago: Aldine, 1967.

Glasersfeld, E. von, "Einführung in den Radikalen Konstruktivismus", in: P. Watzlawick (ed.), *Die erfundene Wirklichkeit. Wie wissen wir, was wir zu wissen glauben? Beiträge zum Konstruktivismus*, Munich: Piper, 1985 (3rd edn).

Glasersfeld, E. von, "Abschied von der Objektivität", in: P. Watzlawick & P. Krieg (eds), *Das Auge des Betrachters. Beiträge zum Konstruktivismus*, Munich: Piper, 1991.

Glasersfeld, E. von, *Radical Constructivism. A Way of Knowing and Learning*, London & Washington: Falmer Press, 1995.

Glasersfeld, E. von, *Radikaler Konstruktivismus. Ideen, Ergebnisse, Probleme*, Frankfurt: Suhrkamp, 1996.

Glasersfeld, E. von, *Wege des Wissens. Konstruktivistische Erkundungen durch unser Denken*, Heidelberg: Carl-Auer-Systeme Verlag, 1997.

Glasersfeld, E. von, *Konstruktivismus statt Erkenntnistheorie*, ed. W. Dörfler & J. Mitterer, Klagenfurt: Drava, 1998.

Gneuss, Ch. & Kocka, J. (eds), *Max Weber. Ein Symposion*, Munich: DTV, 1988.

Goethe, J. W., *Maximen und Reflexionen*, Munich: DTV (*Gesamtausgabe* 21), 1968 (2nd edn).

Goldmann, L., *Sciences humaines et philosophie*, Paris: Gonthier, 1966.

Göttner, H., *Logik der Interpretation. Analyse einer literaturwissenschaftlichen Methode unter kritischer Betrachtung der Hermeneutik*, Munich: Fink, 1973.

Gouldner, A. W., *The Coming Crisis of Western Sociology*, London: Heinemann, 1971.

Gramsci, A., *Il materialismo storico e la filosofia di Benedetto Croce*, Turin: Einaudi, 1957.

Gratzl, N. & Leitgeb, H., "Was ist ein wissenschaftliches Paradigma? Zur Explikation des Paradigmabegriffes", in: *Forschungsmitteilungen des Spezialforschungsbereiches FO 12 der Universität Salzburg "Theorien- und Paradigmenpluralismus in den Wissenschaften. Rivalität, Ausschluß oder Kooperation"*, edition 23, Dec. 2001.

Greimas, A. J., *Du Sens*, Paris: Seuil, 1970.

Greimas, A. J., *Maupassant. La sémiotique du texte: exercices pratiques*, Paris: Seuil, 1976.

Greimas, A. J., "Du discours scientifique en sciences sociales", in: *idem*, *Sémiotique et sciences sociales*, Paris: Seuil, 1976.

Greimas, A. J. & Courtés, J., *Sémiotique. Dictionnaire raisonné de la théorie du langage*, Paris: Hachette, 1979.

Greimas, A. J., *Du Sens II. Essais sémiotiques*, Paris: Seuil, 1983.

Greshoff, R., "Lassen sich die Konzepte von Max Weber und Niklas Luhmann unter dem Aspekt 'Struktur und Ereignis' miteinander vermitteln?", in: R. Greshoff & G. Kneer (eds), *Struktur und Ereignis in theorievergleichender Perspektive. Ein diskursives Buchprojekt*, Opladen & Wiesbaden: Westdeutscher Verlag, 1999.

Greshoff, R., "Notwendigkeit einer 'konzeptuellen Revolution in der Soziologie'? Kritische Überlegungen zu Luhmanns Anspruch am Beispiel von 'doppelter Kontingenz' ", in: *Österr. Zeitschrift für Soziologie* 2, 1999.

Greshoff, R., *Die theoretischen Konzeptionen des Sozialen von Max Weber und Niklas Luhmann im Vergleich*, Opladen & Wiesbaden: Westdeutscher Verlag, 1999.

Gripp-Hagelstange, H., *Niklas Luhmann. Eine Einführung*, Munich: Fink, 1997 (2nd edn).

Grujić, P., *Hegel und die Sowjetphilosophie der Gegenwart*, Berne & Munich: Francke, 1969.

Gurvitch, G., *Dialectique et sociologie*, Paris: Flammarion, 1962.

Habermas, J., *Theorie und Praxis. Sozialphilosophische Studien* (1963), Frankfurt: Suhrkamp, 1972.

Habermas, J., "Vorbereitende Bemerkungen zu einer Theorie der kommunikativen Kompetenz", in: J. Habermas & N. Luhmann, *Theorie der Gesellschaft oder Sozialtechnologie – Was leistet die Systemforschung?*, Frankfurt: Suhrkamp (1971), 1982.

Habermas, J., *Die Neue Unübersichtlichkeit*, Frankfurt: Suhrkamp, 1985.

Habermas, J., *Vorstudien und Ergänzungen zur Theorie des kommunikativen Handelns*, Frankfurt: Suhrkamp, 1986 (2nd edn).

Habermas, J., "Entgegnung", in: A. Honneth & H. Joas (eds), *Kommunikatives Handeln. Beiträge zu Jürgen Habermas', "Theorie des kommunikativen Handelns"*, Frankfurt: Suhrkamp, 1986.

Habermas, J., *The Theory of Communicative Action*, vol. II. *The Critique of Functionalist Reason*, Cambridge & Oxford: Polity and Blackwell (1987), 2004.

Habermas, J., *Moral Consciousness and Communicative Action*, Cambridge: Polity (1990), 2003.

Habermas, J. *The Philosophical Discourse of Modernity*, Cambridge: Polity (1990), 2005.

Habermas, J., *Erläuterungen zur Diskursethik*, Frankfurt: Suhrkamp, 1992 (2nd edn).

Habermas, J., *Justification and Application. Remarks on Discourse Ethics*, Cambridge & Oxford: Polity and Blackwell, 1993.

Habermas, J., *Die Einbeziehung des Anderen*, Frankfurt: Suhrkamp, 1997 (2nd edn).

Habermas, J., *Nachmetaphysisches Denken. Philosophische Aufsätze*, Frankfurt: Suhrkamp, 1997 (2nd edn).

Hagiwara, Y., "Zum Verständnis von Liberalismus bei Popper und Hayek", in: K. Salamun (ed.), *Moral und Politik aus der Sicht des Kritischen Rationalismus*, Amsterdam & Atlanta: Rodopi, 1991.

Haig, B. D., "Grounded Theory as Scientific Method", in: *Philosophy of Education*, 1995.

Halbwachs, M., "La Psychologie collective du raisonnement" (1938), in: *idem, Classes sociales et morphologie*, Paris: Minuit, 1972.

Haller, M., *Soziologische Theorie im systematisch-kritischen Vergleich*, Opladen: Leske & Budrich, 1999.

Halliday, M. A. K., *Language as Social Semiotic: The Social Interpretation of Language and Meaning*, London: Edward Arnold, 1978.

Hance, A., "Pragmatism as Naturalized Hegelianism: Overcoming Transcendental Philosophy", in: H. J. Saatkamp (ed.), *Rorty and Pragmatism. The Philosopher Responds to his Critics*, Nashville & London: Vanderbilt Univ. Press, 1995.

Hansen, K. P., *Kultur und Kulturwissenschaft*, Tübingen & Basel: Francke, 2003 (3rd edn).

Hanson, N. R., *Patterns of Scientific Discovery*, Cambridge: Cambridge Univ. Press, 1958.

Harris, Z. S., "Discourse analysis", in: *Language* 28, 1952.

Hartman, G. H., *Criticism in the Wilderness. The Study of Literature Today*, New Haven & London: Yale Univ. Press, 1980.

Hatim, B. & Mason, I., *Discourse and the Translator*, London & New York: Longman, 1990.

Hauck, G., "Peter Zimas Traum von der moralischen Wissenschaft und der natürlichen Sprache", in: *Ethik und Sozialwissenschaften* 4, 1999.

Haug, W. F., *Kritik der Warenästhetik*, Frankfurt: Suhrkamp, 1976 (5th edn).

Haug, W. F., "Möglichkeiten und Grenzen interparadigmatischer Kommunikation", in: *Ethik und Sozialwissenschaften* 4, 1999.

Hegel, G. W. F., *Lectures on the History of Philosophy*, London & New York: Routledge & Kegan Paul and Humanities Press (1955), 1963.

Hegel, G. W. F., *Science of Logic*, London & New York: Allen & Unwin and Humanities Press, 1969.

Heller, A., *Philosophie des linken Radikalismus. Ein Bekenntnis zur Philosophie*, Hamburg: VSA Verlag, 1978.

Hennen, M., *Krise der Rationalität – Dilemma der Soziologie. Zur kritischen Rezeption Max Webers*, Stuttgart: Enke, 1976.

Henry, P., "Constructions relatives et articulations discursives", in: *Langages* 37, 1975.

Hjelmslev, L., *Prolegomena to a Theory of Language*, Madison, Milwaukee & London: Univ. of Wisconsin Press, 1969.

Hoffmann, D., "Dialogische Theorie – eine Methode zur Überwindung der Widersprüchlichkeit innerhalb der Wissenschaft?", in: *Ethik und Sozialwissenschaften* 4, 1999.

Horkheimer, M., *Anfänge der bürgerlichen Geschichtsphilosophie. Hegel und das Problem der Metaphysik. Montaigne und die Funktion der Skepsis*, Frankfurt: Fischer, 1971.

Horkheimer, M., *Zur Kritik der instrumentellen Vernunft*, Frankfurt: Fischer, 1974.

Horkheimer, M. & Adorno, T. W., *Dialectic of Enlightenment* (1947), London & New York: Verso, 1997.

Huke-Didier, E., *Die Wissenssoziologie Karl Mannheims in der Interpretation durch die Kritische Theorie – Kritik einer Kritik*, Frankfurt, Berne & New York: Lang, 1985.

Husserl, E., *Die Krisis der europäischen Wissenschaften und die transzendentale Phänomenologie*, ed. W. Biemel, The Hague: Nijhoff, 1962.

Husserl, E., *Zur Phänomenologie der Intersubjektivität. Texte aus dem Nachlaß*, Teil I (1905–20), II (1921–8) and III (1929–35), ed. I. Kern, The Hague: Nijhoff, 1973.

Jakobson, R., "On Linguistic Aspects of Translation", in: L. Venuti (ed.), *The Translation Studies Reader*, London & New York: Routledge, 2001.

Jauß, H. R., "Paradigmawechsel in der Literaturwissenschaft", in: *Linguistische Berichte* 3, 1969.

Jay, M., *The Dialectical Imagination. A History of the Frankfurt School and the Institute of Social Research 1923–1950*, Boston & Toronto: Little, Brown & Co., 1973.

Jenkins, R., *Pierre Bourdieu*, London & New York: Routledge, 1992.

Johnson, T., Dandeker, Ch. & Ashworth, C., *The Structure of Social Theory*, London: Macmillan (1984), 1987.

Kant, I., *Critique of Judgement (1790) (including the First Introduction)*, Indianapolis & Cambridge: Hackett Publishing Co., 1987.

Karádi, E. & Vezér, E. (eds), *Georg Lukács, Karl Mannheim und der Sonntagskreis*, Frankfurt: Sendler, 1985.

Keat, R. & Urry, J., *Social Theory as Science*, London & Boston: Routledge & Kegan Paul, 1982 (2nd edn).

Kemp, W., "Wo Rudi Rüssel einen Lehrstuhl hat. Ein Besuch beim Titelhandel", in: J. Wertheimer & P. V. Zima (eds), *Strategien der Verdummung. Infantilisierung in der Fun-Gesellschaft*, Munich: Beck, 2001.

Kettler, D., Meja, V. & Stehr, N., *Karl Mannheim*, Chichester: Ellis Horwood, 1984.

Keupp, H., "Diskursarena Identität: Lernprozesse in der Identitätsforschung", in: H. Keupp & R. Höfer (eds), *Identitätsarbeit heute. Klassische und aktuelle Perspektiven in der Identitätsforschung*, Frankfurt: Suhrkamp, 1997.

Kim, T. H., *Vom Aktantenmodell zur Semiotik der Leidenschaften. Eine Studie zur narrativen Semiotik von Algirdas J. Greimas*, Tübingen: Narr, 2002.

Kipfer, D., *Individualität nach Adorno*, Tübingen & Basel: Francke, 1999.

Kloft, H., "Die Theoría der Griechen. Ein Modell und drei Fallbeispiele", in: K. L. Pfeiffer, R. Kray & K. Städtke (eds), *Theorie als kulturelles Ereignis*, Berlin & New York: de Gruyter, 2001.

Kluckhohn, C., "The Study of Culture", in: L. A. Coser & B. Rosenberg (eds), *Sociological Theory*, New York: Macmillan, 1966.

Kneer, G. & Nassehi, A., *Niklas Luhmanns Theorie sozialer Systeme*, Munich: Fink, 1997 (3rd edn).

Knorr-Cetina, K., *Die Fabrikation von Erkenntnis. Zur Anthropologie der Wissenschaft*, Frankfurt: Suhrkamp, 1984.

Knorr-Cetina, K., *Wissenskulturen. Ein Vergleich naturwissenschaftlicher Wissensformen*, Frankfurt: Suhrkamp, 2002.

Koch, C., "Möglichkeiten und Grenzen der vergleichenden Religionswissenschaft", in: P. V. Zima (ed.), *Vergleichende Wissenschaften*, Tübingen: Narr, 2000.

Koch, E. & Fischer, W., "The Cubic Limiting Complexes in the Tetragonal Lattice Complexes", in: *Zeitschrift für Kristallographie. International Journal for Structural, Physical and Chemical Aspects of Crystalline Materials* 9, 2003.

Kögler, H. H., *Die Macht des Dialogs. Kritische Hermeneutik nach Gadamer, Foucault und Rorty*, Stuttgart: Metzler, 1992.

Kramsch, C., *Language and Culture*, Oxford: Oxford Univ. Press, 1998.

Krieger, D. J., "Wissenschaft als Kommunikation", in: *Ethik und Sozialwissenschaften* 4. 1999.

Kristeva, J., "La sémiologie comme science des ideologies", in: *Semiotica* 1, 1969.

Kristeva, J., *La Révolution du langage poétique. L'avant-garde à la fin du XIXᵉ siècle: Lautréamont et Mallarmé*, Paris: Seuil, 1974.

Kuhn, T. S., *The Essential Tension. Selected Studies in Scientific Tradition and Change*, Chicago & London: Univ. of Chicago Press, 1977.

Kuhn, T. S., *The Structure of Scientific Revolutions*, Chicago & London: Univ. of Chicago Press, 1996 (3rd edn).

Kukla, A., *Social Constructivism and the Philosophy of Science*, London & New York: Routledge, 2000.

Labarrière, P.-J. (ed.), *Témoigner du différend. Quand phraser ne se peut. Autour de Jean-François Lyotard*, Paris: Osiris, 1989.

Laclau, E., "Psychoanalysis and Marxism", in: *Critical Inquiry* 13, 1987.

Lakatos, I., *The Methodology of Scientific Research Programmes*, Cambridge: Cambridge Univ. Press (1978), 1983.

Landowski, E., *La Société réfléchie. Essais de sociosémiotique*, Paris: Seuil, 1989.

Lanson, G., *Essais de méthode, de critique et d'histoire littéraire*, Paris: Hachette, 1965.

Laplanche, J. & Pontalis, J.-B., *Le Vocabulaire de la psychanalyse*, Paris: PUF, 1967.

Lash, S., *Sociology of Postmodernism*, London & New York: Routledge, 1990.

Lecourt, D., *L'Ordre et les jeux. Le positivisme logique en question*, Paris: Grasset, 1981.

Lecourt, D., *Lyssenko. Histoire réelle d'une "science prolétarienne"*, Paris: PUF (1976), 1995.

Lefebvre, H., *L'Idéologie structuraliste*, Paris: Anthropos, 1971.

Lelas, J., *Teorije razvoja znanosti*, Zagreb: ArTresor Naklada, 2000.

Lenk, K., *Marx in der Wissenssoziologie*, Lüneburg: Dietrich zu Klampen Verlag, 1986 (2nd edn).

Lieber, H.-J., *Ideologie. Eine kritisch-systematische Einführung*, Paderborn: Schöningh, 1985.

Link, J., *Literaturwissenschaftliche Grundbegriffe. Eine programmierte Einführung auf strukturalistischer Basis*, Munich: Fink, 1979 (2nd edn).

Lorenzen, P., *Konstruktive Wissenschaftstheorie*, Frankfurt: Suhrkamp, 1974.

Löwith, K., *Von Hegel zu Nietzsche. Der revolutionäre Bruch im Denken des 19. Jahrhunderts*, Hamburg: Meiner, 1986 (9th edn).

Lüdke, W. M., *Anmerkungen zu einer "Logik des Zerfalls": Adorno-Beckett*, Frankfurt: Suhrkamp, 1981.

Luhmann, N., *Soziale Systeme. Grundriß einer allgemeinen Theorie*, Frankfurt: Suhrkamp (1984), 1987.

Luhmann, N., *Ökologische Kommunikation. Kann die moderne Gesellschaft sich auf ökologische Gefährdungen einstellen?*, Opladen: Westdeutscher Verlag, 1986.

Luhmann, N., *Die Wirtschaft der Gesellschaft*, Frankfurt: Suhrkamp (1988), 1994.

Luhmann, N., *Die Wissenschaft der Gesellschaft*, Frankfurt: Suhrkamp, 1990.

Luhmann, N., *Beobachtungen der Moderne*, Opladen: Wetsdeutscher Verlag, 1992.

Luhmann, N., *Die Gesellschaft der Gesellschaft*, 2 vols, Frankfurt: Suhrkamp, 1997.

Luhmann, N., *Einführung in die Systemtheorie*, ed. D. Boeck, Heidelberg: Carl-Auer-Systeme Verlag, 2002.

Lukács, G., *History and Class Consciousness. Studies in Marxist Dialectics*, London: Merlin Press (1971), 1990.

Lyotard, J.-F., *The Postmodern Condition. A Report on Knowledge* (1984), Manchester: Manchester Univ. Press, 2004.

Lyotard, J.-F., *The Différend. Phrases in Dispute*, Minneapolis: Univ. of Minnesota Press (1988), 1999.

Lyotard, J.-F., *The Inhuman. Reflections on Time*, Cambridge & Oxford: Polity and Blackwell, 1991.

Lyotard, J.-F., *Political Writings*, London: UCL Press, 1993.

Lyotard, J.-F., *Postmodern Fables*, Minneapolis & London: Univ. of Minnesota Press, 2003 (3rd edn).

Macherey, P., *Hegel ou Spinoza*, Paris: Maspero, 1979.

Man, P. de, *Allegories of Reading. Figural Language in Rousseau, Nietzsche, Rilke, and Proust*, New Haven & London: Yale Univ. Press, 1979.

Mannheim, K., *Ideology and Utopia. An Introduction to the Sociology of Knowledge*, London & Henley: Routledge and Kegan Paul (1936), 1976.

Mannheim, K., *Strukturen des Denkens*, eds D. Kettler, V. Meja & N. Stehr, Frankfurt: Suhrkamp, 1980.

Mannheim, K., *Konservatismus. Ein Beitrag zur Soziologie des Wissens*, eds D. Kettler, V. Meja & N. Stehr, Frankfurt: Suhrkamp, 1984.

Martin, B. & Ringham, F., *Dictionary of Semiotics*, London & New York: Cassell, 2000.

Marx, K. & Engels, F., *Basic Writings on Politics and Philosophy*, ed. L. S. Feuer, New York: Doubleday-Anchor, 1959.

Marx, K., *Die Frühschriften. Von 1837 bis zum Manifest der kommunistischen Partei 1848*, ed. S. Landshut, Stuttgart: Kröner, 1971.

Marx, K., *Capital. A Critique of Political Economy*, vol. I, Harmondsworth: Penguin, 1976.

Masterman, M., "The Nature of a Paradigm", in: I. Lakatos & A. Musgrave (eds), *Criticism and the Growth of Knowledge*, Cambridge: Cambridge Univ. Press, 1970.

Materialy meždunarodnogo kongressa 100 let R. O. Jakobson, Moscow: Rossijskij Gosudarstvennyj Gumanitarnyj Universitet, 1996.

Maturana, H. & Varela, F., *Der Baum der Erkenntnis. Die biologischen Wurzeln menschlichen Erkennens*, Berne & Munich: Scherz Verlag-Goldmann, 1987.

Maturana, H., "Wissenschaft und Alltag: Die Ontologie wissenschaftlicher Erklärungen", in: P. Watzlawick & P. Krieg (eds), *Das Auge des Betrachters. Beiträge zum Konstruktivismus*, Munich: Piper, 1991.

Maturana, H., *Was ist erkennen? Die Welt entsteht im Auge des Betrachters*, Munich: Piper, 1994; Goldmann, 2001.

Mauron, Ch., *Des métaphores obsédantes au mythe personnel. Introduction à la psychocritique*, Paris: Corti, 1983.

Mecklenburg, N. & Müller, H., *Erkenntnisinteresse und Literaturwissenschaft*, Stuttgart: Kohlhammer, 1974.

Medvedev, P. N., *The Formal Method in Literary Scholarship. A Critical Introduction to Sociological Poetics* (1928), Cambridge (Mass.): Harvard Univ. Press, 1985.

Meja, V. & Stehr, N. (eds), *Der Streit um die Wissenssoziologie*, 2 vols: *Die Entwicklung der deutschen Wissenssoziologie* and *Rezeption und Kritik der Wissenssoziologie*, Frankfurt: Suhrkamp, 1982.

Merton, R. K., *Social Theory and Social Structure*, New York: The Free Press, 1968.

Mészárosz, I., *The Power of Ideology*, London & New York: Harvester-Wheatsheaf, 1989.

Metzler-Lexikon Literatur- und Kulturtheorie, ed. A. Nünning, Stuttgart: Metzler, 2001 (2nd edn).

Mikl-Horke, G., *Soziologie. Historischer Kontext und soziologische Theorie-Entwürfe*, Munich & Vienna: Oldenbourg, 2001 (5th edn).

Mitchell, J., *Feminism and Psychoanalysis*, New York: Random House, 1975.

Mittelstraß, J., *Die Häuser des Wissens. Wissenschaftstheoretische Studien*, Frankfurt: Suhrkamp, 1998.

Mitterer, J., *Die Flucht aus der Beliebigkeit*, Frankfurt: Fischer, 2001 (2nd edn).

Mooy, J. J. A., *Idee en verbeelding. Filosofische aspecten van de literatuurbeschouwing*, Assen: Van Gorcum, 1981.

Morin, E., *Le Paradigme perdu: la nature humaine*, Paris: Seuil (1973), 1979.

Mukařovský, J., "Problémy estetické normy", in: *idem, Cestami poetiky a estetiky*, Prague: Československý Spisovatel, 1971.

Mulkay, M., *Functionalism, Exchange and Theoretical Strategy* (1971), Aldershot: Gregg Revivals, 1992.

Mulkay, M., *Science and the Sociology of Knowledge* (1979), Aldershot: Gregg Revivals, 1992.

Münch, R., *Theorie des Handelns. Zur Rekonstruktion der Beiträge von Talcott Parsons, Emile Durkheim und Max Weber*, Frankfurt: Suhrkamp (1982), 1988.

Münch, R., *Die Struktur der Moderne. Grundmuster und differentielle Gestaltung des institutionellen Aufbaus der modernen Gesellschaften*, Frankfurt: Suhrkamp (1984), 1992.

Munday, J., *Introducing Translation Studies. Theories and Applications*, London & New York: Routledge, 2001.

Musil, R., *Aus den Tagebüchern*, Frankfurt: Suhrkamp, 1971.

Musil, R., "Aphorismen", in: *idem, Gesammelte Werke*, vol. VII, Reinbek: Rowohlt, 1978.

Neurath, O., "Universaljargon und Terminologie", in: *idem, Gesammelte philosophische und methodologische Schriften*, eds R. Haller & H. Rutte, Vienna: Hölder-Pichler-Tempsky, 1981.

Neurath, O., "Pseudorationalismus der Falsifikation (1935)", in: *idem, Gesammelte philosophische und methodologische Schriften*, vol. II, eds R. Haller & H. Rutte, Vienna: Hölder-Pichler-Tempsky, 1981.

Nicklas, H., "Die dialogische Theorie: Eine Baustelle", in: *Ethik und Sozialwissenschaften* 4, 1999.

Nietzsche, F., *Die fröhliche Wissenschaft*, in: *idem, Werke*, vol. III, ed. K. Schlechta, Munich: Hanser, 1980.

Nöth, W., *Handbuch der Semiotik*, Stuttgart: Metzler, 1985.

Parsons, T., *The Social System*, London: Routledge & Kegan Paul, 1951.

Passeron, J.-Cl., *Le Raisonnement sociologique. L'espace non-poppérien du raisonnement naturel*, Paris: Nathan, 1991.

Pasternack, G., *Theoriebildung in der Literaturwissenschaft*, Munich: Fink, 1975.

Pêcheux, M., *Les Vérités de La Palice*, Paris: Maspero, 1975.

Péquignot, B. & Tripier, P., *Les Fondements de la sociologie*, Paris: Nathan, 2000.

Peursen, C. A. van, "Rationality: European or Universal?", in: *Higher Education and Research in the Netherlands* 3/4, "Eurocentrism and Science", 1982.

Peyré, H., "Durkheim: The Man, his Time, and his Intellectual Background", in: E. Durkheim, *et al.*, *Essays on Sociology and Philosophy*, ed. K. H. Wolf, New York: Harper & Row, 1960.

Pfeiffer, K. L., Kray, R. & Städtke, K. (eds), *Theorie als kulturelles Ereignis*, Berlin & New York: de Gruyter, 2001.

Philosophisches Wörterbuch, ed. G. Schischkoff, Stuttgart: Kröner, 1978.

Piaget, J., *Le Structuralisme*, Paris: PUF, 1974.

Pirandello, L., "L'umorismo", in: *idem, Saggi, poesie, scritti varii*, Milan: Mondadori, 1977 (4th edn).

Popper, K. R., *The Open Society and its Enemies*, vol. II: *The High Tide of Prophecy: Hegel, Marx, and the Aftermath*, London: Routledge & Kegan Paul (1945), 1962.

Popper, K. R. *The Logic of Scientific Discovery* (1959), London & New York: Routledge, 2002.

Popper, K. R., *Conjectures and Refutations. The Growth of Scientific Knowledge*, London: Routledge & Kegan Paul (1963), 1972.

Popper, K. R., "Normal Science and its Dangers", in: I. Lakatos & A. Musgrave (eds), *Criticism and the Growth of Knowledge*, Cambridge: Cambridge Univ. Press (1970), 1982.

Popper, K. R., "The Myth of the Framework", in: E. Freeman (ed.), *The Abdication of Philosophy. Philosophy and the Public Good. Essays in Honour of P. A. Schilpp*, La Salle (Ill.): Open Court, Library of Living Philosophers, 1976.

Popper, K. R., *In Search of a Better World. Lectures and Essays from Thirty Years*, London & New York: Routledge, 1992.

Popper, K. R., *Die beiden Grundprobleme der Erkenntnistheorie*, ed. E. Hansen, Tübingen: Mohr-Siebeck, 1994.

Prieto, L. J., *Pertinence et pratique. Essai de sémiologie*, Paris: Minuit, 1975.

Prieto, L. J., "Entwurf einer allgemeinen Semiologie", in: *Zeitschrift für Semiotik* 1, 1979.

Psychoanalysis as an Empirical, Interdisciplinary Science, International Symposium of the Austrian Academy of Sciences, Vienna, 22–24 Nov. 2002.

Quéré, L., "Vers une anthropologie alternative. Pour les sciences sociales?", in: Ch. Bouchindhomme & R. Rochlitz (eds), *Habermas, la raison, la critique*, Paris: Les Editions du Cerf, 1996.

Raible, W., "Roman Jakobson oder 'Auf der Wasserscheide zwischen Linguistik und Poetik'", in: R. Jakobson, *Aufsätze zur Linguistik und Poetik*, Munich: Nymphenburger Verlagshandlung, 1974.

Rasch, W., *Niklas Luhmann's Modernity. The Paradoxes of Differentiation*, Stanford: Stanford Univ. Press, 2000.

Rickert, H., *Philosophische Aufsätze*, Tübingen: Mohr-Siebeck, 1999.

Rinofner-Kreidl, S., *Edmund Husserl. Zeitlichkeit und Intentionalität*, Freiburg & Munich: Alber, 2000.

Rorty, R., *Objectivity, Relativism, and Truth*, vol. I of *Philosophical Papers* (2 vols), Cambridge: Cambridge Univ. Press, 1991.

Ryan, A., *The Philosophy of the Social Sciences*, London: Macmillan (1970), 1980.

Ryan, A., "Popper and Liberalism", in: G. Currie & A. Musgrave (eds), *Popper and the Human Sciences*, Dordrecht, Boston & Lancaster: Nijhoff, 1985.

Saldern, M. von, "Auch Sozialwissenschaftler/innen sind nur Menschen", in: *Ethik und Sozialwissenschaften* 4, 1999.

Sarasin, P., *Geschichtswissenschaft und Diskursanalyse*, Frankfurt: Suhrkamp, 2003.

Saussure, F. de, *Course in General Linguistics* (1959), London: Fontana, 1974.

Sayer, A., *Method in Social Science. A Realist Approach*, London: Hutchinson, 1984.

Schäfers, B. (ed.), *Grundbegriffe der Soziologie*, Opladen: Leske & Budrich, 1986.

Schiffer, W., *Theorien der Geschichtsschreibung und ihre erzähltheoretische Relevanz (Danto, Habermas, Baumgartner, Droysen)*, Stuttgart: Metzler, 1980.

Schlick, M., *Allgemeine Erkenntnislehre* (1918), Frankfurt: Suhrkamp, 1979.

Schluchter, W., *Rationalismus und Weltbeherrschung. Studien zu Max Weber*, Frankfurt: Suhrkamp, 1980.

Schmidt, A., *Zur Idee der Kritischen Theorie*, Munich: Hanser, 1974.

Schmidt, M., "Sozialwissenschaftliche Theoriebildung und Dialogische Theorie. Oder: Brauchen die Sozialwissenschaften einen ideologischen Diskurs?", in: *Ethik und Sozialwissenschaften* 4, 1999.

Schmidt, S. J., "Der Radikale Konstruktivismus: Ein neues Paradigma im interdisziplinären Diskurs", in: S. J. Schmidt (ed.), *Der Diskurs des Radikalen Konstruktivismus*, Frankfurt: Suhrkamp, 1987.

Schmidt, S. J., "Allgemeine Literaturwissenschaft – ein Entwurf und die Folgen", in: C. Zelle (ed.), *Allgemeine Literaturwissenschaft. Konturen und Profile im Pluralismus*, Opladen & Wiesbaden: Westdeutscher Verlag, 1999.

Schülein, J. A., *Autopoietische Realität und konnotative Theorie. Über Balanceprobleme sozialwissenschaftlichen Erkennens*, Weilerswist: Velbrück, 2002.

Schülein, J. A. & Reitze, S., *Wissenschaftstheorie für Einsteiger*, Vienna: WUV Universitätsverlag, 2002.

Schurz, G., "Koexistenzweisen rivalisierender Paradigmen. Eine begriffsklärende und problemtypologisierende Studie", in: G. Schurz & P. Weingartner (eds), *Koexistenz rivalisierender Paradigmen. Eine post-kuhnsche Bestandsaufnahme zur Struktur gegenwärtiger Wissenschaft*, Opladen & Wiesbaden: Westdeutscher Verlag, 1998.

Schütz, A., *Das Problem der Relevanz*, Frankfurt: Suhrkamp (1971), 1982.

Schwinn, T., "Differenzierung und soziale Integration. Wider eine systemtheoretisch halbierte Soziologie", in: H.-J. Giegel & U. Schimank (eds) *Beobachter der Moderne. Beiträge zu Niklas Luhmanns "Die Gesellschaft der Gesellschaft"*, Frankfurt: Suhrkamp (2001), 2003.

Searle, J. R., *Speech Acts. An Essay in the Philosophy of Language*, Cambridge: Cambridge Univ. Press (1969), 1977.

Searle, R. J., "Reiterating the Differences. A Reply to Derrida", in: *Glyph* 1, 1977.

Shklovsky, V., "Iskusstvo, kak priëm", in: J. Striedter (ed.), *Russischer Formalismus*, vol. I (bilingual edn), Munich: Fink, 1969.

Shklovsky, "Svjaz priëmov sjužetosloženija s obščimi priëmami stilja", in: J. Striedter (ed.), *Russischer Formalismus*, vol. I (bilingual edn), Munich: Fink, 1969.

Šik, O., *Plan und Markt im Sozialismus*, Vienna: Molden, 1965.

Simmel, G., *Über sociale Differenzierung*, Leipzig: Duncker und Humblot, 1890.

Smith, J. E., "Hegel's Critique of Kant", in: J. J. O'Malley, K. W. Algozin & F. G. Weiss (eds), *Hegel and the History of Philosophy. Proceedings of the 1972 Hegel Society of America Conference*, The Hague: Nijhoff, 1974.

Sperber, D. & Wilson, D., *Relevance. Communication and Cognition*, Oxford: Blackwell (1986), 1993.

Spinner, H. F., *Ist der Kritische Rationalismus am Ende? Auf der Suche nach den verlorenen Maßstäben des Kritischen Rationalismus für eine offene Sozialphilosophie und kritische Sozialwissenschaft*, Weinheim & Basel: Beltz, 1982.

Srubar, I., "Mannheim und die Postmodernen", in: M. Endreß (ed.), *Karl Mannheims Analyse der Moderne*, Opladen: Leske & Budrich, 2000.

Stagl, J., "Malinowskis Paradigma", in: W. Schmied-Kowarzik & J. Stagl (eds), *Grundfragen der Ethnologie. Beiträge zur gegenwärtigen Theorie-Diskussion*, Berlin: Dietrich Reimer Verlag, 1993.

Stagl, J., *A History of Curiosity. The Theory of Travel 1550–1800*, Chur: Harwood Academic Publishers, 1995.

Stanzel, F. K., *A Theory of Narrative*, Cambridge: Cambridge Univ. Press, 1986.

Stegmüller, W., *Probleme und Resultate der Wissenschaftstheorie und Analytischen Philosophie*, vol. II, *Theorie und Erfahrung*, Zweiter Teilband, *Theorienstrukturen und Theoriendynamik*, Berlin, Heidelberg & New York: Springer, 1985.

Stegmüller, W., *Probleme und Resultate der Wissenschaftstheorie und Analytischen Philosophie*, vol. II, *Theorie und Erfahrung*, Dritter Teilband, *Die Entwicklung des neuen Strukturalismus seit 1973*, Berlin, Heidelberg & New York: Springer, 1986.

Stirner, M., *Der Einzige und sein Eigentum*, Stuttgart: Reclam, 1972.

Stolze, R., *Übersetzungstheorien. Eine Einführung*, Tübingen: Narr, 1994.

Strauss, A. & Corbin, J., *Basics of Qualitative Research: Grounded Theory. Procedures and Techniques*, London & Newbury Park: Sage, 1990.

Strauss, L., "Die Unterscheidung zwischen Tatsachen und Werten", in: H. Albert & E. Topitsch (eds), *Werturteilsstreit*, Darmstadt: Wiss. Buchgesellschaft, 1979.

Stubbs, M., *Discourse Analysis. The Sociolinguistic Analysis of Natural Language*, Oxford: Blackwell (1983), 1994.

Sturmatz, A., *Pippi Langstrumpf als Paradigma. Die deutsche Rezeption Astrid Lindgrens und ihr internationaler Kontext*, Tübingen & Basel: Francke, 2004.

Supek, I., *Teorija spoznaje*, Zagreb: Graficki Zavod Hrvatske, 1974.

Thompson, E. M., *Russian Formalism and Anglo-American New Criticism. A Comparative Study*, The Hague: Mouton, 1971.

Thumerel, F., *La Critique littéraire*, Paris Armand Colin, 1998.

Touraine, A., *Sociologie de l'action*, Paris: Seuil, 1965.

Touraine, A., *Critique de la modernité*, Paris: Fayard, 1992.

Touraine, A., *Pourrons-nous vivre ensemble? Egaux et différents*, Paris: Fayard, 1997.

Trotsky, L., *Literature and Revolution* (1924), London: Redwords, 1991.

Bibliography 271

Van Tieghem, Ph., *Les Grandes doctrines littéraires en France*, Paris: PUF, 1968.

Vischer, F. T., *Kritische Gänge*, vol. IV, ed. R. Vischer, Munich: Meyer & Jessen, 1922.

Volhard, E., *Zwischen Hegel und Nietzsche. Der Ästhetiker Friedrich Theodor Vischer*, Frankfurt: Klostermann, 1932.

Walton, W. G., "V. N. Voloshinov: A Marriage of Formalism and Marxism", in: P. V. Zima (ed.), *Semiotics and Dialectics. Ideology and the Text*, Amsterdam: Benjamins, 1981.

Warmer, G. & Gloy, K., *Lyotard. Darstellung und Kritik seines Sprachbegriffs*, Aachen: Ein-Fach-Verlag, 1995.

Weber, M., "Der Beruf zur Politik", in: *idem, Soziologie, universalgeschichtliche Analysen, Politik*, ed. J. Winckelmann, Stuttgart: Kröner, 1973.

Weber, M., "Die 'Objektivität' sozialwissenschaftlicher und sozialpolitischer Erkenntnis" (1904), in: *idem, Gesammelte Aufsätze zur Wissenschaftslehre*, ed. J. Winckelmann, Tübingen: Mohr-Siebeck, 1973.

Weber, M., "Vom inneren Beruf zur Wissenschaft", in: M. Weber, *Soziologie, universalgeschichtliche Analysen, Politik*, ed. J. Winckelmann, Stuttgart: Kröner, 1973.

Weber, M., *Die protestantische Ethik I. Eine Aufsatzsammlung*, ed. J. Winckelmann, Hamburg: Siebenstern, 1973 (3rd edn).

Weber, M., *Wirtschaft und Gesellschaft. Grundriß der verstehenden Soziologie*, Tübingen: Mohr (5th edn), 1976.

Weingart, P., *Die Stunde der Wahrheit? Zum Verhältnis der Wissenschaft zu Politik, Wirtschaft und Medien in der Wissensgesellschaft*, Weilerswist: Velbrück, 2001.

Wellek, R. & Warren, A., *Theory of Literature*, London: Peregrine Books (1963), 1968.

Welsch, W., *Unsere postmoderne Moderne*, Weinheim: VCH, 1991 (3rd edn).

Wendel, H. J., "Wie erfunden ist die Wirklichkeit?", in: *Delfin* 2, 1989.

Wenturis, N., Van hove & W., Dreier, V., *Methodologie der Sozialwissenschaften*, Tübingen & Basel: Francke, 1992.

White, H., "Vergangenheit konstruieren", in: H. R. Fischer & S. J. Schmidt (eds), *Wirklichkeit und Welterzeugung*, Heidelberg: Carl-Auer-Systeme Verlag, 2000.

Whorf, B. L., *Language, Thought and Reality*, Cambridge (Mass.): MIT Press, 1956.

Wiche, R. T. P., "Dialogische Theorie und dialogische Praxis", in: *Ethik und Sozialwissenschaften* 4, 1999.

Wiggershaus, R., *Die Frankfurter Schule. Geschichte. Theoretische Entwicklung. Politische Bedeutung*, Munich: DTV, 1989 (2nd edn).

Winch, P., "Popper and Scientific Method in the Social Sciences", in: P. A. Schilpp (ed.), *The Philosophy of Karl Popper*, La Salle (Ill.): Open Court, The Library of Living Philosophers (Book II), 1967.

Winch, P., *The Idea of a Social Science and its Relation to Philosophy*, London: Routledge (1958), 1990 (2nd edn).

Winter, R., *Die Kunst des Eigensinns. Cultural Studies als Kritik der Macht*, Weilerswist: Velbrück, 2001.

Witschel, G., *Wertvorstellung im Werk Karl R. Poppers*, Bonn: Bouvier, 1977 (2nd edn).

Witte, E. H., "Teamfähigkeit und Moderation in den Sozialwissenschaften beim theoretischen Diskurs", in: *Ethik und Sozialwissenschaften* 4, 1999.

Wörterbuch der Soziologie, founded by G. Hartfiel, re-edited by K. H. Hillmann, Stuttgart: Kröner, 1972 (3rd edn).

Young, M. & Willmott, P., *Family and Kinship in East London*, London (1957): Pelican, 1969.

Zima, P. V., " 'Rezeption' und 'Produktion' als ideologische Begriffe", in: *idem, Kritik der Literatursoziologie*, Frankfurt: Suhrkamp, 1978.

Zima, P. V., "Dialektik zwischen Totalität und Fragment", in: H.-J. Schmitt (ed.), *Der Streit mit Georg Lukács*, Frankfurt: Suhrkamp, 1978.

Zima, P. V., *Textsoziologie. Eine kritische Einführung*, Stuttgart: Metzler, 1980.

Zima, P. V., "Irrationalität und Totalität bei Broch, Lukács und Mannheim", in: K. Amann & H. Lengauer (eds), *Österreich und der Große Krieg*, Vienna: Verlag Christian Brandstätter, 1989.

Zima, P. V., "Bakhtin's Young Hegelian Aesthetics", in: *Critical Studies* 2 ("The Bakhtin Circle Today"), 1989.

Zima, P. V., *Ideologie und Theorie. Eine Diskurskritik*, Tübingen: Francke, 1989.

Zima, P. V., *Komparatistik. Einführung in die Vergleichende Literaturwissenschaft*, Tübingen & Basel: Francke, 1992.

Zima, P. V., "Der Unfaßbare Rest. Übersetzung zwischen Dekonstruktion und Semiotik", in: J. Strutz & P. V. Zima (eds), *Literarische Polyphonie*, Tübingen: Narr, 1996.

Zima, P. V., *Der unzitierbare Text. Ein Gespräch, initiiert von Peter V. Zima und herausgegeben von Alexander Schwarz, Tausch*, vol. X, Berne, Berlin & Paris: Lang, 1997.

Zima, P. V., "Jan Mukařovský's Aesthetics between Autonomy and the Avant-Garde", in: V. Macura & H. Schmidt (eds), *Jan Mukařovský and the Prague School*, Potsdam: Univ. of Potsdam, 1999.

Zima, P. V., *Manuel de sociocritique*, Paris (1985): L'Harmattan, 2000.

Zima, P. V., *Roman und Ideologie. Zur Sozialgeschichte des modernen Romans*, Munich: Fink (1986), 1999.

Zima, P. V., *The Philosophy of Modern Literary Theory*, London & New Brunswick: Athlone, 1999.

Zima, P. V. (ed.), *Vergleichende Wissenschaften. Interdisziplinarität und Interkulturalität in den Komparatistiken*, Tübingen: Narr, 2000.

Zima, P. V., *Theorie des Subjekts. Subjektivität und Identität zwischen Moderne und Postmoderne*, Tübingen & Basel: Francke, 2000.

Zima, P. V., *Das literarische Subjekt. Zwischen Spätmoderne und Postmoderne*, Tübingen & Basel: Francke, 2001.

Zima, P. V., *Moderne/Postmoderne. Gesellschaft, Philosophie, Literatur*, Tübingen & Basel: Francke, 2001 (2nd edn).

Zima, P. V., *Deconstruction and Critical Theory*, London & New York: Continuum, 2002.

Zima, P. V., "Die Stellung der Literaturwissenschaft zwischen den Kulturen: Eine textsoziologische Betrachtung", in: H. Foltinek & Ch. Leitgeb (eds), *Literaturwissenschaft: intermedial – interdisziplinär*, Vienna: Verlag der Österr. Akademie der Wissenschaften, 2002.

Zima, P. V., "Adorno et la crise du langage", in: *idem, Théorie critique du discours. La discursivité entre Adorno et le postmodernisme*, Paris: L'Harmattan, 2003.

Zourabichvilli, F., *Deleuze. Une philosophie de l'événement*, Paris: PUF, 1994.

Index